D0936452

Days of Anger, Days of Hope

Days of Anger,
Days of Hope

A Memoir of the League of American Writers
1937–1942

Franklin Folsom

University Press of Colorado

© 1994 by the University Press of Colorado

Published by the University Press of Colorado, P.O. Box 849, Niwot, Colorado 80544

The University Press of Colorado is a cooperative publishing enterprise supported, in part, by Adams State College, Colorado State University, Fort Lewis College, Mesa State College, Metropolitan State College of Denver, University of Colorado, University of Northern Colorado, University of Southern Colorado, and Western State College of Colorado.

Excerpt from "A Tribute, And a Nightmare" from *Afternoon of a Pawnbroker and Other Poems*, © 1943 by Kenneth Fearing and renewed 1971 by Bruce Fearing, reprinted by permission of Harcourt Brace & Company.

Library of Congress Cataloging-in-Publication Data

Folsom, Franklin, 1907–
    Days of anger, days of hope: a memoir of the League of American writers, 1937–1942 / Franklin Folsom.
        p.   cm.
    Includes bibliographical references (p.) and index.
    ISBN 0-87081-332-3
    1. American literature — 20th century — History and criticism.   2. Communism and literature — United States — History — 20th century.   3. Authors, American — 20th century — Political and social views.   4. Authorship — Societies, etc. — History.   5. League of American Writers.   6. Folsom, Franklin, 1907– .   I. Title.
PS228.C6F64   1994
810.9′0052 — dc20   94-26
                                                                 CIP

The paper used in this publication meets the minimum requirements of the American National Standard for Information Sciences — Permanence of Paper for Printed Library Materials. ANSI Z39.48–1984

∞

10 9 8 7 6 5 4 3 2 1

For
Mary Elting Folsom

Some other books by Franklin Folsom

For adults:

Impatient Armies of the Poor: The Story of Collective Action by the Unemployed, 1808–1942

America's Ancient Treasures: A Guide to Archeological Sites and Museums in the United States and Canada, 4th revised enlarged edition (with Mary Elting Folsom)

Give Me Liberty: America's Colonial Heritage

The Great Peace March: An American Odyssey (with Connie Fledderjohann)

Exploring American Caves

For young readers:

Red Power on the Rio Grande: The Native American Revolution of 1680

Black Cowboy: The Life and Legend of George McJunkin

The Language Book

Science and the Secret of Man's Past

Sand Dune Pony

Contents

ish intellectuals to reach safety when they had to flee their homeland. The League went on to help save the lives of scores of writers who had been forced to escape from Germany, Austria, Czechoslovakia, Italy, Poland, and France ahead of Fascist forces in World War II.

It was into the organization that was carrying on this kind of work that I came as a full-time official in August 1937. So that the contributions of the League on the literary, political, and humanitarian scenes may not be forgotten, I have set down my recollections of them. I have not attempted anything so ambitious as a literary history of the period. Rather, you will find in the book that follows a series of notes on some aspects of the League's passage through the literary-political firmament, now and then qualified by a backward look half a century later.

Franklin Folsom
Boulder, Colorado

Days of Anger, Days of Hope

1

The League I Found

The beauty of the thirties was its communion among people — its generosity — its willingness to be guilty of folly and its chance to get out of the constricted *I* in what seemed a meaningful way.

— Josephine Herbst[1]

As to my political convictions, I am an anti-Fascist and for democracy, not merely a political democracy but also an economic democracy. I try to do what I can to work with others toward such a goal, through organizations like the League of Women Shoppers and the League of American Writers.

— Leane Zugsmith, circa 1938[2]

"Got a job which is a wow, a lulu and a pip!" With these inelegant words of rapture at escaping unemployment, I began a letter to my parents August 17, 1937.[3] I was to be executive secretary of the League of American Writers.

Before that post at the League fell vacant, I had been busy with unpaid work as a poet and an organizer of a Communist Party unit. Earlier, I had edited newspapers for the Unemployed Council for $8 a week. I had been arrested and beaten up by cops during an unemployed demonstration. I had been arrested for passing out leaflets in support of a strike. I had had jobs on work relief until I was fired for organizing. In the four years since I left Oxford, where I was a Rhodes Scholar, I had seen more of working class life than some writers get a chance to see in a lifetime. Perhaps these brushes with reality were considered an asset when I applied for a job at the League.

At any rate, Isidor Schneider, novelist, poet, and critic, recommended me for the job.[4] Joe Freeman, an editor of the *New Masses*, seconded the recommendation. Apparently, Joe had forgiven me for my

Waldo Frank, novelist, the first president of the League.[6] National Archives photo.

bad housekeeping the previous winter when I house-sat in his country place. He was now publishing weekly paragraphs called "Flashbacks" that I wrote anonymously for his magazine. These were brief reminders of upcoming anniversaries in labor and radical history taken from notes accumulating in my files as spinoff from research I did on the history of organizations of the unemployed.[5] Alexander ("Trachty") Trachtenberg, a Communist Party official and director of International Publishers, had been present in the *New Masses* editorial meeting when it was decided to run my "Flashbacks." Trachty said that if I did the research, he would provide the ideology — a suggestion that did not warm the cockles of my heart and that I never took advantage of.

At no point did Joe Freeman question the "ideology" of my simple anniversary notes. Perhaps he thought I had made better use of his home library than I really had. Be that as it may, I got the League job.

When I opened the desk of Ellen Blake, my predecessor in the League office at 125 East 24th Street in Manhattan, I found the longest one-page epistle I had ever seen. When I held the "Dear Ellen:" line high above my head, the "Yours fraternally — Walter Lowenfels" touched the floor. Poet Lowenfels had fed one end of a roll of butcher paper into his typewriter and then typed on and on and on. The kind of paper he used was available in the butter-packaging plant where he made his living.

I knew the name Lowenfels, but just barely. A few years before, he had been a contributor to little magazines in Paris, where life was exciting and living was cheap and where other expatriates, including the poet and critic Malcolm Cowley, had taken refuge from what they regarded as American philistinism. Most of these writers, Lowenfels and Cowley among them, had returned to the United States when funds from home dwindled and the cost of living in Europe shot up.

This was also a time when the shadow of fascism was beginning to lengthen. Not long after they got home, both Lowenfels and Cowley found themselves deeply shocked, along with millions of others, by the

Great Depression. Both responded to the twin desolations of fascism and unemployment by leaving the ivory tower and moving into political life. Lowenfels went into the Communist Party, and Cowley shifted in the same direction, but not so far.

The Lowenfels letter was an imaginative, enthusiastic list of suggestions of things for the League to do. It included more projects than any large, well-funded organization could manage. The League was small — it had only 220 members — and it was poor.

And what were the members up to? They were filled with great anger and great hope — anger at the violence and destruction of life and culture that fascism

Lincoln Steffens, journalist, member of the League's National Council until his death in 1936. Library of Congress photo.

was spreading, and hope that people everywhere could frustrate the fascist attack on life. One way to hunt for clues to what writers were doing in response to their anger and their hope is to look at what the executive secretary did on a typical day.

I dealt with mail. The first letter I opened might be from a member who offered to provide an affidavit guaranteeing support to a refugee writer trying to enter the United States. Another letter might be a plea for help from within a concentration camp in France. And then might come a report from Western Union on money cabled to world-famous writers, now impoverished. Often the money did not arrive.

One day there is a letter from Louis Aragon in Paris reporting on the assistance being given to anti-Fascist writers by the International Association of Writers for the Defense of Culture, with which the League was affiliated. Later, C. Day Lewis, secretary of the British branch of the association, would write telling us of new problems that refugee writers from Nazi Germany were having as they sought asylum in his country.

There might also be a cantankerous blast from the novelist Nelson Algren complaining that the Chicago chapter of the League was misunderstood by the national office. Another might be a fascist communication, only semi-literate but fully vituperative, urging the League to drop dead. Another might contain a poem from a young writer who in some vague way wanted his words to help the cause.

Lillian Hellman, playwright, member of the League's National Council. National Archives photo.

In that same mail is a note from a printing salesman insisting that we hurry up with the payment of a bill. Where would I get the money? The salesman, I knew, was ill; he had trichinosis, probably contracted from eating in cheap restaurants on 14th Street. His name was Stefan Heym, a man who would later become famous for his novels — and his protests — sent out of East Germany after the war and who had already begun work on *Hostages* (G. P. Putnam's Sons, 1942).

There were always bills. One day after opening an unusually large number of these, I turned for help to Lillian Hellman. In response to my call, Lillian said she would see me. When I arrived at her hotel suite, I told her that the League needed $50. Could she lend it to us?

Lillian said she would, on condition that the money be repaid in two weeks. She was very firm about this. Obviously, she did not put unlimited trust in the financial reliability of the League — or perhaps of the Left.

Two weeks to the day I reappeared at Lillian's suite. She sat on a sofa in front of a low cocktail table, and facing her was a man I didn't know but would meet again before long. Lillian introduced him as a diamond merchant. Between the two, spread out on the table, was more jewelry than I had ever seen outside the window at Tiffany's. The man seemed to be making suggestions for redesigning the bracelets and rings, some of which I later learned had probably been given her by Dashiell Hammett.

I handed Lillian her $50, thanked her, and left.

That week and the week before I had gone without my wages to make sure I could repay the loan, and I was a little miffed that Hellman, so obviously prosperous, was so stingy. But I had to admit that she had given the help I asked for. She often did.[7]

To continue with a typical day at the League: It took time to deal with the flood of letters. In addition, there might be a press release to write about an upcoming lecture, or a committee meeting to discuss plans for a reading from a work in progress, or calls for sponsors for a fund-raising dinner.

Had a hall been found for a lecture on poetic drama in radio? Who was this volunteer who came in off the street and worked endless hours stuffing envelopes and making good suggestions about improving office efficiency? Who was that other volunteer who came well recommended and who seemed interested only in working with the membership files and the files of contributors?

One day I was asked by the author of *Brown Muscles* and *The Arms of Woman Love* (whose name I have forgotten) to aid in starting a children's camp. Another day I received a very crudely sewn black mask from an applicant for membership who called us the "Kaffee Klatsch Klan" and considered us "enemies of the revolution." Next day an English professor in Texas sent a full page of atrocity pictures clipped from Hearst's *American Weekly,* as proof that our contest for student essays on the anti-Fascist war in Spain was aiding and abetting the destruction of Spanish art.

Another day there would be a hastily typed note asking the League to support a trade union picket line called to protest the arrest of striking workers. Or a letter might come from the Philippine Writers League or from Blackie Myers, a wonderfully humorous leader of the National Maritime Union; or a serious one from the usually funny Donald Ogden Stewart in Hollywood.

A desperate, totally impoverished writer's plea for money might be followed by an envelope containing an anonymous five dollar bill. How do you tell a League member that you really have no way to get a writer dying of cancer into a special treatment program supposed to exist in Czechoslovakia? How do you handle the author of a well-known biography of Shelley when he comes into the office seeking help from friendly writers? He is obviously half-starved and in need of money for food and a doctor. He and others gravitated toward the League that they saw offering emotional support and material aid to suffering writers in Europe. It was natural that U.S. writers, among the fifteen million unemployed in the country, should feel that the League's beneficence might well include them.

How do you draft a letter for League vice president Van Wyck Brooks to sign, inviting President Roosevelt to accept honorary membership in the League? And what do you do when Roosevelt accepts? It turns out you do nothing. Roosevelt was a member for two years, but

this fact was never announced. Then, only days after the League protested raids on homes in Detroit where volunteers were alleged to have
been recruited to the Abraham Lincoln Battalion in Spain, Roosevelt
resigned from the League.

How do you handle a letter that accuses the League of being an
apologist for unspeakable crimes Stalin is alleged to have committed,
when you think the charge is mistaken and is irrelevant to the League's
work? (The League was trying to fight fascism and defend culture.) And
how do you feel years later when you find that the letter about Stalin —
whom the League did *not* get involved in defending — was correct? And
how do you feel still later when you learn that some of the letter's authors
apparently accepted money from the CIA, which has also committed
unspeakable crimes?

One day the mail brought from the Writers Union a plea asking the
League to oppose efforts that were being made to terminate the Works
Progress Administration (WPA) Writers Project. I pause over this letter.
I had helped form the Writers Union; it grew out of the Unemployed
Writers Association on whose executive committee I had served. Moreover, I had a special interest in the Writers Project, which had been set
up to provide jobs for out-of-work writers. Before the project was
started, I had been on a committee, with novelist Robert Whitcomb and
poet Leon Srabian Herald, sent by the Unemployed Writers Association
to Washington with a proposal for Harry Hopkins, the WPA adminis-
trator: that jobless writers be put to work compiling guidebooks. Later,
in response to a request from Harold Coy, a Writers Project editor in
Washington, I had proposed the names of writers who I thought would
make good directors of the projects in twenty different states. Ten of my
nominees did become state directors, and the guidebooks the Writers
Project produced are still held in very high regard. Here I should also
note that many League members worked on the Writers Project throughout the country and contributed to some of its most celebrated publications, including *American Stuff,* an anthology of creative writing done by
members of the project on their own time and published by Viking Press
in 1937.

Dipping into the League's voluminous mail could go on and on, but
it is enough to say that from all these communications I soon found out
a lot about the League. I had actually known very little except that it
seemed earnestly trying to be of service to writers. I would have known
more if I had been able to attend the Second American Writers Congress,

held in June 1937, a little more than two months before the day I first opened the mail.

The letterhead I found in my desk made clear that the League's leaders elected at the congress were in the midst of the creative activity of the 1930s. The president, Donald Ogden Stewart, was one of the most sought-after writers in Hollywood. Erskine Caldwell, a vice president, had introduced to the reading public the poor people of the South. Widely read science writer Paul de Kruif was also a vice president. Other vice presidents were Van Wyck Brooks, who was bringing some Puritan values of New England of the past to support egalitarian socialist sentiments in

Meridel LeSueur, fiction writer, poet, League vice president, FBI target. Courtesy of Rachel Tilsen.

the present; Meridel LeSueur, erupting out of radical life in mid-America, and Genevieve Taggard, who were singing from the Left for women; Langston Hughes, with his gentle wit and firm anger, who gave voice to mute rebels, both black and white; and Upton Sinclair, who had been a crusading journalist and novelist for more than three decades.

Another vice president elected at the congress in June was Malcolm Cowley. He had been sufficiently moved by the vigor of the working class around him to write a poem for a recent May Day that was published in *The New Republic* and reprinted in *The Daily Worker* in April 1936. It ended this way:

> From factory gates and convict camps and cabins
> Unpainted, windowless, deep in the Cotton Belt —
> Tensed muscles loosening, a first free breath
> A hundred million times repeated, felt
>
> Then slowly heard, tornado of the mind
> Driving the mist and terror from the head.
> The vault of cloud was split by a sharp wind.
> The sky was suddenly blue and the sun shone red.

In addition to Cowley and the other vice presidents there was a secretary, the gentle, very firm Philip Stevenson. These officers and a small executive committee were the people with whom I would be

Katherine ("Kit") Buckles, early executive secretary of the League. Photo: Schultz, Washington, D.C.

working most closely. In the beginning this committee consisted of Dorothy Brewster, scholar and critic, of Columbia University;[8] Kyle Crichton, an editor of *Collier's Magazine* and, under the name Robert Forsythe, a writer of radical humor for the *New Masses;* George Dangerfield, historian; Marjorie Fischer, writer of children's books; Joseph Freeman; Robert Gessner, poet and novelist; editor Henry Hart; Rolfe Humphries, classics scholar and poet; John Howard Lawson, playwright, critic, and screenwriter; Dexter Masters, journalist and editor of *Consumer Reports;* W. L. River, novelist and screenwriter; Genevieve Taggard, poet; and Jean Starr Untermeyer, poet.

I had learned a little about them and others in the League from an early executive secretary,[9] Katherine ("Kit") Buckles, with whom I had gone to school in Boulder, Colorado. I also learned something about other writers associated with the League from the following notes on the Writers Congress written by Jane Sherman, who was in the large audience. (Jane was an aspiring young writer whom I had met in the early 1930s when she visited Oxford at the time I was a student there.)

Crowds at Carnegie Hall on the opening evening. Young, enthusiastic, eager. The 350 delegates [not all League members] sat on the stage behind the speakers. Archibald MacLeish was chairman — pale, high forehead, lisping voice, seemingly in earnest although one has the suspicion that he merely feels the rising proletarian [literature] movement as *the* thing for the future and has decided to get on its bandwagon. Donald Ogden Stewart . . . Tall, baldheaded, glasses, ineffectual looking, with a scarecrow kind of limpness in his posture. He started out by being merely funny . . . but when he turned serious, his was almost the best speech of the evening. One thing he said that I applauded in my heart: A sense of humor . . . and a liberal education are the two best preparatives for a young person to lead a life of slavery. Liberals are able to see both sides of a question dispassionately and act on neither.

Earl Browder . . . [called] writers to action, not under the Communist banner, necessarily, but under any banner or discipline they chose which resulted in a strong stand against the menace of Fascism.

Joris Ivens . . . dark serious burning-eyed young Dutchman spoke next about the making of his film *The Spanish Earth* in Spain. . . .

Ernest Hemingway was the last speaker and the most enthusiastically received. It was his first public lecture and he was nervous. . . . He spoke clearly, in his own one-syllable words, a deep strong voice, few gestures. He is fine looking, tall, dark, sunburned, heavy-set, wearing rimless glasses when he reads. . . . His main thesis was that the problem of the writer was the same now as it had always been, namely that he should try to write truly and project the truth as he sees it so that it becomes a part of the experience of the reader. He said, about Spain, that any man might become interested in war, as a science . . . but that no man was interested in murder such as was being committed in Spain. Of course, by interested he meant impersonally so, because he certainly advocated every writer fighting vigorously against Fascists.

Tillie Lerner Olsen, novelist, member of the League's National Council, 1935. Photo © Leonda Fink, Courtesy of Bantam Books.

Saturday afternoon, Martha Gellhorn spoke first. She was tall, blond, extremely good looking, with a distinct diction, fine thin hands, restrained gestures, and the dignity of sincerity. She told of her experiences in Spain, where the writers were judged not by their writing but by how good soldiers they were. Not one of them, she said, was there for the local color he could pick up, but because they thought this fight was more important than any writing they might ever do.

Harry Slochower, German exile, said, "Nazi literature uses exclamation points to express deep emotion, and dashes to express deep thought!"

Albert Rhys Williams . . . spoke especially of the nationalist cultures which the USSR was encouraging in minority groups by developing their alphabets, teaching them to read and write, etc.

Sunday afternoon . . . several disruptors got in and beclouded the issue with false questions, slimy implications, and general sabotage.[10] They are indeed a vicious lot, and they were silenced most effectively by Joe Freeman who spoke from the floor saying that this was no time for general revolution, but for the amassing of all and any forces to fight against the stronger enemies of war and Fascism, and anyone who, in writing, speaking or thinking, said otherwise was merely acting as a direct Fascist agent, willingly or not. Then we came to the first speaker of the afternoon.

H·W. L Dana

Henry Wadsworth Longfellow
Dana, drama critic, historian,
member of the League's National
Council, 1941. From *New Masses*,
June 17, 1941.

Henry Hart, a lanky fellow in a well-tailored suit, and pale face, with a marvelous speaking voice, [gave a talk] on Literary Waste, in which he exposed the publishers as predatory businessmen with no interest in books, and went on to say, "If you do not examine your mind carefully every single day, you will be amazed to see how much material you automatically discard because it will not make money." . . . The average talented writer makes about $300 a year for the first ten years.

Those who spoke from the floor included Henry Wadsworth Longfellow Dana, Joe Gollomb, Robert Gessner (who wrote *Some of My Best Friends Are Jews*), A. B. Magil, Albert Bein, Sender Garlin. Next, Granville Hicks spoke. . . . His plea was for active participation, even at the risk of losing the quiet and contemplation necessary for creative work. . . . (I wish SOMEONE would say how they mean "to be active." They don't mean join the party, do they?)

Henry Alsberg, head of the WPA writing project, spoke last, and made a fine plea for closer cooperation with the work he is trying to do with his unemployed writers and the work we are trying to do in the Writers Congress.

One day only a few weeks after I assumed my duties at the League, a letter arrived from *Poetry: A Magazine of Verse.* Out of it fell a check for $100 and the astonishing news that I had been awarded the Harriet Monroe Memorial Prize for a group of poems that had appeared in the June 1937 issue. I assumed that the prize was essentially a gesture of goodwill to the League, and I said as much in a letter to the magazine. It was pleasant to be told by the editor, George Dillon, that he had supported the prize for me, and that he had not known of my connection with the League when he cast his vote. He knew it later, though, because the letter announcing the prize had been addressed to the League office.

One of my poems that *Poetry* had published reflected the contradictory worlds in which I lived at the time the League job came my way:

After Moving to a Quiet Room

Here purrs the pillowing kitten and we read.
The room is radiatored warm and walled
against siren and tremble from trucks, which commerce-called,
stagger below like pin balls that succeed
at last in entering where no pins impede.
Our table baskets fruit, which yesterday sprawled
Rubens-ripe in the market. We are installed.
We smile for speech, and silence is agreed.

But thinking shouts down silence: word-temblors tear
our walls open for the quaking world to use
the cracks in for gateway. Echoes from everywhere
over-run our room, and we pay dues
in deeds to the trembling invaders. The kitten can spare
the world, but we cannot so sinuously choose.

I had come into an organization that was very busy, and I was convinced that so many important writers had never before joined together in such an important cause. And they were my bosses. They were also my resources. With them, and using an armature of politics, I would try to shape something.

I had little from my own experience at the age of thirty to pass along to these talented people, most of whom were older than I, but clearly I had to concern myself with trying to find common ground on which they could stand as they sought to push together against a terrible threat to them all.

In 1937 writers were ready to be organized. As Malcolm Cowley had said of the recent Writers Congress, "People had quit even joking about the Ivory Tower. Almost all writers were 'politicalized,' even the conservatives — and perhaps one should say, the conservatives most of all."

Notes

1. Quoted by David Madden in *Proletarian Writers of the Thirties* (Southern Illinois University Press, 1968), p. xxvii.

2. Quoted by Abe C. Ravitz, *Leane Zugsmith: Thunder on the Left* (International, 1992).

3. All of the author's personal letters cited in this book are in his possession and will ultimately by deposited in Special Collections, Norlin Library, University of Colorado at Boulder.

4. The first time I ever drank hot tea from a tumbler instead of a cup, I did so in the apartment of Isidor Schneider. This custom — as good as any other — came naturally

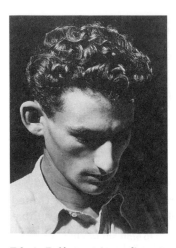

Edwin Rolfe, poet, journalist, veteran of Abraham Lincoln Battalion. Courtesy of Cary Nelson and the Rolfe Archive at the University of Illinois at Urbana-Champaign.

took up arms. Among the writers from France was André Malraux, who helped organize an air force for the republic. Small wonder that the civil war in Spain has been called the Writers War.[3]

Of course, writers were only a tiny minority among the 40,000 men and several hundred women from fifty-two countries who joined the International Brigades of which the Abraham Lincoln Battalion was a part. About 3,000 of these volunteers came from the United States, and the League gave them support in many ways. "Your battles in Spain were but the opening salvo in the war against Hitler which claimed the lives of 50 million human beings. Had you been successful we might have been spared some of the horrors of World War II." This was the opinion of Gene La Roque, a rear admiral retired from the U.S. Navy, director of the Center for Defense Information, who spoke in 1990 at the fifty-fourth anniversary of the Abraham Lincoln Battalion.

What had made Spain so important to volunteers and writers as well as to millions of non-writers throughout the world?[4] Perhaps a glance at history will make this clear.

In February 1936, the Spanish people voted out of office a government dominated by right-wing parties and elected a new government that included not only several parties of the Center but also both the small Communist Party and the larger Socialist Party. Only three years earlier in Germany, Socialists and Communists had quarreled so bitterly that the minority Nazi Party was able to take over.

The new government in Spain, called the Popular Front, represented an effort to reverse this suicidal pattern of sectarian hostility. The Popular Front grew out of a meeting of parties affiliated with the Communist International (Comintern) held in Moscow in 1935. At this meeting, Communists adopted a policy of seeking coalitions with parties and organizations of the Left and Center all around the world. In the United States the League of American Writers reflected this new alignment.[5]

I may have been a little more alert to news about the 1936 Spanish election than were some of my American contemporaries. In the spring of 1931, during an Oxford vacation, I had spent several weeks as a tourist in inexpensive Spain. Although I had gone mainly to see the Alhambra and the paintings in the Prado, I did know that a republic had just replaced a monarchy. The postage stamps I used had "República de España" printed over the likeness of King Alfonso XIII.

The British government, I soon learned, was much more interested than I in this political change. When I returned to England, I was held up at customs, and the boat train for London left without me. For two hours British security officers questioned me only to learn that I knew astonishingly little about Spanish politics. Then they questioned me about Merton, my college at Oxford. My knowledge of that respectable center of learning seemed to make them feel that I couldn't be all bad and they could safely admit me to the United Kingdom. They stamped my passport and let me board the next train.[6]

I have often wondered about this strange little episode. Did someone in the British government, which still ran a big empire in 1931, think that I might have been up to some radical mischief in Madrid? At Oxford I did belong to both the reformist Labour Club and the radical October Club, which was the undergraduate Communist society.

In 1931 the new Republic of Spain was inexperienced and weak — much weaker than the reactionary officers in the Spanish army realized or they might have moved immediately to return the king to power. Instead, the officers sought out military friends in Italy and Germany, as well as political allies in France, Britain, and the United States.

At that time, British interest in political developments in Spain was very real. British investors had put a lot of money into — and were getting a lot of money out of — important Spanish enterprises. They did not want what they regarded as a radical new government to threaten the status quo.

Other countries were interested, too. France had a very conservative and powerful upper-middle class, and it had a common border with Spain. The Catholic church, which supported the monarchy, was powerful in France and in the United States. Here, particularly in the Democratic Party, the Catholics had great influence. The result was that the United States did not offer support to anti-Fascist Spain. In Italy the Fascist government, which had been in power since 1922, looked with alarm at the apparent growth of democracy in the Mediterranean area.

Fascists who would soon take power in Germany had their expansionist eyes looking everywhere.

In Spain, in response to these developments, "the Left began to stir," as Robert G. Colodny, professor of history and also a Lincoln Battalion veteran, has put it in *Spain: The Glory and the Tragedy.*[7] Many Spanish workers wanted more revolutionary action than the government was taking, but in the absence of centralized coordination and leadership, their restlessness did not materialize except in the northern province of Asturias. There miners were numerous and well organized, and a strike in support of more popular control of the government did break out. Although the socialist head of the government favored the aims of the strikers, two generals, one of whom was Francisco Franco, suppressed the rebellious Asturians. Franco brought from Spanish North Africa troops who killed more than 1,000 and imprisoned 30,000 Asturians. Moderate middle-class supporters of the government objected to the terror imposed by Franco's troops, and in 1934 and 1935, they managed to keep the army out of power.

In February 1936, following a victory at the polls of a coalition known as the Popular Front, the Asturian miners whom Franco had imprisoned were released, and immediately they injected a militant spirit into the new government.

Meanwhile, a covert group of Spanish Fascist generals had strengthened their alliances and had become closely linked to Germany and Italy. They decided to move, ostensibly against Communists, although Communists were only a small minority within the Popular Front. In July 1936, the generals acted. A plane chartered in Britain, whose pilots some believed were closely affiliated with British intelligence, ferried General Franco from the Canary Islands to Morocco. On July 15, Italian transport planes airlifted 20,000 Moroccan and Spanish Foreign Legion troops into Spain. These men, very well equipped, moved rapidly toward Madrid.

To defend itself, the Popular Front government asked for help from France, which also had a Popular Front government. But the timid Socialist premier Léon Blum refused to supply arms. His government went further. It proposed that the major countries of Europe adopt a policy of non-intervention, the stated objective of which was to limit the Spanish war to the Iberian Peninsula. In the United States, the Congress and President Roosevelt followed a similar policy, placing an embargo on the export of arms to Spain.

At first, the Soviet Union agreed to non-intervention, but when it became clear the Spanish Fascists could get all the arms they wanted and the Loyalist government of Spain could get none except from Mexico, the Soviet Union reversed its position. At the same time, the Communist International stimulated Communist parties around the world to organize volunteers in support of those who were loyal to beleaguered Spanish democracy. And wherever these international volunteers appeared, there were writers among them. Writers in the United States were also active very early on behalf of the anti-Fascists in Spain. In October 1936, the League of American Writers raised money for a "propaganda motor truck" to be used by the Loyalists.

Popular support of the Loyalist government was widespread in the United States, although the U.S. government placed obstacles in the way of volunteers who wanted to go and fight. The English poet Stephen Spender, who had been an observer in Spain, noted years later in the *New York Review of Books* (September 25, 1969): "On the arrival of the first American volunteers in Spain, Cordell Hull [who was secretary of state] cabled instructions to the American consul in Barcelona that the American nationals in the Brigade should be given none of the protection — not even if they deserted and wished to leave Spain — accorded to American citizens."

A few months after the bombing of Guernica, Malcolm Cowley, Louis Fischer, and Anna Louise Strong represented the League at an international writers' congress in Spain.[8] As the delegates approached Madrid where the congress was to be held, Cowley reported, the following occurred in a village:

> When we went down into the square, we were surrounded by girls and boys, by mothers and grandmothers. The women were saying something very earnestly: All I could catch were the words "friends" and "help us, help us." Towering above the crowd was Stavsky, the Russian writer with a shaven head who looked like a Mack Sennett comedy convict. He made a gesture that nobody would have expected of him: he took the hand of an old woman, bent very low from the waist and kissed it. I saw with amazement there were tears in his eyes, and in the old woman's too, and in my own — except for the children, everybody was furtively weeping.
>
> It was one of those moments of direct feeling, transmitted almost without speech, that you find in Spain and nowhere else in the civilized world. Only afterwards did I learn what the women had been saying. They were asking us to go home and tell our countries that the Spanish people needed guns and airplanes.[9]

Malcolm Cowley, poet, critic, League vice president, 1937–1940; resigned 1940. From *Direction* magazine, May–June 1939.

In the same report, Cowley noted that later, after a bombing raid on Madrid, he and other writers, including Anna Louise Strong, went to the front. Along the way, Cowley saw undernourished children in devastated villages.

"Listen, Anna Louise," Cowley said. "Why couldn't I adopt some Spanish children and take them to the states?"

"If you are serious about it, I can take you to the Children's Bureau in Madrid," Strong replied.

Cowley was serious, but endless obstacles were placed in his way by U.S. consular officials, and he had to leave without the three or four children he had wanted to adopt.

After Cowley returned from Spain, his full report on the congress in Madrid was published in the August 1937 issue of the *Bulletin of the League of American Writers.* I have not seen it in any collection of his writings. I give it here:

A dozen people have asked, "Why was the second writers' congress held in Spain?" There are two answers. First, the congress had been scheduled for Madrid ever since June 1935. The invitation from the Spanish writers had been repeated and re-accepted in June 1936, a month before the Fascists started their revolt. And on November 6, when the Moors were almost in the streets of Madrid, it was publicly announced that the congress would be held there. This June, the International Association of Writers for the Defense of Culture was simply fulfilling its obligations. But also — and here is the second answer — it was showing the sympathy of writers all over the world for the men who are fighting fascism in Spain.

Obviously a congress held in a country at war involved enormous difficulties. The exact date had to be kept secret in order to keep the congress from being bombarded by Fascist planes. Invitations couldn't be sent out widely for fear of admitting spies and provocators. The entire English delegation as originally chosen was kept at home by the British Foreign Office, which refused visas. A new delegation had to be smuggled across the border.[10] Some of the exiled German delegates had to stay in Paris for the same reason. A few of the older and more distinguished writers were physically unable to face the hardships of the trip.

For the fact that the congress was held at all, we have to thank the persistent work of Louis Aragon, the novelist and poet, now editor of the influential Paris daily, *Ce Soir*. Aragon conducted negotiations with writers and governments and got special visas from the French Prefecture of Police — this in spite of the Cabinet crisis. André Malraux handled the problem of getting delegates over the border. In Spain, the poet Rafael Alberti handled arrangements and the Republican Government did its best to help. By the afternoon of Saturday, July 3, about seventy-five foreign delegates had reached Valencia. There were representatives of twenty-eight countries as far apart as China and Chile. And there were a good many delegates of international reputation — Benda, Malraux, Spender, Sylvia Townsend Warner, Alexis Tolstoy, Fadayev, Nexo, Chamson — as well as the Spaniards, Machado, Alberti, Del Vayo, De los Rios, Bergamin, and men from the International Brigades like Ralph Bates, Gustav Regler and Ludwig Renn. The United States was represented by Louis Fischer and Anna Louise Strong (already in Madrid), by Malcolm Cowley (who came directly from New York) and by Langston Hughes (who was delayed in passage and joined the congress only after its return to Paris).[11]

Once in Valencia, the delegates were confronted by two difficulties that proved greater than had been anticipated. In a country fighting for its life, given over completely to defense against a fascist invasion, it was very hard to talk calmly about the literary or theoretical questions that would have occupied the congress in another place, at another time. Speeches had to be immediate, practical, and they could not help being emotional. Then too, language became a serious obstacle. In

Anna Louise Strong, journalist. *Saturday Review of Literature* photo, December 25, 1937. Reproduced with the permission of the Western Historical Collections, University Archives, University of Colorado at Boulder Libraries.

Louis Aragon

Louis Aragon, French poet, novelist, editor, leader of the International Association of Writers for the Defense of Culture. Caricature by Georges Schreiber. From *New Masses*, 1939.

Sylvia Townsend Warner

Sylvia Townsend Warner, British
novelist, speaker at Third American Writers Congress. Caricature
by Georges Schreiber. From *New
Masses*, 1939.

Muriel Rukeyser, poet, FBI target.
Saturday Review of Literature
photo, July 31, 1937. Reproduced
with the permission of the Western Historical Collections, University Archives, University of
Colorado at Boulder Libraries.

Europe at present there is no international
tongue, not even French. The Scandinavian and
German delegates spoke German, the Russian
and Bulgarian delegates spoke Russian, the
Italian and French delegates spoke French.
Everything except French was translated into
Spanish, which the American and English delegates did not understand. The result was that
they missed some of the best speeches, including those by Bergamin and De los Rios. Most of
the translators were busy at the front.

They were especially busy that week because on Tuesday, July 6, the Republicans
started their big offensive west of Madrid. No
cable messages of any sort, except the official
Government communiques translated word
for word, could be sent out of Spain, so that the
congress was not mentioned in the foreign
press. At Madrid, speeches were made to the
rumble of not-so-distant artillery.

Nevertheless, the congress accomplished a
few important tasks. It revealed to the Spanish
people, who feel betrayed by the world, that
they are not fighting alone. It showed foreign
writers the real nature of this war, and the new
society that Spain is building for itself. And
later, at two meetings in Paris, there were resolutions and speeches of a more reflective nature, in Louis Aragon's important paper on
nationalism and art. It was a congress that will
have echoes for a long time to come. Incidentally, Louis Aragon criticized the American
writers and their organizations for still being
too sectarian. He thought we were not paying
enough attention to our own history and nature
as a people.

The American delegation extended an invi-
tation to hold the 1938 congress in New York.
On this invitation — and on another from the
Mexican delegation — action was deferred.

The League was not able to carry through the proposed congress, but it was very busy with many other projects.

Notes

1. Ernest Hemingway met Edwin Rolfe in Spain and years later wrote to him, "Remember I am fonder of you and respect you more than any guy I know." Hemingway to Rolfe, January 1943, Edwin Rolfe Archives, University Library, University of Illinois at Urbana-Champaign.

2. By joining the Spanish Republican Army, both Rolfe and Bessie expressed a deep conviction that was moving most writers. After returning from the war, however, Bessie wondered if he and Rolfe had made the best use of themselves. "There

Agnes Smedley, journalist, member of the League's National Council, 1935, FBI target. National Archives photo.

   is more than one way of fighting Fascism," he said. "A man should do what he knows best." Bessie and Rolfe knew more about writing than about soldiering. Alvah Bessie, *Men in Battle* (Charles Scribner's Sons, 1939), p. 191.

3. The American journalist Louis Fischer had been an early volunteer in the Lincoln Battalion. Communist journalists John Gates and Joe Brandt were soon under arms, as was Carl Marzani. British writers Ralph Bates and George Orwell fought and survived. Christopher Caudwell and Ralph Fox fought and died. W. H. Auden drove an ambulance at the front. Stephen Spender, Pablo Neruda, César Vallejo — these and many others wrote about what they saw and hoped for in Spain. The volunteers included Hungarian-born Arthur Koestler, from Germany, Gustav Regler, and Ludwig Renn. From Italy came political journalists Pietro Nenni, Luigi Longo, Palmiro Togliatti.
   Many League members sought and found ways in Spain to put their writing skills to work on the side of democracy: Ernest Hemingway, Josephine Herbst, John Dos Passos, Theodore Dreiser, Vincent Sheehan, George Seldes, Anna Louise Strong, Lillian Hellman, Joseph North, Dorothy Parker, Martha Gellhorn, James Neugass, Muriel Rukeyser, Langston Hughes, Erskine Caldwell, Henry Hart, Herbert Kline, Liston Oak, Bruce Minton, John Stuart, and James Benet.

4. "Never before in this century had so many authors from different countries written thus passionately from a political point of view concerning a historic event; nor had they been closely identified with a popular movement embracing so many extraliterary functions." Frederick R. Benson, *Writers in Arms: The Impact of the Spanish Civil War* (New York University Press, 1967), p. 40.

5. In support of the Popular Front policy, Georgi Dimitrov, head of the Communist International, who had outwitted Nazi prosecutors when he was falsely accused of setting fire to the Reichstag, said, "We want to prepare and hasten the overthrow of the Fascist dictatorship. We are ready to do all this because we want to save the world from Fascist barbarity and the horrors of imperialist war." Quoted in "U.S. Communists in Spain: A Profile," by Leonard and Levenson, in *Political Affairs*, August 1986, p. 23.

6. During World War II, I was actually deported from the United Kingdom, where I was hospitalized in Scotland following an injury at sea while I was serving with the U.S. Merchant Marine. I had with me a Russian grammar, a book on Marxist philosophy, and a textbook on trigonometry (I was preparing to become a third mate). In the hospital a nurse's aide asked me what newspapers I wanted to read. I requested the

conservative *London Times*, the liberal *Manchester Guardian*, and the Communist *London Daily Worker*. I thought that from these three I might get a fair idea of what was going on. When she heard *"Daily Worker,"* the young woman fled. Soon there appeared not newspapers but two British security officers, who wrote in my passport that the United States War Shipping Administration was responsible for evacuating me from the United Kingdom as soon as possible. I was flown back to the States, while badly wounded G.I.'s, fresh from the Battle of the Bulge, had to come home on a slow ship.

7. Robert G. Colodny, *Spain: The Glory and the Tragedy* (Humanities Press, 1990), p. 15.

8. The Madrid congress in 1937 was the second held by the International Association of Writers for the Defense of Culture. The first was held in Paris in June 1935.

9. *New Republic*, September 22, 1937.

10. Here I think of an example of British policy that had not been made public when Cowley drafted his report. Jessica Mitford in *A Fine Old Conflict* (Alfred A. Knopf, 1977), p. 18, tells of the length to which the British government went to keep British subjects from aiding the Republic of Spain. Mitford and her husband-to-be, Esmond Romilly, a young writer and the nephew of Winston Churchill, were blackmailed into leaving Spain by the British consul in Bilbao. He threatened to deny help in evacuating Basque women and children until Mitford and Romilly departed on a British naval vessel that had been sent specifically to bring them home.

11. After his return from Europe, Langston Hughes said of African-Americans in the Abraham Lincoln Battalion: "They were there in Spain in 1937–1938, American Negroes. History has recorded it; before that time, the leading ambassadors of the Negro people in Europe were jazz-band musicians, concert artists, dancers or other performers. But these Negroes in Spain were fighters — *voluntary fighters* — which is where history turned another page." Quoted by Page Smith, *Redeeming the Time* (McGraw-Hill Book Co., 1987), p. 773.

"Franco: I am an envoy from the gods," by the Spanish artist Clavé, winner of first prize in a contest sponsored by the Postal Employees Union of Barcelona in 1938. An album of six prints submitted for the contest, *Concurso de Caricaturas Antifascistas,* was published by the union's newspaper, *Vanguardia Postal.* In June 1939, Ludwig Renn gave the League a copy of this album. Original in the Franklin Folsom Collection.

International Association of Writers for the Defense of Culture. Before long, he also hinted — but did not actually state — that he was high in the international Communist organization. And did I know where he could stay while he was in New York waiting for his tour to be arranged?

My wife, Mary, and I had a spare room in our apartment. We invited Ralph to use it and he did — for the next six weeks. During all that time he kept us entertained. He told us about his working class origins in Swindon, England. He had been a railroad worker there before he became a writer, and he had a brother who was still working in the railroad shops in Swindon. Along with this proletarian background, he had somewhere picked up an amazing lot of learning. He was a connoisseur of medieval stained glass, and he knew a lot about Middle English and about music. He also knew everybody on the Left in Europe and, soon, in the United States. Words poured endlessly out of him, and food poured endlessly in.

In New York, with speech after rousing speech, Ralph raised thousands of dollars for Spain and then left on a nationwide tour, which was a great success. In time, he went to Mexico where, in fluent Spanish, he continued to agitate for republican Spain. Later he returned to New York, but there was a change in him. For one thing, he ate more than ever, and Millen Brand recorded in his journal that Bates was drinking heavily.

Then one day I came into my office and, to my astonishment, saw Ralph Bates sitting at my desk, going through my papers. He quickly reminded me that he was a member of the executive committee of the International Association of Writers for the Defense of Culture and he thought he ought to know what was going on in the American affiliate. I wondered.

Time and again, Bates talked nervously about trouble he was having getting a valuable Mexican guitar through customs, and about being summoned to Baltimore — why Baltimore? — by a British consul. One day he invited me to a very expensive dinner. Another day he borrowed money from me, although I had learned he had multiple sources of income. (He was an officer in the Spanish Republican Army, a propagandist for the Spanish government, and a paid speaker at fund- raising affairs. In addition, he had royalties from his writings.)

About this same time, he also took Jane Sherman, a League volunteer, to dinner on their first — and last — "date." Jane came to me the next morning with a curious story: Ralph had been at her home, obviously very excited — Jane thought he seemed terrified — and he played her piano madly. At dinner as he stuffed himself with *tagliatelle,* he seemed out of control and miserable. Just as he was leaving, he told Jane to look in *The New Republic* the next day. (He had told me that he wanted a job as foreign editor of that magazine.)

What we saw in *The New Republic* was an article by Ralph that began, "A spectre is haunting Europe, the spectre of a revolution that is dead."[3] He was referring to the military action that the Soviet Union had just taken against Finland, which had placed heavy artillery within range of Leningrad. Bates had made a complete break

Martha Gellhorn, journalist, novelist, speaker at Second American Writers Congress. From *Direction* magazine, May 1940.

with the Communists, and he would be allowed to stay in the United States, which he very much wanted to do.

Later I heard about Ralph from time to time from Marjorie Fischer, a member of the National Council of the League. He had a job teaching writing at New York University, dropped in sometimes at her nearby apartment, and talked about, among other things, the psychoanalysis he was undergoing. I never saw him again to ask what pressure he felt, possibly from the British government, that had made him reverse his life so completely and so quickly. Did his apparent psychological breakdown mean that he was a casualty of the Fascist attack on Spain? No matter what caused his sudden about-face, the days when Bates was a remarkably good writer were all in the past.

Other writers, too, came from Spain, and the League organized speaking tours for them. One was Ludwig Renn, a refugee German and chief of staff of the International Brigades. Renn, whose real name was Arnold Friedrich Vieth von Golssenau, was a German aristocrat, formerly an officer in the Kaiser's army in World War I. In 1928 he published an anti-military novel, *War,* and that year he joined the Communist Party. After Hitler took power, Renn was imprisoned for two and a half years for his opposition to the Nazi regime. Much of the time he was in solitary confinement, the rest of the time in forced labor. One of his tasks was to paste coffee bags together. Even on this job he managed to do some anti-Nazi propaganda. As he explained to his

Ludwig Renn, exiled German novelist, for whom the League arranged a national tour on behalf of republican Spain. From *Direction* magazine, December 1939.

audiences, "It was not long before coffee merchants in distant places began to find anti-Nazi slogans written between the outside paper and the lining of the bags."

In Spain Renn put his considerable military knowledge at the disposal of the Loyalist government, and in 1937 he came to the United States to increase support for the Spanish cause.

Renn entered the United States by train from Canada, and I went to Grand Central Station on a Sunday morning to meet him. He was a slender, impressive man but plainly nervous — he had chewed his fingernails to the quick. Did he always do this or was it evidence of the awful strain, even on a professional soldier, of being in battle and having great responsibilities?

We went from the station to my office, and there Renn made it clear that he was astonished by the nature of his reception. From all of the United States only one employee of the anti-Fascist writers' organization had come to meet him. Was this an indication that American writers attached small importance to the war in Spain?

I had focused my attention on organizing a tour and had completely overlooked the ceremonial side of my job. Renn was miffed. I was humiliated. But he carried through his tour and addressed sixty audiences with success before returning to Spain.[4]

In the summer of 1938, two international anti-Fascist conferences were organized, one in Paris and one in Madrid. The League's National Council asked Theodore Dreiser to represent American writers at those gatherings. He did not immediately agree to go. At the behest of the National Council, my wife and I went in search of Dreiser along the Connecticut shore. There we found him living with his young secretary, who tried her best to keep him from promising to be a delegate. Finally, however, he said he would do what his fellow writers had asked, if I would assure him that the expense money for his trip did not come from the Russians. I gave him this assurance. The money was provided by the International Association of Writers for the Defense of Culture.

Dreiser went to the conference in Paris, then on to Spain. When he returned in July, I joined newspaper reporters on a cutter in New York Harbor that took us to meet him on board the *Laconia*. I found him on deck in a line of passengers waiting to have their papers examined. The instant he saw me, he stepped out of the line, took my arm, and said with great earnestness, "Folsom, we have to get milk to the Spanish children!"

Dreiser made a number of speeches urging aid to Spain.[5] I arranged for League members to hear him at the City Club, which I had joined in order to get facilities for just such gatherings. Later he spoke at a dinner given for him by the League at the St. Moritz Hotel, September 15, 1938. The dinner raised $1,500 for aid. At a White House lunch with President Roosevelt, Dreiser pleaded for the U.S. government to send food to Spain. His plea was not successful.

I did not tell Dreiser, either before or after his talks, something I had not realized when he questioned me about the source of money for his European trip. It *had* been in large part paid for by the Russians. The Soviet Writers Union was the largest single affiliate of the International Association of Writers for the Defense of Culture. Accordingly, it made the largest contribution in the form of dues to the organization's treasury. I had not thought of this obvious fact when I gave him my assurance that he was not traveling on Russian money. But it was what he saw — not the Russian money — that determined what he said when he returned.

With encounters like that with Dreiser in mind, I wrote to my father on November 7, 1938:

> My job is as interesting as anybody could wish for: This week-end's schedule will give you some idea. We had the treasurer of the British Association of Writers (corresponding to ours) as our guest in the country over the week-end. . . . We had a fine time. Come Sunday afternoon I had to choose between a Connecticut meeting of writers, an interview with Heywood Broun, and an interview with one of the wealthiest women in the United States. I chose the latter. . . . You see I am trying to raise money for the League and I think I succeeded, but I'm not yet boasting. The check hasn't come. . . .
>
> I'm deep in all kinds of plans these days: how can we keep America from becoming the victim of the hysterical anti-semitic propaganda that always accompanies and precedes fascism? (We're getting out a pamphlet on this.) How can America's progressive writers make use of the radio (we're calling

a conference on this)? How can the writers of this country contribute to maintaining peace, and work for the establishment of economic justice? I also have to build up daily committees to go to Ellis Island to visit the veterans of the Abraham Lincoln Battalion who are being held there prior to deportation to their deaths in fascist countries. The fact that these aliens, though some of them have lived in this country for fifteen or twenty years, were willing to give up their lives for democracy, seems to be of no importance. The officials are bent on deporting them as if they were criminals — and deporting them to certain death, in spite of the fact that they fought in defense of democracy. Their deportation and death will make the entry of fascism into this country all the easier. . . . Then I have to write and send letters to the *Herald Tribune* (or get them written) proving that what they have just printed on behalf of Rebel Spain is a lie which has been refuted by every eye witness of the incident for a year and more now since the incident. (The H.T. yesterday revived the theory that Guernica was destroyed by the retreating Loyalists, although every newspaper man present, and every civilian who escaped described the destruction as being a thoroughgoing bombing by the Rebel (German) planes.

I don't recall how — or if — my anti-communist father responded to this catalogue of my activities in the literary-political world, but I do recall one of the projects that soon took much of my time. Following the lead set by British anti-Fascist writers, the League decided to query American writers about Spain. Donald Ogden Stewart, president of the League, sent a letter to over 1,000 writers in this country asking, "Are you for or against Franco and Fascism? Are you for or against the legal government and the people of Spain?" Four hundred eighteen writers replied. Millen Brand, Dorothy Brewster, Harry Carlisle, and Groff Conklin, serving as editors, compiled a pamphlet, *Writers Take Sides,* listing those who answered and including excerpts from typical letters.

Writers Take Sides did not include a letter that came from Max Eastman, once a supporter of *New Masses,* then a follower of Trotsky, and later an editor of *Reader's Digest.* In line with the prevailing fashion in League circles, the small number of Trotskyist writers in this country were not invited to submit their views on Spain. But somehow Eastman got an invitation, and I thought that since we had asked his opinion, we ought to publish his reply, although it was hostile to the elected government of Spain. The Communist Party thought otherwise. I, with some other League members — I don't recall which ones — met for a long afternoon with League member Moissaye Olgin, editor of the *Freiheit,* the CP's Yiddish language newspaper. Olgin gave us the full range of the CP arguments against Trotskyism. Who were we to pit our political inexperience against that of the Party? We all caved in and pretended in *Writers Take Sides* that Trotskyists did not exist. They *were* few, and I think they were wrong about Spain, but it was no contribution to anti-Fascism to say that only one of the writers polled by the League had objected to the Popular Front when, in fact, two had objected, and about a dozen Trotskyists had not even been polled.

Not counting Eastman, 410 of the replies favored the republican government and opposed Franco. Seven writers claimed to be neutral, and one, Gertrude Atherton, was opposed to the Loyalist government. No list of the writers who did not reply has survived. The list of those who did reply is in Appendix G.[6]

Robert S. Lynd, sociologist. *Saturday Review of Literature* photo, April 24, 1937. Reproduced with the permission of the Western Historical Collections, University Archives, University of Colorado at Boulder Libraries.

Another League activity peculiarly suited to an organization of writers was a sale of manuscripts and letters held on March 25, 1938, at the Barbizon-Plaza Hotel, for the benefit of the Medical Bureau of the North American Committee to Aid Spanish Democracy.

Of our plans for the manuscript sale, Van Wyck Brooks wrote: "I think this is a grand idea. I was thinking it was about time for us to do something more about Spain. And couldn't we make it a bang-up sale and get some kind of ms. from every decent writer in the country? It would make a great impression if we could prove in this way that every writer who is worth a nickel is a hundred per cent for the Loyalists."[7]

A committee headed by Marjorie Fischer solicited the manuscripts we were turning into commodities for sale. Among the committee members were the playwright and novelist Philip Stevenson, journalists Edith and Samuel Grafton, and novelist Edwin Lanham.

Contributions turned up from unexpected quarters and were testimony both to the widespread revulsion against fascism and to the many friends that League members had in the writing community. From all points of the literary compass came many whole manuscript drafts of well-known books and chapters or pages from other works, all by

Marc Blitzstein, composer, play-wright, FBI target. National Ar-chives photo.

contemporary authors in the United States, Britain, France, the Soviet Union, and by writers in the German, Czech, and Austrian diaspora. Some of the contributions were handwritten — true manuscripts; others were typescripts, often with handwritten corrections. And there were many letters by authors living and dead.

Living donors included Albert Einstein, Henri Barbusse, Romain Rolland, Booth Tarkington, Edna St. Vincent Millay, Van Wyck Brooks, William Carlos Williams, Fannie Hurst, Louise Bogan, Upton Sinclair, Thomas Mann, Archibald MacLeish, Elinor Wylie, H. G. Wells, Edgar Lee Masters, Edna Ferber, and Thornton Wilder. In addition, dealers in rare manuscripts and letters dipped into their stocks and contributed letters from Jack London, Eugene Debs, John Reed, Sir Arthur Conan Doyle, and others from the past.

At the sale, which went on until three in the morning and netted $5,000 (enough in 1938 dollars to buy several ambulances), celebrities did the auctioneering. One of these was the German refugee writer and wounded veteran of the International Brigades, Gustav Regler. Others were actors Lionel Stander, Jean Muir, and Will Geer and the German dramatist Ernst Toller. Marc Blitzstein performed part of his *The Cradle Will Rock* as he auctioned off the much-corrected script of the opera. Everything was sold, even autographed copies of the handsome catalogue that had been designed by the eminent book designer, Milton Glick.

How League members felt about the sale was reflected in lines from a poem that Rolfe Humphries wrote for the occasion:

> Lucky, to buy and sell
> While men in Spain are dead
> Who battle for a world
> Where books may still be read.[8]

Humphries put a great deal of effort into the League. But one day in 1939, when he came to the office on some matter about Spain, he showed in his own gruff way that committee work did not exclude other activities. I knew that Rolfe found pleasure in many directions — his duties as a Latin teacher in a private preparatory school, his membership in the Communist Party, his afternoons watching Big League baseball or horse racing, and on the day in question he didn't go straight into the discussion for which he had come. Instead, he plunked down on my desk the April-September issue of *Poetry: A Magazine of Verse.* In it was an ode he had written for a Phi Beta Kappa occasion at Columbia University, where Nicholas Murray Butler was president.

What I saw was full of classical allusions, and I couldn't make sense of it. I must have shown my perplexity as I looked up at Rolfe, who was grinning. He leaned over and ran a finger down the left side of each of the pages on which the ode was printed. I followed the initial letters of the lines and saw spelled out: NICHOLAS MURRAY BUTLER IS A HORSES ASS.

As Rolfe Humphries was writing his prosodic swipe at a reactionary university president in New York, the Loyalist army in Spain was facing increasing difficulties, due in part to a reactionary policy that prevailed in Washington. With this in mind, the League, in December 1938, sent a letter to the hundreds of writers whose addresses we kept on file. We asked them to sign a petition to President Roosevelt. The petition read:

Events of recent months in Czechoslovakia, which has lost its independence, and in Germany, which has intensified its persecution of Catholics and Jews, make us realize the necessity of approaching you once more with the earnest hope that you will find it in your power to raise the embargo on arms to the friendly government of Spain. Since Spain will be the most natural base of operations for Fascist penetration of Spanish speaking America, we consider that it is doubly urgent that Spain be preserved as a democracy.

If America raised the embargo on Spain, it would not only act in its capacity as a defender of freedom and democracy in this hemisphere, it would take a decisive step in protecting one of the few remaining democracies in Europe and strike a serious blow to the Nazi plans for world domination. Moreover, raising the embargo on Spain would be an immediate and practical defense of the Catholics and Jews in Germany, for economic pressure on Hitler seems the only language he can understand.

We commend you for the steps you have taken to make known the outraged feeling of Americans at the treatment of Jews and Catholics in Germany, and we wish every success to your policy of protecting North

Carl Van Doren, biographer, critic, FBI target. From an etching by Theodore Brenson reproduced in *New Masses*, October 21, 1941.

"I am the official translator in this country of Marx and Engels," he said.

Why Leonard had chosen to put forward this of his many distinctions, was not clear, but Madame de la Nux did not seem disturbed. She graciously offered us drinks. Would Mr. Mins open the soda bottle?

Leonard was a man of action. He took the bottle, surveyed the kitchen, saw what he wanted, and strode over to a counter. With one swift motion he jerked the bottle down; off came the cap, leaving a deep gouge in the soft metal counter.   ·

At about this point Madame de la Nux decided that perhaps $2,000 was a bit much to put into the new committee. She wrote out and handed me a check for $1,000 and rather quickly bade us good night.

It was not until some time later that the mystery of this woman's interest in Spanish refugees was solved. We found out, just how I forget, that she had bought a place on the Spanish Intellectual Aid committee at the behest of her husband, who was an official in the French Foreign Office. The French government wanted an easy way of knowing what was being done to spirit Spanish intellectuals — including Communists — through France.

Whether Madame de la Nux and her principals thought they got their money's worth, I do not know. But we did manage, in spite of all the efforts of the French government to the contrary, to give real help to quite a number of devoted Spanish anti-Fascist writers, teachers, and artists.

And Leonard Mins? He was later subpoenaed to appear before the House Un-American Activities Committee. There he turned up nattily dressed, wearing a Homburg hat, and he confounded the members of the committee by quoting Catullus to them — in Latin.

The effects of the Spanish Loyalists' defeat — and by ugly events that preceded it — were soon felt among those who had been helping the republic. Some individuals took up positions closer to those of the winning side.

The evils that go with any war were not manifested only by the Fascists. Authorities, who seem to have been Communists, had José Robles, the interpreter for John Dos Passos, shot as a spy, although he may not have been one.[11] At any rate, a bullet quickly made it impossible to investigate fully the charge against him. This military execution outraged Dos Passos and helped to drive him from the community of writers who had joined in defending democracy in Spain. Indeed, it seems to have played a role in changing the whole direction of Dos Passos's political life. He ultimately became very conservative.[12]

John Dos Passos, novelist, who turned against the League and the Popular Front in Spain. *Saturday Review of Literature* photo, April 9, 1938. Reproduced with the permission of the Western History Collections, University Archives, University of Colorado at Boulder Libraries.

Other writers, too, had to deal with both the positive and the negative aspects of Stalinism. On the positive side, the Russians were sending to Spain material aid that the United States refused to give; and Communists were risking their lives. On the other hand, some of the Communists who were giving military advice were martinets, rigid and violently suspicious, and powerful enough to order executions. Many writers who were somewhat aware of Stalin's paranoia still focused on the good that many Communists were obviously doing, and they remained loyal to the Popular Front. Among the English writers, George Orwell came out of the war intensely hostile to the Popular Front and to Communism. He had been attached to a POUM military formation. POUM was an acronym for *Partido Obrero de Unificación Marxista,* which the Communist Party, perhaps mistakenly, regarded as a Trotskyist organization.

Spanish Trotskyists objected to policies of the Communist Party in the Popular Front. Anarchists, who were more numerous, objected on principle to centralized government authority and so opposed the Popular Front. In the murky arena of sectarian squabbles, it is difficult even after fifty years to separate fact from fabrication. POUM, for example, claimed that the CP engaged in provocations that were used as pretext for bloody suppression of the POUM organization. The Communists for their part saw POUM as objectively helping Franco. They even claimed that Franco was actually using POUMists as spies and disruptors. Tension was high, and at that very time violent purges and frame-ups were marring the political scene in the Soviet Union. It is not unreasonable to suspect that these purges spilled over into Spain, channeled there through Soviet citizens and sympathizers, some of whom were in the military. At any rate, about a thousand POUMists were killed, and executions are said to have been carried out in the ranks of the Abraham Lincoln Battalion. The U.S. Communist leader, Earl Browder, told his friend Philip Jaffe that he discovered in Spain that two heroic leaders of the Lincoln Battalion, Dave Doran and Robert Merriman, were executed, not killed in military action as reported.[13]

Such events sent some of those who knew about them reeling away from the Left and the Popular Front, and their reactions lessened the effectiveness of the League and other anti-Fascist organizations. Many knew nothing about this grim underside of the war. Informed or uninformed, the majority of those who began as supporters of the Popular Front still felt committed to do what they could, so that a government chosen by the Spanish people might survive and fascism be stopped.

Writers, when they paused to reflect, were discovering that political life was not simple, and it would become more complex. Meanwhile, the League continued to grow.

Notes

1. For a list of those who took part in translating or adapting the ballads, see Appendix C.

2. Humphries to E. Merrill Root, Box XIV, Rolfe Humphries Papers, Special Collections and Archives, Amherst College Library, Amherst, Mass.

3. Ralph Bates, "Disaster in Finland," *The New Republic,* December 13, 1939, p. 221.

4. When Spain collapsed, Renn escaped to France, where he lived underground and wrote a book, *Warfare: The Relation of War to Society* (Oxford University Press, 1939). Then he escaped from France, went to Mexico, and there became president of the Free Germany organization. After World War II, he became a professor of anthropology in East Germany. He died in 1979.

5. The speeches given by Dreiser in Paris, at the City Club and at Hotel St. Moritz, are in the Dreiser Papers, Special Collections, Van Pelt Library, University of Pennsylvania.

6. Una Jeffers, whose husband Robinson Jeffers, the poet, was neutral about the war in Spain and who never joined the League, said, "What's so wrong with Hitler? He doesn't smoke or drink or go with women." — Ella Winter, *And Not to Yield* (Harcourt, Brace and World, 1963), p. 132.

7. Brooks to League, LAW Papers, Bancroft Library, University of California, Berkeley.

8. At the Writers Congress in June 1939, Langston Hughes read the names of forty-five writers from nine countries who had given their lives in the fight against fascism.

9. The text of the petition to Roosevelt is in the LAW Papers, UC–Berkeley.

10. A copy of Dreiser's telegram is in my possession. I do not recall the wording of the cable to the Pope.

11. Hemingway in *For Whom the Bell Tolls* "depicted the spy-disease, the Russian syphilis." Gustav Regler, *Owl of Minerva* (Farrar, Straus and Cudahy, 1960), pp. 292–293.

12. The fate of José Robles did not drive his son away from support of the republican government. Constancia de la Mora in *In Place of Splendor* (Harcourt, Brace, 1939) reported that Elliot Paul knew the boy and said, "I never knew such sadness — and such firmness." The wife and daughter of Robles also remained very active in support of the republican government. Constancia de la Mora commented, "What John Dos Passos could not forgive the Spanish people, the man's wife and children understood."

13. It was a problem like this that a woman called Hedda commented on in Joseph Freeman's *An American Testament* (Farrar and Rinehart, 1936), a book that the Communist Party disapproved of. Hedda said (p. 598), "Telling people the truth is the most difficult art in the world. One must know how to do it, just as one must know how to lead an army. Good intentions alone will get you nowhere. Your truth, awkwardly stated, may turn out in effect to be a lie."

Members of the Abraham Lincoln Battalion in Spain, including writers Alvah Bessie (second row left) and Edwin Rolfe (third row left) with Joseph North a visiting U.S. journalist, (first row left) Courtesy of Cary Nelson and the Rolfe Archive at the University of Illinois at Urbana-Champaign.

British novelist Ralph Bates (left) and poet Edwin Rolfe in Spain. The League organized a speaking tour for Bates in the United States. Courtesy of Cary Nelson and the Rolfe Archive at the University of Illinois at Urbana-Champaign.

Ernest Hemingway and Ludwig Renn near the Guadalajara front in Spain following a Loyalist victory there. Joris Ivens photo.

4
Rescuing Refugees

Today America finds herself host to 85 percent of the surviving intellectuals of Europe.

— Gustav O. Arlt, Professor of German
University of California, Berkeley, 1943

Soon after Hitler became chancellor of Germany in January 1933, Nazis threw books into bonfires throughout the country. At the same time, they began to exclude Jews from all cultural life and to bar from all political life Communists, Socialists, and others who opposed them. To German writers, these assaults on freedom meant that they could no longer practice their profession in their homeland. In order to write — in order to stay alive — they had to go to a foreign country. Anywhere was better than the Third Reich.

Very soon after Nazis set fire to the parliament building, the Reichstag, as a pretext for establishing Hitler's dictatorial power, men and women of letters quietly left their homes, their belongings, their friends and tried to slip across the German border. Some didn't make it and were never heard from again. Almost all talented authors left. An exception was aged Gerhardt Hauptman, dramatist and author of *The Weavers*, who was friendly to the Nazis. Many writers sought refuge in France. A few went to England, others to Austria, Czechoslovakia, or Spain. Then, as the Nazis increased the area they controlled, writers had to flee again from Spain, from Austria, from Czechoslovakia. Ahead of Hitler's armies, some escaped to Scandinavia, only to move on from there.

As fascism changed the political climate of Europe, France ceased to be hospitable to anti-Nazis, although it had welcomed them in the days of the French Popular Front government. Under Premier Edouard Daladier, writers were sent to concentration camps and treated with

Jules Romains, exiled French novelist. Portrait by Georges Schreiber in *Saturday Review of Literature,* October 19, 1940.

great hostility. Men and women who had already fled once or twice now had to flee again, this time from behind barbed wire.[1] And where can you go without identity papers and without money? Many in the literary diaspora hoped for refuge in the United States, but this country would not admit, sometimes even for transit, writers who were Communists — or who were believed to be Communists. They had to go elsewhere. Some found shelter in Chile. Many settled in Mexico. Before the migration ended, French writers joined it. Jules Romains, president of PEN (Poets, Essayists, Novelists) came to New York. Sigrid Undset had to leave Norway with nothing but a handbag.

To deal with this vast human and cultural tragedy, a number of committees became active in rescue work, but often they concentrated their efforts on non-Communists, and some committees would not knowingly give any help to Communists. Howard L. Brooks, a representative of the Unitarian Service Committee in France, in 1941 said, "Race, color or creed made no difference whatsoever, but not a single Nazi or Communist ever received our help."[2] Varian Fry, who acted as the representative in southern France of the Emergency Rescue Committee, said, "I had to be careful not to help . . . a Communist masquerading as a democrat."[3] The anti-Communist mood in influential quarters in the United States was such that relief agencies were willing, in effect, to leave Communist refugees to certain death at the hands of the Nazis.

Reminding us of the anti-Communist mood at this time, League member John Sanford, in his autobiographical *A Very Good Land to Fall With,* records this conversation with a doctor he consulted. The doctor asked, "What do you do for a living?"

"Write," Sanford said. "I call myself a writer."

"What do you write about?"

"Oh, I don't know. People, I guess."

"People!" the doctor said. "What the hell are you — a Communist?"[4]

As a result of such hostility, the plight of the anti-Nazi Communists in Europe was desperate. To help them, indeed to help any writers, the

League set up an Exiled Writers Committee with headquarters in New York.[5]

Exiled writers themselves worked
with the committee if they were lucky
enough to reach New York, even tempo-
rarily. One of these was the Czech novelist,
Franz Weiskopf, who was representative
to the League from the International Association of Writers for the Defense of Culture. He was fluent in several languages
and conducted a prodigious correspondence in all of them. His energy and ability
were such that only days after he reached
New York, he was selling articles written
in English about developments in Europe.
Soon his anti-Nazi novels began to appear

Walter Schoenstedt, exiled German fiction writer. From *Direction*
magazine, December 1939.

in English in the United States. *The Firing Squad* (Alfred A. Knopf, 1944)
portrayed both the inner corruption of the Nazi regime and the Czech
resistance to the Nazi invaders. *Dawn Breaks* (Duell, Sloan and Pearce,
1942) gave a vivid picture of the guerrilla warfare conducted in Czechoslovakia against Hitler's forces. In addition, Weiskopf introduced readers in the United States to Czech and Slovak literature with the
publication of *Hundred Towers*, (L. B. Fischer, 1945), an anthology of
translated selections from the writings of his compatriots. After the war,
Weiskopf became at different times minister plenipotentiary of Czechoslovakia to the United States, ambassador to Sweden, and ambassador
to China, all the while continuing to write.

Ambrogio Donini, an Italian journalist who had been professor of
comparative religion at the University of Rome, advised the committee
about Italians in concentration camps who needed help.

Few writers in the United States knew more about what was hap-
pening to German writers than did Martha Dodd, daughter of William
E. Dodd, who was U.S. ambassador to Germany from 1933 to 1937.
Martha Dodd gave enormous help with fund-raising and introductions
to people who could solve problems, while at the same time, her book
Through Embassy Eyes (Harcourt, Brace and Co., 1939) was offering
readers a close look at what went on inside Germany under the Nazis.
Ironically, Martha herself was to become a refugee. When witch-hunting

Ellen Conried, poet, photographer, volunteer on the Exiled Writers Committee. Courtesy of Ellen Conried Balch.

The refugees who used these dangerous secret routes often traveled on forged passports, used aliases, and passed along bribes to border guards. Consequently, the minutes and reports of the Exiled Writers Committee sometimes had a mysterious, conspiratorial quality. The records are vague at just the points at which normal curiosity would ask for specific facts. "—— recently arrived in New York from a concentration camp in France." "The Exiled Writers Committee is sending $5 a month to B ——, G ——, L —— in a concentration camp in the unoccupied zone of France." And so on. The committee was operating a kind of underground railroad, and it took precautions against snoopers working for French intelligence or for newspapers more interested in sensation than in the safety of human beings, or for the FBI, as I discovered much later when I was able to inspect some of the FBI files. As a result of our caution, it is now impossible to construct a detailed record of many of the rescues in which the committee participated.

Nevertheless, the committee very often succeeded in frustrating the Nazis and their French puppets and the FBI, whose common goal was to silence independent voices. What follows are stories of rescues about which at least some information has survived.

One writer in flight was Anna Seghers. At the age of twenty-eight she had won the Kleist Award, the highest literary honor in Germany. Five years later, her books were banned and burned, and she was interrogated by the Gestapo. Somehow, she managed to escape to Paris with her husband, Laszlo Radvany, and their two children. In Paris she continued to write, helped to found the German Writers Protective League, and was active as an anti-Nazi editor. When France declared war on Germany, Seghers's husband, a Hungarian sociologist, was interned, and she and her children went into hiding. In time she escaped from the occupied north of France into a part of the country not yet under direct German control. The Exiled Writers Committee located her, got visas for her and her children, and raised passage money to Martinique, where they were interned. From there they managed to reach Santo

Domingo. The committee then brought them to New York, where they were stopped at Ellis Island.

The manuscript of Anna Segher's novel *The Seventh Cross* had preceded her. The Exiled Writers Committee had a portion of it translated and sent to Maxim Lieber, a literary agent. Together, he and I went to see Seghers on Ellis Island. Lieber had with him a contract for the book. *The Seventh Cross* (Little, Brown and Co., 1942) became a Book-of-the-Month Club choice and later a movie, from which the fact that her hero was a Communist was entirely cut out. At any rate, some of Anna Seghers's words managed to enter this country although she herself could not. On

Albert Einstein, honorary League member. National Archives photo.

Ellis Island I watched her sign the contract for her book about the underground struggle against the Nazi terror and learned why she was being detained. An Immigration Service doctor had said her teenage daughter had "an incurable disease of the central nervous system." This meant that the girl was medically inadmissible, and the Immigration Service, humanely, did not believe in separating parent and child.

The fact was that the girl, who had been a hunted — and haunted — refugee for years, had a tic. Her face twitched a little. The examining doctor observed this from a distance of twenty feet, never closer, and the result was that she and her left-wing mother could not take asylum in the United States.

In Mexico Anna Seghers, with two other exiled writers, Ludwig Renn and Egon Erwin Kisch, established a German-language, anti-Nazi publishing house that managed to bring out twenty books by writers who had been driven from their homeland. Seghers was also very active with about thirty other anti-Nazi refugees in an organization called Allemania Libre (Free Germany), which published a newspaper by the same name. In addition, she learned Spanish and lectured on German culture in the Workers's University. After the defeat of nazism, she returned to East Germany, where she continued to write, and became one of the founders of the World Peace Council.[13]

On Ellis Island, in December 1939, I also met Egon Erwin Kisch, a Czech newspaper man who was regarded as the creator of the journalistic form known as reportage. He had a transit visa to the United States, and soon he too would have to move on to Mexico. Before his departure from Europe, he said, he was confined in a little village. "Couldn't have any mail. No one knew my address. Two shirts in a suitcase. One socks. All ready to go to a concentration camp at a moment's notice. One day an American newspaper man said 'I'm here on behalf of American writers. You have to go to America.' 'That's fine but I have no money.' He said, 'We'll fix that.' And here I am."[14]

And indeed he was. On the ferry that carried us from Ellis Island to Manhattan, Kisch grew more and more tense. When the vessel edged into the slip, he moved up to the chain stretched across the bow, behind which passengers were supposed to wait. The moment the ferry bumped, Kisch, his clumsy overcoat flapping, clambered over the chain, ran forward, and leaped onto the pier. There he fell to his knees and kissed the ground, the dirty ground of freedom. He had visited the United States some time before and knew something of our folkways. His first request, when I caught up with him, was for a hot dog.

After meeting Kisch, I read his *Sensation Fair* (Modern Age Books, 1941) in translation. It was full of rich and colorful accounts of events in Europe to which he had been eyewitness, as well as tales of his own life. One episode was surely unique: a passionate love affair he had with one-half of a pair of Siamese twins.

After the war Kisch returned to his homeland. Among the honors he received there was one he specially treasured: He was made mayor of his hometown in Czechoslovakia.

Another European with whom I had dealings on Ellis Island was Otto Katz, a Czech political writer, who also wrote under the name André Simone. Otto had a presence that acquaintances agreed was appropriate for an ambassador. When he entered a room, people looked his way, although he engaged in no stage business, so far as I could see, that was designed to attract attention. He might have made a good actor, but he was a good journalist, a good historian of the contempory scene, and an editor under Willi Muenzenberg of *The Brown Book of the Hitler Terror*.[15] And he was good company, as my wife and I found when he visited us at a little cabin we rented in the country.

One day I got word that Otto had been taken into custody by the Immigration and Naturalization Service, even while the country was

Egon Irwin Kisch (left), exiled Czech writer, in Spain. From
Direction magazine, May–June 1939.

gearing up for war against Adolf Hitler, the most zealous of all anti-
Communists. Otto was awaiting on Ellis Island the kind of hearing that
usually led to deportation. But he could be released pending the hearing
if someone would post bail. The Exiled Writers Committee had some
money but not enough.

I phoned Lillian Hellman, who knew and liked Otto, told her about
his plight, and asked if she could contribute the additional amount
needed to arrange for his release.

"I haven't got it," she barked. Then she added, "But if you will come
to my apartment at midnight, I'll have it."

When I knocked on her door that night, a maid appeared. She
obviously expected me and led me into the big drawing room, where
empty bottles and glasses were everywhere. There had been a party —
but not a soul was about. The maid went to the mantle over the fireplace

and got an envelope addressed to me. In it was the cash I had asked for. The next day Otto Katz was free. (A macabre sequel to Otto's story appears in Chapter 13.)

Many other writers still needed our help. In the course of arranging for food packages, steamship fares, or fund-raising events, League members quite often stopped by the League office. Some, it seemed to me, came to regard it as a sort of social club. They dropped in, hoping for some literary conversation and companionship, although all the place usually offered them was two rooms full of employees and volunteers stuffing envelopes. A member of the Exiled Writers Committee who appeared frequently was Robert Carse, a sailor turned writer, always sociable but not always sober. One day he came in obviously bent on business rather than pleasure, but what he had to say made me wonder whether it was one of his drinking days.

This is the tale he told: A political writer, whose name I have forgotten, was in Le Vernet, the concentration camp for "undesirables." German troops were fast advancing on Le Vernet, and because the man was a secretary of the German Communist Party, he would surely be killed when they reached the camp.

However, it was still possible, said Carse, to save this man's life. His wife was in Marseilles, and if we could get $1,000 to her immediately, she could use it to bribe a guard at the camp to let her husband escape.

This sounded a little like one of Carse's melodramatic sea stories. Nevertheless, I rushed down to the Communist Party headquarters to see if Carse knew what he was talking about. I was assured that he did. But where could I get $1,000? Up the street from the League office was the office of *Friday* magazine, an anti-Fascist journal edited by Dan Gilmore, a radical young man who had inherited wealth. I told him Carse's story — now my story — and asked for the money. Dan was cautious. He obviously wanted to find out if I was talking sense. In less than an hour, he had satisfied himself that I knew what I was doing. He wrote out a check.

It was impossible at that time to cable money from the United States to France; we did not have diplomatic relations with the Vichy regime there, but funds could be transferred through Mexico. I hopped into a cab and went to the office of the diamond merchant I had once met in Lillian Hellman's apartment. He took the check and within an hour a diamond merchant in Mexico City was cabling money to Marseilles to the wife of the man who was in such danger in Le Vernet.

After all this, there was silence — except for the news a few days later that the German army had taken over Le Vernet. Then came word that the thousand dollars had arrived too late. The man it was to save was dead.

I had no desire to hurry up to *Friday* magazine with this news, and it turned out that I didn't see Dan Gilmore again for a long time. He went into the army when the United States entered the war. I went into the Merchant Marine, and our paths didn't cross until the war was over and we both had children in the Downtown Community School. There I had become director of adult education, and one of my chores was to organize a fund-raising dinner. Dan bought tickets. Now, I decided, I would have to tell him that his money had not reached Marseilles in time. As I helped to arrange the seating of guests at the dinner, I swallowed hard and placed Dan at the table where I would be.

The day of the dinner, a small item in the *New York Times* caught my eye. The man who was supposed to be dead had just attended in Germany an important gathering that was concerned with the collaboration of Socialists and Communists!

I dropped everything and rushed the few blocks to Communist headquarters. "The story is correct," I was told. For some reason everyone concerned had assumed I knew what had happened.

The cabled money had arrived in Marseilles on schedule. The guard at Le Vernet had been bribed, just as planned. Shortly thereafter, a corpse was taken out of the camp bearing the tags of the German journalist. At the same time, the journalist was allowed to leave, presumably with false identification. He went directly toward the advancing German army, passed through the lines, and remained — underground — in German-held territory for the rest of the war.

I was able to tell this story to Dan Gilmore that night at the Downtown Community School dinner.

Another rescue of a very different kind involved Benedict Freistadt and his son and daughter. Freistadt, who was better known under his pen name, Bruno Frei, began, after World War I, as an author of books about Vienna. From that city he moved to Berlin, where he became an editor of an anti-Nazi newspaper. When the Nazis seized power, Bruno, with his wife, Maria, and their teenage children, Hans and Lisa, escaped first to Prague, then to Paris. There, on June 3, 1940, during the only Nazi air raid on that city, a bomb killed Maria.

Bruno Frei, exiled Austrian journalist. From *Exil in Lateinamerika,*
by Wolfgang Kiessling.

Soon after losing his wife, Bruno was
sent to Le Vernet, and Hans and Lisa
stayed in a series of orphanages. Finally,
although they were as much Catholic in
origin as Jewish, they ended up in a Jewish
orphanage in southern France. At this
point, the Exiled Writers Committee got
visas that allowed the children to join their
father and board a French vessel, the *Win-
nipeg,* bound for the French island of
Martinique in the Caribbean.[16] There, in
the ship's steerage, they found they were
fellow passengers of Gerhardt Eisler, who
would later become a well-publicized target of the House Un-American Activities
Committee, and Albert Norden, who after
the war would become an important political figure in East Germany.

Only one day out from Martinique, an anti-Nazi Dutch warship
captured the vessel because it was French and France was now almost
completely controlled by the Germans. The Dutch diverted the vessel to
Trinidad, which the British controlled. There Bruno and the children
were again interned.

Soon the Exiled Writers Committee obtained Mexican visas for all
three. But Bruno hoped that the children could get into the United States,
where he thought they would have a better education than in Mexico.
That would be possible if a U.S. citizen legally adopted them. Bruno
himself could not enter the United States because of his Communist
politics.

The Exiled Writers Committee sent out word that Hans and Lisa
were seeking an American parent. Before long, a Mrs. Miller, a school-
teacher in Evanston, Illinois, volunteered. Mrs. Miller satisfied the immigration authorities that she had adequate income and housing
arrangements, and the adoption went through. The generous mother-
to-be drove to New York. The children came from Ellis Island, and in
the League office I introduced the tense, bright-eyed boy and the timid
girl to their new parent.

First off, Mrs. Miller took Hans and Lisa on a shopping spree. They
needed clothes — American-style clothes — to start their new life. Then

from New York, crossing the country by car to Evanston, she showed them some of their new homeland. Bruno Frei proceeded to Mexico, where he stayed until the end of the war.[17]

Most of the writers rescued by the League kept on writing in spite of their separation from the peoples and the languages so essential to them. Those in New York also organized and gave financial help to their colleagues in Mexico, Argentina, and elsewhere in Latin America. Exiles for whom the League had found employment in Hollywood contributed much to the lively intellectual activity of that community. In Mexico City they set up the Heinrich Heine Club, which gave German-speaking writers a way of encouraging each other and of keeping alive German literary tradition. In a periodical that soon reached 20,000 readers worldwide, they published news and articles about what was going on in their homeland and in the resistance to the Nazis.

Max Schroeder, exiled German editor, critic. From *Max Schroeder: Zum Gedenken* (Berlin: Aufbau-Verlag).

Otto Katz, who spoke English well, lectured repeatedly in Mexico City about current events to groups of tourists from the United States. He and others, with whom Lázaro Cárdenas, president of Mexico, and Lombardo Toledano, leader of the Mexican trade union movement, became friendly, had the effect of increasing among Mexicans an awareness of the dangers of nazism.

After the defeat of Hitler, Max Schroeder, who had suffered greatly in the French concentration camp at Le Vernet, worked at publishing amid the ruins of Berlin. His first project was to make available to German readers the best books that writers had produced while they were in exile. In one way or another, the writers rescued by the League did much more than stay alive. They kept German literature alive, and if the government of East Germany fell short of their dreams for a society full of human warmth and marked by equality for all, they were not the cause of its failure.

Notes

1. For a list of German and Austrian writers taken into custody in November 1939, see Appendix I.

2. Howard L. Brooks, *Prisoners of Hope: Report on a Mission* (L. B. Fischer, 1942), p. 13.

3. Varian Fry, *Surrender on Demand* (Random House, 1945), p. 24.

4. John Sanford, *A Very Good Land to Fall With,* vol. 3 (Black Sparrow Press, 1967), p. 164.

5. The personnel of the committee varied from time to time. For a list of members who helped at one time or another see Appendix C.

6. Brooks, p. 158.

7. For a list of others who endured stays in Le Vernet, see Appendix I.

8. All Humphries letters referred to and his diary are in the Humphries Papers, Special Collections and Archives, Amherst College Library, Amherst, Mass.

9. In 1986 one of Enge's nephews, Daniel Menaker, an editor of the *New Yorker,* wrote a long piece for that magazine about his uncle, who had just died at the age of ninety. This piece grew into a novel, *The Old Left* (Alfred A. Knopf, 1977).

10. Rolfe Humphries visited Tourlaque on March 28, 1939, noting laconically in his diary that the Fascists entered Madrid that day. He had earlier attended a meeting with Menaker and Aragon in Paris.

11. In April League members George Seldes, Isobel Walker Soule, Shaemas O'Sheel, Vincent Sheean, Martha Dodd, and Arthur Kober joined a committee that protested the arrest of fifty-three picketers at the French consulate, objecting to French policies.

12. Alvah Bessie, *Men in Battle* (Charles Scribner's Sons, 1939), p. 20.

13. Ella Winter said she spent "unexpectedly gay hours . . . of the gallows' humor variety" with Anna Seghers in Germany after the war. "We laughed together [about] American and German pots calling German and American kettles Nazi or anti-Nazi according to the degree of de-Nazification claimed but hardly carried out since American officials neither understood nor desired that process." Ella Winter, *And Not to Yield* (Harcourt, Brace and World, 1963), pp. 260–261.

14. Benjamin Appel, "The Exiled Writers," *The Saturday Review of Literature,* October 16, 1940.

15. *The Brown Book of the Hitler Terror* (Alfred A. Knopf, 1933) presented in graphic detail the provocation the Nazis designed as pretext for suppressing all opposition. "The second-in-command [in preparing the book] was Otto Katz, a Czech journalist and considerable linguist, aged forty-three, with a thin-lipped, hard-bitten face, lined with suffering, that had hitherto been known only to the higher agents of the Comintern, and a tendency to lean his head over on his right shoulder. He was always very neatly dressed." Gustav Regler, *The Owl of Minerva* (Farrar, Straus and Cudahy, 1960), p. 162.

16. Wolfgang Kiessling, in *Exil in Lateinamerika* (Leipzig: Verlag Philipp Reclam jun, 1980), tells this story about Bruno Frei's escape from France. He traveled under his real name. When he went to pick up his visa in Marseilles, he was ordered to see "the Boss" — a white-haired woman supervisor. "Are you Bruno Frei?" she asked and looked at a list she held. Then, "Here is your visa, Mr. Freistadt," she said and shook his hand. "Bruno Frei, who is wanted by the Gestapo, is not on our list. Good luck Mr. Freistadt."

17. After the war, Bruno Frei returned to Europe and resumed his life as a journalist, becoming editor of *Das Abend.* Lisa, too, returned to Europe. Hans, a brilliant student, remained in the United States. He got a Ph.D. in physics and won a fellowship to work for the Atomic Energy Commission. He made no secret of the fact that he was a Communist, and his fellowship was soon canceled. Now blacklisted, he could find no

steady employment in his field anywhere, even in post-war Europe. Finally, he changed professions. In Canada he went to medical school and became a physician. Because of the U.S. citizenship that came with the adoption the League had arranged, Hans was able to return to the United States, where he has engaged successfully to this day in his second profession.

This is a scene from the anti-Hitler motion picture, PROFESSOR MAMLOCK, the most powerful attack on Nazi Germany that ever reached the screen. The author, Friedrich Wolf, is in a concentration camp, not in Germany, but in France,

RELEASE FRIEDRICH WOLF!

From a flier circulated early in 1940 by the League as part of its work for exiled anti-Nazi writers.

Louis Aragon, French poet, novelist (left) and Theodore Dreiser, American novelist, in Paris where Dreiser represented the League at an international congress. Courtesy of Special Collections Department, Van Pelt Library, University of Pennsylvania.

The Exiled Writers Committee mailed out this signed print by William Gropper with a request for contributions. Photo courtesy of Emmanuelle Germaine.

5

Penthouse Panhandlers

The mere knowledge of your readiness to help has saved many of us from the last step.

— Lion Feuchtwanger, speaking at the Exiled Writers Committee dinner at the Hotel Commodore in New York, October 17, 1940

The League had a big dinner October 17 for exiled writers which, to the amazement of all, brought in nearly $15,000 clear profit. . . . None of this is going to stick in the League office on the way through, and there is no knowing where I'll collect the $450 back wages due me.

— Franklin Folsom, to his mother, October 21, 1940

How did the League and its Exiled Writers Committee raise the money needed to help save writers from Hitler? We raised it by begging, and we begged in many ways. In October 1940, working with a committee of prominent publishers, we held a Pan-American dinner at which Pearl Buck, Edna Ferber, William Saroyan, and Fannie Hurst spoke in support of the rescue work of the League, to which Pearl Buck, but not the other three, belonged. A year later, Lillian Hellman and Ernest Hemingway invited guests to another fund-raising dinner, and again writers who were not League members joined in making the appeal.

Direct-mail appeals frequently went out from the League office. In one, we audaciously included a signed William Gropper print that few recipients were brazen enough to keep without sending in a check. A pamphlet, *We Must Save Them All*, quoted from letters we had received from writers in concentration camps. This moving document went out to a large mailing list. We also sold Christmas cards that included this poem by Rudolf Leonhard, written in Le Vernet concentration camp and translated by Jean Starr Untermeyer:[1]

Lion Feuchtwanger, exiled German novelist, speaker at Exiled Writers Committee dinner. Drawing by Georges Schreiber. From *Saturday Review of Literature*, October 19, 1940. Reproduced with the permission of the Western Historical Collections, University Archives, University of Colorado at Boulder Libraries.

William Gropper, artist. His print showing refugees was used by the Exiled Writers Committee in fund-raising. From *New Masses*, June 17, 1941.

Christmas Song

Now here we are all
In the straw, in a stall
Not uneasier than Him
Who lay in Bethlehem.

Here in these narrow boxes
Neither the ass nor ox is.
Here mouse and rat are free —
We keep them company.

Here wise men from the east,
The greatest and the least,
Light reigns in the heart,
No kings take part.

No incense here nor myrrh,
Yet each a shepherder
'Neath poorer roof than thatch
For himself keeps good watch.

The mothers send their sighs
As gifts — Could they surmise
Children in snow and damp
With us at Vernet Camp?

Our stall is like all stalls,
Our fall like other falls,
Togetherness is great
That stamps a common fate.

Here is a rubbish heap
First stand in forest deep —
The forest from Camp is far —
Yet here too burns a star.

We mailed out urgent appeals, such as this one:

FOLLOWING CABLE RECEIVED FROM MARSEILLE: "END OF OCTOBER A DIRECT BOAT WILL LEAVE FROM CASABLANCA, NORTH AFRICA, FOR VERA CRUZ, MEXICO. NO TRANSIT VISA NECESSARY. KEEPING TEN RESERVATIONS FOR YOUR WRITERS. PASSAGE PAYABLE IMMEDIATELY NEWYORK. AWAITING A REPLY URGENTLY." WE NEED FIVE THOUSAND DOLLARS AT

ONCE TAKE ADVANTAGE THIS OFFER AND RES-
CUE TEN ANTI-NAZI WRITERS FROM FRENCH
CONCENTRATION CAMPS AND INCREASED GE-
STAPO ACTIVITY RESULTING VICHY COLLABO-
RATION TREACHERY. BEG YOU, YOUR FRIENDS,
AIRMAIL GENEROUS CONTRIBUTIONS TODAY
TO SAVE THESE MARKED MEN AND WOMEN
THUS ENABLING THEM CONTINUE WORLD
STRUGGLE AGAINST HITLERISM. THIS POSSIBLE
ONLY WITH YOUR IMMEDIATE HELP.

[signed]

DASHIELL HAMMETT EXILED WRITERS COM-
MITTEE 381 4TH AVE. N.Y.C.2

Ferdinand Bruckner, exiled German writer. From *Direction* magazine, May–June 1939.

Paralleling the work in New York, a committee in Hollywood, at one point under the energetic leadership of Ella Winter, brought in many thousands of dollars from the film community.[3] Then, with the committee, she helped twelve refugees to get work in the film industry after they arrived. Ella Winter not only had energy, she had personal experiences that gave her momentum. After World War I, she had done relief work in Europe, where she saw firsthand what it meant to be a refugee. Fluent in German, she later spent time in Germany and observed nazism close up. In addition, she knew many of the European writers who were fleeing for their lives. Aided by a committee of screenwriters in Hollywood, she organized nationally publicized dinners.

One dinner, on November 26, 1940, raised $6,000. Sheridan Gibney and Edward G. Robinson presided. Heinrich Mann, Genevieve Tabouis, Emil Ludwig, Donald Ogden Stewart, Helen Gahagan, Paul Muni, Garson Kanin, and Sidney Buchman spoke. Many film stars were in the audience, and part of the program was carried on a national broadcast by CBS. On November 10, 1941, the League committee, together with other committees, raised $8,500 at another dinner chaired by Louis Bromfield and Ida Lupino. The speakers included Walter Duranty, Sir Cedric Hardwicke, and Heinrich Mann. Orson Welles and Wendell Willkie sent telegrams of support.

Fund-raising also went on in private homes in several major cities. One cocktail party in Philadelphia, addressed by the Czech novelist F.

Franz C. Weiskopf, exiled Czech novelist, diplomat. From *Direction* magazine, October 1939.

C. Weiskopf, who had escaped from Europe with our help, was in the home of the poet Katherine Garrison Chapin, wife of Francis Biddle, the U.S. attorney general. Another financial success was a gathering in the home of Martha Dodd. And a contribution came from at least one writer who had left the League because of policy disagreements, Malcolm Cowley. He had received an anonymous article about Fascist maltreatment of refugees, translated the article, and sold it, but he had no way of passing along to the original author any of the money he received from his translation. He solved the problem by making a generous donation to the Exiled Writers Committee.

Another fund-raising device was the League's publication of a record album called *Behind Barbed Wire,* made up of songs from concentration camps sung by Bart van der Schelling, a wounded veteran of the International Brigade.[4] Still another way of raising money was a sale of books contributed by 500 writers, most of whom were not League members.

The committee developed and used very successfully another technique, already mentioned, that was peculiarly suited to a writers' organization helping writers. It held very professional auction sales of manuscripts, typescripts, and letters.[5]

In preparation for our sale at the Hotel Delmonico, I went to Lillian Hellman and asked her to contribute the manuscript of *The Little Foxes.* She agreed — on one condition. I had to promise to bid $200 for it if no other bid went that high. Lillian would reimburse me after the sale.

I promised.

We tried to stage each sale almost as a theatrical production, with one celebrity auctioning off the manuscript of another celebrity. With this in mind, we asked Lillian Hellman's former husband, the playwright and author Arthur Kober, to auction *The Little Foxes.* To provide publicity for the entire sale, we had retained Ivan Black, the well-known Broadway press agent. It was only at the beginning of the sale, however, that I thought to ask Ivan how he might stimulate authentic bids on

Hellman's manuscript. He thought a moment, then exclaimed, "I've got it!" and dashed out the door.

Ivan had not returned when the Hellman manuscript was announced, and Arthur Kober had tipsily staggered to the lectern. All he could say to encourage bidding was "Lillian's a wunnerful woman, a wunnerful woman."

I was about to make the bid I had promised when Ivan Black hurried in, escorting a man who called out "Two hundred dollars!" Kober manged to declare the manuscript sold. *The Little Foxes* had gone to I. J. Fox, owner of a prestigious fur store that bore his name.

William Saroyan, novelist, speaker at Exiled Writers Committee dinner. *Saturday Review of Literature* photo, August 14, 1937. Reproduced with the permission of the Western Historical Collections, University Archives, University of Colorado at Boulder Libraries.

Another manuscript at this sale involved Aline Bernstein as the donor, not as the author. Bernstein, a distinguished stage designer and writer on stage design, who had been elected to the National Council at the Third American Writers Congress, was a vigorous, middle-aged woman, wife of a Wall Street broker. She had many friends in the theater and another connection well known in the book world: She had had a love affair with Thomas Wolfe, who was many years her junior.

Over the years when they were together, Bernstein had given Wolfe several thousand dollars, and he, out of affection for her, had given her the manuscript of *Look Homeward Angel*, which, when it was published in 1929, was called by one critic "the greatest novel of our time." As their relationship began to fall apart, Wolfe in some of their quarrels gave vent to strong anti-Semitic feelings. How Bernstein, a Jew, felt about this, we can guess. Soon she was also troubled because Wolfe began some curious negotiations about the manuscript he had given her. To Bernstein's chagrin, he began to regard it as repayment for the money she had given him. Bernstein was offended. She had thought the gift expressed affection and was not simply a business transaction. In time, however, she acquiesced and agreed to sign a document saying that she had the manuscript in exchange for money.[6]

Theodor Balk, exiled German writer. From *Exil in Lateinamerika,* by Wolfgang Kiessling.

Arnold Zweig, exiled German writer. Portrait by Georges Schreiber in *Saturday Review of Literature,* October 19, 1940.

When Bernstein learned that the Exiled Writers Committee was planning a manuscript sale to rescue anti-Nazi writers, she offered *Look Homeward Angel,* on condition that whoever bought it must give it to one of three libraries — the New York Public Library, the Library of Congress, or the Harvard University Library.

One day, shortly before the auction, a messenger arrived at the League office with a huge, heavy package. I opened it and found inside the immense, original wordage from which literary agent Elizabeth Nowell and Maxwell Perkins, editor at Scribner's, had helped Wolfe to fashion *Look Homeward Angel.* When I piled the manuscript on the floor, it reached almost to the level of my desk top.[7]

Look Homeward Angel brought $1,700 at the sale — a fair amount considering the stipulation that the buyer had to give it away. The manuscript is now with other Wolfe papers at Harvard, and the words of an anti-Semite who loved a Jewish woman served well in helping to rescue anti-Nazi writers, many of whom were Jews.

As the Exiled Writers Committee prepared for one of its auctions, I toured the country organizing for the League and soliciting manuscripts from League members. In Los Gatos, California, I called at the home of the iconoclast Charles Erskine Scott Wood, white-bearded and in his eighties. There I obtained a few pages of *Heavenly Discourses* — delicious, impious satires that spoke of a rebel spirit of another generation. Wood's wife, the poet Sarah Bard Field, also contributed a manuscript, but I was not much cheered by my stop in the Wood home. The feeble old man said he was no longer writing. "I'm just waiting for death," he said, and death came soon after my visit.

Also in Los Gatos, I visited the home of John Steinbeck, who was one of the vice presidents of the League. I had wired ahead announcing my imminent arrival, but there hadn't been time for an answer before a cab dropped me off in front of Steinbeck's hillside house. In the front yard, an elderly lady was fussing with the lush flowers and shrubs.

I introduced myself and asked to see Mr. Steinbeck.

John Steinbeck, novelist, League vice president, 1939–1942. From *Direction* magazine, May–June 1939.

"He's not here, but my daughter Carol is. She's his wife. Come on in." I waited a few moments in the big living room, which had a superb view — and a tall bookstand with an open copy of *Webster's Unabridged Dictionary.*

Soon a handsome young woman appeared.

"So you're the son of a bitch who's been sending us telegrams," she said.

I gulped, but reminded her about the Exiled Writers Committee sale and said that I had come to ask for the manuscript of *The Grapes of Wrath.*

"You can't have it. It's mine," she snapped, then explained that she was in a great hurry. She was going to San Francisco with friends, who appeared at that moment in the other end of the big room and remained there.

"If you want to talk some more about the manuscript, you can do it while you scrub my back, I've got to take a bath."

I declined to be of assistance, but she asked me to wait. "Do you want to see the manuscript?" she asked when she returned. Of course I did.

"Come along, then." In her bedroom she reached up to a high closet shelf and brought down what looked like a big bookkeeping ledger. It was *The Grapes of Wrath,* all in Steinbeck's handwriting. The final word was in Norwegian or Swedish, and she said it meant, "The End."

The ledger went back up on the shelf, and it was not because I had ungraciously failed to scrub a lady's back that my effort on behalf of exiled writers did not succeed. Some time later, I thought I could guess

Ernst Bloch, exiled German philosopher. From *Direction* magazine, May–June 1939.

why Mrs. Steinbeck wanted to keep the manuscript. She had guided and goaded Steinbeck through his work on the book and even suggested its title. It was hers in more ways than one. It was even dedicated to her, and it might someday be a financial resource for her. Her marriage was soon to come to an end, and Carol Henning Steinbeck did eventually sell the manuscript. It is now in the University of Virginia Library.

Usually more successful than my efforts to get the Steinbeck ledger, the Exiled Writers Committee, between 1939 and 1941, raised $37,000 with an overhead of 23 percent. *The New York World Telegram,* in September 1941, attacked the committee, claiming that an audit of its funds had never been published and alleging that we had collected $1,176,000 for Spain. Would that we had!

Our activities never equaled the need, but as Heinrich Mann, addressing the committee over a national CBS hookup, said, "Your power is far-reaching. Be certain that the future and the law of life as well as history belong to you. Despair of the future? *Never,* so long as mankind in his heart loves liberty."

Notes

1. Rudolf Leonhard, "Christmas Song," in LAW Papers, Manuscripts Division, Bancroft Library, University of California, Berkeley.

2. Hammett appeal for Exiled Writers Committee, October 16, 1941, LAW Papers, Bancroft Library, University of California, Berkeley.

3. At a writers' congress in Hollywood in 1943, Thomas Mann spoke of a special problem that plagued twentieth-century exiled writers. He said:

    The exile of Victor Hugo, for example, was child's play compared with ours. To be sure, he sat as an outcast far from Paris on his island in the ocean, but the spiritual link between him and France was never broken. What he wrote was printed in the French press; his books could be bought and read at home. Today exile is a total exile, just as war, politics, world, and life have become total. We are not only physically far from our country but we have been radically expelled from its life both in the purpose and, at least for the present, in the effects of our exile. Our books are outlawed, just as we ourselves are; they exist only in translations. In fact, since the conquest of the European continent by the enemy, they exist only in English. We can count ourselves fortunate that it is still so, that that which we produce exists at all, for every writer will feel with us what it means to exist only as a literary shadow, to live only a translated and denatured life.

I can confirm that Victor Hugo did live comfortably while in exile. By sheer chance, I obtained lodging, during an Oxford vacation, on the island of Guernsey in the house in which Hugo lived when he was banned from mainland France. In this roomy dwelling I found poignant evidence of family life. Hugo had marked on a doorjamb several dates with the increasing heights of his children. The successive owners of the house had never painted over these markings.

4. I have not been able to locate a copy of this album.

5. A detailed, step-by-step handbook on how to arrange a manuscript auction was prepared for the committee by rare-book dealers. A copy of this document is with the League papers in the Bancroft Library in Berkeley.

6. For information about Bernstein's relations with Wolfe, see Carol Klein, *Aline* (Harper and Row, 1979), pp. 135–136, and Donald David Herbert, *Look Homeward Angel: A Life of Thomas Wolfe* (Fawcett Columbine, 1988).

7. I had another interest in the manuscript of *Look Homeward Angel*. Much of it had been typed by Eleanor Buckles, sister of Katherine Buckles, early executive secretary of the League. Eleanor and Kit had lived only a block from my home when we were all going to school in Boulder, Colorado.

Sleeping arrangements in a French concentration camp where writers were confined with other exiles. Unitarian Universalist Services Committee photo. Courtesy of Andover-Harvard Theological Seminary.

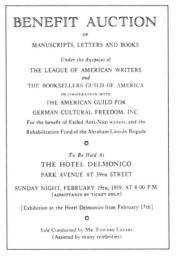

The Exiled Writers Committee raised funds for refugees in collaboration with publishers and booksellers.

6

We Hold These Truths

I am a writer and I am also a Jew. I want to be quite sure that I can continue to be a writer and that if I want to say that greed is bad or persecution is worse, I can do so without being branded by the malice of people who make a living by that malice. I also want to be able to go on saying that I am a Jew without being afraid of being called names or end in a prison camp or be forbidden to walk down the street at night.

— Lillian Hellman at an American Booksellers Association luncheon[1]

Thousands of Jews who fled from the Nazis into Czechoslovakia had to leave that country for France as the German army spread its terror. Then they had to flee France when Hitler expanded his control. While this was going on in Europe, Nazi sympathizers were busy spreading race hatred in the United States. Many scores of anti-Semitic organizations and publications were springing up in our land. To counter this growing assault on human dignity, the League, in November 1938, sent out a letter to a cross section of opinion makers:

What do you know about anti-Semitism in this country? What would you do to stop it if you were chosen to lay down a program? The League of American Writers would hold your answers to these questions in high value.

We would like you to imagine that you had been invited to address a highly selected group of the nation's leaders in the professions and arts on this subject, and that, for ten minutes, you were to tell them what you know about anti-Semitism in your field, whether it is dangerous, whether it is growing or decreasing, and what measures should be taken against it.

If, in four to five hundred words, you make this contribution of your mind and spirit to the world's struggle against race hatred, the League of American Writers would be proud to place your thoughts in the hands of thousands of the nation's leaders.

Henry Pratt Fairchild, sociologist, contributed to *We Hold These Truths*. From *Direction* magazine, November 1939.

We are publishing a book — a convention on paper — made up of such statements by seventy-five of the country's best authorities. Your page in the book would become part of the essential data which the nation must consider in making up its mind on this question-that-must-be-answered.

The Twentieth Century, which opened with the promise of light, threatens to close in great darkness. Flames may again climb about the victims at the stake. So dreadful is the danger that we feel privileged to make this claim upon your time.

Speed is essential, for the wave of revulsion sweeping the country against the new Nazi excesses will result in the formulation of a new national policy — and you hardly dare give up your part in the shaping of that policy. Will you tell us by an early post when we may expect your article . . . ? Or, better, will you send the article itself?[2]

While responses to this appeal were coming in, I visited a room maintained by a man who worked for Jewish organizations. Along the walls stood row after row of file cabinets that contained appalling information about the extent of anti-Semitic activity in the United States. Here I found the names and addresses of the organizations, publications, and individuals that were spreading hate. So that people might see proof of the magnitude of the problem facing this country, I collected these addresses for use in *We Hold These Truths,* the League publication we were planning.[3] I also went for a long conference in the home of Albert Maltz, the handsome, earnest playwright, novelist, and screenwriter who had undertaken to write, anonymously, an introduction to the pamphlet. Our work together began a friendship that lasted until his death in 1985.

In his introduction, Maltz showed how throughout history reactionaries had used attacks on minorities to divert the attention of people from their real problems. Some of the replies that made up the body of the pamphlet touched on this theme. Others had a wide variety of reasons for their answers. Dr. Walter B. Cannon, president of the American Association for the Advancement of Science and co-chair of the

Medical Bureau and North American Committee to Aid Spanish Democracy, pointed out one of the absurdities of anti-Semitism: Doctors in fascist countries, as they did their work, were greatly dependent on discoveries made by Jewish scientists and physicians.

"I do not believe in a social torture of any group or race or sect," wrote Theodore Dreiser in his contribution, which he insisted on copyrighting. He was sensitive on the subject of anti-Semitism because he had been accused of being a Jew baiter.

Support for our campaign against bigotry came from all quarters. Thomas E. Dewey, who would before long be the Republican candidate for president of the United States, contributed a brief piece. So, too, did Earl Browder, general secretary of

W. L. River, novelist, screenwriter, vice president of the Hollywood chapter, 1941. From *Direction* magazine, July–August 1939.

the Communist Party. In between the political poles represented by these two were labor leaders of different persuasions, writers of all kinds, and leaders in various religious faiths. All of these contributors gave support to our human rights effort. As George Albee said in an article in *Direction*, "Thanks to the League of American Writers the only writer today who does not know what he has to fear from Fascism is the writer who is too deficient in curiosity to ask."[4]

A good deal of publicity accompanied the publication of *We Hold These Truths*, and most of the 25,000 copies we printed were sold or given to opinion makers or libraries. One distribution effort we made did not succeed. Early in March 1939, in response to information that the Book-of-the-Month Club planned to circulate Hitler's *Mein Kampf* as a book dividend, a League committee consisting of Leslie River, Marjorie Fischer, Jean Starr Untermeyer, and me visited Harry Sherman, head of the book club. We wanted to persuade him not to give Hitler's anti-human words the kind of circulation Hitler wanted for them. Our anti-Nazi zeal was such that we easily forgot that we were also anti-censorship. We failed to persuade Sherman not to circulate *Mein Kampf*. We also failed to get the club to accept our alternate proposal to send

Margaret Culkin Banning, novelist, contributor to League pamphlets. *Saturday Review of Literature* photo, June 12, 1937. Reproduced with the permission of the Western Historical Collections, University Archives, University of Colorado at Boulder Libraries.

along a copy of *We Hold These Truths* with each copy of Hitler's anti-Semitic tirade.

Usually we were alert to attempts at censorship. When citizens in Oklahoma were harassed and arrested for selling radical literature, the League sent to the governor a protesting petition signed by 400 writers. The League also joined other organizations in legal action on behalf of an Oklahoma bookseller charged with criminal syndicalism. When Ernest Hemingway's *To Have and Have Not* was banned in Detroit in July 1939, the League — with Archibald MacLeish, Van Wyck Brooks, and Thornton Wilder taking the lead — began a strong campaign against this act of censorship.

In other ways, the League tried to protect the rights of writers. When the State Department, in October 1938, refused to admit to this country John Strachey, author of *The Coming Struggle for Power*, we protested and pointed out that Strachey's cousin, Major James Strachey Burns, had been admitted although he was an honorary member of the Italian Fascist Party. That same year when Queens College revoked an invitation to Ernst Toller to speak on "Social Drama," we protested.

When the WPA writers went on strike, the League supported them, and when the Roosevelt administration tried to reduce the number of jobs provided by the WPA, we protested vigorously. When the librarian at the University of Montana was fired for engaging in union activity, we campaigned for his reinstatement. When the Immigration and Naturalization Service tried to deport Harry Bridges, the militant leader of the West Coast longshoremen, we placed members on his defense committee, and the Hollywood chapter published a pamphlet, written by Dalton Trumbo, telling the story of the government's anti-Bridges vendetta. The first edition was 100,000 copies, and it quickly sold out.

The League also responded to the centuries-old discrimination against African-Americans. We did this in part by including African-American writers in all our activities. Langston Hughes and later Richard Wright were vice presidents. Other black members were: Arna Bontemps, Gwendolyn Brooks, Countee Cullen, Frank Marshall Davis, Ralph Ellison, Arthur Huff Fauset, Jessie Fauset, Eugene Gordon, Eugene Holmes, Alain Locke, Marian Minus, Margaret Walker, Theodore Ward, and Frank Yerby. Claude McKay was also a member briefly.

Langston Hughes, poet, playwright, journalist, League vice president, 1937–1941, FBI target. From *Direction* magazine, May–June 1939.

Not all writers from minority groups received this same attention. No conscious policy was involved here. We just didn't know where to reach those in some groups. We were in touch with Puerto Rican writers and rescued one, Emilio Delgado, who was in Spain when the Fascists took over there. A poet of Chinese origin, T. S. Tsiang, was a League member. We campaigned for citizenship for another Asian writer, Younghill Kang. We had active relations with many writers in Latin America and in the Philippines but little contact with Latino or Native American writers in the United States.

Hostile criticism of the League seems not to have included charges that it was sexist. (The term was not heard in those days among either the League's friends or its enemies, nor was "ageism." Mercifully, youthism, has not yet been invented, so far as I know.) Women were always in the leadership of the League. Eleanor Flexner, later the author of *Century of Struggle: The Women's Rights Movement in the United States* (Harvard University Press, 1975) took an active part in our work. Lillian Hellman, a good complainer, certainly did not tax us with discrimination against her. Of forty contributors to *Writing Red: An Anthology of American Women Writers, 1930–1940*, edited by Charlotte Nekola and Paula Rabinowitz (The Feminist Press, 1987), twenty-one were League members at some point, and most of these remained members as long as the organization existed.

Notes

1. Quoted by William Wright, *Lillian Hellman* (Simon and Schuster, 1986), p. 168.
2. The League members who signed the letter were the Catholic novelist Margaret Culkin Banning, the playwright George S. Kaufman, humorist and fiction writer Ruth

McKenney, and Donald Ogden Stewart, filmwriter. Letter included in *We Hold These Truths* (see note 3).

3. This 128-page pamphlet was published by the League in March 1939. A list of the contributors is in Appendix G. A copy may be seen in the LAW Papers, Bancroft Library, Berkeley.

4. George Albee, "The Writers' Organizations," in *Direction*, 1 (Nov.–Dec. 1938): 6.

7

Writers Teach Writing

Today we are entering a period when artists of Shelley's stature are more necessary than scientists or engineers.

— Malcolm Cowley, *The New Republic*, May 23, 1934

The League did a good many things to help beginning writers master their craft. Most important, it established a writers' school in the fall of 1937. A course in writing for children was taught by Marjorie Fischer; there were others in poetry and fiction writing, and one that may have been unique in the whole country — it introduced young trade unionists to labor journalism. Harold Coy, experienced in the field, was its teacher.

From this start the school expanded steadily, and it attracted students from all over the city of New York. One slender black teenager came from Harlem — walked all the way because he did not have a nickel for the subway fare. He wanted to study short story writing under Mary Elting, who, with the students in the class, soon discovered that here was a writer of rare talent. When the students found that he was walking a hundred blocks to class and then another hundred blocks back to his home, they quietly found ways of seeing to it that he had subway fare. That young writer's name was James Baldwin.

A student in an early poetry class was Eve Merriam, who later became noted for her poetry and plays and her children's books. Before she died in 1992, she was a national officer of the Author's Guild. Another student very quickly became a successful writer for pulp and confession magazines, winning several prizes offered in the field.

Outreach to young people took other directions, too. A poetry program, created by Genevieve Taggard, had an audience of half a million high school students in New York City classrooms. Rolfe Humphries

Norman Corwin, poet, radio writer, teacher in the Writers School. From *Direction* magazine, Summer 1940.

Genevieve Taggard, poet, member of the National Council, LAW treasurer, teacher in Writers School. Photo by Ellen Conried Balch.

assisted a group of young poets who met frequently and read to each other and discussed their work.

At the height of the war in Spain, the League offered prizes totaling $1,000 for the best essays by students on "The anti-Fascist struggle in Spain today in relation to the general welfare of American citizens of tomorrow."[1] Later, at the suggestion of Rolfe Humphries, we ran a nationwide poetry contest for young writers. This turned out to be an embarrassment. The winner, an African-American, had not read the rules carefully and did not realize that he, a well-established mature poet, was not eligible.

In various ways, the League maintained close contact with the American Student Union and with the National Council of Teachers of English. After the Third Writers Congress, in 1939, we ran a weekly lecture series under the general heading "Find Yourself in Writing," and later we gave enthusiastic support to a group of young actors called the American Youth Theater, who put on plays in a hotel auditorium they were able to rent.

Dramatist Barrie Stavis taught at one union headquarters a class for young workers who wanted to write plays, and several unions provided scholarships for students to attend classes at League headquarters. League members Eli Siegel and Martha Millet helped to build a group of young labor poets independent of the League.

The League sought to be of use not only to young writers but also to labor, which was organizing apace all over the country. Time and again, the League sent representatives to labor conferences, thus putting writers in direct touch with workers in a variety of contexts. Time and again, writers joined picket lines in support of protests, strikes, and programs. Often these demonstrations became more than ritualistic evidence of solidarity. In one early picket line of special literary interest, well-known authors paraded back and forth on fashionable Fifth Avenue in front of the offices of the *American Mercury* magazine, then edited by Lawrence Spivak. In his autobiographical book, *Total Recoil*, Kyle Crichton reported:

Edwin Seaver, novelist, member of the National Council, teacher in Writers School. From *Direction* magazine, Summer 1940.

> Things got a little rough in the second week of the strike, and the police began making arrests. That only added fuel to the fire. One afternoon the strikers were being cheered on by a large crowd. The police arrived in force. Some of them came on horseback; others tumbled out of a big patrol wagon. There were boos and jeers from the strikers; the cops began breaking up the picket line and grabbing the more obstreperous strikers. They were hustled into the Black Maria.
>
> When the wagon was jammed to the roof, the driver stepped into the front seat — and then there was a pause. There was no key for the ignition lock. The driver looked in panic all over the front seat and the dashboard; then he began going through his pockets. The happy uproar among the prisoners was joined with the curses of the cops, who were trying to keep some sort of order among the captives. The curses were aimed at the poor driver, who at last threw up his hands helplessly and sank into his seat in despair. Amid the happy howls of the prisoners and the jeer-

Alexander L. Crosby, labor journalist, teacher in Writers School. Courtesy of Alexander C. Crosby.

ing laughter of the bystanders, the police sheepishly opened the door of the patrol wagon and transferred their charges to taxicabs. Some of them got away in the confusion, there were abortive chases; it was one big glorious mess that reflected no credit on the police department.

What had happened was very simple. Emmett Gowen, the writer from Tennessee, had simply reached in at the peak of the excitement and snatched the ignition key from the dashboard. Just as quietly and effectively, he had dropped it through a street grating into a sewer. Everybody agreed that this

Leane Zugsmith, novelist, and
Carl Randau, the first president of
the Newspaper Guild, husband
and wife. Photo by Lotte Jacobi,
Courtesy of Ruth Zugsmith.

was far more satisfactory than sticking pins in a mounted cop's horse. I'm sure the police don't know to this day what happened to the key.[2]

As a result of a great variety of such episodes, writers learned a good deal, and the life of workers began to appear in radio programs, plays, and novels, often written by teachers in the LAW Writers School. For example, two of these novels, *A Time to Remember* (Random House, 1936) and *The Summer Soldier* (Random House, 1938) came from the typewriter of Leane Zugsmith, who taught fiction writing.

The League tried, though without success, to set up an agency to help writers place their work in labor publications. As an alternative, we campaigned to persuade members to contribute to the Federated Press, an organization that supplied news to trade union newspapers.

Term after term, the Writers School grew. Young people who had talent sharpened their skills, and they, together with others less talented, had the experience of direct, frequent, personal contact with professional writers who shared a vision of writers as citizens engaged in the critical enterprise of defending democracy against fascism.[3]

From New York the Writers School reached out to young people far from the city. At the Highlander Folk School in Monteagle, Tennessee, the League ran a summer writers' conference in 1940. In 1941 we conducted another conference in the White Mountains of New Hampshire. There we were reminded that not all problems facing democracy were in Europe. The site for the conference had to be changed because the hotel with which arrangements had originally been made insisted that no blacks or Jews be allowed to attend.

In Hollywood a major school developed and offered training for those interested in writing for the film industry. It also offered classes in fiction and poetry writing and in the history of American literature.

Before the League's schools closed down in 1942 in New York and later in Hollywood, more than 3,000 young people had attended classes, and in New York they had formed a Young Writers League. From time to time, the schools ran forums that were of general interest and to which students were admitted free or at a reduced rate. Students were also encouraged to attend the numerous readings from work in progress and other lectures run by the League, as distinct from the schools. One lecture series, called "Literature in the World Today," covered the work of writers in many countries.

In a variety of ways, the Writers Schools represented an organized effort to continue and expand the tradition of pro-people's literature that had roots around the world and certainly in the United States.

Eda Lou Walton, poet, critic, teacher in Writers School. League of American Writers photo.

Notes

1. The judges in this contest were Elliot Paul, Clifford Odets, Robert Morss Lovett, Jean Starr Untermeyer, Genevieve Taggard, H. V. Kaltenborn, and Donald Ogden Stewart.

2. Kyle Crichton, *Total Recoil* (Doubleday and Co., 1960), pp. 43–44.

3. For a list of teachers in the League's Writers Schools, see Appendix H.

8

Fighting Words

Don't mourn, organize!

— The words of Joe Hill before he was executed,
quoted by Dorothy Parker at the Third American Writers Congress

In his journal entry for April 7, 1939, Millen Brand wrote,

Dank [the nickname everyone used for me] and I and Dorothy Brewster
discussed topics for the main speakers at the [Third] Writers' Congress. We
thought of three parallel topics for Thomas Mann, Eduard Beneš [former
president of Czechoslovakia] and Juan Negrin [former prime minister of
Spain] — the restoration of democracy in Germany, Czechoslovakia, and
Spain. There's talk in the air of forming an organization, world-wide, for
restoring the world's lost democracies. We laid out topics for other speakers,
Hemingway, Dorothy Thompson, etc.[1]

Out of many consultations like this one with Millen Brand and
Dorothy Brewster, the plan for the congress grew. Everybody was taking
part in the preparations. Rolfe Humphries, returning from his travels on
a Guggenheim Fellowship, landed in Philadelphia at noon May 15. His
first stop that afternoon in New York was the League office. The next
day he attended a League dinner meeting. The following evening he
chaired a council meeting. On May 29, he and Henry Hart met Louis
Aragon, who came from France on the *Normandy*.[2] We were all busy,
busy, busy.

We wrote to President Roosevelt inviting him to speak at our
Carnegie Hall meeting. He declined. We searched for a new League
president to relieve overworked Donald Ogden Stewart. I went with a
committee to see if Vincent Sheean would take on this responsibility. He
declined, saying he did not feel he was sufficiently gray and bearded for

the job. Stewart had to be pressed to serve for a second term, and I leave to him the telling of the full story of the congress. It is to be found in his *Fighting Words* (Harcourt, Brace and Company, 1940).

Two months after Millen, Dorothy, and I had our first idea for the big public meeting, Mann and Beneš appeared for the actual event. Negrin, Hemingway, and Thompson were not there, but others were on hand to take their places. Plans for all the sessions that were open only to writers had developed in somewhat the same way — that is, collectively. Commenting on a great change that had taken place since the 1920s, when "writers like cats, regarded every colleague as a rival," Malcolm Cowley reported in *The New Republic*, "Considering that [the congress] had been organized as a collective undertaking by writers, who are individualists by definition and quite unused to organizing their own lives or anything more complicated than a chapter in a novel, it was something to feel proud about. . . . It will certainly encourage writers to think of one another not as rivals but as partners in the same undertaking and as human beings to be treated with consideration."[3]

When the congress was over, Cowley returned to his home in Connecticut, and there, he said, "hoeing between the bean rows in my garden, I reflected that this congress, in addition to the high aims that were set for it and partially achieved, might serve a humble and an unexpected purpose. It might help to establish human relations among writers." More than a year later, when he had resigned from the League following policy differences about the non-aggression pact that Germany and the Soviet Union had signed, Cowley still had warm

Dorothy Parker, poet, humorist, League vice president, 1940, FBI target. From *Direction* magazine, May–June 1939.

Millen Brand, novelist, poet, member of the National Council, 1940–1941. From *Direction* magazine, May–June 1939.

Vincent Sheean, journalist, League vice president, 1939–1940. From *Direction* magazine May–June 1939.

feelings about the congress. "It was an extraordinary affair, perhaps the greatest achievement of the League of American Writers."[4]

Cowley had not been able to attend the poetry craft session of the congress and so did not hear Dorothy Parker's remarks there that closely paralleled his own feelings. Of the writers of 1939, she said, "They know you cannot find yourself until you find your fellow men — they know there is no longer 'I'; there is 'We.' " During one session of the congress she sat in the audience, waiting her turn to speak from the platform. I was in a seat just behind her. Over her shoulder I watched her write out her speech on a big notepad. It was simply the words that Joe Hill spoke before his execution: "Don't mourn, organize!"[5]

What I thought of the congress went into an immodest letter I wrote a week after it ended. The letter was addressed to my mother and father, the latter of whom, particularly, took a dim view of my politics:

Dear Mom and Dad:
A. Franklin Brewster Folsom, recently elected to membership in the Descendants of the American Revolution, a member of the City Club of New York, and of other equally distinguished but sometimes unmentionable organizations, begs to inform you that he was unanimously elected by a rising vote to serve for two more years as Executive Secretary of the League of American Writers, soon to be the League of American Writers, Inc. You know how it is, everybody rises and there's one poor devil in the room sitting in his chair looking down his nose wondering how he can put a stop to this awful proceeding. I've got a fairly long nose and couldn't put a stop to it for some time. Anyway, at the end of the Third American Writers Congress, I still seem to have some friends. . . . Other officers elected, at least two of them I regret to say, also by a standing vote, were Thomas Mann, Honorary President, and Donald Ogden Stewart, President. . . . B. The Congress was a great success (in case the point has not been made, Folsom organized the Congress). There were about 450 delegates, 38 of them from foreign countries: Chile, Brazil, France, England, the Philippine Islands, exiles from Italy, Germany, Czechoslovakia, not to mention at least one strange visitor from a world very foreign to literary affairs, which rumor

has it is known by the name of FBI. It all started like this. Months ago Folsom wrote a long plan of what he thought should happen and then people began to quibble and much as Folsom hates to admit it, the quibblers chewed off many rough edges. Quibblers then became known as nibblers. And the Congress was under way. Hundreds of invitations by telegram, thousands by letter went out, and the net result was cooperation of the most important writers organization (the Authors League of America) in our Congress, support from the most important labor organizations, greetings from Mayor La Guardia, from Haile Selassie, the President of Cuba, the President of the Mexican Confederation of Labor, the President of the Philippine Islands, and a score of others.

Eduard Beneš, former president of Czechoslovakia, speaker at the Third American Writers Congress. From *Direction* magazine May–June 1939.

Carnegie Hall, which is the auditorium for fine music, was almost filled for the opening night of the Congress. Nearly 3000 present. Vincent Sheean, Heywood Broun, Langston Hughes, Donald Ogden Stewart, Sylvia Townsend Warner, Thomas Mann and Eduard Beneš spoke. Broun, Mann and Beneš were broadcast by shortwave radio to all of Europe and we had arranged in advance so that Czechoslovakia knew when the broadcast would go on. Then a collection speech by one of the leading correspondents of the *New York Herald Tribune*. Fifteen hundred dollars cold cash for the aid of exiled writers was raised, $500 of this from a famous Hollywood producer who shall be nameless. Following the Carnegie Hall meeting there was a reception for the speakers and stray celebrities, including Tom Mooney who made a great hit and who managed to get his hand shaken at $2 per for the benefit of exiled anti-Fascist writers.

Next morning literary events began to happen, simultaneously and with extremely unliterary precision. America's poets had the best get-together they have had since the days of the Abolition movement when they cooked up rhymes they thought would be of use to somebody. (Don't take my word for this — look at this week's issue of the *Saturday Review of Literature*.) Fiction writers, with the public excluded, decided to forego fiction for the truth, and instead of seeing in each other merely a group of annoying competitors, found a friendly audience of distinguished colleagues. Oliver La Farge was chairman and everybody whose name is coming in with the rising tide was a speaker. Ditto the dramatists. Except that Lillian Hellman was chairman.

Heywood Broun

Heywood Broun, journalist, a founder of the Newspaper Guild. Caricature by Georges Schreiber. From *New Masses*, 1939.

Donald Ogden Stewart, screenwriter, playwright, League president, 1937–1941, FBI target. Courtesy of the Academy of Motion Picture Arts and Sciences.

Exiled writers (the center of German literature is now in New York) had their innings Sunday afternoon, and the crowd stood in moving silence and wept as the names of scores of writers who have been killed as victims of fascism were read.

Saturday afternoon ten million people listened in on the program over a nationwide radio hookup. The program was about radio, by radio's leading writers and editors. The heads of the three major networks were there, and H. V. Kaltenborn was chairman. The point of it all was that good literature can be produced on the air; good pro-democratic, anti-fascist literature. And the movies went to town Saturday night, with important papers from Hollywood and about Hollywood, and with samples of movies which Hollywood won't let touch on civil liberties themes. Sunday morning two of the most famous creators of America's growing folk literature were present in person and sang their original songs and told their stories.[6] Present with them were scholars and writers whose works are enriched by reference to the literature created by the people.

Dorothy Parker, Dashiell Hammett, William Rose Benet, a half dozen screen writers who struggle along on a thousand a week, Richard Wright, the brilliant new Negro novelist, Langston Hughes the Negro poet, Peador O'Donnell, Irish peasant novelist, Pietro Di Donato our brick-layer friend whose book has just been chosen by the Book-of-the-Month Club, Ella Winter widow of the late Lincoln Steffens now wife of Donald Ogden Stewart, Mike Gold, columnist for the *Daily Worker*, Kyle Crichton, an editor of *Colliers*, Hilton Smythe, editor of the *Saturday Review of Literature*, W. H. Auden, British poet — and so on were swarming all over the New School for Social Research where the meetings took place. They felt a good deal more communal and friendly than the isolated writer of the past could ever have believed. In the entire Congress there was only one small squabble, and it was of no importance. America's major writers were all agreed and friendly — they wanted to work together to preserve democracy and culture. And those who couldn't come, like Hemingway and Steinbeck and MacLeish sent their words of support and regret.

A special edition of *International Literature,* with important statements by all of Russia's leading writers was got out in time for the Congress and copies sent over especially for the delegates.

The upshot of all of this is that Folsom is thinking of growing a beard, wearing a scarlet-lined cape and taking on peculiar and impressive mannerisms. Aside from these tendencies, which are entirely his own idea, he is being bothered to hell by a bunch of gadflies he formerly considered as personal friends who are trying to make him get up on his hind legs and make speeches. Or maybe write articles — god knows what. The point seems to be that America's writers suddenly find themselves having been at an important Congress and now they have got to create somebody important who ran it. I prefer wood chopping.

It appears that tomorrow afternoon there is some kind of party with various assorted authors present at which Folsom has to appear and be guest of honor. He's staying up all hours of the night to get this letter dictated to his fond frau so as to avoid the possibility of spending any time preparing a few well-chosen words. Two years of teaching public speaking certainly took a tuck in my soul. Louis Aragon, who spoke at several of the sessions and who came over from France, seems to be the main cause for my present distress.[7] He

John L. Spivak, journalist who exposed Fascist priest Father Coughlin. From *New Masses,* December 5, 1939.

Meyer Levin, novelist, Chicago representative on National Council, 1938, 1940. *Saturday Review of Literature* photo, May 13, 1937. Reproduced with the permission of the Western Historical Collections, University Archives, University of Colorado at Boulder Libraries.

seems very much annoyed at having a famous organization cluttering up the literary scene with nobody famous to boss it around. I prefer wood chopping.

Health OK.

Mike [our son] OK.

Finances KO.

Your loving son

After the congress the League felt poised for a big year, but on August 23, a big change came. The Soviet Union and Germany signed a non-aggression pact. The Popular Front, which had made possible the Third American Writers Congress, was very suddenly a thing of the past.

Notes

1. Millen Brand Journal, April 7, 1939, Rare Book and Manuscript Library, Columbia University, New York City.

2. After Aragon returned to France, he was captured by the Germans, escaped, then had to make frequent moves to keep ahead of the Nazi advance. He was able to reunite with his wife, Elsa Triolet, and both of them continued to write, in spite of everything. He was even able to say in a letter to *The Clipper,* June 1941, "It is just as possible to write in Nice [as in Paris], and there is sun here, it is warm, etc."

3. Malcolm Cowley, "Notes on a Writer's Congress, " *The New Republic,* June 21, 1939.

4. Malcolm Cowley, "In Memoriam, " *The New Republic,* August 12, 1940.

5. Many people have reported Dorothy Parker's witty comments. Kyle Crichton in *Total Recoil* remembers a different person: "People who meet Dorothy Parker for the first time are invariably amazed. They find it impossible to believe that this quiet, soft-voiced, almost humbly considerate woman is the Dorothy Parker who once terrorized New York with her coruscating wit."

6. Aunt Molly Jackson and Pete Seeger.

7. When I conferred with Aragon in his hotel room, he was very insistent that I seek more publicity for myself. As he talked, I noticed that he had rearranged the furniture in the room so that his typewriter was directly in front of a big mirror. I was later told that he had a similar mirror in the office of the newspaper he edited in Paris. How could he work that way? But how many authors have written as much as Aragon, and of such variety and excellence?

John Reed. From a painting by Robert Hallowell reproduced in *New Masses*, June 6, 1939.

9

The Communist Party and the League

In the place of the old bourgeois society, with its classes and class antago-
nisms, we shall have an association in which the free development of each
is the condition for the free development of all.

— *The Communist Manifesto*

We all felt free, within fairly large limits, to disagree with Party functionaries.

— Granville Hicks, *Where We Came Out*, written after he left the Party

I owe my literary development to the Communist Party and its influence.
. . . It gave me my first full-bodied vision of Negro life in America.

— Richard Wright, interview with Alfred David,
Daily Worker, February 25, 1938

The leaders [of the CP] varied from the intelligent and heroic — even saintly
— to the talmudic and vulgarly opportunistic.

— Cedric Belfrage, *The American Inquisition*

Did the Communist Party control the League of American Writers?
Most critics have answered this question with an accusatory "Yes." I also
answer "Yes," but with a very specific definition of "control." Remembering my father, a successful football coach, I know that a coach
"controls" a team as all of its members work together to win. Not only
that, every member of a team, from star to substitute, qualifies the nature
of the control exercised by the coach. And so I suggest that rather than
asking if the CP controlled the League, it would be more illuminating to

ask, "Did the League contribute to what it summarized as resisting fascism and defending culture, and did the CP help the League in these endeavors?" To this question I believe the answer must also be, "Yes."

To explain why I say this, it may help to take a backward glance at the years before the League was founded in 1935. There had been harbingers of political and collective activity by writers. *New Masses* stirred up fusses. So too did the Workers Drama League. Writers had been prominent in the effort from 1920 to 1927 to prevent a miscarriage of justice in the case of Nicola Sacco and Bartolomeo Vanzetti, foreign-born anarchists who had been charged with murder.[1] In 1931 Sherwood Anderson, Theodore Dreiser, Waldo Frank, Edmund Wilson, Malcolm Cowley, and Mary Heaton Vorse took considerable risks when they went to Harlan, Kentucky, where coal operators were using violence to break a strike led by the National Miners Union. In 1932 many writers joined a committee, called Professional Groups for Foster and Ford, to support the Communist presidential candidates.[2] In 1934 Myra Page, Grace Lumpkin, John Howard Lawson, and Jack Conroy went to Birmingham to support and to write about an inter-racial strike there.

In the early 1930s when friends gathered for a little social life as a break from picket lines, committee meetings, union meetings, Party meetings — meetings, meetings, meetings — they might exchange confidences. Time and again, some enthusiast present revealed that he or she expected the revolution would come before long and certainly it would rid this country of unemployment and exploitation and corruption. Malcolm Cowley in *The New Republic*, April 12, 1935, put it this way. "The farmer says, 'if they don't stop foreclosing our mortgages, there's going to be a revolution.' The Congressman says, waving a sheaf of letters from his constituents, 'Unless the present situation is remedied, we must face the possibility of revolution.' "

Beginning earlier — at the time of the Wall Street crash in 1929 — and continuing for several years, writers had joined artists in forming John Reed clubs, which were dedicated to creating art and literature with a social vision. John Reed Club writers scorned ivory-tower literature — the tradition of individualistic creation in isolation from society. Theirs was a break from the notion, current in the 1920s, that art should be created for its own sake.

These clubs took their name from John Reed, Harvard graduate, poet, and journalist, who had sympathetically reported the revolutionary activities of Pancho Villa in Mexico before World War I. Later Reed

Edmund Wilson, critic, hostile to the League. *Saturday Review of Literature* photo, Dec. 25, 1937. Reproduced with the permission of the Western Historical Collections, University Archives, University of Colorado at Boulder Libraries.

was in Petrograd when the Communists took power in 1917. His popular book, *Ten Days That Shook the World,* was a work of both literary skill and sympathetic passion for the October Revolution with which it dealt. Reed died while still a young man, but in radical circles he was remembered as a founder of the Communist Party in the United States.

Soon after the first John Reed Club was established in New York City in 1929, branches appeared in a dozen other cities. The members were mostly young people, and they were revolutionary in mood. In New York the club established a school for beginning writers. One who taught there was Joshua Kunitz, a literary scholar very familiar with Russian culture, whose Ph.D. dissertation at Columbia was on the treatment of Jews in Russian literature. Other teachers in the school were Kenneth Burke, a critic, Horace Gregory, a poet, and Edward Dahlberg, a novelist and writer of memoirs. In addition to their classes and lectures, the clubs also published magazines. Within five years they had started or supported: *Left Front, Left Review, Leftward, The Cauldron, Blast, Dynamo, Anvil, Hammer,* and *Partisan Review.*

One of the magazines, *Anvil,* had come into existence independently of the John Reed clubs, but it later merged with *Partisan Review.* Another, *Rebel Poet,* got its impetus from the Industrial Workers of the World — the IWW — also called the Wobblies. It was printed in an old cow shed, and its contributors joked that the U.S. Postal Service finally closed it down because it was too unsanitary to be sent through the mails.

In November 1930, John Reed Club delegates went to an international gathering of like-minded writers in Kharkov in the Soviet Union. Among them were two Communists, Mike Gold and John Herrmann, and non-Communists Josephine Herbst (who was married to Herrmann) and Matthew Josephson. From this meeting, attended by representatives from many countries, the Americans received a good deal of stimulation. Soon the clubs in the United States were increasingly vigorous. I almost said they prospered, but prosperity is not a word suited to these groups of young people, who were almost always poor, as they tried to cope with the Great Depression. By 1934 the John Reed clubs had created a great deal of interest in what was called proletarian literature. This was writing supposedly done from a working class point of view. It was often about workers, was sometimes by workers, and was always intended to further the interest of workers and to expand literary concern for a much-neglected area of life in the United States.

The Communist Party had contributed greatly to the establishment of the John Reed clubs. But when the Nazis took over Germany, the Party decided that a more powerful form of writers' organization was needed — one that would attract established writers who had more influence than did John Reed Club members. As a first step, a group that included editors and writers for *New Masses* issued a call for an American writers' congress. It was held April 25–27, 1935, and at its end those present voted to establish the League of American Writers.

"There was nothing conspiratorial about the party's domination of the League," says Daniel Aaron in *Writers on the Left* (Harcourt, Brace and World, Inc., 1961), "nor did it bother to conceal its influence. The writers who came to New York, in [April] for the congress did not need the party to tell them that more than twenty million were on relief and that the Third Reich menaced the peace of the world. As fellow travelers, many had already worked with members of the party on various issues and felt no hostility to the principles outlined in the League's program."[3]

In the process of changing over from support of the John Reed clubs to organizing the League, there were losses and awkward situations. Writers who focused on the stimulation that the clubs had given to young authors were upset. One of them, Richard Wright, recounts the story in his *American Hunger:*

[A] national John Reed Club congress . . . convened in the summer of 1934 with left-wing writers attending from all states. But, as the sessions got under way, there was a sense of looseness, bewilderment, and dissatisfaction among the writers, most of whom were young, eager, and on the verge of doing their best work. No one knew what was expected of him, and out of the congress came no unifying idea. Through conversations I learned that the members of the New York John Reed Club were in despair at the way in which the congress was drifting, but they took care to conceal their disapproval. This puzzled me, for I felt that the problem should be brought into the open for discussion. But I was glad to hear the New York Commu-

Richard Wright, novelist, poet, League vice president, 1941. From *Direction* magazine.

nists express horror at the brutal way in which the Chicago Communists made demands upon the Chicago John Reed Club membership. One astonished New York comrade declared:

"A Chicago Communist is a walking terror!"

As the congress drew to a close, I attended a caucus to plan the future of the clubs. Ten of us met in a Loop hotel room and, to my amazement, the leaders of the club's national board confirmed my criticisms of the manner in which the clubs had been conducted. I was excited. Now, I thought, the clubs will be given a new lease on life. Writers would now be free to make their political contributions in the form of their creative work.

Then I was stunned when I heard a nationally known Communist announce a decision to dissolve the clubs. Why? I asked. Because the clubs do not serve the new People's Front policy, I was told. That can be remedied; the clubs can be made healthy and broad, I said. No, a bigger and better organization must be launched, one in which the leading writers of the nation could be included, they said. I was informed that the People's Front policy was the correct vision of life and that the clubs could no longer exist. I asked what was to become of the young writers whom the Communist party had implored to join the clubs and who were ineligible for the new group, and there was no answer. This thing is cold! I exclaimed to myself. To effect a swift change in policy, the Communist party was dumping one organization, scattering its members, then organizing a new scheme with entirely new people![4]

In one way, Richard Wright was correct. The Party's action was wasteful of human resources. But Wright also underestimated the danger to all writing — to all culture — that led to the abrupt change in the Communists' emphasis. Adolf Hitler, though far from Chicago, was a very real threat to writers in mid-America, including those who were young.

In 1937 when Wright moved to New York — and before long into national leadership within the League — he did not repeat his charge that young writers were being ignored, and indeed they were not, although they no longer had an organization that was largely their own.

The Communist Party had a political blueprint in mind when it urged the formation of the League and the dissolution of the John Reed clubs. In retrospect, it is possible to see that the clubs could have continued to live a useful life at the same time the League of American Writers carried out its broader strategy in the effort to defeat Fascism. The CP's decision that the death of the John Reed clubs was essential to the birth of the League was clumsy and undemocratic. But what more graceful, more productive decisions were being made by the Democratic Party, the Socialist Party, the Socialist Workers Party (Trotskyists), or anyone else? To ask the question is to answer it. In the mid-1930s the parties of fascism, throughout the world, stood in direct opposition to writers, indeed to all enlightenment. In the United States, less far to the Right than the Fascists, the Republican Party certainly did not concern itself with support for literature.

And the Democrats? Up to the time of the WPA Writers Project, no parties except the Communist and the Trotskyist tried to do anything. This meant the Democrats made no mistakes of commission. Many Democrats did join the League, and for two years the most important member of the party, President Franklin D. Roosevelt, was an honorary member. But the Democratic Party as a whole showed no interest, and some of its leading members were as hostile to the League as were most Republicans. In fact, the government agencies that the Democrats controlled resisted the League's proposals about Spain and other matters and finally helped put the League out of business.

The only other national groups that called themselves parties were very small organizations in certain localities or on the Left. Some Socialist Party members and supporters participated in the League up until late in 1939 — Van Wyck Brooks among them. But the Socialist Party did nothing to associate itself with the anti-Fascist activities of the organization.

The Socialist Workers Party was strongly opposed to the Popular Front, which the League endorsed. The SWP did take literature seriously but had a special complaint about the League: It had abandoned what they considered a necessary revolutionary course.

No political party or group, Right, Center, or Left, was bestirring itself on behalf of writers and their readers with anything like the earnest vigor shown by the CP. Nevertheless, literary historians have attacked the CP for its activity, and they have not called to task the other groups for their inactivity.

The CP had come ill prepared for its involvement with writers. It was an organization that focused on workers and working class issues and needs. When writers, under the impact of the Depression, began to move to the Left in considerable numbers, the CP had no well-developed way of responding to them. John Reed, a writer and CP leader, was long gone. The Party official who seemed closest to writers was Alexander Trachtenberg, head of International Publishers, the Party's publishing house. He had done graduate work in economics at Yale and had edited Marxist books and pamphlets. Although Trachty had limited firsthand knowledge of creative writers, in the early days of the League he was very active in its affairs. He could give advice of several kinds. As a longtime participant in organizations, he knew how to get things done — a skill not common to writers who were unused to working in groups. If the Exiled Writers Committee, for instance, wanted to have a fundraiser in Chicago, he could find out who was the best Party person or sympathizer to get it started. (He did not at any time — nor did anyone else acting for the CP — ever give funds to the League, so far as I know.) On occasion, of course, he passed along the thinking of the CP about practical ways to influence the political scene.

When it became clear, in the fall of 1937, that the League needed larger offices, it was no doubt Trachty who proposed that we look at space that was available at 381 Fourth Avenue, the building in which he had his office.

If I wanted to consult Trachty, I only had to step into the elevator and go up a few floors. One day I did this after I had a visit from a young man, very plainly dressed, as were a great many people in the Depression years. What he wanted was help in a publishing venture that he explained with an intensity that compelled attention.

His idea was this: He would scout around for good, progressive books that had not reached the audience they deserved. He would buy them from publishers at cost or less, then sell them at an affordable price to members of a book club that he proposed to start. All he needed from the League was a job, sponsorship, some organizational help, and introductions to people who could provide some financing. He would be happy to let the League play a big role in choosing books to distribute.

This seemed to me a plan that could get enthusiastic support from both League members and publishers. So I took the elevator up to the International Publishers office. There Trachty sat, short and plump, behind his big desk piled all over with books and pamphlets and papers.

I outlined the idea and asked him, as an old hand at book distribution, what he thought of it.

Trachty exploded. I don't remember what reasons he gave for scorning the proposal, but he spluttered such vehement objections that I knew I would have problems with him and the Party if I tried to add a book club to the League's already full quota of work.

I took the easy way out and let the young man look elsewhere for help. This he did, and he got it. Before long his Book Find Club put into the hands of 36,000 readers its first selection — Albert Maltz's anti-Fascist novel, *The Cross and the Arrow.* The club's founder, who went on to make it a success, was George Braziller, later the founder of a publishing house that bore his name.

Alexander Trachtenberg, director of International Publishers, member of the Executive Committee, 1935–1937. Courtesy of International Publishers.

Clearly, it seemed to me, Trachty had less-than-complete wisdom about publishing and, perhaps, about politics, too. Perhaps it was his clumsiness — or it may have been his habit of talking at great length while he was deciding what he really wanted to say — that led to his replacement as an adviser to the League. Whatever the reason, I changed from occasionally consulting him in his office to meeting V. J. Jerome, sometimes conspiratorially on street corners.[5]

V. J., small, absentminded, scholarly looking, was born in Poland, spent his boyhood in London, and then came to the United States. He graduated from City College and had mastered several languages. When he first became involved with the Party, his main interest was poetry, but later he developed a great preoccupation with Marxist theory and finally became editor of the Party's theoretical journal, *The Communist.*

V. J.'s first wife was Frances Winwar (Francesca Vinciguerra), a literary critic and biographer. Later he was married, until her death, to Rose Pastor Stokes, a famous working class radical who had been the wife of I. N. Phelps Stokes, a millionaire Socialist. When I first encountered him, V. J. was married to Alice Hamburger, much younger than

V. J. Jerome, novelist, poet, cultural director of the Communist Party. Courtesy of Fred Jerome.

he and as cheerful and outgoing as he was reflective and shy. Under the name Alice Evans, she was executive secretary of the New Theater League. Later she was a teacher and psychologist, with a special interest in working with autistic children. She and V. J. had two sons; one of them, Fred, was the same age as our son, and the two boys attended the same school. With this as a point of contact, the Folsoms and the Jeromes saw a good deal of each other. One summer we shared a house in the country.

The V. J. I saw there could be very funny, singing ribald songs as we sat around our home-made swimming pool on a warm summer evening. During his holiday with us, he was completing his autobiographical novel, *A Lantern for Jeremy* (Masses and Mainstream, 1952) — a simple, touching story of Jewish boyhood.

Jerry surprised us one day when he asked if he could ride our bicycle. He had not been on one since his childhood in London. Clad only in shorts, he wheeled the bike up the hill behind the house. Recalling English bikes as he rolled downhill, he felt for levers on the handlebars that would operate the brakes. Our brakes were controlled by pushing backward on the pedals. V. J. took a violent spill on the gravel road.

To prevent infection, Mary applied iodine over a huge scraped area of his bare back. V. J. uttered not a sound. Later when I commented on his fortitude, he said he regarded enduring the pain as practice for the day when he might have to undergo torture. So far as I know, this day never came, but he did serve a term in prison after being convicted under the Smith Act.[6]

Because V. J. was interested in poetry, I ventured on one occasion to show him a sonnet I had written that told something of my discovery of Marxism:

A Nova in Our Night

"In plain English, Nova Herculis is a star which blew up, becoming a new solar system about 1200 years ago, and it took all those years for the light from that explosion to reach us. . . . In ten days the 'nova' or new star had increased over 100,000 times in brightness." — News Item.

When steel bites granite or diamond digs at glass,
thin sparks begin to shower, forming a wide
and scintillant corolla, then dropping beside
the night they darken, die and let the darkness pass.
These sparks shed quicker nearer light, surpass
in speed this Nova here whose darkness died
during our own Dark Ages. Its sheen tried
twelve hundred years to leap the sky's crevasse.

When steel-sharp men lathe life, we quickly find
new sparks which burgeon brightly in our sight,
but when a daring spacious ordered mind
grows to a dazzling universe, the light
from it lingers in reaching dark mankind:
And Marx was such a nova in our night.

V. J. read my words, then showed me a poem of his own that he dug out of a desk drawer filled with manuscripts. I didn't think it was very good, and I don't recall what I said about it, but I do remember what V. J. said about my sonnet. He proposed that I delete "Marx" from the last line and insert "Lenin" in its place.

I was not impressed. It would not serve my purpose to rip out "Marx" and pry in "Lenin." It was Marx — deeper in time than Lenin — around whom my image had formed. By no stretch of the imagination, however, was I being ordered to improve the politics of my poem, although Jerome's tendency was clear. Some other CP members have complained that he rigidly found fault with their writing and made proposals for changes that seemed like orders.[7] I can see how they might have bridled at such criticisms.

V. J.'s first major involvement with professional writers in the commercial world came when the CP sent him to Hollywood to help develop Party organization, which in turn would stimulate union organizing and anti-Fascist action among screenwriters. In his dealing with them, he was handicapped; he had published very little, and, I believe, felt insecure with writers. He tried to compensate by being over-assertive.

Exchange of criticisms of manuscripts was very much a part of literary life at that time — certainly of literary life on the Left. John Howard Lawson and Dalton Trumbo engaged in vigorous analysis of one another's work. "Your comments, received this morning, were *exactly* the kind of thing I was looking for. No, Jack, you do not lose *this* friend because of criticism. I wasn't looking for 'It's wonderful!' — I was looking for 'It's wrong here, and this is why.' " So wrote Trumbo to Lawson on one occasion.[8]

Not all writers responded amicably to criticism from Lawson and Jerome (who criticized each other's work), and in 1957, according to Victor Navasky in *Naming Names,* (p. 302), Jerome wrote this to Albert Maltz: "In looking back on the field of my own activity, the cultural field, I can see now that the method was by fiat, the purpose — clarification through discussion — was less than served. 'Long is the way and hard that out of hell leads up to light.' " I can't help wondering how literature on the Left might have been different if Jerome had come to his 1957 conclusion twenty years earlier.

Jeromes's "fiats" were of two kinds — one having to do with the content of writing, the other with organizational matters. Content was not my concern as a League official, and I did not always accept Jerome's organizational proposals. I think of one street corner rendezvous with him. He liked meetings that had a clandestine air, although it would have been much better for the League's health if he, as a League member, had brought his ideas to the organization in the ordinary democratic way. He proposed, where nobody would overhear, that I have the League arrange a well-publicized reception for a German Communist novelist who had somehow got into the United States in spite of the government's anti-Communist screening process. It seemed to me that Jerome was proposing the reception solely because the German was a Communist. Nothing was said about him as a writer. The proposal that the League honor him did not come from within the League; it was an intrusion of sectarian politics. I told Jerome I would have nothing to do with the project. He was furious, but the matter ended there.

On another occasion, Jerome met me on a street corner and asked me to pass along to John Howard Lawson in Hollywood word that novelist Harry Carlisle, a very active League member, had "come under suspicion."[9] Party writers were no longer to rely on him as they had been doing for years. Dutifully, I sent the warning to Jack Lawson, I forget by what means.

It wasn't long before Harry appeared in my office, where he tried to find out who had turned off the faucet of goodwill — the flow of comradeship. I thought it my duty to pretend ignorance, and I can remember still the pained look on Harry's face when he blurted out the news that suddenly no one trusted him. He was deeply hurt, and I was deeply ashamed that I had mechanically carried out an order — one that should have gone through the Party apparatus and not through me.

Why didn't I ask Jerome to explain the reason for his unusual request that I transmit Party orders? I don't know. Why didn't I ask what Harry's supposed crime was? I don't know. On other occasions, I had resisted Jerome. Possibly I did not do so this time because I knew that Harry had married Viola Ilma, about whom the CP had grave suspicions.[10] She had been a self-appointed leader in a youth organization and, as she says in her autobiography, had been much interested in meeting with important Fascists in Germany and Spain. Still, she may only have been a naive opportunist. Whatever the reason for Jerome's order or my acceptance of it, I had not solved a problem that has plagued revolutionary movements — the problem of how to balance skeptical inquiry, which is essential, with loyalty to a collective, which is also essential. I later thought I knew how some Russians must have felt when they carried out orders to ostracize someone — or worse — only to find out too late that the orders were dreadfully wrong.

I am confident the order was wrong in the case of Harry Carlisle. He was foreign-born — English in origin — and the Immigration and Naturalization Service hounded him for years, finally in 1962 driving him out of the United States.

Jerome tried to be helpful to the League, but he was not a practical organizer. His interest was in theory. Often he seemed to me rather like a Jesuit or Talmudist. He could always point to a classical text that supported his point of view — a method of citing authority that was not always helpful to writers finding their way in a complex world different from the world in which classical authors had lived.

In addition to occasional conferences with Jerome, I — and other Party members in the League — got advice when we went to what were called fraction meetings. These were caucuses of Party members, and they dealt not with organizational details but with matters of basic policy. Fraction meetings were held before congresses and whenever there were major changes on the political scene that required new thinking. At one of these meetings, held just before the Third Congress

Earl Browder, general secretary, Communist Party, speaker at the Second League Congress, 1937. National Archives photo.

in 1939, Earl Browder spoke and had this to say:[11] "It is among the writers particularly that the Party made its first big advance in influence in the broad cultural field."

Browder was referring to Party activities among writers who worked in a situation somewhat like that of workers in industry — in the big studios of Hollywood. Among other writers, those who worked in isolation on their books or plays or poems, he said the Party's influence had been slower, particularly in the two years since the Second Congress in 1937. This was the period during which I had been working for the League, when it had more than tripled in size. Browder urged CP members in the League to be:

> outspoken in the defense not of the Communist Party line but in the line of President Roosevelt . . . in the line supported by the majority of the people of America and the writers should contribute to the winning and consolidation of an ever-growing majority of the people behind the policy of concerted action by the United States with other democratic powers to stop fascist aggression. . . . The writer, the artist, is the welder of the unity of the people, the fighter against everything that is the enemy of this unity.

An enemy of this unity, Browder emphasized, was the influence of Trotskyism, which manifested itself "among writers in particular." He spoke of the "disruptive ideology" of Trotskyists and said: "The struggle against Trotskyism is not merely a struggle against an ideology that is hostile to our Communist answers to all the problems of society, but it is a struggle against an immediate destructive and wrecking influence in the broadest progressive movement of the day."

While emphasizing the need for building anti-Fascist unity, Browder noted that CP members were only a minority in the League and that Communists should fight anti-Communist tendencies in the organization by demonstrating in action that "they are good collaborators in solving the immediate tasks before the organization."

Browder was never a League member, but he signed the call to the First Congress; he was an invited speaker at the Second Congress in 1937, and I consulted him at one point, I forget about what. As I remember, he gave advice that seemed to me to be helpful.

Very few Party members knew that another CP leader, William Z. Foster, thought it possible that some kind of arrangement might develop between the Soviet Union and Germany. Because of Browder's prominence and influence in the Party, most members were ill prepared to understand the non-aggression pact that Stalin and Hitler agreed to in August 1939.

Only days after the League held its anti-war Fourth Congress in June 1941, the Nazis broke their non-aggression agreement and invaded the Soviet Union. The United States, which had been gearing up for war on the side of the French and British empires, suddenly and surprisingly found itself an ally of the Soviet Union. In this astonishing new situation, what should the League do to continue its usefulness? I wanted helpful ideas and sought a meeting with Earl Browder.

Browder ducked. He might have said that he did not know what our anti-Fascist writers' organization should do in the circumstances. But he just evaded, and it wasn't long before he engaged in larger evasions. Within a very few years, he proposed the dissolution of the Communist Party, and soon after that he was cast out of the Communist movement. In time, he got a job with the Fund for the Republic as a paid consultant on a series of books about Communism that were certainly not pro-Communist. I had seen an able man, a man I admired, collapse.

When Browder was in prison, convicted of passport fraud, I did see William Z. Foster on two or three occasions. Foster was a League member and had written more books than had many other League members, but he was ill at ease among writers. He preferred workers, whom he understood. He did attend the final session of the Third Congress, at which resolutions were to be acted on, although he did not take the floor. After the session I asked him why he had not contributed to the discussion.

"There was no need to," he said. This I took to be his way of saying that we writers had shown what he thought was good sense. He spoke only when he felt he had to. He did not waste energy. Because he was not well, he organized his life to get the most out of it with the least effort. Trachty, who published Foster, once asked me if I had ever noticed how many chapters Foster had in some of his books. I hadn't noticed.

Lionel Berman, leader in cultural section of the Communist Party, founder of Frontier Films. Courtesy of Hortense Socholitsky.

"Fifty-two," Trachtenberg said. "Foster writes a book a year at the rate of a chapter a week. He runs on schedule — a habit he got from his long experience as a railroad worker. Trains run on schedules."

I liked this story enough never to have endangered it by checking Foster's books to see if Trachty was telling the truth.[12]

As I think of Foster, I recall a visit I had one day from Mrs. Raymond Gram Swing, wife of a well-known radio commentator. She was doing some volunteer work for the League, and I asked her why her husband was not active in our organization. "He thinks the League is too much controlled by the Communists," she said. And as she spoke, I wondered if she was looking at my desk calendar. On it was written, "W. Z. Foster, 3:15 pm."

In June 1938, I wrote this to my parents about the relation of my politics to my job:

> I never have discussed my politics with any [non-Party] League members. I never have denied being a Communist — no one has raised the question. The members of the League like the work the League is doing, and I am the guy that does the League's work. Many non-Party members [I am sure] suspect I am a Communist, but they so thoroughly approve of the line I follow that they have no objections and that is just what any sensible person would say is a sensible solution. But [now] this crazy question has to come up. The book editor of a prominent publishing house who is trying to break up the League by saying I am a Communist was present [at a meeting, the exact occasion for which I have now forgotten]. Also present were the head of the Book-of-the-Month Club and sundry others. I was on trial. And do you know that no one dared ask me whether I was a Communist or not? They hadn't the courage, and they in the publishing business are thoroughly aware of the influence of the League.

A letter I wrote on July 6, 1940, to the Communist *Daily Worker* speaks in a different way of the League and its relations with the Left:

> The splendid support which the *Daily Worker* has given to the anti-war program of the League of American Writers deserves recognition and

thanks. I am pleased at all times to have our work publicized and commented on in your columns, and I was particularly pleased that you gave a
good deal of space in your Saturday edition to the meeting on Wednesday
night which we organized jointly with TAC [Theater Arts Committee].

However, a false impression may gain currency as a result of one passage
in the article. There are a great many courageous and honest liberals in the
League of American Writers who are opposed to war and whose activity at
this moment is in strong contrast to that of the noisy but unrepresentative
group of pro-war writers. Remarks which I am afraid may be interpreted
as blanket abuse of all liberals were wrongly attributed to me in the article
by your reporter. Specifically, I am quoted at one point as referring to " . . .
all the various weak-chinned, weak-kneed liberals, social democrats and
self-seeking gentlemen of no principles." As you probably know, liberals
constitute the overwhelming majority of the League membership, and I
hope you will find opportunity to re-emphasize the impressive number of
honest liberal literary men and women who risk the displeasure of pro-war
editors, publishers and producers by taking an open stand at this time with
the people and against war.

Please do not conclude that I want to restrain the just anger of anyone
against the recent "liberal" converts to the pro-war camp, far from it. I have
only contempt for the fancy rationalizing we see a few writers engaging in
to explain why present comfort under the protection of the war-makers is
more honorable than enduring usefulness in the ranks of the peace-loving
people. No condemnation of these liberals is too strong. But I am sure you
will agree that it is necessary to seek the most effective way of exposing and
isolating agitators for war. Accordingly, I am sorry that your paper and my
organization were both placed in a false light by the remarks carelessly
attributed to me in your Saturday edition.

The League of American Writers is overwhelmingly against America's
entry into this war. This position is one of dignity and importance. We have
no need of appearing so unconvinced of the intelligence of our position that
we excitedly bolster up our self-confidence by indiscriminate name-calling.

Again let me thank you for the considerable attention you have paid to
the efforts of American writers to save peace and to enrich our cultural
heritage. May I ask that, in justice to the many honest liberals in the League
and to the organization they loyally support, you publish this letter.

Very truly yours,
FRANKLIN FOLSOM,
National Executive Secretary.

The letter was published.

In the five years I worked for the League, only two members asked
me if I was a Communist. The first time this happened, I was so surprised

Joseph North, editor of *New Masses*, member of the National Council, 1939–1940. Caricature by Georges Schreiber. From *New Masses*, June 27, 1939.

that I made a flat denial. I was afraid that any other answer would hurt the League. My interrogator was Grace Flandrau, who had invited me to an elegant lunch at the Algonquin, apparently to spring this question.

The second questioner was Oliver La Farge. I evaded. I said I was too busy working for the League to have time for activities that did not contribute to helping the League achieve its goals.

These replies have long bothered me. There were surely better methods of protecting the work of the League. I might, for example, have found a way of getting the questions withdrawn. We were all in an organization because we agreed on — among other things — the principle of the Popular Front. Any published writer could belong and should be judged only on his or her performance in relation to these aims. I might have diverted the questioners to considering whether my performance ran counter in any way to the aims of the League's members. I might have helped Flandrau and La Farge to realize that they should not ask about political affiliations. That was the kind of thing that was done by the political police — by the FBI.

Not being quick-witted enough for a reply along these lines, I suffered because I had lied, and lying was not good for the League — or the Party.

In spite of blunders such as those I made with Oliver La Farge and Grace Flandrau, I managed to serve for a few years as a channel through which flowed some of the energy of writers as they enlarged their roles on the civic scene.

So much has been done by the media, by academia, and by politicians to screen out the realities of the Depression years, that I find it difficult to report — so that it can be believed — the warmth that came from the Party in the 1930s. In one way or another, this warmth affected the lives of hundreds of writers and hundreds of thousands of others. As they worked together trying to cross the rough terrain that separated them from an expanding future, a new mood of selfless companionship developed that set people to finding worth in each other.

Sometimes that same warmth brought with it light that simultaneously provided much-needed illumination and blinded us to what lay in the shadows. Hidden there was an ugliness that has drawn so much attention that we forget the light itself.

In this ambiance, my method of work in the League council often followed a pattern: After receiving suggestions from all quarters, I drew up a plan for a project that I believed would serve the League's aims and the wishes of the members. I prepared this plan in some detail, then submitted it to the council. There it was discussed and revised. When finally adopted, it became the property of the whole council, and the members went to work to put it into effect. With this method, I think I helped writers to move toward that part of the population that needed a better future. My role in doing this was that of a technician, not that of an ideologue. But a technician was useful.

The Party was useful to the League — and to literature — as Malcolm Cowley acknowledged after he had left the League because of his objection to its stand on the German-Soviet non-aggression pact. In a letter December 17, 1940, to Kenneth Burke he said: "The CP did play a central role [in the literature of the last ten years] not by giving all the answers but by stating the problems that people argued about."[13]

Notes

1. For a list of writers who took active part as picketers or protesters in the campaign to save Sacco and Vanzetti, see Appendix D.

2. The names of writers on this committee appear in Appendix E.

3. Daniel Aaron, *Writers on the Left* (Harcourt, Brace and World, Inc., 1961), p. 284.

4. Richard Wright, *American Hunger* (Harper and Row, 1977), pp. 190–191.

5. Party leaders and some members assumed rightly that they were under FBI surveillance, and they took many precautions to ensure the privacy of their communications with each other. One such defensive measure was to meet where eavesdropping was unlikely — on street corners, for example. Jerome, it seemed to me, carried precautions to unnecessary lengths.

6. The Smith Act, which President Roosevelt signed into law in 1940, forbade "teaching and advocating" the overthrow of the United States government by force and violence. Commenting on one of the trials that took place following passage of this act, Supreme Court Justice Hugo Black said, "The petitioners are not charged with attempt to overthrow the government. . . . [The indictment] is a virulent form of prior censorship of speech and press which I believe the First Amendment forbids."

7. One instance of Jerome's orthodoxy is reported in Victor S. Navasky's *Naming Names* (Penguin Books, 1981), p. 294:

"I have always made my own judgments on my work and not been affected by judgments coming from any political source," said John Howard Lawson. When [Lawson's play] *Processional*, originally produced . . . in 1935, was revived in 1939, it was violently attacked by the Communist papers as an example of Dada and surrealism. "I can't recall that that had any devastating effect on me," Lawson said. He got a frantic telegram from V. J. Jerome saying the play went against all the principles of socialist realism. Lawson replied, "Sorry, I disagree. Besides, forty people's jobs depended on it, so I let it run." Lawson also remembered the time Michael Gold criticized one of his plays as the work of a "bourgeois Hamlet. . . . I didn't like it, but it wasn't the end of the world."

8. Dalton Trumbo to John Howard Lawson, December 18, 1956, Lawson Papers, Special Collections, Morris Library, Southern Illinois University, Carbondale, Ill.

9. Harry Carlisle was a leader in the John Reed clubs and later organized many important functions for the League. Always, I think, he was well loved by those with whom he dealt. I never discovered why Jerome sent the strange order to shun him.

10. Viola Ilma, *The Political Virgin* (Duell, Sloan and Pearce, 1958), pp. 61–67.

11. Remarks of Earl Browder to writers' meeting, May 16, 1939. Box 2, Item 1 in the Draper collection, Robert W. Woodruff Library, Emory University, Atlanta.

12. Some years after the League days, I had a long conversation with Foster, but not about politics. He spoke about nutrition and the vegetarian diet he found beneficial to his health, and he talked about Shakespeare. He knew the plays more thoroughly than I did, and I had studied them at Oxford.

13. Malcolm Cowley to Kenneth Burke, December 17, 1940, Special Collections, The Newberry Library, Chicago, Ill.

10
Human Rights and Wrongs

It ain't what a man doesn't know that makes him a fool, but what he knows that ain't so.

— Josh Billings

One area in which the League was tried and found wanting was its response to the infamous trials in Moscow, far removed from the center of American literary and political life but little farther away than Spain, in whose civil war the League had become deeply involved. Beginning in August 1936, a series of proceedings in the Soviet capital led to the execution of prominent figures who everyone had assumed were loyal to the stated goals of Soviet society. In the first trial sixteen leading men were condemned. A few months later, seventeen more were convicted of horrendous crimes. Six months later, several high military officers were tried and shot. And that was not the end. The terror spread.

But what did these trials have to do with writers in the United States?

Many writers here, having experienced the devastating effects of the Great Depression and deeply alarmed by the awful deeds of expanding fascism, had come to hope that socialism could serve humankind better than the staggering capitalist system. These writers, I among them, believed that the Soviet Union was a socialist country and was making advances that held great promise for all who did — or wanted a chance to do — useful work. The Soviet Union seemed to be a basically good society, and we hated to see some of its old revolutionaries turn against it, as the prosecutors in the Moscow trials claimed they were doing. I, and many others, assumed that those convicted were guilty as charged. Not every League member, however, shared that belief. For example, League members Philip Rahv and William Phillips, who were among the editors of *Partisan Review*, disagreed. They and others seemed to rely

Walter Duranty, *New York Times* Moscow correspondent, speaker at the Second Writers Congress. *Saturday Review of Literature* photo, July 3, 1937. Reproduced with the permission of the Western Historical Collections, University Archives, University of Colorado at Boulder Libraries.

on information they received from Trotskyist sources. Because the League refused to condemn the trials as unjust, Rahv and Phillips, together with the novelist James Farrell and the critic Edmund Wilson, began to attack the League on several counts.

One common complaint was the claim that the League took orders ultimately from Moscow. It was true that the League wanted to resist injustice anywhere and that the League did remain silent about the Moscow trials, which Phillips, Rahv, and others maintained were frame-ups. It was also true that the trials *were* gross miscarriages of justice. Nevertheless, many League members — who yielded to no one in the desire for justice — thought that the trials were fair. These writers were not ordered by the Communist Party, supposedly acting for the Soviet Union, to believe the defendants were guilty. It seemed to them that the evidence required this conclusion.

The press reports that cast doubt on the fairness of the Moscow trials came from sources habitually hostile to socialism, which had often been proved wrong in the past. On the other hand, Sender Garlin, a League member who had been active in the John Reed Club and on *Partisan Review*, covered all the Moscow trials and was convinced that the defendants were guilty. Sharing his view were the U.S. ambassador, Joseph E. Davies, and the *New York Times* correspondent Walter Duranty, both of whom witnessed part of the trials. In the more than fifty years that I have known Sender Garlin, I have found him to be a hard man to fool, but fooled he was by the trials: so was I and so were a good many others. I had a full supply of prejudices against Trotskyists. They, it seemed to me, made themselves vulnerable by objecting to many of the good things the League was doing or wanted to do.

A commission of inquiry into the charges against Leon Trotsky in the Moscow trials met in Mexico in mid-April 1937. It seemed to me at the time that the commission's findings were merely a self-serving ploy arranged by Trotsky.[1] I did not believe the findings, and I did not think the proceedings relevant to the work of the League. Our work was certainly not to sponsor revolutionary Communism. It was to defend peace and bourgeois democracy from attack from the Right.

The list of injustices to which the League did not object goes on. We did not oppose the trial of U.S. Trotskyists who, on December 8, 1941, were sentenced to prison under the Smith Act. This act, signed into law by President Roosevelt in June 1940, rendered illegal "teaching and advocating the overthrow of the United States government by force and violence." Severe penalties were provided for "teaching and advocating." In other words, this was a thought control measure. Its first use was against Trotskyists who were influential in trade unions in Minneapolis, and the League did not object as it should have. So far as I recall, this lapse in our resistance to injustice did not come as a result of orders from the Communist Party. The League had been so roundly abused by the Trotskyists that we could not see that we would be defending ourselves if we defended them from this assault on their freedom of thought. A few years later, when the Communist Party was persecuted under the Smith Act, writers who had belonged to the League were not so silent.

The League was weakened by its blindness to the truth about the Moscow trials and, four years later, to the principles involved in the Smith Act trials of the Trotskyists. But our League's very obvious activities against fascism continued to be appealing. The organization kept on growing.

We were deeply concerned about the concentration camps in Europe, but as the United States became involved in the war, we were silent when our government, in February 1942, set up its own concentration camps for Americans whose crime was that they had chosen Japanese ancestors. The Communist Party did not protest the maltreatment of the Nisei, but I don't recall that any Communist leader — or anybody else — suggested that the League, too, ignore this injustice. If we were aware of the concentration camps, we put no energy into facing the problem they presented. We were entirely focused on winning the war against fascism in Europe and Asia. We were, however, generally aware of the attention that the FBI was paying to writers, even if we didn't know all the details of the scrutiny to which we were being subjected.

The building of twelve concentration camps designed to receive Communists was still several years in the future, following the passage by Congress of the Emergency Detention Act, which was part of the Subversive Activities Control Act of 1950.[2] Radicals were never rounded up and put in these camps, but the government maintained them in readiness for more than twenty years, until the Emergency Detention Act was repealed in 1971. I didn't learn until many years later that I was on J. Edgar Hoover's list of citizens scheduled to be interned when and if . . .

Notes

1. David Aaron, *Writers on the Left* (Harcourt, Brace and World, Inc., 1961), pp. 447–448, lists many of the writings, pro and con, that dealt at the time with the Provisional American Commission for the Defense of Leon Trotsky that preceded the Commission of Inquiry Into Charges Against Leon Trotsky.

2. The Act authorized "the detention of each person as to whom there is reasonable ground to believe that such person probably will engage in or probably will conspire to engage in, acts of espionage or sabotage." The Emergency Detention Act of 1950, 64 Stat. 1019, Sec. 103 (a).

"One thousand nine hundred and thirty-eight years later — And for this I let myself be crucified?" by the Spanish artist Fontanals, winner of third prize in a contest sponsored by the Postal Employees Union of Barcelona in 1938. An album of six prints submitted for the contest, *Concurso de Caricaturas Antifascistas,* was published by the union's newspaper, *Vanguardia Postal.* In June 1939, Ludwig Renn gave the League a copy of this album. Original in the Franklin Folsom collection.

11

Political Police

Gee, but I'd like to be a G-Man
And go Bang! Bang! Bang! Bang!
Just like Dick Tracy, what a "he man"
And go Bang! Bang! Bang!
I'd do as I please, act high-handed and regal
'Cause when you're a G-Man there's nothing illegal.

— Harold Rome, 1937[1]

A complete review of the FBI files would reflect the fact that President Roosevelt used the FBI far more than any other president — and for things that were *not* within our jurisdiction.

— Cartha De Loach, assistant director of the FBI until 1970[2]

Where suspicion fills the air and holds scholars in line for fear of their jobs, there can be no exercise of the free intellect. Supineness and dogmatism take the place of inquiry.

— William O. Douglas, dissent,
Adler v. Board of Education, 342 U.S. 485(1952)

The government policy of scrutinizing writers has had a long history, much of which has been told by Victor S. Navasky in *Naming Names* (Penguin Books, 1981), Herbert Mitgang in *Dangerous Dossiers* (New York: Donald L. Fine, 1988), and Natalie Robins in *Alien Ink* (William Morrow and Company, 1992).[3] But none of these books is centrally concerned with the League of American Writers. Navasky focuses on congressional harassment. Mitgang is primarily interested in the shameful spying done on prominent writers in the literary mainstream. He omits most of the less well known writers and most writers on the Left, and so does not bring to light the effect that spying may have had on their contribution to American life and literature.

Robins, in her more detailed study of some writers, makes clear that she strongly objects to this attention from the FBI, except possibly in the case of people who were really Communists.[4] These, she alleges, as did the ineffable J. Edgar Hoover, were real threats to the United States. So, in spite of three well-researched books about writers and the political police, and many other books about governmental repression in general, there is still something to say about spying on the League and its members. This surveillance increased as the government prepared for war. "In 1936, and again in 1938," says Robins, "the President issued secret oral instructions to [J. Edgar] Hoover to investigate *all* subversive activities, including communism."[5]

In 1938 the House Committee on Un-American Activities (HUAC) began to function, with Martin Dies as chairman. (By 1947 J. Parnell Thomas was chairman, and Richard Nixon was a member.) The committee was supposed to investigate "un-American" (whatever that meant) propaganda activities, but it served no legitimate legislative function, spent a vast amount of money, and ruined many lives.

At one of HUAC's hearings in Washington, Walter S. Steele, a professional Red-baiter on the staff of the *National Republic,* testified against the League. The League was not aware of this hearing and had no opportunity to rebut his charges, but the general assault did not go unnoticed. On October 3, 1938, Donald Ogden Stewart, representing the League and several thousand members of the Hollywood Anti-Nazi League, made a nationwide radio broadcast on NBC, in which he denounced Martin Dies and condemned the activities of HUAC.

In harmony with HUAC, the FBI became increasingly watchful of the League; the Roosevelt administration dropped many of its progressive programs, including the WPA Writers Project, and moved closer to entry into the war, which France and England were still hoping to turn against the Soviet Union. At this time, someone with easy access to the League office obtained the League membership list and various letters. The method of this burglary appears in a report dated October 7, 1941, in the FBI files: "There is transmitted herewith one roll of Kodak microfilm, 35 millimeter film taken with a Graflex photorecord camera at 1/2 second Fll. This film has been developed at the New York Field Division. The photographs contained herein were secured through a confidential source who had access to the files and membership list of the above named organization."[6]

Other information in the FBI file, stemming from an anonymous "confidential source," included news — not at all confidential — that the League deplored the imprisonment of the Communist leader Earl Browder. And there was correspondence with Corliss Lamont, who asked for the League's membership list in order to distribute copies of *The Soviet Power* by the Dean of Canterbury. Also the FBI had filched a letter from the novelist and poet Millen Brand, in which he sponsored the application for membership of Susan B. Anthony II, great-niece of the nineteenth-century feminist. The League was still attracting members.

In July 1939, Congress passed "An Act to Prevent Pernicious Political Activities," popularly known as the Hatch Act. One provision of this act was used to limit the political freedom of federal employees, among whom were writers.

Immediately following the non-aggression pact between Germany and the Soviet Union, government intrusion into the lives of citizens increased. In early September, J. Edgar Hoover ordered agents in charge of FBI offices throughout the country to make reports on persons of German, Italian, or Communist sympathies. This order was issued on Hoover's own initiative, but on September 6, President Roosevelt directed Hoover to do what he had already begun doing. On that same day, Hoover reported to the attorney general that the New York Police Department had decided to create an "espionage" squad that would soon have 150 members.[7]

Writers and their works were already suspect. In 1920, soon after Hoover began his career with the Department of Justice, he created what came to be known as the "Book Review Section." What did this file have to say about books by members of the League? I applied to the FBI for such information, and a limited number of pages on writers was made available to me. Because large portions of the files were blacked out, and because the FBI was so slow in producing them, I could not make a real survey of its book reviewing. But here is a sample:

In 1923 Upton Sinclair, later a vice president of the League, complained vigorously in a long telegram to the FBI that the agency was interfering with his right to freedom of speech. Sinclair had been scheduled to talk about his novel *The Goose Step* at a meeting of the University Club in Pasadena. The engagement was canceled when the chairman got information that Sinclair was "disloyal to the government" and was "under constant surveillance." What Sinclair did not know was that the FBI had in its file a report on his novel *The Brass Check* ("not obtained from undercover sources"). The book was, said the report, "A Socialist commentary upon American journalism" that "attempts to show that the press is capitalized." Nor did Sinclair know that the directing manager of the Associated Press, according to a memorandum in the file, "Has in his possession a confidential report on the book, *The Brass Check.*"[8]

Upton Sinclair, novelist, League vice president, 1937, 1939, FBI target. Portrait by Hugo Gellert. From *New Masses*, October 18, 1938.

I skip now to an FBI review, dated March 3, 1941, that dealt with *Faith for Living*, by the eminent social critic Lewis Mumford, a League member but not a very active one. Mumford is described as being "an intellectual agnostic," and "a little farther to the left than the exiled writer Thomas Mann." A long, bored summary of his book ends: "The author's prescriptions [for the ills of democracy] go on ad infinitum."[9]

As I searched, I noticed that Rex Stout's file contained a long, hostile review of his *The Doorbell Rang* (Viking Press, 1965), a detective story that is very uncomplimentary to the FBI. J. Edgar Hoover could not abide criticism, but what could he do about Stout's picture of his agency? I found no clear evidence that he did anything to sabotage *The Doorbell Rang* itself, but I did find a memorandum from Hoover to an unidentified person (obviously an FBI official), instructing this person that he/she could "diplomatically" say "Stout has been a member of, affiliated

Erskine Caldwell, novelist, journalist, League vice president, 1937–1941, FBI target. From *Direction* magazine, Summer 1940.

with, or has lent his name and prestige to numerous organizations which have been affiliated with communist groups or identified as communist fronts."[10] Hoover, who had done much to make this country paranoid on the subject of communism, was adroitly labeling Stout a Red, although Stout was a vociferous anti-Communist.

Of more direct relevance to the League was information I found in the file of best-selling novelist Erskine Caldwell, a League vice president who, in 1942, published *All-Out on the Road to Smolensk,* an eyewitness account of Soviet resistance to the Nazi invasion. The FBI review began "Erskine Caldwell, a well known pink American author," and ended "on the whole the book is interesting." Hoover recommended that "this individual be considered for custodial detention in the event of a national emergency."

Theodore Dreiser's file showed that he, too, was listed among those who were to be put in a detention camp if and when some unspecified crisis occurred. Because no complete search of the files on writers has yet been possible, there is no way of knowing how many were on Hoover's Custodial Detention List (later re-named the Security Index).

Scheduled to join Dreiser and many others in a concentration camp was John Howard Lawson, famous for his plays, films, and scholarship. Surveillance of Lawson was particularly intense, and his file included such matters relevant to national security as this: "7PM Lawson was observed putting trash out at curb." The report on his active relationship to the League is entirely blacked out in his file on the excuse that leaving this entry intact could reasonably be expected to reveal the identity of a "confidential source" — in other words, an informer in the League.

Another writer subjected to intense surveillance was League vice president Langston Hughes, a very popular African-American writer. Time and again, people wrote to the FBI to ask if Hughes was a Communist. Usually they asked because he was being considered, or had been announced, as a speaker before some organization. One who made such an inquiry was George Bush, at the time a congressman from Texas.

Hoover diligently replied to these (and other such) inquiries. He explained that he could not give out information from the FBI files, but then he went on to list public sources of negative information about Hughes, including testimony given against him before the Dies committee. What Hoover thought of Hughes's writing is not always revealed, but copies of many of his poems appear in his file. A favorite for FBI attack was "Goodbye Christ," which Hughes withdrew from circulation in the 1950s, as he himself finally went into retreat during the terror of the McCarthy period.

Hughes was not the only poet whose writings were collected by FBI agents. Many poems by many writers are buried in the vaults of the J. Edgar Hoover Building in Washington, along with essays and short stories and dramatic pieces. It occurs to me that some enterprising publisher might do well to put a researcher to work on these voluminous FBI files. An anthology of the literary creations that Hoover regarded as threats to national security would be fascinating reading.

Book reviewing was only one component in Hoover's hysteria-building activities. Beginning in 1939, according to Natalie Robins, Hoover sent Roosevelt two or more reports every day. "Whatever went into [an FBI file] stayed there," historian David Caute tells us. "If someone called a man a vegetarian, and this information was filed, and if subsequently the man proved to the loyalty board that he ate meat every day, and thus was 'cleared,' his file would continue to record the allegation of vegetarianism."[11]

Trotskyists and Stalinists (and radicals opposed to both) are treated as equally objectionable. In fact, J. Edgar Hoover seems to have regarded all radicals as interchangeable parts of one anti-American whole. The well-known journalist Dwight Macdonald, for instance, made it onto the Security Index of the FBI as a "native-born Communist," although at that time neither the CPUSA (Stalinists) nor the Socialist Workers Party (Trotskyists) would have defined him as a Communist.

In 1940 Congress passed and the president signed the Voorhis Act, requiring Communist organizations to register with the government and giving the executive branch the power to deny entry to anyone whose ideas were found to be dangerous. A little later, Attorney General Francis Biddle prepared a confidential list of "subversive" organizations. The League was on this list and remained on it when it was expanded in 1947 by Attorney General Tom Clark under President Truman's orders, although the League was no longer in existence. Once a League member, always a subversive.

The League office was surely bugged and its phone was no doubt tapped, although such of the FBI files as have been released do not provide proof of this.[12] Athan G. Theoharis says that, in the 1940s and later, almost all organizations regarded as leftist by the FBI were subject to this kind of surveillance.[13] And there were other curious happenings not immediately provable as FBI activity.

For example, one day in July 1939, my secretary, new on the job, came into my office looking startled and uncertain.

"There is a man out here who says he is from Moscow and wants to see you."

I wasn't expecting anyone from Moscow, but I said to show the gentleman in.

"I'm Harry Magidoff," my visitor said. "I bring you greetings from the Union of Soviet Writers."

The League did correspond with the organization of Soviet writers who were, like us, part of the International Association of Writers for the Defense of Culture. I thanked Mr. Magidoff and for a few minutes we engaged in chitchat. Finally my visitor asked, "Do you have any messages you want to send to the Soviet Writers Union?"

"No," I said, and went on to explain that if we did have a message, which wasn't often, we would either write or cable.

End of conversation.

Next day at about the same time, my secretary, looking very puzzled indeed, came in and said,

"There is a man out here who says he is from Moscow and wants to see you."

I was intrigued and asked her to show him in.

"My name is Harry Magidoff," he said. "I bring greetings from the Soviet Writers Union."

I believe I managed to conceal my astonishment. This man bore no resemblance to the Harry Magidoff I had seen the day before. When he offered to take back any message we might want to send to the Soviet organization, I repeated what I had told the other Harry Magidoff, and in a few minutes said goodbye.

I knew there was a Harry Magidoff. He had been a foreign correspondent in Moscow, and he had recently returned to the United States. I had never seen him, however, and didn't know which — if either — of my two visitors might be the real newspaperman. I still don't know, nor does a journalist named Harry Magdoff, an editor of *Monthly Review* whom I consulted, thinking I might have got the Magidoff name wrong. He wonders, as do I, if at least one of the Harry Magidoffs was an FBI agent on a fishing expedition.

HUAC continued to pursue the League. In September 1939, it sent a letter asking for our file of correspondence on fascism, nazism, and communism. We replied that we would supply such information if properly served with a subpoena. No subpoena ever came, why I don't know.

This legalistic evasion was not the League's only response to HUAC. On March 6, 1940, Oliver La Farge, author of *Laughing Boy,* and a council member, acting for the League, wrote to Senator Norris urging him to press for action against the FBI, which had raided homes in Detroit where recruiting was alleged to have taken place for the Abraham Lincoln Battalion. Norris did protest, and the harassment of Detroit citizens stopped. Shortly thereafter, President Roosevelt resigned from the League.[14] At about the same time, Donald Ogden Stewart and Dorothy Parker, before a large crowd in Hollywood, put on a skit satirizing Martin Dies, head of HUAC. "When Martin Comes," the skit was called, and it depicted Dies as getting Karl Marx mixed up with Harpo Marx.

George Seldes, journalist, League vice president, 1939–1941. From *Direction* magazine, November 1939.

A few months later, League vice president George Seldes was listening to the radio as it brought reports of additional advances by the Nazi blitzkreig in Europe. Mingled with this news was an attack by Congressman J. Parnell Thomas of HUAC on the League and other anti-Nazi organizations.

Seldes, a former correspondent for the *Chicago Tribune,* was angered because he heard the League called part of a fifth column and a front for the Communist Party. He knew a good deal about what a "fifth column" really was: He had been in Madrid when the term was originated by Fascists to describe their agents in that city who were sabotaging the republican cause. Earlier, Seldes had seen fascism spread. He had even known Mussolini personally before he became a dictator and when he was still a socialist newspaper reporter. They had covered peace conferences together.

Immediately after the Thomas broadcast, Seldes rushed off a letter to me proposing that the League demand time on the air to answer Thomas's attack. I acted on the suggestion, and on August 31, 1940, Seldes addressed a nationwide audience on the CBS network. In his talk

Vida Dutton Scudder, critic, teacher at New Hampshire Writers School. League of American Writers photo.

he told who in the United States were the real Fascists, and he reported on the many pro-democratic activities in the League. He said:

In Germany, Italy, France, Spain, Fascism came after every liberal, labor, progressive, had been labeled "red," communist subversive, and suppressed. The formula worked in Europe; there are many who are using it in America. Is Mr. Thomas attacking us because we believe in civil liberties for everyone, not only Republicans, and Democrats, but all minorities, parties, groups and individuals? . . . As a matter of simple fact the communist members of the League are *a small minority*, but they accept majority decisions, work harmoniously with Republicans such as Margaret Culkin Banning, and Clyde R. Miller, with a large number of members who are Democrats and American Labor Party members such as Martha Dodd and Wellington Roe, with Socialists such as Upton Sinclair and Vida Scudder.

The League of American Writers is not a Communist Party front. It is not a front for anything except literature, democracy, peace.[15]

Hundreds of letters supporting Seldes's opposition to Thomas and HUAC poured in after the broadcast. Today I can't help regretting that Seldes was not able in his talk to discuss the criminal activities for which Thomas was later indicted. Thomas got caught padding his payroll and went to prison in the 1950s, a period during which he had again attacked writers. Unfortunately, Seldes did not have a crystal ball and could not know that screenwriter Lester Cole, a League member, would one day serve time in prison alongside Thomas, who had helped send him there after Cole invoked the First Amendment to the Constitution rather than become an informer.

The FBI had a bizarre interest in another writer, the playwright Maxwell Anderson, who was never very active in the League or in any group that was accused of being Left. Nevertheless, as Herbert Mitgang reports:

The FBI special agent in charge of the New York office received a communication in October 1942 from J. Edgar Hoover labeled *"Maxwell Anderson — Internal Security — C"*. The message from on high said: "The New York field division is requested to conduct an appropriate investigation to develop background and activities of subject Anderson with reference to his possible Custodial Detention. A summary report should then be submitted in accordance with prior bureau instructions summarizing all pertinent information concerning this individual contained in the files of the New York office and including the information incorporated in this letter."[16]

Kenneth Fearing, poet, novelist, teacher in Writers School. Caricature by Georges Schreiber. From *New Masses*, 1939.

The poet Maxwell Bodenheim had a different story to tell in 1940, in a letter to Ben Hecht, quoted by Natalie Robins:

The galoriously [*sic*] democratic FBI has threatened me with arrest and a trial for perjury unless I turn stool pigeon and informer and give reams of information regarding names of Party members, places where members recruited others, etc., in return for which the government would restore my $21.90 WPA job (just a little deal between friends). If I do not sign certain papers the FBI declares that I will be arrested.[17]

Bodenheim did not become an informer, nor did Dorothy Parker, to whom the FBI paid a great deal of attention. She was active not only in the League but in a number of other organizations, including the Joint Anti-Fascist Refugee Committee (JAFRC). On one page in her file is this notation: "Strict care must be exercised that the existence of this important source of information [the JAFRC informer] will not be known to any outside agency."

Those helping refugees were suspect in the eyes of the FBI, and the FBI was suspect in the eyes of Dorothy Parker. According to *New York Post* columnist Leonard Lyons (April 7, 1955), two agents went to Parker's apartment to question her about her influence in the organizations she worked with. "Mrs. Parker's two pet dogs romped all over the room, paying no attention to her commands to stay put. When the questioners asked about the extent of her influence on the committees, Mrs. Parker replied, 'My influence? Look at these two dogs of mine. I can't even influence them.' "

Not only those who helped refugees but also the refugees themselves were regarded suspiciously by the FBI. Some were subject to intense surveillance, even after they left the United States for Mexico. The file on Ludwig Renn reveals that the FBI intercepted his letters to people in the United States. It dutifully records, for example, that Renn wrote to Thomas Mann thanking him for the gift of two books. Nothing to suggest that Renn was working against the interest of the United States appears in the file, but it does include this information: Renn had an office in which he conducted business as president of two organizations, Free Germany, and the Latin American Committee of Free Germans. His office, the file tells us, was "under the constant care of an armed watchman who neither drinks nor has proved amenable to bribing." That report came from the civil attaché of the U.S. embassy in Mexico, who was so diligent in keeping tabs on Renn that he sent specimens of Renn's typing and handwriting to the FBI to be tested for evidence that secret ink might have been used. The results of the tests were negative.

Renn at that time was heading a movement to unite all German refugees into one strong anti-Nazi organization. The United States was then at war with Nazi Germany, but some U.S. agencies obviously did not welcome help from exiled German writers. Whether or not Renn's group knew about the surveillance, they made a brave effort in Mexico to keep German culture alive. They published books and periodicals, held lectures, and encouraged each other to be creative. A book about their activities appeared in East Germany after the war.[18]

Almost everyone in the anti-Fascist literary world was affected in some way by the police activities of the U.S. government. Even I, though barely visible as a writer, was a target of the FBI before I became an official of the League. An account of my experience with the political police appears in Chapter 12, but perhaps I should add this about the effects the surveillance had on me. In 1936 I was encouraged by a faculty member at the University of Washington to apply for an instructorship there, for which I seemed qualified. I was not hired. The professor who had asked me to apply told me that one of the three scholars I had given as references had told the University that I was a Red. The professor could not find out which of my three "friends" had informed on me. At that point, I decided not to waste more time trying to get a job in academia.

In time, unlike some League members who were forced out of writing by the tactics of the FBI, I was forced into writing, and I used pseudonyms. Of these I had eight before I deemed it safe to use my own name.[19] At first, I wrote mainly for children, learning the trade from my wife who was already established in this part of the literary marketplace. It was a part that did not seem to interest the political police, and it was accordingly a kind of safe haven for liberals and radicals, a number of whom became editors as well as writers.[20]

For some reason, poets, who had comparatively small audiences, were not free from attack by the FBI and HUAC. Kenneth Fearing gave wry voice to all of them with these lines:

> Stranger, whoever you are, and whatever your final destination may be,
> I give you, freely, a name to conjure with:
> In heaven: Martin Dies, Chairman of the Membership Committee,
> In hell: Martin Dies, President of United Coke & Coal.[21]

Notes

1. Quoted by Ward Churchill and Jim Vander Wall in *The Cointelpro Papers: Documents From the FBI's Secret War Against Domestic Dissent* (South End Press, 1990), p. xxii.

2. Quoted by Natalie Robins, *Alien Ink* (William Morrow and Company, 1992), p. 73.

3. Many books have dealt with government surveillance of citizens in general. I have found Athan Theoharis's *Spying on Americans* (Temple University Press, 1978) and *The Boss* (Temple University Press, 1988), with John Stuart Cox, particularly informative. *Freedom Under Fire: U.S. Civil Liberties in Times of War* (South End Press, 1990), by Michael Linfield, is valuable for part of the story.

4. "For a long while, at least during the mid-thirties, the forties, and the early fifties, the CP was a potential danger worthy of much of Hoover's concern. . . . The CP did want to get rid of American democracy, and was willing to defraud even its friends and acquaintances in an attempt to accomplish its goals." Robins, p. 79.

5. Robins, p. 73.

6. Copies of the FBI files on the League and on me are in Special Collections, Norlin Library, University of Colorado, Boulder. When I applied to the FBI for the League file, I received — after a long delay — only about thirty pages. Professor Harvey E. Klehr of Emory University applied for the same file and received about 1,000 pages. These he was kind enough to let me borrow and photocopy.

7. Theoharis and Cox, p. 179. My efforts to locate the files of this "espionage" squad were unsuccessful.

8. Another item in the Sinclair file provides a sad contrast to Sinclair's earlier protest. In a letter, written in 1952 during the McCarthy period, he humbly asks Hoover to check

his anti-Communist novel, *The Return of Larry Budd*. Hoover obliged and had eleven, single-spaced typewritten pages full of "corrections" and suggestions sent to the author. Sinclair, of course, had long since resigned from the League.

9. Lewis Mumford File, FOIA Reading Room, J. Edgar Hoover Building, Washington, D.C.

10. Rex Stout File, FOIA Reading Room.

11. David Caute, *The Great Fear* (Simon and Schuster, 1978), p. 271.

12. "FBI warrantless wiretapping of domestic 'subversives' began in 1940 under Roosevelt's directive, and the FBI also began implanting 'bugs' against domestic subversive targets in 1940 without any clear authority to do so. The FBI placed twelve taps and bugs in 1940, and ninety-two in 1941." Robert Justin Goldstein, *Political Repression in Modern America* (Schenkman Publishing Co., 1978), p. 254.

13. Athan G. Theoharis and John Stuart Cox, *The Boss: J. Edgar Hoover and the Great American Iquisition* (Temple University Press, 1988), p. 10.

14. Right-wing screenwriter Morrie Ryskind reported to HUAC that Sidney Hook "called up the White House and informed them of the nature of the League, and the President's membership was withdrawn and all publicity on that was withheld." HUAC, *Hearings Regarding the Communist Infiltration of the Motion Picture Industry*, 80th Cong., 1st sess., U.S. Government Printing Office, 1947, 183.

   Another innacurate version of this episode came from Earl Browder, when he cast himself as an adviser to President Roosevelt in an interview taped many years after the event: "Browder: Before the American Writers League went out of existence Roosevelt had sent in his application to join it, and under my advice it was quietly returned to him with the advice: 'Don't get mixed up in this. There's going to be a lot of controversy about it.' " I found the transcription of the Browder interview in the Oral History Research Service of Butler Library, Columbia University, New York City.

15. A copy of Seldes's broadcast is in my possession.

16. Herbert Mitgang, *Dangerous Dossiers* (Donald L. Fine, 1988), p. 150.

17. Robins, p. 99.

18. Wolfgang Kiessling, *Exil in Lateinamerika* (Leipzig: Verlag Philipp Reclam jun, 1980).

19. These were: Benjamin Brewster, Chase Elwell, Michael Gorham, Horatio Jones (also H. D. Jones), Troy Nesbit, Lyman Hopkins, Philip Stander, and Samuel Cutler.

20. For a fascinating, detailed account of how a writer and union organizer (not a League member) confronted harrassment by HUAC and blacklisting in the 1950s, see Emmanuel Fried, *The Un-American: Autobiographical Non-Fiction Novel* (Buffalo, N.Y.: Labor Center Books, 1992).

21. Kenneth Fearing, *New and Selected Poems* (Indiana University Press, 1966), p. 110.

John Howard Lawson, playwright, screenwriter, critic, League vice president, 1941, picketing later when he was one of the Hollywood Ten. Courtesy of Special Collections, Morris Library, Southern Illinois University at Carbondale.

A page from the FBI file on John Howard Lawson.

12

Fingermen Are All Thumbs

One thing is certain: most of the writers were watched [by the FBI] because of *what they thought.*

— Natalie Robins, *Alien Ink*

William Steele Sessions [FBI Director, 1987–1993]: "I have no information about any list of writers that is being maintained. I categorically deny that we have any files on writers simply because they are writers."

— Natalie Robins, *Alien Ink*

"I may want to commit a crime someday, and I understand that criminals leave fingerprints at the scene." This was my explanation to the young woman in the police station when she asked why I wanted a set of my prints.[1]

The officer gulped. For a moment I thought she was going to call for reinforcements, but she tried again on the off chance that I might be the harmless, white-haired old man I looked to be. (This happened in 1979, a full thirty-seven years after my days at the League.)

"Why do you really want them?" She smiled soothingly as she asked.

I told her. "Although the FBI has long had my prints, they don't seem to feel happy about them and have asked for my help."

"Why does the FBI want them?"

"I've asked for my FBI file under the Freedom of Information and Privacy Acts. The Bureau apparently isn't sure I am who I claim to be, even after I sent them all my past addresses, plus a sworn notarized statement saying I am who I say I am."

That glimpse of comforting red tape gave the young officer the sense of security she needed, and she proceeded to besmudge herself and me and record the fingerprints, without which the FBI was immobilized.

I had debated whether or not to comply with the request for prints. But so far as I was aware, I had not in seventy-two years done any harm to my fellow Americans, nor was I known to be wanted for any crime I did not commit. So I decided to send the prints in and thus remove the latest pretext for evasion in the J. Edgar Hoover Building in Washington.

But perhaps the FBI really doubted that I was the Folsom I claimed to be. I remember visiting the Department of Justice about the time the United States entered the war against fascism. My mission was to persuade the department to release from Ellis Island one Ambrogio Donini, a distinguished professor of comparative religion at the University of Rome. He was being held on the pretext that he had a brother in the Fascist Italian Navy. The charge was true — as far as it went. Ambrogio Donini did have a Fascist brother, but Ambrogio was thoroughly anti-Fascist. In time the "confusion" was resolved and Ambrogio re-entered the United States (see Chapter 13 for details). But the day I was in the Justice building on his behalf, I didn't get out before I saw what I assumed was a stage prop left ostentatiously on a desk I would have to pass. It was a fat folder, and lettered on it was "Frank Folsom."

Was the Justice Department or the FBI accustomed to leaving folders about citizens lying around this way? I doubted that it was standard operating procedure. Possibly the folder was filled with blank paper, bulking it out so it looked impressive. But then it occurred to me that perhaps some fellow whose name resembled mine might have had *his* file enlivened with sinister material about me.

In due course, I found there was such a possibility. At the very time I was in the Justice building, one Frank Folsom was serving as chief procurement officer for the Navy Department. The FBI might have been asked to take a look at someone who had massive government funds to spend, particularly if the FBI was inclined to get him mixed up with Franklin Folsom. I, after all, was pretty obviously a dangerous character.

The possibility that Frank Folsom and Franklin Folsom could occasionally be mistaken for one another seemed more likely some time later, when Frank had risen in the world and was head of the Radio Corporation of America (RCA), and I had sunk to being a free-lance writer. A letter, somewhat as follows, came one day to my home:

"Dear Mr. Folsom, It is our privilege to remind you that your annual contribution of $5,000 to the Boy Scouts is now payable."

Five thousand dollars was about what I earned in a whole year of writing — that is, a good year.

But back to my request for my FBI file. One day I did receive a sample of what I might expect if I persisted. It included little of interest, and on many of the pages almost every line had been blacked out with a marking pen — to protect "national defense" or the identity of informants. However, I did persist.

Finally, I received word that the FBI had got its act together, but first, the law required the bureau to notify me that the file it had assembled consisted of "more than 25 pages." There was no indication whether it ran to twenty-six pages, or 260, or 26,000. I had heard what happened to Corliss Lamont when he asked for his file. The FBI included photocopies of a lot of books and pamphlets he had written and published.

In a panic I insisted that I not be billed for photocopies of the forty-four books I had published. Also I wanted excluded from my file all the considerable material I had written, edited, and distributed for the League of American Writers.

More delays.

I like to think it took time for the FBI to whittle down my file by eliminating such things as books for third-graders about cowboys and Indians. But finally a bill came for $29.70. After I sent a check for this amount, I received 297 photocopied pages. A quick glance told me that much material was being withheld. There was almost nothing, for instance, about the years when I was executive secretary, first of the League of American Writers, then of the New York Council of American Soviet Friendship. It was because I held these jobs that I was listed in the FBI's Security Index as a "Key Figure." I complained to the bureau about its inattention to a matter of such obvious importance, according to the FBI scale of values, and a few more pages dribbled in, this time without a bill.

From what I have received thus far, I have learned much about myself that I did not know, for instance, that I sometimes go under the name Benjamin Webster. (Had someone heard that I wrote several children's books under the name Benjamin Brewster?) I am also known to the FBI, although to no one else, as Fred Franschi. I must remember to write the family of the late Frank Folsom and ask if he ever used those names, perhaps for ceremonial purposes in connection with his duties as a knight of the Sovereign Order of Malta.

The file reveals that it was "Confidential Informant T-2," a person "of unknown reliability," who originally put the name Benjamin Webster into my record — where it is later repeated as a fact to be relied on, without any reference to its dubious origin.

My file also registers that I lived exactly where my printed stationery and the telephone directory said I lived. How much this information cost the taxpayer, no one will ever know. Many different informants, possibly copying each other, but surely drawing different paychecks, came up with the same data. Here was one fact the FBI had straight.

At least thirty "Confidential Informants," some identified by such symbols as "N" or "200" and others as "T-1," "T-2," and so on through "T-25," sent in reports about me to supplement the researches of an undetermined number of special agents. Here is a tidbit from a 1953 report by one of the special agents: "Subject's car was observed parked in front of the New Brunswick Theological Seminary." I was there all right, attending a meeting of people interested in stopping the war in Korea. At least the FBI had evidence that I personally attended a meeting I had done my damnedest to publicize.

Not only did I find such records about myself, but I also got at least one startling bit of news about my wife of more than forty years. She, it seems — totally without my knowledge or her own — had taught for three years (one informant said five years) in the Communist Workers School. Clever woman.

Another discovery really made me look in the mirror. The FBI was afraid of me! J. Edgar Hoover ordered his special agents not to interview me, saying, "Because the subject is self-employed as a writer, authority to interview the subject is denied." At least eight times, agents were ordered *not* to interview me. *Because I am a writer.*

And because I was an official of a writers organization, I was dubbed a "Key Figure." I have hesitated about drawing attention to this classification because persons really familiar with the Communist Party will smile at the notion that I was a "Key Figure" in the revolutionary movement. A keen participant certainly, but equally certainly, not key — unless, of course, I underestimated the FBI's regard for writers. Many of the best in the country belonged to the anti-Fascist organization I served.

Although the FBI avoided me (and my wife, also a writer), it did muster enough courage in 1955 to interview my non-writer mother, then seventy-six.

On with my file. I found a note, dated February 27, 1955, that I was marked "Tab for Detcom." (All applicants for their FBI files should ask the bureau to supply a glossary with the files.) Does "Detcom" refer to those deemed suitable for placement in detention camps for communists? Attorney General Biddle in 1943 ordered Hoover to do away with his Detention Index. But I understand Hoover was adept at evading such orders. He simply changed the labels on his files. Five days after I was marked "Tab for Detcom," orders came through not to tab me for Detcom — whatever that was.

One thing I learned will be of great interest to the earnest Republican who owns tourist cabins on the ranch adjoining the site of what was then my home in Colorado. The FBI thought that I made at least part of my living by pocketing the rents paid by tenants in *his* cabins. Writing is a bad way to make a living, but not that bad.

Now comes a memorandum, dated November 1, 1963, from "SAC Newark" (does that mean Special Agent in Charge, Newark?) to "Director FBI" (I know what that means) about Franklin Brewster Folsom. A diligent researcher has dug up my middle name (from a rare copy of *Who's Who in America?*), but the body of the memorandum dispenses with this frill. It's about Franklin Folsom, and it's a "reliability memorandum regarding subject," meaning me. Moreover, there were apparently seven copies of it deemed "suitable for dissemination." Dissemination to whom? How reliable is this "reliability memorandum?" Does it include data about Frank Folsom? There is no way of telling from the file in front of me. The "reliability memorandum" itself is missing.

Much earlier, May 18, 1950 (the files arrived in no discernible order and certainly not chronological order), Louis Budenz, a one-time Communist turned professional informer, in an interview with the FBI identified me as a "concealed Communist." He presumably got paid for this testimony. On February 5, 1951, Budenz deleted the name of Franklin Brewster Folsom from a list captioned "400 concealed communists revealed by Louis Budenz." No doubt Budenz drew his pay for work on February 5. Then, in June, he was back at the same stand. He identified Franklin Folsom as one of these "concealed communists." Later, perhaps on the same day, perhaps on another — this is not clear — Budenz, re-interviewed, "was unable to satisfy himself of the identity of Folsom and his Communist affiliations." Another paycheck.[2]

A still earlier entry from Confidential Informant "N" reported April 28, 1942, that I was talking to a "Reliable Informant" — a Communist Party member. (The FBI considered such a person reliable?) This Reliable Informant told the Confidential Informant that I was the "Party wit" of the League of American Writers. Party wit — that's a nice touch. A kind of counter–court jester? Could this hearsay of hearsay really mean that someone thought I was the Party "Whip" — no doubt scourging Party writers who did not toe the Party line?

I must note, before I leave Confidential Informant "N" and apparently other informants who were no more observant, that in 1936 (one of the several dates on which the file says I joined the Party), I collaborated on a paperback book with Frederick Engels Menaker, and the title was *The Life of the Party*. More observant than the FBI, Joseph Freeman, then editor of the Communist magazine, *New Masses*, saw our paperback on a newsstand. Expecting to find some meaty political matter, Joe bought a copy. He was furious when he realized that he had invested in a collection of parlor games for adults. But perhaps here I do the FBI an injustice. Someone in the bureau may have read the book, found out what it was, and sagely left mention of it out of my file. Whether it was the FBI or not I don't know, but a book buyer did order from University Microfilms a photocopy of this long-out-of-print publication. A few years ago, I received a check for the royalty due on a single copy.

At the end of 1946, there was a kind of summary report on me for the year. On page nine of this report, I am reminded that a real estate agent obtained a tenant for the summer for my New York apartment. The tenant, who called herself Countess Mariella de Pisa, I learned after the lease was signed and I couldn't do anything about it, claimed to be a very close friend of the Italian Fascist marshall Pietro Badoglio. He, the lady assured me, was at that moment in the United States under an alias — although many anti-Fascist refugees were being denied entrance. My file would have been much more interesting if it had thrown some light on how Badoglio got into this country — and whether he used my apartment. Whoever gave him a visa may know the full story.

Time and again, my file suggests tantalizing questions like this, then provides no answer. For instance, why did the FBI continue to spend money trying to establish that I really was a member of the Communist Party, when I had sworn that I was in a statement filed with the

Department of Justice at the time I became a staff writer for TASS, the Soviet news agency? To hold this job, I had to register as an agent of a foreign power and to answer questions about my political affiliations. I simply told the truth. I now tell it again when I say that I engaged in no political activity of any kind as long as I worked for TASS. And, perhaps surprisingly, the FBI does not contend that I did. That task was left to the Senate Internal Security Subcommittee, which may have tried, through me, to link the U.S. Communist Party, TASS, and the Rhodes Scholarships in a remarkable conspiracy.

It was my schooling that fascinated the subcommittee:

> Mr. Morris [subcommittee counsel]: Now what has been your education?
> Mr. Folsom: I decline to answer that question for the reasons stated.
> Mr. Morris: You mean you refuse to tell us where you went to school?
> Mr. Folsom: You have my answer.
> Mr. Morris: Because you might possibly be giving testimony against yourself?
> Mr. Folsom: Yes.
> Senator Johnson: Did you finish any college?[3]

Neither the senator nor Mr. Morris seemed willing to understand why I wouldn't say anything on such an innocent subject, if indeed it was innocent. The reason, of course, was that if I gave testimony on that or any other subject, I would lose my protection under the Fifth Amendment, which I pleaded, as well as pleading the writers' amendment — the First. If I surrendered the protection of the Constitution, the Senate subcommittee could probe freely into my personal beliefs, which it had no business doing. It could demand that I give names of associates whose efforts to achieve a better world I thought demanded respect, not harassment. Since I wouldn't discuss my politics except where and when I chose to, and since I wouldn't inform on decent people, I availed myself of the Fifth Amendment for the purpose for which it was intended — to protect the innocent weak from those who misused power.

I didn't suspect what the subcommittee might have been fishing for until later when Courtney Smith, American secretary of the Rhodes Trust, reported to a gathering of Rhodes Scholars that the *Chicago Tribune,* always alert to save America from Britain, had been warning its readers that the Rhodes Trust was engaged in some kind of skulduggery. The trust may have its faults, not the least of which is the source of its funds in racist South Africa, but the trust is certainly not in cahoots with the American Left or the Soviet Union to do you-know-what. But perhaps the *Tribune* or the Senate subcommittee or somebody may have had something. It was at Oxford that I joined the October Club, the Communist undergraduate organization, which at the time was headed by Frank Meyer, who later found an editorial post on the *National Review* more congenial to him.

One of the things I couldn't find out from reading my file was whether it was a "friend" or an FBI burglar who at one point swiped my personal address book. And there is no hint about what annoyances, or worse, may have been caused persons whose names appeared in that book. There

Irwin Shaw, playwright, screenwriter, novelist, teacher in Writers School, FBI target. League of American Writers photo.

was, however, a clear implication that those listed there were all to be watched because of their association with me. Did special agents quiz Dr. Milton Levine, for instance? He was our pediatrician, and I never saw him except on medical business. And who was Dr. Benjamin Brockin? I have forgotten, unless he was the surgeon I saw only at the operation on the leg I broke during my wartime, Merchant Marine service.

Another name in my file was Frank Aydelotte. How he would have laughed if he had found out that the FBI was keeping an eye on him because of me. I can't be sure now why I saved his address. Perhaps, like the FBI, I just squirreled away information long beyond the time it might have had meaning. I had known Aydelotte years before when I taught at Swarthmore College, where he was president. Also he had preceded Courtney Smith as American secretary of the Rhodes Trust, which had financed my three years at Oxford. The notion now crosses my mind that the FBI may have leaked to the *Chicago Tribune* and the equally patriotic Senate Internal Security Subcommittee the alarming news that the name of the American secretary of the Rhodes Trust was in the address file of a Key Figure in the Security Index.

Newspapers have received material from FBI files, although the bureau is forbidden by law to give out such material. A reporter on the Scripps Howard *Rocky Mountain News* told me he was sure a lot of "information" he had about me came from the FBI. And he relied on this information when the *Rocky Mountain News,* in 1961, led several Colorado papers in a campaign against me and my wife. We were at the time on the staff of a writers' conference at the University of Colorado.

Before the conference opened, I noted in a news story that the university had hired Dr. Frank Oppenheimer (brother of Dr. Robert Oppenheimer) to teach physics. Frank Oppenheimer had some years before been fired from another university because he had not told the truth about his politics when he appeared before an investigating committee.

"This is one fellow I am not going to look up in Boulder," I told Mary. My reason was that I had seen Frank Oppenheimer's name in a United Press story one day while working at TASS. The story said that Frank Oppenheimer had testified before HUAC that he had joined the Communist Party under the name Frank Folsom. The story was killed before any paper carried it, so nobody was likely to remember it except me.

During the twenty-one days of the writers' conference, the class Mary and I taught attracted more and more people because of the continuing publicity about us. One of those who asked to join the class was a children's librarian. To reward us for letting her audit, this young woman invited us to dinner at her parents' home in Boulder. Her father turned out to be the physicist Edward U. Condon, who had been hounded out of a government job by Cold War witch-hunters. After I had told him my story about Frank Oppenheimer, I repeated what I had said to Mary, "There is one fellow I am not going to look up in Boulder."

"You're going to meet him in a minute," Condon said, and very soon a slender man came through the doorway across the room. When we met I asked, "Did you join the Communist Party under the name Frank Folsom?"

"Yes," Oppenheimer replied and, in response to my further questions, explained how he happened to use that name.

"When my wife and I joined the CP in California, we were advised to adopt party names. We thought fast." Prisons were much on their minds as they took the dangerous step of joining an organization that was deemed subversive by the FBI. Two well-known California prisons were San Quentin and Folsom. Oppenheimer continued, "My wife Jacqueline took the surname San Quentin, I became Frank Folsom."

The FBI does not give up easily. On April 30, 1968, when I was nearly sixty-one, this note was inserted in my file: "A re-evaluation of subject's

subversive activities, his physical well being and potential dangerousness [*sic*] continue to warrant this subject's inclusion in
the Security Index." If my physical well-be-
ing made me eligible for the Security Index
when I was sixty one, does It make me
eligible today when I am eighty-six? How
decrepit do I have to be to be purged from
the index?

And how about my CIA file? More
than a year after I applied for it, I got this
letter: "Dear Mr. Folsom: Would you ad-
vise whether you were ever associated
with the Radio Corporation of America,
and if so in what capacity? We are asking
you this since we have information which
may or may not pertain to you."

Louis Untermeyer, poet, FBI target. *Saturday Review of Literature*
photo, February 2, 1938. Reproduced with the permission of the
Western Historical Collections,
University Archives, University
of Colorado at Boulder Libraries.

I wrote back: "I am not now nor have I
ever been associated with R.C.A."

Long silence.

Finally a package came from the CIA, and I was reminded by it that
over a period of more than thirty years I had exchanged a few letters
with persons I had known in the States who were visiting or living in
Moscow. Less-political letters would be hard to find, although I don't
know why I shouldn't exercise my human right to discuss politics if I
want to. But the CIA methodically noted the dates of these letters, to
whom they were sent, and who wrote them. Then someone interested
in handwriting got busy with communications sent to me by Vladimir
Kazakevich, a Russian émigré who had returned to his homeland after
living in the United States for some years.[4]

"Kazakevich's last two items to Folsom," notes the handwriting
expert (or was he or she a cryptanalyst?) "have been addressed to
Franklin Folsam and he has called him Franklyn on the inside. It is not
known whether this has any special significance. The 'a' in Folsam
(correct spelling 'Folsom') has a hook on it, but all the other 'a's in his
correspondence do not have this hook." Apparently, it never entered the
head of the CIA graphologist that English might be a second language
for Kazakevich and that on occasion he might lapse into Russian habits
of selecting vowels and shaping them as he wrote longhand. But I

Katherine Anne Porter, novelist, FBI target. National Archives photo.

suppose that if you are in the spy-and-conspiracy business, you think everybody else might be, too.

But that is not all. The CIA had given me photocopies of these letters, thus providing me absolute proof that an important branch of the United States government violated my constitutional rights. Under separate cover, I planned to bill Rhodes Scholar Stansfield Turner, director of the CIA, for damages, in the wake of a 1978 decision by federal court justice B. Weinstein of the Eastern District of New York. Justice Weinstein awarded Corliss Lamont $2,000 for letters of his that had been opened by the CIA, and he also awarded $1,000 each to Victoria Wilson, Rodney Driver, and Stanley Faulkner, whose mail had been similarly tampered with. How the judge arrived at his figure for damages is not as clear as his denunciation of the CIA. This left me in a quandary about how much to charge Turner. Perhaps $1,000 a letter would be a good figure, and if I got more than $2,000, I could give the difference to the National Emergency Civil Liberties Committee, of which Corliss Lamont was chairperson.[5]

From material related to the Soviet Union, my CIA file jumps to heavily "sanitized" (their word) stuff having other connections. Here is an entry: "Dispatch is withheld in its entirety." What could this mean? The date is August 20, 1964. I begin to remember. My wife and I were on the coast of Wales, living in a cottage lent us by an old Oxford friend.

I recall more. This was the month of the Tonkin Gulf incident. When I first heard of this caper, I was dead certain that it was designed as a pretext for military action against North Vietnam. But the *Times of London* thought otherwise. That journal overnight accepted the official U.S. account of the affair.

For the august *Times* to acquiesce so meekly seemed undignified, and I wrote a letter saying so and protesting the United States action in Tonkin Gulf. In my communication I requested space in the *Times*, not only as an American visitor but also as a graduate of a British university.

One day a letter arrived from the *Times'* editor-in-chief. With it was the letter I had written to him. He said he was returning it "for my own good."

Did the "dispatch," which the CIA admits relates to me, also relate to word the CIA received from the *Times*? The CIA knew very well that I had just come from six weeks in the USSR, where I had been gathering material for a children's book on that country. They even knew I had a contract with a leading Bible publisher (Thomas Nelson) to do the book. Had I, while visiting a children's camp in the Pamir Mountains near the Soviet-Chinese border, received instructions to write just such a letter? Or had I simply "remembered the *Maine*"?

In addition to this mysterious "dispatch" withheld for "security" reasons, page after page of my file is almost completely blacked out. There is no telling, for instance, if reports sent to Washington from Mexico refer to me or to the head of RCA or to some other Frank Folsom. I certainly have been to Mexico several times. While I was there, I did look up some of the good people who had fled the United States during the McCarthy period, but I spent much more time visiting archeological sites and museums than I did chatting with old Lefties.

I even did some work on children's books, and in the course of this activity, I was photographed twice in the State Department–supported Benjamin Franklin Library in Mexico City. It happened this way: I had left my name at the embassy, where I had gone hoping that their business library would have the name of the new editor and the new address of one of my publishers. Not finding what I needed, I walked to the Benjamin Franklin Library to make a second try. There, immediately after my arrival, the reference librarian snapped pictures of me in the stacks and in front of the circulation desk. With the ink scarcely dry on my signature at the embassy and two snapshots to go with it, the spooks should have felt pretty sure who it was they were spooking. But where are these photos? They don't turn up in my file. Was the CIA still worried it might be sending me a photo of the head of RCA?

There is no way of knowing how much of the taxpayer's money was being spent on surveillance of me in Mexico, but it is a safe guess that there, as elsewhere, the government's fingermen were all thumbs. Perhaps I should try to find out more of what was going on from Philip Agee, who flitted in and out of Mexico before he wrote his book about the CIA.[6]

pause. What from my file may be in somebody else's? And I don't mean any file labeled "Frank Folsom."

So ended my encounter with my FBI files, but I have wondered why, in view of this file, plus the testimony of informers against me, I was never subpoenaed to testify before the House Un-American Activities Committee. These possible explanations of HUAC's omission have occurred to me: (a) I was deemed too obscure and too likely to be uncooperative to produce the kind of headlines that HUAC sought; (b) I was an embarrassment to the Department of Justice. I had a brother, Fred G. Folsom, Jr., who had been at one time chief of the civil rights section of the department's Criminal Division and who later served for many years as the head of the tax section of that same division. Hoover doubtless would have considered this fact harmful to the department's carefully managed public relations if the press had got it.

It is easy to laugh at the FBI as an assemblage of fingermen who are all thumbs, but the often-idiotic, often-malevolent operations of government agencies were in reality no laughing matter.

Notes

1. The account I give here of my adventures with my FBI file is from an article by the same name that appeared in *CounterSpy* (November 1980–January 1981) and in *The American Oxonian* (Winter 1981).

2. "Edwin Lamb, lawyer and owner of radio stations got an admission from Budenz that after 1953 he had received $70,000 for the testimony he had given." Bud Schultz and Ruth Schultz, ed., *It Did Happen Here* (University of California Press, 1989), p. 386.

3. Senate Committee on the Judiciary, *Hearing Before the Subcommittee to Investigate the Administration of the Internal Security Act and Other Internal Security Laws, on Scope of Soviet Activity in the United States*, 84th Cong., 2d sess., April 17, 1956, pt. 16.

4. See note 6, Chapter 16, for more about Kazakevich.

5. I did sue the CIA and was awarded $1,000.

6. Philip Agee, *Inside the Company: CIA Diary* (Stonehill Publishing Company, 1975).

43

NY 100-25825

'B7c

B7c

The Chicago Defender, national negro weekly newspaper published in Chicago, Illinois, according to PM, December 27, 1945 cited JAMES GOW, playwright and ARAUD D'USSEAU for the racial amity honor roll for their play "Deep are the Roots." It set out that this honor roll was intended to honor persons who distinguished themselves in 1945 by improving race relations.

Confidential Informant ████ whose identity is known to the Bureau, b7D advised that GOW was a speaker on "Our Ties with Soviet Artists" in the literature panel of the Cultural Conference of the NATIONAL COUNCIL OF AMERICAN SOVIET FRIENDSHIP, November 18, 1945. HOWARD FAST also spoke.

B7c

It is noted that the JEFFERSON SCHOOL is the su████████ the Communist ███████ Workers School.

Confidential Informant T-7 advised that FRANKLIN FOLSOM received a letter from VLADIMIR MANSVETOV inviting him to a meeting of the Association of Russian Writers, 514 West 153rd Street, New York City in 1941. FOLSOM referred this letter to V. D. KASAKEVICH at 44 West 71st Street, New York City. KASAKEVICH said that MANSVETOV was an anti-Soviet, was a Socialist, and was interested in the advancement of cooperatives. He would not have written to FOLSOM if he had known that FOLSOM knew KASAKEVICH and another individual named YAKHONTOFF. He warned FOLSOM not to have anything to do with MANSVETOV.

Time magazine on January 10, 1944 carried an article naming KASAKEVICH as a long-time Communist and an editor of the Maxist quarterly, "Science and Society". It was indicated that he was a lecturer at the JEFFERSON SCHOOL.

-10-

The FBI kept track of playwright James Gow, a classmate of Franklin Folsom at the University of Colorado.

13

Blacklists, Graylists, and the Gallows

Woke up this morning
FB eye under my bed
Said I woke up this morning
FB eye under my bed
Told me all I dreamed last night, every word I said.

— Richard Wright, "The FB Eye Blues"[1]

The FBI is opposed to writers — because they're saying the same thing people feel — only the writers say it better.

— Amiki Baraka[2]

The impact that the political police, including the forerunners of the CIA, had on writers of the pre-war years often extended into later decades. A case in point concerns the exiled Czech writer, Otto Katz, mentioned in Chapter 3. Katz, after being harassed by the U.S. immigration authorities and forced to sit out the war in Mexico, was victimized by U.S. intelligence after he finally returned to his homeland. The byzantine story begins in 1952, when the press carried reports that Katz had been hanged in Czechoslovakia as a traitor, after being found guilty of working for a capitalist intelligence organization.

I could not believe that the man I knew had worked against the interest of his compatriots. Then years later, another news story reported a Czech court had found that Katz, and others who had been hanged with him, were not guilty after all. Otto Katz was "rehabilitated." Little good this did him in his grave.

If Katz was innocent, how could he have been found guilty? Twenty-two years after he was executed, I came across a book, *Operation Splinter Factor,* by Stewart Steven, a journalist for major British newspapers, who seems to have had excellent connections with British intelligence.[3] In great detail, Steven reported a secret plot that led to the execution of Katz and many of the brightest Communist leaders in Eastern Europe.

The plot began when a Lt. Col. Josef Swiatlo, one of the most powerful Polish Communists, let British intelligence know that he wanted to defect. British intelligence turned Swiatlo over to U.S. intelligence.[4] Allen Dulles, who would soon become head of the CIA, told Swiatlo in effect, "Very well, we will give you asylum, but only if you stay in Eastern Europe for a while and do a chore

Otto Katz (André Simone), exiled Czech writer, FBI target. From *Exil in Lateinamerika,* by Wolfgang Kiessling.

for us." The chore was to persuade Stalin, who was paranoid, that a lot of very able Communist leaders in Eastern Europe were really spies and secret agents of hostile countries. Swiatlo did as he was told — did it very well — and the Communist leadership in Eastern Europe was decimated. After Stalin's death, the Czech government learned about Dulles's "Operation Splinter Factor," as the plot was called, and it was then that Otto Katz's innocence was discovered and made known.

A happier future unfolded for Ambrogio Donini. He was a Communist, a fact that the Immigration and Naturalization Service missed when it admitted him to the United States, where he became editor of an anti-Fascist Italian language newspaper, *L'Unita del Popolo.* After the United States entered the war, Donini was arrested and taken to Ellis Island. The League protested Donini's arrest, and I with other League members went to Washington to ask Attorney General Francis Biddle to release him. We had some hope that Biddle would do so because Donini's newspaper carried valuable propaganda for the Allied cause. Furthermore, Biddle's wife, the poet Katherine Garrison Chapin, was a League member. She had held a fund-raising party for the Exiled Writers Committee in her home in Philadelphia.

Whether Biddle responded to us — or to his wife — we don't know, but Donini was released to resume his editorial work in Manhattan. There, by chance, he lived across the street from my wife and me, and his and our small sons were playmates.

On one occasion, after the League was no more and when I was recuperating from the injury received in the Merchant Marine, Ambrogio came in to cheer me up. He reminded me that the League had helped to save the lives of some of the most important people in Europe, among them the political writer, Pietro Nenni, leader of the Italian Socialist Party.

Ironically, as the war drew to a close, the United States reversed its position on Donini. Instead of trying to expel him from the country, the government would not let him leave. Donini wanted to resume life in Italy, but the State Department did not want him to return to his homeland, where he might work against the kind of government sought by the United States. In time, however, he did go back and was elected a Communist senator in the national parliament to represent a district adjacent to the Vatican.

While exiled writers associated with the League were of great interest to the Immigration and Naturalization Service, the FBI and other agencies kept close watch on many (perhaps all) League members who were United States citizens.[5] The nature of the FBI's surveillance and meddling varied from one person to another, and the effects on the writers varied as well. Lester Cole, who in time would go to prison for refusing to cooperate with the House Un-American Activities Committee, was amused to note that during one period the FBI did not keep him from working as a screenwriter. He and other anti-Fascist writers found themselves in demand. The studios had discovered it was profitable to turn out anti-Fascist films, and those who opposed fascism knew best how to write the scripts.[6]

The attentions of the FBI to Ella Winter were numerous and persistent. An early incident provoked this comment from her:

> I soon learned a new political lesson, that the current America would stand for almost any kind of horror, murder, rape, sadism, but not radical activity. One day in San Francisco, when I was about to go on a lecture platform, I overheard my Christian name spoken by a group of burly men I didn't know. When I asked my chairman who the strangers were and why they were looking at me so peculiarly, he laughed a hearty laugh. "The FBI," he said.

"But why should the FBI be here?" "You've committed an act," he said. "But I haven't done a thing!" "Oh yes, you're writing a book; that's a very dangerous act."[7]

Another time when Winter was about to board a ship to go abroad during the war, two FBI agents appeared and insisted on examining her handbag. In it were letters from her husband and from poet Muriel Rukeyser, and some poems that May Sarton had copied and sent her as a going-away gift.

Ella Winter, journalist, member of the National Council, 1938, 1941, FBI target. Courtesy of Pete Steffens.

The agents claimed they had to look in these intimate documents for possible messages for the Nazis, written in invisible ink.

"I'll throw them in the sea," Ella threatened.

"You are inside the territorial waters of the USA," the agents said. "You can't do that."

Ella put the letters in a nearby trash can and set fire to them.

"We said you can't do that," an agent said.

"I know," Ella replied, "but I just did."

The agents' bluff had been called. They let her go.

At another point, the FBI stole Ella Winter's private diary, and at times they kept an around-the-clock watch on her husband, Donald Ogden Stewart, a leader in the Hollywood Anti-Nazi League as well as president of the League. Such intense surveillance did not go unnoticed by those who employ writers. Markets for their work dried up.

Stewart has recorded how his blacklisting occurred. At the studio where he worked, he was asked to see the legal department. There he was told he had to clear himself. "I just didn't," he said. "It wasn't bravery.... I felt and still feel so very proud of those years ... and to say that I had been duped ... was just not true. So that was the end of my Hollywood career."[8]

By 1952, in search of an outlet for Stewart's plays, the couple moved to London. When I saw them there in 1964, Ella was having no luck finding a publisher in the States who would take a book she had written. She asked me for help, and I tried but without success. Don's work, too,

Lester Cole, screenwriter. One of the Hollywood Ten. Courtesy of Sheila Schwartz.

was boycotted in the United States. Both he and Ella lived abroad the rest of their lives.

Troubles with government repression, and the blacklisting to which it led in private industry, did not all begin at the same moment. Some screenwriters who were under surveillance were blacklisted before official blacklisting began in 1947. John Howard Lawson, an active leader in the League and the first president of the Screen Writers Guild, was fired by Columbia Studios when he refused to contribute to the election campaign of a Republican candidate for the governorship of California.[9]

HUAC conducted flank attacks as well as frontal assaults on writers — and on freedom of thought — and it created at least one blacklist to be used against readers as well as writers. On May 16, 1941, in the nation's capital, agents of the committee appeared with a subpoena at the Washington Cooperative Bookshop. They demanded the list of twelve hundred members of this non-profit co-op, and when the woman who was chair of the organization tried to escape with the list, the agents forcibly took it from her. With the list in their hands, HUAC had an instrument for blacklisting a considerable number of government employees and for frightening them away from books sold at the shop and from attending lectures and seminars the co-op conducted with speakers, most of whom were League members.

Four days after this raid had reminded many co-op members of the Nazi book burnings, 375 of them held a vigorous protest meeting. After the meeting, more than 100 new members joined the bookstore, replacing the fifty-six who had been frightened into resigning.

A few days later, League member Eugene C. Holmes told the story at the Fourth American Writers Congress in New York. Holmes, an African-American who taught philosophy at Howard University, saw the ugly event as part of a repressive drive toward a war that, while pretending to be anti-Fascist, was really supportive of the British Empire in its competition with the German Reich. Clearly, the raid was one of the increasing attacks on freedom with which writers had to cope.

Lester Cole as a prisoner, after his refusal to cooperate with the House Un-American Activities Committee. Danbury Federal Correctional Institution photo.

HUAC had its own agenda, and even a public break with the League was not insurance that a writer could depend on. Congressman Martin Dies, chairman of HUAC, did not forgive Malcolm Cowley his long and active past in the League and other organizations. Dies, with the aid of newspaper columnist Westbrook Pegler, succeeded in forcing Cowley to resign from government work during the war. Cowley left his post as chief information analyst in the Office of Facts and Figures and took up the precarious life of a free-lance writer.

As the hysteria that was initiated by the FBI and carried on by HUAC expanded, Congress imposed heavy penalties on several government employees who had been League members. On November 15, 1943, it voted to deny the use of federal funds for payment of salaries to Goodwin Watson, professor at Columbia, William E. Dodd, Jr., son of the former U.S. ambassador to Germany, and Robert Morss Lovett, government secretary of the Virgin Islands.

The HUAC offensive against writers continued after the war. In 1946 it went after the Joint Anti-fascist Refugee Committee (JAFRC), which the League of American Writers had helped form. HUAC demanded the records of the JAFRC, and when the executive board refused to provide them, the board members were cited for contempt and were sent to prison. Two of those imprisoned had been League members — Howard Fast and Dashiell Hammett.

In the fall of 1947, HUAC began a concentrated campaign in Hollywood — a campaign that guaranteed the headlines the committee

Ring Lardner, Jr., screenwriter, Hollywood Exiled Writers Committee. One of the Hollywood Ten. Courtesy of Ring Lardner, Jr.

sought. First, the committee called witnesses who could be depended on to give alarmist testimony about Reds in the movie industry. Then came a series of "unfriendly" witnesses, one of whom, Bertholt Brecht, the Exiled Writers Committee had helped.

At one point the dialogue between Brecht and committee counsel Robert Stripling went like this:

Mr. Stripling: Mr. Brecht, is it true that you have written a number of very revolutionary poems, plays, and other writings?

Mr. Brecht: I have written a number of poems and songs and plays in the fight against Hitler, and of course, they can be considered, therefore, as revolutionary because I, of course, was for the overthrow of that government.

The Chairman:Mr. Stripling, we are not interested in any works that he might have written advocating the overthrow in Germany of the government there.[10]

As an experienced fugitive from fascism, Brecht took precautions. He reserved, under another name, a seat on a plane leaving for Europe at a time just after the hearing would end. Then he appeared before the committee, gave truthful but canny answers to questions, and left the country while HUAC was still unaware that an "unfriendly" fish has escaped its net.[11]

Ten of those called by the committee in Hollywood hoped to defend the Constitution and free speech by pleading the First Amendment. All ended up in prison, after being found guilty of contempt of Congress. Eight of them were writers and members of the League: Alvah Bessie, Lester Cole, Ring Lardner, Jr., John Howard Lawson, Albert Maltz, Sam Ornitz, Robert Adrian Scott, and Dalton Trumbo. The other two were Edward Dmytryk and Herbert Biberman, both directors.

Whatever, in the days of the League, had set the "Hollywood Ten" into motion against oppression continued to motivate most of them. With the exception of Dmytryk, they did not turn "friendly" during the long years that followed their imprisonment, after which they were blacklisted and forced to write under pseudonyms or work at a variety of low-paid, non-literary jobs. Some became refugees from their own country. Maltz, Trumbo, and Lardner moved to Mexico.[12]

Ernest Hemingway, novelist, League vice president 1939–1940. National Archives photo.

The threat of prison and loss of jobs that these unfriendly witnesses fled was affecting the entire literary community. When the Hollywood Ten were summoned before HUAC, they sent telegrams to Carl Sandburg, John Steinbeck, William Faulkner, and Ernest Hemingway asking for support. According to Nancy Schwartz, they did not receive a single reply.[13]

Not only did two former League vice presidents, Steinbeck and Hemingway, remain silent during this attack by HUAC on freedom of thought, but the pressures were such that Dmytryk became an informer. He was not the only informer from Hollywood. On these, all of whom were former Communists, Albert Maltz had this scathing comment:

> Various individuals sought to find justification for becoming informers by blaming the Communist Party for something it did. . . . But no matter what the Communist Party's sins were, even if they had been magnified a hundred times in the case of each of these individuals, it would not have explained why they were cooperating with a committee that was trying to provide thought control in the United States.[14]

One government intrusion that affected more than a few League members was this: In Hollywood some writers went for treatment to Ernest Philip Cohn, who presented himself as a psychotherapist and a CP member. Cohn convinced a number of his patients to be informers before HUAC. Those who were informed on were blacklisted, their careers ruined.[15]

So apprehensive did one TV writer become that he hired an investigator to check up on him and thus provide proof that he was not a "subversive." Indeed, he was not a Communist, but the investigator, in the course of his inquiries, had asked a number of network executives about the writer's politics. The executives assumed that the mere existence of an investigation should make anyone cautious about hiring the writer, and thereafter he simply could not get work.[16]

Samuel Ornitz, screenwriter. One of the Hollywood Ten. Courtesy of Sheila Schwartz.

How many writers became unemployed because they were being hounded by the FBI or HUAC or some private agency? There is probably no way to get an accurate figure, but the experiences of a few suggest what was going on in the lives of many.

Horace B. Davis, a writer on economics (who had been with Theodore Dreiser in 1931 on a writers' committee that investigated a miners' strike) was driven out of one teaching job after another by the FBI. He was still a target in 1967, when he protested at the Pentagon against U.S. military actions abroad. He was arrested then, along with Norman Mailer.

The FBI had a long-standing interest in novelist Myra Page (Mrs. John Markey), an active League member. At one point agents came to the Markey home, ostensibly to find out if the Markeys were fit parents. (Mrs. Markey was a leader in the local PTA). Thereafter, their daughter had nightmares, and their son was denied a federal job because of FBI reports about his mother. During this same period of McCarthyism, Viking Press cancelled Myra Page's contract for a novel; it was later published in 1950 by Citadel Press as *With Sun in Our Blood;* then in 1986 it was republished by the Feminist Press as *Daughter of the Hills.*

Harvey O'Connor, a labor journalist who had been active in the Chicago chapter of the League, was an unfriendly witness before the McCarthy committee in 1952. He claimed the protection of the First Amendment — the freedom of speech amendment — and he refused to cooperate with McCarthy's efforts to frighten writers. Congress found him guilty of contempt, and McCarthy said O'Connor was "the most contumacious witness ever to appear before the committee." O'Connor later said he would like to have that statement carved on his gravestone. He took the congressional finding of contempt to the appellate court, which reversed the verdict not on the grounds of the First Amendment but because it violated the Sixth, which guarantees a fair trial. Score one against McCarthy.

Another victory over the ineffable McCarthy committee was won by Arthur Miller (not a League member). He refused to provide the names of Communists, was cited for contempt, and when he appealed, his conviction was overturned on a technicality.

The effects of McCarthy harassment extended into other government areas. In 1953 the State Department began to remove books from United States Information Agency libraries around the world. Several hundred books by forty writers, most of whom had been League members, were targeted.[17]

Other governmental assaults on writers took many forms. Sometimes an official intervened directly. J. Edgar Hoover turned over material to journalists who used these leaks to isolate writers from publishers and the public. Hoover also supported other actions that were taken against writers. For example, when the Polish-American Council in Chicago condemned Nelson Algren's novel, *Never Come Morning,* Hoover wrote approvingly to the Polish group and announced that its action would be put in the FBI file.

Alvah Bessie, novelist and screenwriter, as a volunteer in the Abraham Lincoln Battalion in Spain. One of the Hollywood Ten. Courtesy of Cary Nelson and the Rolfe Archive at the University of Illinois at Urbana-Champaign.

Publishers, whether or not they were coached directly by the FBI, sensed when a manuscript was likely to be disapproved by the political police, and they usually played it safe. Howard Fast has told how Little, Brown caved in to pressure and refused to publish his *Spartacus.* Outraged, Angus Cameron, an editor at Little, Brown, left the firm. No other house dared to bring out the book, and Fast had to publish it himself.

Albert Maltz, who had also been published by Little, Brown, left these notes among his papers:

> The Literary Penalties Resulting From My Blacklist
> And Imprisonment.

> Most literary careers are cumulative . . . i.e., the result of a total body of work upon critics and readers, rather than the effects of one book or one play, etc. Thus, the careers of James Gould Cozzens, Irwin Shaw, Eudora Welty, Thomas Mann. By 1947, when the Washington hearings took place, my literary position was a good one, notwithstanding my left-wing public

Albert Maltz, novelist, playwright, screenwriter, League vice president, 1941. One of the Hollywood Ten. National Archives photo.

stand. The first effects of the blacklist came with *The Journey of Simon McKeever* in 1949, before the case [against the Hollywood Ten] had been lost. It received only half the press reviews of *The Cross and The Arrow,* and was banned for film production . . . with all that this means for soft cover reprint, public attention to a work and an author, etc.

With the loss of the case in 1950, the following resulted:

a) No soft cover reprint of any of my books.
b) No radio or television use of my stories.
c) No magazine outlet for my stories.
d) No chance of writing films.
e) An end to anthology and college text use of my stories.
f) I was dropped by Little, Brown and could get no other trade publisher for "A Long Day."
g) "A Long Day" received no reviews.

In short, for a full decade I was blacked out of the American literary world. Whatever position I had had, was banned, and no cumulative career was possible.

The Sinatra debacle in 1960 has blacklisted me for a second time. [Sinatra, in an ad in *Variety,* announced that he had hired Maltz to write a screenplay; then, when pressured by the American Legion, the Catholic War Veterans, and the Hearst press, Sinatra reneged.] As I write, eight months have passed since then, and I have had no offer to write a screenplay even on the black list.

Where am I now? . . . The McCarthy atmosphere has lightened, but:

a) It may return.
b) Meanwhile, although Dalton Trumbo has broken through, no one is knocking on my door to do a film under my name.
c) I am still in the position where: (1) editors will be afraid to use my stories in magazines — (2) or, if printed in magazines, in anthologies and college texts — (3) or in television.
d) No novel of mine can be used by a major film company.
e) Even if I succeed in getting a regular publisher for my new novel, there will be critics who ignore it out of personal prejudice, and it will run up against all the blacklist hangovers in film, television, libraries, etc.

> Thus, the case for using a pseudonym is a good one. But, I must be serious about it and really keep it secret.[18]

FBI agents haunted some writers who were unwise enough to allow them an initial interview. One such victim was the former League member Kyle Crichton, who had been an editor of *Collier's Magazine* and a contributor to *New Masses* under the name Robert Forsythe. FBI agents even looked in the walls of his house for Russian rubles that they fantasized might be hidden there. Crichton's son Robert has said: "I was always conscious that he had not been released from his ordeal. Once on the disloyal list, you are on it forever. There is no statute of limitations for stigma and hurt. No one was buying his pieces. It was not a blacklist, but a graylist, and he was worried about money."[19]

Most of those being harassed by the FBI — or HUAC, some state investigating committee, or one of the publications that published lists of alleged Reds — worried about money. They often had other worries too. Ring Lardner, Jr., and Howard Fast, for example, were denied passports, as were others who were not writers.

By the 1950s the persecution became unendurable to F. O. Matthiessen, a League member and Harvard professor. He was subject to intense, hostile investigation by a committee of the Commonwealth of Massachusetts, and he committed suicide.

How does one gauge the effect on a writer when an FBI agent has been following him or her, opening mail, listening to all phone conversations? What is the effect on writing when the government sets up concentration camps to receive writers (and others) whose thoughts are unacceptable? What happens to literature when writers are surrounded by a hostile environment of newspapers, magazines, radio stations, teachers, preachers, all deeply beholden to the Establishment?

No matter how a writer responds to repression, the exercise in constriction by those in power is usually reflected somehow in the words he or she manages to use. Some writers turn to very private writing, or very evasive writing. Some look inward. Some deal with little things to which no one is likely to object. They turn away from large social themes.

Commenting on this phenomenon, Howard Fast, one of the League members who had to endure prison and a loss for a while of all outlets for his writing, has said, "The FBI killed the social novel."[20] This was a casualty, the consequences of which are still pushing American writing away from the great tradition of social literature in this country.

Notes

1. Richard Wright, "The FB Eye Blues," *Richard Wright Reader* (Harper and Row, 1978).

2. Quoted in Natalie Robins, *Alien Ink* (William Morrow and Co., 1992), p.64.

3. Stewart Steven, *Operation Splinter Factor* (J. B. Lippincott Co., 1974).

4. Josef Swiatlo was vice director of Poland's Ministry of Public Security.

5. A partial list of League members who were under government surveillance: Ernest Hemingway, John Steinbeck, Richard Wright, F. O. Matthiessen, Maxwell Bodenheim, Theodore Roethke, Howard Fast, Ella Winter, Donald Ogden Stewart, Malcolm Cowley, Vincent Sheean, Nelson Algren, Lillian Hellman, Dashiell Hammett, James T. Farrell (both while he was a member and later), Waldo Frank, Langston Hughes, Edna St. Vincent Millay, and Maxwell Anderson. There were many others.

6. Nancy Lynn Schwartz, *The Hollywood Writers' Wars* (Alfred A. Knopf, 1982), pp. 77–78.

7. Ella Winter, *And Not To Yield* (Harcourt, Brace and World, 1963), p. 172.

8. Quoted by Pat McGilligan, *Backstory* (University of California Press, 1986), p. 348.

9. In 1955, in the midst of the Fearful Fifties, for a celebration of John Howard Lawson's birthday, Donald Ogden Stewart sent this cable from London: "Can't remember anyone named Lawson. Absolutely deny sending this cable admitting his courage integrity intelligence . . . Donald Ogden Schminks." For the same occasion Martha Dodd wrote from exile in Mexico: "Dear Jack: I respect and love you, Jack, for many things, above all for the warm and wonderful integration of your life and work. I greatly esteem the struggle and dedication that went into the achievement of this rare synthesis. A long, good, fruitful life to you. Devotedly Martha Dodd." John Howard Lawson Collection, Special Collections, Morris Library, Southern Illinois University at Carbondale.

10. House Un-American Activities Committee, *Hearings Regarding the Communist Infiltration of the Motion Picture Industry*, 80th Cong., 1st sess., October 30, 1947.

11. James K. Lyon, *Bertolt Brecht in America* (Princeton University Press, 1980), p. 326.

12. Some facts about the very real blacklist in the film industry are elusive, but a chart offered by Michael Linfield, in *Freedom Under Fire: U.S. Civil Liberties in Times of War* (South End Press, 1990), p. 225, gives an idea of what was going on. Linfield shows the employment record of nine of the Hollywood Ten. The tenth, Edward Dmytryk, is not included, presumably because he became an informer, thereby guaranteeing himself continued employment. Linfield's chart defines employment in terms of screen credits for the authorship of film scripts, both before and after the HUAC hearings:

Alvah Bessie	5 credits, 1943–1948	then none
Herbert Biberman	7 credits, 1935–1947	then none until 1968
Lester Cole	36 credits, 1932–1948	then none until 1970
Ring Lardner, Jr.	10 credits, 1939–1948	then none until 1965
John Howard Lawson	16 credits, 1929–1947	then none
Albert Maltz	7 credits, 1932–1948	then none until 1969
Samuel Ornitz	26 credits, 1929–1945	then none
Adrian Scott	11 credits, 1940–1947	then none
Dalton Trumbo	27 credits, 1936–1945	then none until 1959

13. Schwartz, p. 261.

14. "The Citizen Writer in Retrospect: Albert Maltz," interview by Joel Gardner, 1983, University Library, University of California, Los Angeles, pp. 825–826.

15. Victor S. Navasky, in *Naming Names* (Penguin, 1981), pp. 130–131, says:

    The hearings quickly gave rise to free-lance blacklisters — some of them nonprofit, like the American Legion, the Catholic War Veterans, or Hollywood's Motion Picture Alliance for the Preservation of American Ideals (MPAPAI); others, free enterprisers of the blacklist, like the American Business Consultants and Aware, Inc., which published, listed and cleared names for pay. The Committee itself got into the act with annual reports that conveniently listed names and namers in the appendix, which could be clipped and pasted by the free lancers. Not only in scandal sheets such as *Confidential* but in national magazines and newspapers, political and gossip columnists supplemented and subtracted from the "official" lists by giving two-line case studies in repentance and/or subversion.

16. Eric Bentley, *Thirty Years of Treason* (Viking Press, 1971), p. 708.

17. Robins, pp. 272–273.

18. Albert Maltz Collection, Special Collections, Mugar Memorial Library, Boston University. Eventually, a few of Maltz's books were published, but not in the mainstream press.

19. Robert Crichton, "My Father the Un-American," *New York,* March 10, 1975.

20. Fast made this statement in the course of a conference on anti-Communism on the Harvard campus in 1988, which I attended.

"Unless something is done soon; there will be
deaths by the hundreds when winter comes."

So writes an anti-Nazi author about his colleagues who are facing their
second winter in a French concentration camp. These are the men whose
books you have read with pleasure, the men who brought the culture of
Germany, Italy, Spain, Austria, Poland and Czechoslovakia into your home.
These are the men whose fearless stand against fascism has brought them
to suffering, persecution and exile.

Now their shelter is a concentration camp, their reward for resistance to
Nazism, internment. Now they face another winter of cold, hunger, sickness.
And the wonder is that every letter they write proves their spirit is strong. Will
their hatred of Hitler is still strong.

How much longer can such courage endure? Each letter tells how much
the mere knowledge of the interest of American writers has served to maintain
the morale of these refugees. But each letter also tells of their desperate need
for help, their imminent danger of being seized by the Gestapo. Can we afford
to let the voices they raised against oppression be silenced? As the picture on
the reverse shows, "S.O.S.!" is the cry that comes to us from across the Atlantic.

This cry no longer comes from some 20 writers, thanks to $13,200 which
was raised at a dinner we held on October 17th, in cooperation with a committee of leading publishers. Passage to Mexico has been bought for these
fortunate exiles. But at least 75 others are awaiting our help. It now costs
$600 per person to get them safely out of France to Mexico; while they wait
in Lisbon for their chance to board the over-crowded boats, they must live.
They must have food, money, medicine. And they count on us, democratic
Americans, to bring them to the safety of the New World.

Can you fail to hear their cry this Christmas? "S.O.S!" They will be
grateful for whatever contribution you can make towards the best gift we
can send them—security, safety and a chance to write again.

THE NATIONAL BOARD OF THE LEAGUE OF AMERICAN WRITERS, INC.
(Officers of the National Board are: Donald Ogden Stewart,
PRESIDENT; Ernest Hemingway, Langston Hughes, Dorothy
Parker, Meridel Le Sueur, George Seldes, Vincent Sheean, John
Steinbeck, and Richard Wright, VICE-PRESIDENTS.)

This copy of a publicly distributed League appeal for funds to help exiled writers remained
classified in the FBI files for four decades.

14

The Pact

This morning came the news about the Russo-German mutual assistance Pact over the wireless. Although I expected this, I felt shattered when I actually heard it. We are living at a time when we see the forces behind events, and the direction which may take years to be revealed, with a blinding clarity. The question does arise: what are we fighting for? Though this is not quite in the form the Germans put it to us. We aren't fighting for Poland.

— Stephen Spender[1]

In early summer 1939, League members were aware of some, though certainly not all, of the political maneuverings in Europe that would affect the writing community. Britain and France had already, at Munich, agreed to let Hitler move into Czechoslovakia, and he had done so. Although the Spanish war was still going on, Britain and France — and soon afterward the United States — had given diplomatic recognition to Franco. During this period the Soviet Union had proposed several times that all countries threatened by the expanding Fascist aggression should take joint steps to resist it. This proposed collaboration, which became known as collective security, did not win support.

The Soviet Union had other worries, too. For example, the very influential Lord Halifax, a member of the British cabinet, had said he hoped a way could be found to come to terms with Hitler by leaving him free to move east. Not everyone in high position in Britain agreed. On May 15, the British chiefs of staff pointed out in a confidential memorandum that if Britain rejected an alliance with the Soviet Union, that country might enter into some kind of agreement with Germany, which was, in fact, at that time making proposals for such an agreement. This, and other high-level maneuvers that were more visible, served as signals that the danger of expanded war was very real.

The National Council of the League, in response to such ominous developments, tried to shape for itself policies appropriate to the increasing concern of all anti-Fascists. On July 19, the council adopted a statement that said in part:

> We hate war, but recognize that war already exists, and may be forced directly upon ourselves unless we can effect a united opposition to warlike nations. Common sense compels us to acknowledge the value of the Soviet Union as a factor for peace, and as writers we cannot ignore the power and contribution of its living literature. We hold this position regardless of our individual opinion of the Soviet Union's internal political system.[2]

Events continued to move rapidly in Europe. The Soviet Union by now had every reason to doubt its chances for practical arrangements with Western powers. On July 21, it announced the opening of trade talks with Germany. Four days later, the British government made a gesture toward negotiation with the Soviet Union, but it sent only low-level negotiators to Moscow. They traveled by the slowest possible means of transportation, and they had no real power to reach agreement. Talks in Moscow with these officials and with a French delegation dragged on, and by mid-August, the Soviet government finally decided that the French and British had no intention of coming to any real arrangement for mutual security.

Meanwhile, anti-Fascist writers in the United States continued their activities. On August 14, League members Dashiell Hammett and Lillian Hellman and four hundred other intellectuals signed a statement denouncing a recently formed group called Committee for Cultural Freedom, which alleged that the USSR was not different from what the committee called other "totalitarian" states. Such an allegation, the four hundred intellectuals argued, would hurt relations between the USSR and other peace-loving nations. This document, although not officially produced by the League, reflected the mood of many League members.

On August 20, Hitler sent a message to Stalin saying that a serious crisis might arise any day and that it might involve the Soviet Union unless Stalin agreed to sign the non-aggression pact for which Germany had been pressing. On August 21, the Soviet Union signed the pact, which seemed a means of getting Germany to agree not to attack.

News of the pact created shock waves throughout the world. President Roosevelt, who was aboard a ship at sea, cut short his voyage and rushed back to confer with his advisers. The British and French governments were furious. Their strategy — to turn Hitler eastward — had suffered a real setback. In the media and in government circles, Stalin was portrayed as a traitor to the anti-Fascist cause.

Perhaps some writers who followed high-level diplomacy were not surprised by the pact. Most, however, were taken unawares. How should they respond? Discussions went on everywhere. The Communist Party was in turmoil from bottom to top. Some members of the Politburo held that the Soviet Union was justified in signing the pact. Some, following Earl Browder, held that in the new situation Communists should place their support behind the policies of President Roosevelt, which were increasingly pro-British. Almost immediately, writers divided along those same lines. Many years later, Albert Maltz, when he was no longer in the Communist Party, reflected the opinion of one group of League members: "The Soviet Union had every right to sign the Non-Aggression Pact: the British and French had been signing non-aggression pacts with Hitler from 1935 on. So their screams were only those of people whose plans had fallen to the ground."[3]

Writers in Europe were also divided. Gustav Regler, the day after the announcement of the pact, volunteered to serve in the French army, although his wounds from service in the International Brigade in Spain had not yet healed. Nevertheless, he was arrested and sent to Le Vernet, the same concentration camp that held German Communist leaders. While the Communists remained in the camp, Regler, a former Communist, was released following appeals by Ernest Hemingway, Eleanor Roosevelt, and Martha Gellhorn. Later, when Regler was in Mexico, Hemingway, Mrs. Roosevelt, John Dos Passos, and Jay Allen vouched for him, and he was admitted to the United States.

Soon after the pact was signed, Soviet armies moved into Poland and then into the Baltic states. This made some sense militarily, because it created a buffer area along the border that German forces might attack. Nevertheless, writers who felt friendly to the Soviet Union had to consider a troublesome fact: Neither Poland nor the Baltic states had been consulted. They had not invited the Soviet Union to bring in armies.

Rumors had it that the Soviet Union and Germany had secretly agreed, imperialist fashion, on spheres of influence in eastern Europe, an allegation that the Soviet Union denied. In fact, the Soviet Union *had* entered into a secret agreement. In 1989 the Soviet government finally admitted that there were secret protocols defining spheres of influence in eastern Europe between Germany and the USSR.

It is possible for reasonable men and women to disagree about the real meaning of the German-Soviet pact. No one doubts that it was an event of enormous importance. But were supporters of the Soviet Union, who regarded themselves supporters of peace, justified in refusing to criticize the USSR for signing it? The Soviet Union had much to gain from it if it was observed, but also much to lose from such a pact — the goodwill of many liberals and the whole international structure of the Popular Front. Many non-Communists suddenly came to believe that Communists were not trustworthy allies.

The signing of the pact produced bizarre responses. The Communist leader Earl Browder, at a press conference in New York on August 25, said that the pact would bring peace. War began within a week. *The New Republic*, many of whose editors were League members, editorialized that the rupture between the Soviet Union on the one hand and Britain and France on the other was so profound that it "is doubtful if they can get together again for years even in time of supreme need." In less than two years, Britain and France were actively allied with the Soviet Union.

The League's decision about how to regard the pact was not easy. I described the situation to my parents in a letter on October 6, 1939:

> The League has been very quiescent while we figured out a policy which would satisfy a reasonable number of our 800 members. A lot of them, it appears, are decidedly disturbed by the spectacle of a war in Europe in which so far only a neutral socialist state has benefited. There are really significant political problems and just how strong the League is going to be in the near future it is difficult to say. The Dies committee has shown every indication of persecuting us and is already laying a very strong foundation for a campaign to make illegal any honest minority group. If Dad thinks I am being hysterical, I hope he'll leave some little loophole for himself so that he can at least pay me a social call in a concentration camp. There has never been a time when American civil liberties have been so seriously threatened and when so many people's liberties have been endangered.

To some League members the pact made perfectly good sense. One of these was John Sanford, who was traveling by auto in the West, out of touch with almost everyone, when news of the pact broke. This was his reaction:

> It's a crime-story. We hire an assassin named Hitler to kill our enemy, Stalin. Our gunsel's no fool, though: he knows that once he does his job, *We'll* kill

him. So he joins up with the goat we gave him, and before we know it, he'll make a goat of us.

"And is that what The Faithful will be cheering for?" [his traveling companion asked.]

You touched the newspaper, saying, "This is another disaster for the rich. They learned nothing in 1917, and they've learned nothing since. They're still out to kill the Devil, Socialism, but they'll wind up killing themselves."[4]

Some of the members of the National Council wanted the League not only to condemn the Soviet Union for signing the pact, but also to become active in support of Britain. Van Wyck Brooks, a vice president and a Socialist, carried on a concerned correspondence with me on the one hand and with Malcolm Cowley and Newton Arvin on the other. (Arvin, a literary critic and college professor, was a League member but not an officer, as both Cowley and Brooks were.)

John Sanford, novelist, Hollywood Executive council, 1940. With his wife, screenwriter Marguerite Roberts, he defied the House Un-American Activities Committee. She was blacklisted for ten years. Photo by Marguerite Roberts.

"I hate the idea of breaking up the League over some point of policy of a foreign nation," Brooks wrote to Arvin. Brooks's biographer tells us that Cowley and Arvin tried to persuade Brooks not to resign.[5] So did I. I wrote to him on October 11:

> There was a long and serious discussion at a well-attended Board meeting last Wednesday after I read your first letter. (The second had not arrived). The upshot of the discussion was to appoint a new committee on policy and instruct it to work speedily. There were three points on policy on which there was complete agreement at the Board meeting: 1.) the need for the League to do all it could to keep America from being involved in the present war; 2.) a campaign to preserve civil liberties, threatened now as never since the League was formed; 3.) a campaign to give whatever financial and spiritual assistance we can to writers who are exiles from fascism and reaction or who are in any way war casualties.
>
> Only today, I learned (indirectly from Erika Mann) that *all* of the exiled German and Austrian writers (up to the age of 60) who are now in residence in France have been put in concentration camps in France. There are of course anti-fascist Spanish writers who have been in camps for upwards of

Newton Arvin

Newton Arvin, critic, resigned
from the League, 1939. Caricature
by Georges Schreiber. From *New
Masses*, 1939.

eight months. French writers who question the
sincerity of Daladier's motives have been arrested. The need for our assistance, in other
words, increases daily, and if our League does
not help, I'm afraid no other group will.

We are having a manuscript sale again this
year to raise funds for exiled writers and would
be honored to have you join Dorothy Canfield,
Louis Bromfield and Donald Ogden Stewart in
signing a letter of appeal for manuscripts. You
may very well think it inadvisable to sign a
League appeal until your questions about our
policy have been answered, and if so I shall of
course understand.

I don't know what more I can say regarding
your queries about our policy. There seems to
be a general feeling that we may do a great deal
of harm to the League by rushing into print at
this confused moment with a statement of any
kind on the actions of the Soviet Union. Some
League members disapprove those actions, or
at least are puzzled by them. Others see them
as a blow to the imperialist ambitions of the
right-wing governments of France and Eng-
land as well as to the aggressive intentions of the Nazis. And no matter what
most League members think, they all find that events are moving so fast
that whatever is said today becomes outmoded tomorrow. Has there ever
been a time when events moved so fast?

Caution, in other words, is the dominating mood of the Board. And a
feeling that the League is important — more important now than ever —
united the Board in an effort to find a common ground on which all good
American writers will take pride in standing.

If we were to take a stand critical of the Soviet Union at this juncture we
might precipitate an inner League controversy which could easily end the
League's existence. Some of the hardest workers in the League approve the
Soviet's action. These people will not readily acquiesce in a public criticism
of the Soviet Union — and yet they will work hard for civil liberties, for
keeping this country at peace, for aiding the unhappy writers of Europe, for
improving and increasing the work of our Writers Schools (Hollywood now
has a thriving school) etc. A resolution criticizing the Soviet Union would
be tantamount to expulsion of a group that has been very loyal and useful
to the League. All the Communists in the League and many others would
resist such a move out of an honest conviction that humanity has been as
well served as could be under the circumstances by the recent turn of affairs

in Eastern Europe. And now would hardly seem to be the time to split the ranks of progressive writers by excluding the Left. Certainly nothing would be more pleasing to American reactionaries. The whole point of the League seems to me to be that writers of Left and Center have found a common ground which does not limit their individual freedom in any way but which does serve well to make the United States a better place — and a better place for literature.

We have had only three resignations since the German–Soviet Pact — and over the week-end alone there were four applications for membership. This is encouraging — particularly since some Trotskyites have chosen this moment in which to issue a letter implying that the League has gone out of existence (or will do so soon). Our silence on the European situation has been seized on by them as an occasion to ask us a series of questions designed to embarrass us. Fortunately most League members are aware of this group's long record of hostility to the League, and will not be misled by the seemingly respectful air of the letter. At least the letter indicated that our League was more active than any other writer's organization: and if this humble employee of the League has his way the organization will continue to be active — very active — and will refrain from taking any stand which would endanger the League's unity. We have so much on which we can agree, that I'm wholeheartedly opposed to wrangling about points on which agreement seems remote at this moment. Perhaps in the not too distant future the amount of agreement on the meaning of international events will be much greater than it is now.

But most important, I hope nothing in our actions, or statements — or silences — will lead you to think that the League is no longer worthy of your support.

Could you come to our next board meeting Wednesday, October 18, to discuss these matters with the other officers entrusted by the Congress with conducting the affairs of the League? I'm hoping to get several of the Vice-Presidents to be present. Steinbeck is in town, I hear. The meeting may take on a very important character. It will hear the report of the committee which has been drafting a statement of policy.[6]

To my letter, Brooks sent this reply from Westport, Connecticut, dated October 17, 1939. So far as I know, it has never been published in full.

Thank you for your letter, which I have read with interest and with sympathy for you. I value the League highly, as you know; and have hesitated to permit what might seem a matter of theory to interfere with its many practical uses, in bringing writers together, in aiding refugees, in forwarding international relations, etc. But, valuable as these things are, there is

Van Wyck Brooks, critic, League vice president, 1937–1939, resigned from the League, 1939. From *Direction* magazine, May–June 1939.

something else that is more important; and on this point your letter is not reassuring. I think a policy of caution is absolutely fatal; and I am therefore obliged to resign from the League. From this date, — for the present anyway, — I cease to be a member.

You suggest that our "foreign policy" cannot be aired and must therefore remain under cover. But our members, who know Freud, know what that means. What cannot be aired breeds poison, and this will surely be true in the case of the League. Meanwhile, if it is not aired, it becomes a veiled defense of Stalin, whose methods are now openly undemocratic. (And even if Stalin's ends were known, and these ends were democratic, it would be Jesuitical to defend his means. Can Jesuitism ever be democratic? And this Jesuitism openly defends aggression. Under these conditions, a League whose primary purpose is to defend democracy becomes a farce.) This Jesuitism is a worm at the core of the League that will eat away its fabric, and the League can have no health until it is killed. There is only one way to deal with worms and poison, and this is not the way of caution, — which [may?] serve politicians but is ruinous for writers.

May I add that it seems to me degrading for an American League to hinge its policy, even incidentally, on another country. When are we going to stop this preposterous game of button, button, who's got the button, we have the button and have always had it?

When the League finds its head and decides to be an American League, I shall be one of the first new members.

Excuse the somewhat tart tone of this letter, which is addressed to the League alone. I am writing in haste, — although my present action is final, — but with the deepest admiration for your own devoted work.[7]

As Van Wyck Brooks was resigning from the League, W. H. Auden, on November 1, 1939, was joining.

Other League members had different reasons to be troubled by the pact and the course of the war. Some had emotional ties to France. After World War I, Archibald MacLeish had lived in Paris, as had other American expatriates. Memories of this time may well have been in his mind when Nazi troops entered the city June 14, 1940. At any rate, the very next day he urged the United States to declare war on Germany.

Malcolm Cowley, too, was unable to accept the view that France was more interested in turning Hitler eastward than in taking collective measures to prevent the spread of war.[8] He also took an uncharacteristically dramatic position in the debate: At one council meeting Cowley moved that he himself be expelled from the League. The motion was unanimously defeated, but Cowley did resign on May 23, 1940. At that same meeting Rolfe Humphries, Donald Ogden Stewart, and Ella Winter had supported a pro-British resolution. Philip Stevenson, Dorothy Brewster, Leslie River, Albert Maltz, Millen Brand, and Harriette Ashbrook had opposed the resolution. Harry Carlisle and Henry Hart, who were absent, also opposed it, as did I.

Johannes Steele, journalist, speaker at Exiled Writers Committee Dinner, October 9, 1941. *Saturday Review of Literature* photo, July 24, 1937. Reproduced with the permission of the Western Historical Collections, University Archives, University of Colorado at Boulder Libraries.

Some writers who had emotional attachments to England moved toward support of Britain during the Battle of Britain. Ella Winter was one of these. She was born in the British Empire (Australia) and received her secondary school and college training in London. I might easily have been among those who agreed with her. English literature had been my delight during my three years at Oxford. At that same time, however, I began to see imperial Britain in a new way. I had stumbled onto information about the ghastly foundation upon which rested the graceful life so visible in the part of England I knew best. I had encountered facts about the dreadful treatment of Africans by the British in South Africa, the source of the money on which I lived comfortably as a Rhodes Scholar. I had seen thousands of elephant tusks, neatly sorted according to size and stored in a warehouse along the Thames, waiting for the day when Africa's impoverishment could enrich the lives of wealthy consumers. I had biked across Ireland, until recently a British colony, and had seen poverty more painful than I had ever encountered. I had learned something of the crimes committed by the English in the subcontinent of India.

First, the promotion in this country of such a will to peace as will insure our abstention from the war in Europe.

Second, determined resistance to the increasing attacks on civil liberties, in whatever guise they are made, and against whatever progressive groups, and combined with this, a continued effort to extend cultural, intellectual and political freedom to all classes and minorities.

Third, unremitting opposition to fascism, whether open or concealed, at home or abroad, and assistance to the writers who are victims of fascism, or wartime oppression.

We ask the approval of the membership of the League of American Writers for these three basic activities, and for the principle that unity for action best serves the hopes of mankind.[1]

Three hundred and thirty-seven League members approved this policy. Twenty-four opposed it, and some resignations came in. Quite a number of writers did not know what stand to take. Although about half the League members did not vote, the number of those members who paid their dues remained about three times as large as it had been when I began working for the League.

Some of the council members who signed the statement of policy really wanted a statement more supportive of Britain and of Roosevelt's increasingly pro-war stand. The next step of this minority was an effort to take over the council. Aided by Malcolm Cowley, long one of the League's most active members, this group held meetings and tried to develop plans. I don't know what transpired at those meetings, but I do know that an assault on me as the executive secretary soon began.

At a council meeting, I was sharply attacked for releasing funds for the bail of Otto Katz, the Communist who had been arrested and taken to Ellis Island. I had obtained the supporting votes of a majority of the Exiled Writers Committee before releasing funds, but I was criticized for not locating all the members of the committee and getting their votes. Since the majority had approved using the funds for bail, I had not thought it necessary to force Katz to stay on Ellis Island while I went through the ritual of finding the remaining committee members and polling them. Clearly, as a matter of courtesy and of democratic procedure, I should have found some way to serve the interests both of Katz and of the committee members who I knew had begun to oppose certain League policies following the pact.

Millen Brand recorded in his journal what he saw happening:

June 22, 1940.

I drove to New York Wednesday. . . . Arrived just in time for a League National Council meeting where Dank was under fire: Marjorie Fischer and two other members of the Exiled Writers Committee, Nora Benjamin and Mrs. Untermeyer, were angry that Dank had put up exiled writers funds for bail for Otto Katz, to get him off Ellis Island and save him from possible deportation. Five of the committee had voted for it and in the rush, these three weren't consulted. Quite a fuss. Then at twelve twenty when the Council was half dead from fatigue Oliver La Farge introduced a pro-war resolution, apparently hoping to rush it through or at least make trouble. He and Marjorie and Malcolm Cowley and a few others have formed an opposition clique with the intent of making things hard for the League: so it looks. . . . (Loaned five hundred dollars to the Fund, to help out in the Katz bail.)

Things look decidedly difficult at the League.[2]

Opposition in the League made itself felt in another way. Suddenly old friends on the council demanded to see the League checkbook so they could study it, obviously hoping to find some irregularity that would be an excuse to call for my resignation. I produced it immediately and watched with interest as Marjorie Fischer studied it. She found nothing amiss except my handwriting, which left a good deal to be desired. Fischer was busy in other ways. She traveled to Hollywood, where she reported to LAW members "on conditions throughout the country," according to a Hollywood chapter *Bulletin.*

On October 31, 1939, still reflecting about his resignation, Brooks had written to Malcolm Cowley:

Now about the League, I must say at once that I do not propose to publish a statement about it. If there were no Dies Committee, I might do so; but I am not willing to give politicians a chance to stick their noses into the affairs of writers. As for the rest, I cannot agree with you that the new statement of policy straightens things out. If this stated in the spirit what it states in the letter, I might feel differently, perhaps. But the actions and mood of the League are quite discordant with the statement in paragraph II: "It is not necessary for the League to take a stand on international questions such as the meaning of the Soviet policy and of Franco-British policy!" The bulletin that brings this statement *takes* a stand. The League at every meeting takes a stand. And this stand is always against Franco-British policy, and it is always favourable to Soviet policy. It is even, by implication, favourable to Hitler. I do not question Elliot Paul's report on France Today. But what about the British report on the Germans, in the *N.Y. Times* this morning? Do

Elliot Paul, novelist, journalist, contributor to the League *Bulletin. Saturday Review of Literature* photo, July 31, 1937. Reproduced with the permission of the Western Historical Collections, University Archives, University of Colorado at Boulder Libraries.

you think it is false because it is British and because the *Daily Worker* does not print it? As for the question of war-aims, the British aims at least *may* change. I am almost certain that they will; and, as they have not yet been published, I really don't see why one should pre-judge them. As for the Hitler war-aims, they *cannot* change; and one does not have to prejudge what has been published. For Hitler has not wholly gone back on *Mein Kampf.* I say nothing about Stalin, and I urge no one to read Souvarine's book, for I have not read it myself; but I gather that it contains some [illegible word] facts. Take Stalin as you will. You still give the benefit of the doubt to Hitler, and you dwell on the sins of France and England. Is this American? Is it democratic?

Now here is the basis of my quarrel with the League. It simply is not *in the American grain.* For there is an American grain, and I wish to live with it, and I will not live against it knowingly. I believe in a socialized world and a socialized country; and so, for a wonder, do most American writers. But we know that this country can only be socialized *in the American grain.* History, psychology and anthropology tell us this, even if common sense fails to do so; and I am sure that if the League were in the American grain almost every writer would have to join it. As things are, it is rightly suspect by American writers, for, while we are democratic, the League is not so. It actually violates its professions. (You say we should not attack Russia without also attacking the English. But the League does attack the English. Can you really see the League attacking Russia?) And therefore I say that I cannot rejoin until the League accepts this fact and throws itself in line with the American grain. It is not sufficient to say now that the League is opposed to Fascism. In so far as its aim is negative it must oppose *Fascism and Dictatorship together,* whether the professed dictatorship of Hitler, the unprofessed but actual dictatorship of Stalin, the alleged dictatorship of the proletariat or the veiled dictatorship of Daladier. All these dictatorships are undemocratic. They are so in essence and in method; and if the League is to be an American League it must openly and unqualifiedly cease to support them. *And we must have no members who are not writers, in the substantial sense of this tortured word. We must have no mere political sitters-in.*

Will you consider this a letter to the League? And will you kindly read it at one of the meetings? After that, do chuck it away; and I should rather not discuss it. I shall watch the League with the deepest interest, but I have nothing more to say at present. Meanwhile, I reserve the right to keep copies of this statement for members of the League and other friends.[3]

Clifford Odets, playwright, member of the National Council, 1935, 1941, FBI target. From *New Masses*, June 17, 1941.

Life in the League did not become more settled in the following weeks. On November 3, 1939, the Soviet Union took steps to remove Finnish artillery emplacements that were within firing distance of Leningrad. At a meeting of the Hollywood chapter on January 25, 1940, Sheridan Gibney, retiring president, introduced a resolution "condemning Russian aggression against Finland." After much discussion, the resolution was unanimously voted down, although it was not easy in the United States to see justification for this Soviet military action outside its borders. It was only later, when Finland sided with Nazi Germany against the Soviet Union, that the defensive nature of the Soviet action became more apparent. Meanwhile, the pact was having profound effects on the affairs of writers not only in the United States but also in other countries. In France the headquarters of the International Association of Writers for the Defense of Culture could no longer operate because of government pressure. The British section of the association was having serious policy debates, as were the German exiles, both the writers among them and the non-writers. The author Heinrich Mann, chairman of the German Peoples Front, issued a statement of policy that was directed to the German people as a whole. This statement indicated that the pact had not caused the German Left to modify or abandon its unqualified opposition to the Hitler regime.

What was going on at council meetings was reflected in a May 15, 1940, entry in the journal of Clifford Odets, who was never very active in the League.

Went up to the offices of the League of American Writers where there was to be a discussion of an antiwar resolution which Henry Hart had drawn

Kenneth Burke, novelist, critic, member of the Executive Committee, 1935, Program Committee, 1937. From *Direction* magazine, April 1938.

up. I had not met most of the people who were there, Folsom, I. [Isidor] Schneider, Myra Page, but [Samuel] Grafton and L. [Lillian] Hellman I knew. Most of the discussion did not interest me, although it helped clarify some of my feelings about the war and a course in relation to it. But the entire evening I was trying to orientate myself in relation to the people, a curious lot, most of them Communists. The latter were for the resolution, the others more hesitant and wavering since it came out for complete denunciation of help for the allies. They decided to meet again next week, in the meantime appointed a new committee to draw up a new declaration. [Albert] Maltz and [George] Sklar were there too.

This Henry Hart, as I noticed before, is a curious duck. It occurred to me that he might be an interesting possibility for executive director for the Group [Theater].[4]

The turbulence among writers was also reflected in a letter from Malcolm Cowley to Kenneth Burke, May 24, 1940, after Cowley had resigned from the League. Burke had been with Cowley in the League in its very first days. "I have been planting trees and brooding over world affairs and between the two activities I can't think, let alone write. Last night I resigned from the League — no fight I just couldn't stand the party line on the war," Cowley wrote.[5] The resignation was still on Cowley's mind seven months later when he wrote again to Burke: "Anyone who was as close to the radical movement as I was is going to be deeply shaken by breaking his connections with it. . . . You want to justify yourself, while blaming yourself — the double drive that one finds in all books by ex-radicals."[6]

Cowley incorporated his letter of resignation in a *New Republic* review of Donald Ogden Stewart's *Fighting Words,* a book about the Third American Writers Congress. In reply, the council wrote to *The New Republic:*

In his review of "Fighting Words" Mr. Cowley took the occasion to publish his letter of resignation from the League of American Writers. This presented a version of the League's activities and policies by one who was opposed to them. It would only be fair to the League and to your readers to present the League's version. It might be added that Mr. Cowley saw fit to give his letter to the public before there was any opportunity for the National Board to consider it.

Mr. Cowley intimates that a large section of the League has resigned. In the critical eleven months of the war, resignations from the League have totalled fewer than one hundred out of a membership of eight hundred, during which time the League has added thirty new members. This record speaks well of the League's activities and policies as carrying out the will of its membership during a difficult period when it was subject to attacks from the Dies Committee and other reactionary groups and individuals.

When differences developed regarding the political attitude of the League, efforts were made to arrive at a minimum agreement under which the League could maintain its unity and continue its work. That it continued under these conditions to carry on valuable work Mr. Cowley himself admits, though he mentions only one of its activites. That Mr. Cowley and a few others no longer wish to collaborate in this work is deeply regretted by the League, but the work will go on.

Thomas, Mann, Nobel Prize, 1929, exiled German novelist, honorary League President, 1939. Portrait by Georges Schreiber from *Saturday Review of Literature*, October 19, 1940. Reproduced with the permission of the Western Historical Collections, University Archives, University of Colorado at Boulder Libraries.

The difference between the position of the League and of the few Board members who resigned was that they favored measures which seemed to the majority of the League to lead to involvement in the war. The opinion of the majority of the League was given in its recently issued statement from which we quote:

"We yield to no one in our unalterable hatred and opposition to fascism. We have helped create the genuine anti-fascist spirit of the American people. . . . In regard to the defense of America, we take our position in the front line of the defenders of our American peace, our American democracy, our American civil liberties, and we will defend these against foreign invaders as we defend them against enemies at home. A defense of seacoasts and towns is incomplete if it does not also defend these American treasures. We insist, therefore, that the military defense program not be made an excuse for attack on social legislation or on the liberties of the people, for if that is done the defense program will be a concealed invasion of precisely the fascist type it proposes to guard us against; and therefore, we deplore the use of a defense program to arouse hysteria under the cover of which

Granville Hicks, critic, member of the Executive Committee, 1935; resigned 1939, FBI target. From *New Masses.*

attacks have already been made upon the Walsh-Healy Act, upon the trade unions and our civil liberties."[7]

In this statement we associate ourselves with the published resolutions of labor and other progressive forces of America.

To suggest that this means that the League has joined company "with the appeasers and the reactionaries," with "Father Coughlin and Henry Ford," is an affront to the whole progressive movement and serves "to confuse American democracy rather than to defend it."[8]

The New Republic published the letter on August 26, 1940.

Other resignations from the League took other forms. Rolfe Humphries summarized the League's voluminous international correspondence — noting wryly that in some sections of the International Association of Writers, the debate following the pact had been more civilized than it had been in the League — then announced that his duties as secretary were complete. He resigned the position and that of council member, but he did not send a letter of resignation.

Another who departed in this period was Thomas Mann, honorary president. His resignation was not ostensibly because of the pact, but was a protest against an article Elliot Paul had written for the League *Bulletin*. This article was a vigorous attack on the pro-Fascist policies being pursued by the government of France, which Paul had very recently observed at firsthand. It seemed curious then, and it seems curious now, that Thomas Mann should choose this article as a pretext for leaving the League. Obviously, it was the pact that was on his mind and his objection to Paul's attack on France seems to have been an oblique way of saying that the League should be regarding France as a potential ally against Hitler and not as the Nazi puppet that it was.

Other prominent writers who resigned from the League following the pact were Granville Hicks,[9] Archibald MacLeish, Paul de Kruif, Lewis Mumford, Heywood Broun, Walter Duranty, Lewis Gannett, Louis Fischer, Max Lerner, Bruce Bliven, Matthew Josephson, and Kyle Crichton. For Crichton, in particular, the pact was very traumatic. Because of it he took to his bed, believing he was having a recurrence of tuberculosis, which he had had in earlier years. Medical tests proved his self-diagnosis was wrong.

Josephson wrote an open letter in which he set forth his thoughts on the pact. I don't recall where — or if — this letter was published, but I found a copy among his papers in Yale University's Library. After reviewing the situation that led up to the pact, Josephson concluded that neutrality was the course that progressive Americans should follow. That was exactly the course that the League decided to follow, but Josephson inexplicably resigned. Years later, when I organized a

Matthew Josephson

Matthew Josephson, historian, member of the Executive Committee, 1935; resigned, 1940. Caricature by Georges Schreiber. From *New Masses,* 1939.

slate of candidates in the Authors Guild, Josephson supported my candidacy for the guild council. I wondered then — and still wonder — if this support was a way of saying that he had had second thoughts about leaving the League when we actually did what he recommended.

Oliver La Farge, who had been very active in efforts to get the League to take a pro-British position, also wrote a long letter of resignation. Years later, he still looked back with distaste on the League's debate at the time of the pact, but apparently he bore me no grudge. He generously gave me comments on my young-adult novel, *Search in the Desert* (Funk and Wagnalls, 1955) which, like his *Laughing Boy,* was set on the Navaho Reservation.

Other members who did not hold office in the League sent letters of resignation, among them the talented novelist Albert Halper. In his case, the wonder was that he had ever joined the League. He was not a joiner. Almost the only permanent commitment in his life seems to have been to his writing. His relationships to individuals and to groups usually seemed transitory.[10]

Another who left the League (and the Communist Party) at this time was Robert Gorham Davis, an associate of Granville Hicks and Daniel Boorstin. Like Hicks and Boorstin, Davis became an informer. To the House Un-American Activities Committee he said in 1953, "I do feel it necessary to have all possible information about the activities of the Communist Party itself for security reasons."[11]

Angna Enters, novelist, actress. From *Direction* magazine, November 1939.

At the time when some writers were leaving, others joined the League. They were not so well known as many of those who had departed, but they were evidence that the League still had vitality. It retained more than 700 of the 820 members who had supported its program before the pact, and many of them worked very hard preparing for the Fourth American Writers Congress, scheduled to be held in the spring of 1941. (The non-resigners were not issuing statements, as many of the resigners were doing.) The League was not so badly crippled as those who had led the migration out of the organization wanted to believe. "You would be astounded," said Murray Kempton, "how few party members — and for that matter, even fellow travelers — left because of the Nazi-Soviet Pact."[12] The resignations had not been a fatal blow. That was still to come and would have less to do with mistakes made by the League than with power used against it.

As I think back on the effects of the pact, I recall little more than the impression that some members followed the principle of "When in doubt, shout."

It does me little credit that I do recall in detail sharp attacks made on me personally by council members I had thought were my very good friends. Did I forget the more important happenings at council meetings because I dismissed all arguments that went contrary to my own beliefs? I had come from a family that had little tolerance for "wrong" views. One of my grandfathers was typical of the stiff-necked brood. If a discussion of the relative merits of different religious denominations came up, he was sure to say, "The Baptists are a little the rightest."

I probably was one of those guilty of raising a dogmatic voice against those who wanted the League to come down on the side of Britain. It is also possible that I don't recall the bitter words exchanged because I was not central in the debate. The minutes of the council meetings record that I chaired some of them, and in this position I was not free to be fully partisan.

One thing I do know. Malcolm Cowley (not a Party member), who helped organize the pro-British faction, and Rolfe Humphries, a Party member who quietly shared Cowley's views, were both unhappy about the debate. Humphries put his distress into this poem:

With a Resignation, Untendered

Wars and evil abroad in the world, we bicker;
    Energy gone to waste
Hating each other, morose and furious children,
    Caught, shamefaced,

In a deadlock over MacLeish, or the phrase of a sentence
    Paragraph three, line four;
Follow the party line, or cavil against it,
    Hate or obey the Ninth Floor.[13]

Not even huddled for comfort together, like cattle,
    Or the poor refugees,
Waiting, head down, for the storm to be over, secure
    Under the dangerous trees.

Having done here all I can, I take my leave,
    Elsewhere to find
Strength more enduring than any a league can give
    In my own mind,

On the sunny side of a hill in the afternoon,
    Or in bed at night alone,
Try to develop the terrible strength I need,
    And have not yet known,

Consign my voice to grave and resolute silence,
    Nor add one syllable,
To all this pitiful ugly dissolution,
    And so farewell.[14]

Resigning from the League (and the CP) was a painful experience. In 1940 Humphries sought psychoanalytic help and clearly, he withdrew into the private world of his lyrics and his classrooms.[15] Cowley tried for a while to continue public activity, doing propaganda work for the government, but as I have said, reactionaries in Congress and the press would not allow this. He was driven from his job.

Half a century after the debate, it is possible to note that strong forces drove one group of writers toward support of the U.S. government as it

Paul de Kruif, science writer, League vice president, 1937; resigned, 1939. From *New Masses*, April 12, 1938.

prepared for war and confirmed the opposing group in its rejection of the government's foreign policy. The writing community was definitely split. What divided it? Was it poor judgment on the part of the League's National Council? Was it blind obedience to orders coming from the Communist Party, as had been alleged? Was it shortsighted self-interest on the part of liberals? Or was it something else?

Clearly, some Communists on the council did not want the League to take a stand against the pact and for Britain, and they acted in harmony with the policy that came to prevail in the Communist Party. I think, however, it is fair to say that they acted not on orders but as their consciences dictated. Some non-Communists on the council agreed. Others who had been Communists until recently opposed the pact and supported Britain, as did some liberals on the council.

As I review the controversy fifty years after being in the midst of it, it seems to me that no decision the League could have taken would have held all the members together. Anti-fascism and anti-communism do not make a stable blend, because a key element of fascism is opposition to communism. It was not surprising that a hundred writers turned away from the League. They found a variety of doors through which to leave, but no matter which exit a writer chose, it often tended to open on professional opportunity. In contrast, the League had nothing to offer members who remained loyal, nothing except fellowship and a continuing chance to serve. These were currencies not readily accepted by the grocer and the landlord.

On one level, both responses to the pact were acts of faith. One group had faith that the Soviet government had sought peace in its own self-interest, an interest that coincided with the interest of people everywhere. The writers who opposed the pact had faith in what they regarded as the democratic essence of the United States and British governments and in the anti-Nazi protestations of the press. And then there was Phillip Rahv, who had opposed the League ever since 1937.

According to Mary McCarthy, he said that, after the pact, he sometimes awoke at night in a sweat, asking: "And what if Stalin is right?"[16]

Notes

1. LAW Statement to Members, *The Bulletin of the League of American Writers* (hereinafter *LAW Bulletin*), January 1940, LAW Papers, Bancroft Library, University of California, Berkeley.

2. Millen Brand journal, June 22 1940, Rare Books and Manuscripts, Butler Library, Columbia University, New York.

3. Van Wyck Brooks to Cowley, October 31, 1939, Malcolm Cowley Papers, Special Collections, Newberry Library, Chicago.

4. Clifford Odets, *The Time Is Ripe: The 1940 Journal of Clifford Odets* (Grove Press, 1988), pp. 154–155.

5. Cowley to Kenneth Burke, May 24, 1940, Malcolm Cowley Papers, Newberry Library.

6. Ibid., December 17, 1940.

7. The Walsh-Healy, or Public Contract Act, was designed to give the government the power, in all its contracts, to set wage standards, working conditions, and hours. It was intended to defend labor against a recent Supreme Court decision that declared important aspects of the New Deal unconstitutional.

8. *The New Republic*, August 26, 1940.

9. Years later, Granville Hicks explained to the House Un-American Activities Committee something of what had been going on in the League following the Soviet-German non-aggression pact. He said, "There were a good many of us who hoped during the fall and winter of 1939–40 that the League would be taken away from the Communists, but it proved to be impossible, and so most of us simply quit."

10. Albert Halper, *Goodbye, Union Square: A Writer's Memoir of the Thirties* (Quadrangle Books, 1970).

11. U.S. Congress, House Committee on Un-American Activities, *Communist Methods of Infiltration (Education) Hearings*, 83rd Cong., 1st and 2d sess., 1953–1954, February 25, 1953, pts. 1–9.
    During a break in the Writers Congress of June 1939, at an outdoor cafe on Fifth Avenue near the New School where the congress was taking place, I introduced Davis and pulp writer Hope Hale to one another. They soon got married.

12. Murray Kempton, quoted in Natalie Robins, *Alien Ink* (William Morrow and Co.), p. 105.

13. "Ninth Floor" was the term often used for the national headquarters of the Communist Party, which were located on the ninth floor at 35 East 12th Street in New York.

14. Rolfe Humphries, *Collected Poems of Rolfe Humphries* (Indiana University Press, 1965), pp. 54–55.

15. Richard Gilman and Michael Paul Novak, eds., *Poets, Poetics and Politics: America's Literary Community Viewed From the Letters of Rolfe Humphries* (University Press of Kansas, 1992), p. 20.

16. Mary McCarthy, Intellectual Memoirs (Harcourt, Brace Jovanovich Publishers, 1992) p. 86.

16

Hostiles, Turncoats — and Loyalists

If it hadn't been for you I wouldn't have turned into a stoolie for J. Edgar Hoover. I don't think you have the foggiest notion of the contempt I have had for myself since the day I did that thing.

> — Sterling Hayden, writer and actor, in his autobiography, *Wanderer*, said to his analyst after becoming an informer

Just for a handful of silver he left us,
    Just for a reband to stick in his coat —

> — Robert Browning, in "The Lost Leader," 1845, referring to William Wordsworth

After God had finished the rattlesnake, the toad, the vampire, He had some awful substance left with which He made a scab.

> — Jack London, quoted in *C.I.O. News*, September, 13, 1946

There is no error so monstrous that it fails to find defenders among the ablest men.

> — Lord Acton, in a letter to Mary Gladstone, April 24, 1881

The shattering problems of the 1930s — unemployment, fascism, war — demanded great responses, and the League of American Writers was one of many collective efforts of people who tried to make such responses. For its efforts the League won praise, but it also drew severe criticism. Some individuals and groups spent a good deal of energy calling attention to what they considered the League's weaknesses, or worse, its betrayals. Beginning early, criticism came from one particular group of writers who, to one degree or another, were following the teachings of Leon Trotsky. He had been an active leader in the Russian Revolution but in 1929 was exiled by Stalin. Trotsky took a keen interest in literature, and his sensitivity to literary problems gave him credentials among writers.

Many of those influenced by Trotsky's theories were scornful of the League because it included writers who had very large audiences in film, slick magazines, and the so-called pulps. The Trotskyists' focus was more on ideas than on action, and they usually seemed little involved in rendering day-to-day service to other writers or to people generally. As the League tried its damnedest to do what it considered good deeds, these critics jeered at its flaws — which included a non-critical stance on the human rights record of the Soviet Union.

On the larger scene, the Trotskyists opposed the Popular Front in Spain and elsewhere because it was not, they said, sufficiently revolutionary. For the same reason, they attacked the League, which supported the Popular Front as a defense against the growing menace to all culture — to all humanity.

Clearly, the Popular Front was not revolutionary. It had a much more modest role. It simply tried to place roadblocks in the way of the rapidly advancing danger of Hitlerism. This could be done, but by no stretch of the imagination could the seemingly more revolutionary Trotskyists' answer to fascism prevail. The social forces needed to carry through the anti-capitalist revolution they proposed simply did not exist. As someone said to me, you don't keep on trying to climb a peak while you are being attacked by a grizzly bear.

Still, it does not follow that all steps taken by the Popular Front — or by its Communist component — were justified. The Popular Front and the Communists within it did make tactical errors, but that did not mean that the overall strategy was wrong. There was no justification for directing major energies against Spanish Communists instead of against Fascists, and this, it seemed to me, was what Trotskyists were doing. They were proposing to junk a whole auto when they found it had a faulty carburetor and a flat tire.

Even before the Popular Front days, there had been a great churning in the little pot of Left politics. Lovestoneites, who were on the right of the Left, bubbled away until they vanished.[1] Trotskyists, on the left of the Left, were more durable. They, too, were expelled by the CP; then —

James T. Farrell, novelist, member of the National Council, 1935; became an active opponent of the League. National Archives photo.

seeking an alliance that would give them greater influence — they fused with the American Workers Party, called Musteites after the name of their leader, A. J. Muste. Then they entered the Socialist Party. In the course of the continuing ferment, the Trotskyists left the Socialist Party and split into two new parties. All of this turmoil has been traced by Alan Wald in *The New York Intellectuals: The Rise and Decline of the Anti-Stalinist Left in the 1930's to the 1980's.* After the success of the Popular Front, Wald says, "the stream of intellectuals toward Trotskyism virtually ceased."[2]

While the Trotskyists were at the peak of their activity, all the writers they influenced were hostile not only to the CP but also to the League. In their lexicon the two were interchangeable terms. One evidence of Trotskyism's influence was the resignation from the League of writers James T. Farrell and John Dos Passos. Another evidence was the reversal in politics of the magazine *Partisan Review.* After beginning as a journal independent of the League but in which League supporters were dominant, it came to a halt in 1937 for lack of funds. Before the editors could raise the money they needed, and before the League could decide whether it might be published under League auspices, two of its editors, William Phillips and Philip Rahv, began publishing *Partisan Review,* in December 1937, as an anti-Stalinist, anti-League journal. They simply appropriated the magazine's subscription list and title and went into action.

Partisan Review, as its name suggests, began as a contentious periodical, and it remained such, except that the objects of its wrath were now the very people who had been its founders and early supporters. In the course of its changeover, it became more cerebral, more remote from mass movements of people, and only a generous subsidy from a rich "angel" kept it going. No organization of writers developed around it, although its editors made efforts to establish a kind of counter to the League.[3]

An organization of anti-Stalinist intellectuals that included writers did grow up — the Committee for Cultural Freedom, headed by John

Dewey and Sidney Hook. On May 15, 1939, its manifesto, with ninety-six signatures, appeared in the *New York Times*. Leon Trotsky, in exile in Mexico City, thought that a more revolutionary organization was required, and he proposed the formation of the International Federation of Independent Revolutionary Art. In response to his initiative, the League for Cultural Freedom and Socialism appeared in New York on June 3, 1939, by no accident on the eve of the Third American Writers Congress. James T. Farrell supported this new group, and Dwight Macdonald was a central figure in it.

At this time, by an odd coincidence, Macdonald and I lived in adjoining apartments on East 10th Street in Manhattan. An indication of the mood of the times was this: Neither he nor I ever spoke or even nodded as we passed in the corridor. It was left to our wives to be more civilized. On occasion when they met, they discussed their babies, who were about the same age. I have wondered if Dwight Macdonald ever came to think our shunning each other was as silly as it now seems. I don't have to wonder, however, what Trotsky thought of Macdonald, who was his disciple, if only briefly. Harry Roskolenko, a Trotskyist, has reported that Trotsky said, "Everyone has the right to be stupid now and then, but Comrade Macdonald abuses the privilege."[4]

In some respects, *Partisan Review* did not hew closely to Trotsky's line. For example, Trotsky supported the Soviet occupation of eastern Poland following the German-Soviet non-aggression pact. He also supported the Soviet military action against Finland, but *Partisan Review* was anti-pact and anti-Soviet all along the line. The editors held that those who refused — as did the League — to condemn the USSR for signing the pact were in effect enemy agents. In this, the magazine paralleled the position of the reactionaries in Congress.

It is not necessary here to try to trace the stages by which Phillips and Rahv and their friends moved from support of the League to hostility toward it. When the Popular Front passed into history, following the pact, *Partisan Review* lost the enemy that had been a prime reason for its being. It continued, however, vehemently anti-communist, as did less literary folk such as J. Edgar Hoover, Congressman Martin Dies, and a growing number of their friends in Washington. No one, I am sure, would be tempted to describe the *Partisan Review* of recent years as even remotely radical.

To most of the long series of attacks that came from those influenced by Trotskyism, the League remained silent. Many League members did, however, join others in signing a statement that appeared on August 15, 1939, in reply to a Trotskyist diatribe against the Soviet Union. This was only a few days before the signing of the pact set off a new round of criticisms that had more serious effect within the League.

As the members of the League council debated what its position on the pact should be, *Partisan Review* published a letter signed by writers, some of them supporters of the Committee for Cultural Freedom and some members of the League for Cultural Freedom and Socialism. The letter jeered at the League of American Writers for its silence about the pact and asked this series of questions designed to embarrass the League:

1. What is the character of the present war? Is it an imperialist war or a war of the democracies against Fascism?
2. What is the role of the Stalin Regime in this war? Did the Stalin-Hitler pact advance the cause of world peace or did it promote Fascist aggression? Does the League approve of the partition of Poland between Germany and Russia?
3. Does the League still hold that the United States should cooperate with the Soviet Union in order to stop the onward march of Fascism?
4. Does the League still maintain that the United States should adopt a "collective security" policy? If so, what countries should be included in such a common front?
5. Does the League of American Writers still consider the Communist Party to be a force for peace, democracy, and socialism?[5]

This letter appeared after the Third American Writers Congress, but there had been several actions against the League at the time of the congress in June 1939. In one of these, the poet Florence Becker Lennon and fourteen other writers picketed the congress, protesting the League's support of the Popular Front.

The National Council of the League noted that none of the fifteen picketers — all of whom had joined the League earlier — had used organizational channels to discuss their grievances. Nor had they paid their current dues. None of them supported the League's position on the Popular Front, and the council terminated the membership of all fifteen. Florence Becker Lennon immediately protested and tried, without success, to get other writers to support her — and to oppose the League as a whole.[6] Her opposition to the Popular Front went beyond the literary world. She raised money to send a volunteer to Spain to join the military force maintained by POUM (Partido Obrero de Unificación Marxista), which was at odds with the government of the Spanish republic. At one point, POUM forces and certain government forces led by members of the Communist Party engaged in armed combat. As can be expected, each blamed the other for the conflict, but one thing was clear: The friction within the republican forces worked to the advantage of Franco.

Incidents of violence in Trotskyist-CP relations were not limited to Spain. One of these had a curious connection with the League — a connection I still do not understand. One day, probably in 1939, a young man named Sheldon Harte joined the volunteer group in the League office, recruited by Emily Grace, another volunteer, to stuff and seal envelopes.[7] Harte didn't stay around long, and I probably would have forgotten him if I hadn't seen his name in a news story in the spring of 1940. He had been murdered in Mexico City, where he was a guard in the well-fortified villa in which the exiled Trotsky lived.

At that time the Mexican painter David Alfaro Siqueiros, a Stalinist, along with others had apparently tried to assassinate Trotsky. Was Harte killed by Stalinists because he was loyal to Trotsky? Was he killed by Trotskyists — or Stalinists — because he was part of a Stalinist plot? If Trotsky himself knew, the information went with him to his grave, so far as I am aware. Trotsky was soon murdered by a man who seems clearly to have been an agent of Stalin. Why had Harte volunteered to work for the League? Was he friend or foe, or just a young romantic who wanted to be where something interesting was going on? I wish I knew.

What became of the Trotskyists who so actively opposed the League? Alan Wald gives us information about their later political trajectories: " Many of them were involved with the conservative 'Committee for the Free World' led by Midge Decter and her husband, *Commentary* editor Norman Podhoretz. This predominantly pro-Reagan organization achieved considerable notoriety when, in April 1981, it ran an advertisement in the *New York Times* to 'applaud American policy in El Salvador.' "[8]

Some of the criticisms of the League came from writers who had never been active in the organization or whose activity had been only in the first year or so of its existence. Two who made a hostile, public resignation were Bernard D. N. Grebanier and Frances Winwar, husband and wife, both members of the League's National Council. They had participated in League work almost up to the time of the Third American Writers Congress in June 1939.

Bernard D.N. Grebanier, poet, critic, theatrical director, chair, New York chapter of the League; resigned, 1939. Bernard Grebanier Collection, Boston University, Department of Special Collections.

Frances, who was Italian in origin (her birth name was Francesca Vinciguerra), wrote books about English literary figures of the Victorian period. She had at one time been married to V. J. Jerome, who later became a leader in the Communist Party.

Bernard, trained as a concert pianist, became a teacher of English at Brooklyn College and wrote poetry, plays, and literary criticism. At one time he had resisted the American Legion when it demanded that he be fired because he was allegedly unpatriotic. Later, when he was head of the New York chapter of the League, he was a member of the Communist Party.

I first thought something strange was going on when Bernard came to the League office and used the phone to discuss loudly with someone a rather considerable sum of money he owed in Communist Party dues. Every Party member knew that he or she should keep Party and League business separate and should never use the League phone to transact Party business. The phone was doubtless tapped. Not long after this strange little incident, Grebanier and Winwar resigned from the League.

By December 1940, Grebanier had become an informer against Brooklyn College colleagues.[9] At a private hearing before the Rapp-Coudert committee of the New York state legislature, Grebanier named more than thirty Brooklyn College employees as members of the Communist Party. Some of them lost their jobs, but most did not, because no witnesses could be found to corroborate his testimony.

In an effort to find out what had sent Grebanier and Winwar into action against the League, I dug into his jumble of papers, which have been deposited in the Boston University Library. I found very little that threw direct light on his defection from the League and the betrayal of his fellow teachers, but it was clear that he had solidified himself in his job. An official dinner, replete with tributes, was held in his honor when he retired. I did find violent, abusive letters he sent to his brother — letters in which Grebanier resisted increasing his contribution to their mother's support. Also I found the manuscript of a poem about Judas — many pages of iambic pentameter couplets on the theme of betrayal.[10] As I went through Grebanier's vast outpouring of words, a bust of him was right behind me, looking over my shoulder. How long had the real Grebanier looked over my shoulder at the League?

I cannot leave these notes about the League's enemies without recording that we had foes other than Trotskyists. One story may set the balance straight.

In the late summer of 1938, when native Fascists were increasingly active, I went to Salt Lake City as an invited speaker at the Utah Writers Roundup. Many at this gathering were writers of westerns, and I extended to all of them an invitation to join other writers throughout the country in a common effort to prevent the spread of fascism and war. My talk had been well publicized and the meeting hall was full. A number of men were even standing in the side aisles and across the back of the room.

A reception followed the meeting. As the affair began to break up, a young fellow asked if he could give me a lift back to my hotel. My hosts hadn't discussed transportation with me, and I accepted. A moment later someone touched my arm. It was the elderly, rugged-looking novelist who had chaired the meeting. He drew me to one side.

"What did that guy want?" he demanded.

"He offered me a ride back to my hotel."

"You can't go with him!" the old man snapped.

"Why not?"

"He is the leader of the local Silver Shirts.[11] Didn't you see those men lined up around the room as you spoke? They are all Fascists — members of the Silver Shirts. They would gladly take you for a ride, all right — a ride from which you might not come back."

I hope I collected my wits enough to thank the firm old man at my side. I know I asked him how it happened that he was so careful about my safety.

"I'm an old Wobbly," he replied, as much as to say that no further explanation was needed for his display of anti-Fascist solidarity.[12]

I didn't have the presence of mind to ask if he had known Joe Hill, the IWW songwriter who had been framed and executed there in Salt Lake City in 1915, for a murder he did not commit. I was reminded, however, of the direction in which the League could look for friends when it was threatened.

Sherwood Anderson, novelist; resigned, 1939, FBI target. National
Archives photo.

In the following year, 1939, while the French and British governments continued to avoid military efforts to destroy nazism, and while they kept toying with schemes to get Germany to move against the USSR, the political work of the League centered around keeping the United States out of the developing war and opposing the growth of domestic fascism. This emphasis was in harmony with a large body of public opinion. The Gallup Poll reported that nearly three-quarters of the people in the United States wanted to stay out of the war in Europe. On June 14, 1941, *The New Republic* published the result of a poll among 241 opinion makers that included all the recent contributors to that magazine. Those questioned in the poll were offered a choice of seven different policies. The one that proved most popular was the one closest to that of the League. It called for military and financial aid to Britain, but only after Britain had entered into "a bloc of anti-Fascist powers (including Russia) and had given binding assurances that she is fighting for democratic aims."

In addition to resisting and exposing native Fascists, the League tried to carry on the tradition of Randolph Bourne and other writers who had resisted U.S. involvement in World War I, into which President Wilson had led the country shortly after he was elected on an anti-war platform. The National Council of the League set up a Keep America Out of War Committee,[13] headed by Eleanor Flexner. At one point Flexner reported that the committee was facing problems as it fumbled around trying to find the right projects for citizen-writers to undertake.[14] Before long, however, it settled on an idea that an organization of writers could carry through to the benefit of the peace movement as a whole: compiling a bibliography of novels, pamphlets, articles, songs, plays, recordings, radio scripts, memoirs, films, and art that could serve to strengthen people's resolve to stay away from a war that really wasn't against fascism. At first glance, a bibliography might not seem to be a very exciting device for adding energy to a popular movement, but the compilation was soon much in demand.

The Keep America Out of War Committee also prepared and circulated a press release that contained alarming information about what had happened to children in World War I. This release was picked up mainly by trade union papers. Another product of our anti-war campaign was the song "The Yanks Aren't Coming," for which Harold Rome wrote the music and lyrics and which the League published. Also, Sol Funaroff and Ben Maddow arranged a two-hour program at the Newspaper Guild Club where Morris Carnovsky and others read anti-war poems by Nelson Algren, Joy Davidman, Kenneth Fearing, Langston Hughes, and William Carlos Williams. In New York, League writers took part as citizens in the 1941 May Day parade made up of labor and Left organizations.

William Carlos Williams, poet; resigned 1939, FBI target. From *Direction* magazine, December 1940.

Acting for the National Council, Albert Maltz wrote a statement, "In Defense of Peace," that was signed by nearly 350 writers. The commercial press almost totally ignored the statement, although most newspapers did carry a great deal of material that supported the increasing U.S. involvement in the war.

At this same time, the Northern California chapter of the League produced and distributed a four-page pamphlet, "Writers Oppose War! Keep Your Heads!" Another pamphlet, "The Yanks Aren't Coming," by Northern California League member Mike Quin reached such a huge

Ralph Bates, British novelist, resigned from the League at the time of the Soviet-Finnish war. From *Direction* magazine.

audience nationwide that the right-wing newspaper columnist Walter Winchell called Quin one of the most dangerous men in America. In Hollywood Dalton Trumbo, author of the widely circulated novel *Johnny Got His Gun* (J. B. Lippincott, 1939; reprint, Lyle Stuart, 1970), also turned to pamphleteering. He discussed, among other things, the inconsistency of those who had opposed the Soviet military action in Finland:

> I bow to no one in my admiration of and my sympathy with the Finnish people. But I am, in the interest of American neutrality, obliged to ask, "why only Finland?" Did the help of the world go out to China, Spain, Ethiopia, Austria, Albania, Czechoslovakia? On the contrary! People who wished to assist these nations in the defense of their democracy were harassed, held up to public ridicule, and finally smeared with the libel of being subversive to democracy! As a result, seven nations fell before brute force and dictatorship.

Using a new art form made popular by the WPA Theater Project, the Hollywood chapter prepared a Living Newspaper, "America Declares Peace," that was presented before an audience of 20,000. The Hollywood chapter also published Guy Endore's "Let's Skip the Next War" and another pamphlet, "Washington's Cliveden Set," by Bruce Minton, which pointed out the pro-Nazi views of important figures in Washington that paralleled the views of pro-Nazi politicians in England who were called the Cliveden Set.

While the League and its members were finding these ways of speaking out, they were increasingly busy making preparations for the Fourth American Writers Congress, which was designed to be a major statement against the war.

Notes

1. Jay Lovestone, at one time a CP leader, was expelled from the Party in 1929.

2. Alan M. Wald, *The New York Intellectuals* (University of North Carolina Press, 1987), p. 7. Wald further states:

   > Appraisals of the New York intellectuals have been made by at least a dozen scholars, and there have been book-length studies of such individuals as Hannah Arendt (who entered the tradition at a later date), Saul Bellow, Max Eastman, James T. Farrell, Clement Greenberg, Mary McCarthy, Dwight Macdonald, Delmore Schwartz, Lionel Trilling, and Edmund Wilson. Even more striking has been the production of autobiographical and semiautobiographical works by the New York intellectuals themselves. Such memoirs include not only the acclaimed trilogy by Alfred Kazin, the sensational revelations of Norman Podhoretz (another late-comer), and the ironical "confessions" published by Mary McCarthy and Dwight Macdonald in the 1940s, but also numerous books and sketches by Lionel Abel, William Barrett, Daniel Bell, Leslie Fiedler, Albert Halper, Michael Harrington, Sidney Hook, Irving Howe, Irving Kristol, George Novack, William Phillips, Harry Roskolenko, Diana Trilling, Lionel Trilling, and Bernard Wolfe.

3. "Philip Rahv and I actually went to one meeting of the League of American Writers — and created a rumpus — it must have been '37. We were against the League of American Writers and they were against us." William Phillips, quoted in Natalie Robins, *Alien Ink* (William Morrow and Co., 1992) p. 89.

4. Harry Roskolenko, *When I Was Last on Cherry Street* (Stein and Day, 1965), p. 158.

5. LAW Papers, Bancroft Library, University of California, Berkeley.

6. I had forgotten this incident when, twenty-five years later in 1964, Florence asked me to read some of my poems on a radio program she conducted in New York over radio station WEVD (the EVD was for Eugene V. Debs). I agreed to do so. The program was scheduled for the night before May Day, and I wrote a poem for the occasion. Just before I went on the air, Florence impishly reminded me that I had participated in expelling her from the League. This did not exactly put me at ease as I read my verses, but I got through the program. When I returned home, I found Mary was distressed. There had been only silence on WEVD at the time I was supposed to be on the air. What had happened? I found that the U.S. military had put up a shield of some kind around the broadcasting antenna of the station, ostensibly because the signal would interfere with some Air Force exercises. I was tempted to wonder if the Air Force was worried that I might issue a call to the workers of New York to seize power on May Day. Years later, Florence again invited me to read poems on a radio program she ran in Boulder, Colorado. At long last, she and I had established a kind of united front, and following her death in 1984, her family arranged a memorial service in a synagogue and asked me to speak. I did so.

7. Emily Grace, trained in classics at Bryn Mawr and Yale, later married a White Russian émigré, Vladimir Kazakevich, an economist who worked for the National Association of Manufacturers and the National Chamber of Commerce. After the war he, with other White Russian émigrés, was invited to go to the Soviet Union to help rebuild the country. He accepted the invitation, and Emily went with him. In Moscow she began research in ancient Greek history, particularly slavery in Greece, and she continued in this work until her death in Moscow in the late 1980s.

8. Wald, p. 7.

9. *New York Times*, December 20, 1940. See also Ellen W. Schrecker, *No Ivory Tower: McCarthyism and the Universities* (Oxford University Press, 1986), pp. 78–79.

10. The theme of Judas and betrayal also fascinated another council member. In *The Judas Time* (Dial Press, 1946), Isidor Schneider dealt with the subject from a very different point of view, as did council member Lillian Hellman in *Scoundrel Time* (Little, Brown and Company, 1976).

11. The Silver Shirts were a fascist organization founded by William Dudley Pelley.

12. A Wobbly was a member of Industrial Workers of the World — the IWW.

13. For a list of committee members, see Appendix C.

14. Eleanor Flexner had just published *American Playwrights, 1918–1938* (Simon and Schuster, 1939). I had known her, daughter of the educator Abraham Flexner, when I taught at Swarthmore College, where she was a student . In the academic year 1930–1931 we were both students at Oxford.

This Art Young cartoon, "The Big Shots," appeared in *Direction* at the time of the Fourth American Writers Congress.

Many writers who had been League members continued, after the League ceased to exist, to support principles for which the organization had stood. Here novelist and screenwriter Dalton Trumbo (center in light suit), film director Herbert Biberman (behind sign), novelist and screenwriter Alvah Bessie (at far right) and others of the Hollywood Ten, appear on the eve of entering prison for refusing to become informers. With Trumbo, holding a sign, are his children. Courtesy of the John Howard Lawson Collection, Special Collections, Norris Museum, Southern Illinois University at Carbondale.

17
The Yanks Aren't Coming

Oh, the Yanks aren't coming,
aren't coming, aren't coming.
The Yanks aren't coming over there!

— Harold Rome

We Americans produce 90 percent of the world's natural gas, not counting
the speeches of Senators and Congressmen on Saving Democracy.

— Theodore Dreiser in *America Is Worth Saving*

Man, take your gun; and put to shame
earthquake and plague, the acts of God.
You maim the crazy and the lame.

— Jacob Bronowski in *The Clipper*, June 1941

The attitude of great poets is to cheer up slaves and horrify despots.

— Walt Whitman, quoted by Genevieve Taggard
at the Fourth American Writers Congress

By June 1941, war in Europe had become essentially a contest
between the forces of the British Empire and those of an expanded
German Reich.

On June 6, at the public meeting in Manhattan Center that opened
the Fourth American Writers Congress, Richard Wright told the 3,000
members of the public gathered there:[1]

Bitter and obstinate memory separates 15,000,000 Negroes from this war,
memories of hypocrisy, of glib promises easily given and quickly betrayed,

The League published this song by Harold Rome at the time
of the Fourth American Writers Congress.

of cynical exploitation of hope, of double-dealing, memories which are
impossible to forget or ignore. . . .

In short, Negro memory in the United States is forced to recognize that
the character of the present war in no wise differs from the previous world
war. Moreover, there is ample evidence at hand that the current war is
nakedly and inescapably an imperialist war, directed against the Negro
people and working people and colonial people everywhere in this world.

From the Negro point of view, what is this evidence? I cite the following:
On October 9 of last year, the White House secretary, one Stephen T. Early,
after a conference between Roosevelt and the so-called Negro leadership,
announced to the public the following statement:

"It is the policy of the War Department that services of the Negroes will
be utilized on a fair and equitable basis."

Immediately following this lip-service to democracy, following this
sweeping idealistic falsehood, the White House secretary went on to announce the *true* policy:

"The policy of the War Department is not to intermingle colored and white enlisted personnel in the same regimental organizations. This policy has been proven satisfactory over a period of years, and to make changes would produce situations destructive of morale and detrimental to the preparations for national defense."

Parenthetically, I'd like to ask this audience a question: If the United States is really anxious to stop Hitler, does it not seem logical that the morale of the Negro and white troops of the International Brigade, who beat back the Fascists from the gates of Madrid, is a good morale for our troops? I'd like to ask, has there ever fought a more determined army than that wall of men, black and white, who, standing side by side for many months, endured all that Germany and Italy had to hurl at them? Evidently, that is *not* the kind of morale they are planning to instill into the United States Army, which is being created allegedly to fight Fascism and spread the Four Freedoms.

Francis Faragoh, screenwriter, member of the Hollywood Exiled Writers Committee, 1941. Courtesy of Sheila Schwartz.

The White House secretary went on to state the "democratic" policy of the crusade for the Four Freedoms:[2]

"For similar reasons, the War Department does not contemplate assigning colored reserve officers other than those of the Medical Corps and Chaplains to the existing Negro combat units of the regular army."

In view of the above Fascist statement, one must conclude that, insofar as the Negro is concerned, it is an imperialist war, a war which continues and deepens discriminatory tactics against the Negro people, against progressive people, against labor unions, professionals and intellectuals. Such a statement reduces Roosevelt's Four Freedoms to a metaphysical obscenity! . . .

Who can deny that the Anglo-American hatred of Negroes is of the same breed of hate which the Nazis mete out to Jews in Germany? . . .

One of the main purposes of this report on the state of feeling among Negroes is to inform you emphatically that reaction and restrictions are hitting us now, that lynching is on the increase, that a wave of terror impends, not only against us, but against you as well.

A few nights ago, the following words were spoken by Secretary of State Cordell Hull over the radio:

Edward Newhouse, novelist, New York Publicity Committee, 1937. *Saturday Review of Literature* photo, July 31, 1937. Reproduced with the permission of the Western Historical Collections, University Archives, University of Colorado at Boulder Libraries.

Fielding Burke, novelist, critic, member of the National Council, 1935. Courtesy of Southern Historical Collection, Wilson Library, University of North Carolina at Chapel Hill.

"The key to their economic program is contained in one word — conquest. Every territory that they conquer is reduced forthwith to an economic master-and-slave relationship. The economic structure of the enslaved country is forcibly reshaped and systematically subordinated to the economy of the ruling or conquering country. Within the entire tributary area, autarchy or economic self-sufficiency is set up as the central feature of economic policy. At the center of this widespread web of captive nations, the master country wields its vastly enlarged powers. . . ."

The moment I heard those words, I felt and thought that the Secretary of State was describing the policy of the United States toward its single largest minority, the Negro people. Then again I thought that maybe he was describing the policy of the United States toward Mexico, or some other country in Central or South America. I reasoned as follows: The Negro people, 15,000,000 strong, represent a captured nation over which the 48 states wield a vast power, economic, political, social, and otherwise. And, truly, the United States has earned the name of "enemy" in South America. But as I listened, I was soon set aright. I discovered that the Secretary of State was not describing the imperialist policy of the United States, but the imperialist policy of the German High Command! The two policies were so identical that I could not distinguish between them! . . .

The universal demand for peace is the secret weapon of the masses of the common people! It is a weapon which Hitler, Churchill and Roosevelt fear more than any bomb! . . . And that is why the warring nations dare not mention their war aims, save in the most general terms. They are afraid.

When the voice sounds for peace, the Negro people will answer it.[3]

Richard Wright's voice was by no means the only one from black America to command attention at the congress. Langston Hughes, a vice president of the League who was then on the West Coast, wrote this as he signed the call to the gathering that he could not attend, "The League of American Writers has been one of the few cultural organizations to take up the fight for the artistic and economic equality of the Negro artists." At one panel of the congress devoted to radio, the audience heard a selection from a radio series, "Native Sons in the Arts," written by Frank Griffin and Earl Burroughs. So far as anybody knew, this was the first radio series in the country that dealt with the lives of African-American artists.

Herbert Aptheker, historian, teacher in Writers School, on his return from North Vietnam with Tom Hayden and Staughton Lynd in 1966. Courtesy of Herbert Aptheker.

A leading white historian of black America, Herbert Aptheker, reminded the assembled writers of the more than 250 slave revolts and conspiracies that were part of the African-American tradition. Now, he said, there was a link between the rebellious spirit of slaves and the assertive literature being produced by the descendants of slaves.

As they listened, writers held in their hands the latest issue of *The Clipper*, published by the League's Hollywood chapter specially for distribution at the congress. In it Carey McWilliams wrote: "The racism of the Nazis is intolerable to us; yet today, in Mississippi, it is a felony to advocate racial equality.... We are menaced by Fascism from within as well as from without. If we forget this fact, we forget it at our peril."

Aware of the "menace within," Ralph Ellison, a black League member, had worked diligently to help prepare the congress. His special contribution had been developing plans for a national League magazine to parallel *The Clipper*. Another African-American, Eugene Holmes, also expressed concern at the increasing attacks on writers. "This is a period in which the areas of expression are being restricted. It is a period in which ... the defense of this freedom is becoming more hazardous."

The grim reality that there were more and more limitations on freedom was Dashiell Hammett's concern at the public meeting. Bitterly he said:

Art Young, cartoonist, speaker at Fourth American Writers Congress, 1941. From *Direction* magazine, Summer 1941.

Square Players, the Neighborhood Playhouse, and the Provincetown Players) appeared in the same year. The American intellectual suddenly awakened to a belated and ineffectual awareness that war and destruction were sweeping his world away. There was a market for a certain kind of protest."

Living ties to this rebel past were present at the congress in the persons of Henry Glintenkamp and Art Young, both veteran contributors of artwork to the *Masses*, a magazine that had been suppressed by the government following the country's entry into World War I. The much-loved cartoonist Art Young made his own wry contribution to the discussion of illusions that were being spread in the new martial upsurge. He told this story:

> A little boy was lying on the floor, surrounded by papers, and he was drawing pictures. His mother said, "Willie what are you drawing now?" "I'm drawing a picture of God," Willie replied. "Oh, Willie," his mother said, "you mustn't do that. No one knows what God looks like." "Well mother," Willie replied, "they will know when I get through with this."

Other light moments brought variety to some of the panel discussions, which included the theater, screenwriting, poetry, criticism, labor journalism, fiction, radio writing, young writers, juvenile writing, and Latin America. The overall mood, however, was earnestness and anger. A bad war was raging in Europe, and artists and writers wanted to do all they could to keep this country out of it. They also wanted to give aid to those who were seeking to enlarge life for any group of citizens. Donald Ogden Stewart, Richard Wright, Ralph Ellison, Viola Brothers Shore, John Howard Lawson, and others, during a break in the congress proceedings, joined strikers on a Newspaper Guild picket line. Ruth McKenney, author of *My Sister Eileen,* at one meeting proposed forming a women's committee to defend a woman in Oklahoma who faced a prison term because she had sold literature opposing the drive toward war. Speaking unscheduled from the balcony in one session, a Canadian writer told of Fascist-like repression going on in his part of the British Empire, and he set off a spontaneous collection to finance publishing the talks being made at the congress.

Fiction writers at their panel began work on a plan for cooperation with the education committee of the Congress of Industrial Organizations (CIO), and writers for the labor press had a panel of their own. Fred Myers, editor of the *Guild Reporter*, said that labor journalism was opening up for writers, adding, "I am completely qualified to tell you what the standards of the labor press should be because I received most of my journalistic training from William Randolph Hearst. The rule is simple. I just do what I never did be-

Ralph Ellison, novelist, planner in 1941 of a League magazine. National Archives photo.

fore." Colleagues of his were responsible for an award for excellence given by the League to the *NMU Pilot*, the organ of the National Maritime Union. As the panel's discussion proceeded, the Federated Press announced it had taken a poll of U.S. labor editors and found that 60 percent of them opposed any U.S. involvement in the war in Europe. The League was in good company.

Some panels were organized by the United American Artists and the American Artists Congress, CIO. Speaking for the artists, Rockwell Kent said:

> Some of us are old enough to remember what happened in the last war, to remember those betrayals and remember what suckers were made of so many good people in America. There was a literature about the war that a certain distinguished American writer has repudiated.[4] Writers had no right to tell the truth about that, because if they tell the truth about that, how in God's name when the next war comes can we again make suckers of the people?

Artists also made themselves felt in other ways during the proceedings. They mounted an art exhibit and held an auction of their works. The poets, songwriters, and folksingers' panel drew an especially animated audience. With the veteran poet Alfred Kreymborg in the chair,

Rockwell Kent, artist, memoirist, speaker at Fourth American Writers Congress. From *Direction* magazine, February 1941.

Alfred Kreymborg, poet, playwright, member of the National Council, 1941. League of American Writers photo.

Isidor Schneider and Joy Davidman spoke for poets by reading verses by Meridel Le Sueur and "America's Young Black Joe," by Langston Hughes. Earl Robinson, Elie Siegmeister, Marc Blitzstein, Leadbelly, Burl Ives, Tony Kraber, and the Almanacs performed, and the audience often joined the singing.

The congress was not simply a single-focus rally against war, although it was vehemently anti-war. In the theater panel, John Howard Lawson presented a substantial paper on the relation of the theater to society.[5] Lem Ward, director of *Processional* and *One-Third of a Nation*, offered data on and analysis of the current theater, together with a backward glance at the marvelous WPA Federal Theater, which had been killed by Congress June 30, 1939. The panel also heard this special letter to the congress from the Red Dust Players of Oklahoma:

I wish every one of you could have been with us on our last Tuesday's booking for the Oklahoma Tenant Farmers Union up in Creek County. It's sharecropper's part of the state, rolling hills covered with red sand. What hasn't been bled out by the oil wells has been blown away by the wind. We were off the highway, some ten miles from the nearest town, in a little Negro church, playing by light of five oil lanterns that the audience had brought with them. Our audience came from 20 miles away in all directions. Some of them we had to fetch in ourselves. The admission was ten cents, children under six, free — but we felt we should have paid them for the pleasure of performing. One old man toted a sack of flour into town and sold it to raise the admission for himself and kids, and one family mortgaged their old sow. One woman said she would've stayed up all night seeing it over and over, and one woman said it's been ten years — maybe longer — she'd forgot just when — since she's "clupped her hands together" last. But they clupped and they laughed way down deep, Negro and white together, and scraped their feet on the floor, and said yes, sir, that's the truth: that's the way it is, and we sang "We Shall Not Be Moved.". . . And it was Bill Titus's *Tillie the Toiler* — Bill Titus buried in Spain, and Black and White hands together in a church in Oklahoma, and it's the same fight.

Edgar Snow, journalist, FBI target. *Saturday Review of Literature* photo, January 1, 1938. Reproduced with the permission of the Western Historical Collections, University Archives, University of Colorado at Boulder Libraries.

In the screenwriters panel, and also in others, there was a tendency to present collective performances or papers. People working together had prepared this complex event, but all was not harmony outside the congress. The newspaper *PM,* which did not share the League's anti-war position, did say that "hordes swarmed the ballroom floor" for the meetings at the Commodore; but the press was generally hostile when it took any notice of the gathering. It had been hostile in advance. The *New York World-Telegram* ran a pre-congress attack by one of its columnists, to which Donald Ogden Stewart replied. He said the article was simply "name-calling" and "Red baiting" and did not deal with the purpose of the congress, which was "to discuss how best to resist the drive toward war and reaction."

Not only the press but also the government had made difficulties. Two writers from Cuba — the poet and scholar Juan Marinello and the poet Nicolas Guillén, who was black — were denied visas by the State Department. In addition, Edgar Snow disappointed us. After his recent return from witnessing exciting events in China, we had sent him a copy of the call to the congress, invited him to speak at the public meeting, and asked him — as we had asked all the other speakers — to send the text of his talk early so we could mimeograph it for the press. Snow agreed to speak but was slow to send in his text; when we finally saw his remarks, we were alarmed. He called for aid to Britain — in other words, for increased involvement in the war. He was speaking against the meaning of the call.

Richard Wright and I, and another person, whose identity I forget, went to see Snow at the Chelsea Hotel where he was staying. Dick and I explained that he could not use the public meeting of the congress for opposing the League's policy. The meeting at which he had been invited to speak was a rally in support of the League's position, not a forum for a debate on what that position should be.

Snow was furious. He refused to prepare a different speech, but he did come to the public session. He sat quietly in the rear of the hall and let the meeting take its course — a course that the audience approved with vigorous applause.

In this incident, we did not see ourselves as censors, any more than editors regard themselves as censors when they reject for an anthology an article that runs counter to the announced purpose of that book. We were against censorship.

In many ways the mood of the 1941 congress was confrontational and reminiscent of the militancy of the John Reed clubs and the First American Writers Congress. For one thing, writers and artists joined together in the Fourth Congress as they had done in the John Reed clubs. This coalition of creators from different fields was vehemently anti-Establishment, more so than it had been at the Third Congress, although I noted in my 1941 report that "at the last Congress, the great majority of writers present . . . [could] see, step by step, the preparations being made by the great empires of the world to engage in military struggle with each other if necessary, but preferably with the Soviet Union — of whose peaceful policy the League had taken friendly notice on more than one occasion." Those attending the congress believed that the United States was gearing up to enter a war that gave no promise of benefits to the men who would do the fighting or to the civilians who would finance it.[6] And they objected to the fact that the U.S. government — as war preparations increased — gave less and less support to the arts. The House of Representatives, with Roosevelt's acquiescence, had killed the Federal Theater Project and was weakening the Writers Project.

One visible symbol of the mood of the Fourth Writers Congress was the presence among the speakers of Mike Gold, the Communist writer who had been little involved in League affairs after the First Congress. Mike had not found the right voice with which to speak prominently at the Second and Third Congresses — the gatherings that had led into the Popular Front phase of League activity. He did, however, make a contribution to the Fourth Congress. The full text of his talk appears in an anthology of Gold's writings that was prepared by the late Michael Folsom, my son.[7]

Mike Gold, novelist, critic, prominent Communist literary figure. Courtesy of International Publishers.

> The Thirties [said Gold] compares favorably with the Civil War decade, the greatest single chapter in the history of American culture. Its importance lies in its mass character. Therefore, no single Emerson or Walt Whitman stands out, though thousands of potential Emersons and Whitmans were formed. They are still young. Many will be drafted into the army. They will not surrender their souls to the army sergeant or to the literary Fuehrers now on the scene. Democracy still has a future in America — as it has all over the struggling world. The present war interrupts the democratic renaissance of the Thirties. But that renaissance and its literature will in turn end the system of war and profit.
>
> Let us persist.

Mike Gold's paper, and the other papers of the congress, were never published together in book form. The magazine for which Ralph Ellison had drawn up a prospectus never appeared. The organization of young writers that had been proposed at the young writers' panel never came to full life. The revival of the Group Theater, called for by the theater Panel, was not to be. Nor was there to be a handbook for labor journalists, which had been projected by the panel on labor journalism, or the Pan-American writers' congress proposed by the Latin American panel.

Two weeks after the end of the League's anti-war congress, Hitler sent his armies eastward against the USSR. Now, with massive Soviet armies fighting Hitler, the nature of the war had completely changed. The League's officers, elected on the final day of the congress, had been instructed to oppose war and to carry out many projects in defense of culture; they now found themselves having to support war as the necessary means of defending culture.[8]

Following the congress but before the Nazi assault on the USSR, the Hollywood chapter of the League held a meeting attended by more than 400 writers and announced a prize contest for a production in dramatic form on the subject of any one of eight resolutions adopted at the congress. In addition, it published in *The Clipper* (July 1941) a report on the congress by Wilma Shore. Her story of the event included this:

> People sat close together on little black chairs and they kept bringing in more black chairs all the time but there were never enough. Those who couldn't find seats sat on the floor or stood in the rear or along the walls, shifting from one foot to the other as the hours passed, but not leaving. That was how it was. . . . Picture all those people sitting side by side, close not only physically but because they all believed in the same things and were there to say them and hear them said. Grand Central is right next door. Far underground the trains are always leaving. . . . They go all over the country. From the Fourth Writers Congress the clear and brave things we heard there will go all over the country too, and people will know that writers are not afraid to speak the truth.

The writers were not afraid, but it was a different truth they had to speak almost as soon as the delegates were back in their homes.

Notes

1. One hundred and ninety-five League members from eleven states attended the congress. In addition, 121 non-member writers were present, plus 65 individuals who signed up as auditors for the entire congress. Five hundred auditors registered for single sessions. Including foreign writers, exiled writers, young writers, and representatives of mass organizations, the total registration for the congress came to 1,055.

2. President Roosevelt, in his message to the U.S. Congress, January 6, 1941, said the Western powers were fighting for four freedoms: "freedom of speech and expression, freedom of religion, freedom from want, and freedom from fear — everywhere in the world."

3. Unless otherwise noted, Richard Wright's speech and all other speeches, documents, and papers quoted in this chapter are in the papers of the Fourth American Writers Congress in the LAW Papers, Bancroft Library, University of California, Berkeley.

4. Kent was referring to Archibald MacLeish. Kent spoke at the public meeting.

5. In December 1945, John Howard Lawson, in accordance with the wish of Theodore Dreiser, spoke at length at Dreiser's funeral, as recorded (p. 478) in Robert Lingeman, *Theodore Dreiser: An American Journey, 1908–1945* (Putnam, 1990):

    > Lawson's talk — or lecture — was a scholarly summation of Dreiser's literary career, relating his works to American society, emphasizing the social consciousness and the desire for equity that ran through all his books. He reminded the mourners that Dreiser's decision to become a member of the Communist Party [as he had done six months earlier] was the logical consequence of his life and work, and warned that fascism was abroad in the land.

6. Writers not present at the Fourth Congress also shared this view. One of them was the Danish novelist Martin Andersen Nexo, who sent this message to the congress:

    > There are two ways of leading and governing a people — only two. Either help them to a steadily increasing production, enable them to work towards steadily improving living conditions. Or start them forging weapons, make them starve, more or less

unwillingly, take the bread out of their mouths and convert it into armament; cover the people with armor and plate, with golden promises of a place in the sun, a Utopian life at the expense of other people, if only they comply in the matter of armament. There are no other ways than to work or to rob others of their work!

7. Michael Folsom, ed., *Mike Gold: A Literary Anthology*, with an introduction by Michael Folsom (International Publishers, 1972), pp. 243–254.

8. For a list of officers elected at the congress, see Appendix B.

18
Good Neighbors

Trujillo [the Dominican dictator] is a son of a bitch, but he is *our* son of a bitch.

— Widely attributed to President Franklin D. Roosevelt (although the Roosevelt Library at Hyde Park can find no source for it)

At the time of the Latin American panel of the Fourth Congress, a few gray-haired writers may have remembered that William Jennings Bryan, when he was a congressman in the late 1890s, made the word *imperialism* part of the vocabulary of ordinary Americans. Bryan argued passionately that the United States should not become one of the world's empires:

> Imperialism finds its inspiration in money, not in duty. There is no limit to the ambition of an imperialist. With money-making as his object, he is willing to declare himself the appointed agency of the Almighty to conquer and hold in subjection any weaker people for the purpose of securing their trade. . . . Compare, if you will, the swaggering, bullying, brutal doctrine of imperialism with the golden rule and the commandment "Thou shalt love thy neighbor as thyself."[1]

Any connection between government policy and the Golden Rule had not been part of President James Monroe's doctrine in 1823, when he declared that Latin America was for the United States and no one else to exploit. In succeeding decades, North American investors very actively took title to railways, mines, plantations, and property of all kinds in neighboring Latin American countries. When demands for special privileges in those countries were not met, U.S. armed forces often took over. The record of military interventions, between 1900 and the early years of the Depression, included one in Guatemala, one in Mexico, and two in Haiti; four each in Nicaragua, the Dominican Republic, and Cuba; six in Panama; and seven in Honduras.

By 1930, in half the Latin American countries, finances were largely directed by North American business or government agencies.[2] At that same time, the journalist Walter Lippmann commented, "We think of ourselves as a kind of great, peaceable Switzerland, whereas we are in fact a great, expanding world power. . . . Our imperialism is more or less unconscious."[3] This notion was certainly in the minds of some in Herbert Hoover's administration when a "good neighbor" policy toward Latin America began to be discussed. And Franklin Roosevelt, in his first inaugural address said: "I would dedicate this nation to the policy of the good neighbor." A few years, later he announced that the United States was "definitely opposed to armed intervention. We have negotiated a Pan-American convention embodying the principle of non-intervention."[4]

This did not mean, however, that the United States now kept hands off the political, economic, and cultural affairs of its southern neighbors. In fact, said historian Irwin F. Gellman, non-intervention was never "an absolute reality — only an illusion that was valuable in popularizing the Good Neighbor policy."[5] And *imperialism* remained a word in the lexicon of many Latin American writers. They had not forgotten that a court still controlled by the United States military in Santo Domingo had sentenced the poet Fabio Fiallo to prison for criticizing U.S. occupation of his country — after occupation ended. Editors and writers were imprisoned in Haiti even after U.S. Marines withdrew in 1934, following a nineteen-year occupation.

Roosevelt had a special interest in Haiti. He had been there in 1920, and boasted that he had written the constitution that the U.S. military managed to impose on that country. North American banks had controlled Haiti's finances ever since World War I. In 1914 a navy gunboat was sent there to carry off $400,000 in gold that was taken from the Haitian National Bank and ended up in the National City Bank in New York. It just happened that the president of both banks was American financier Roger Farnham.

In 1915 United States Marines under Major Smedley Butler invaded Haiti, supposedly to keep Germany from establishing a base there during World War I. "Glorified bill collecting" was what Butler called his job — that is, making sure that Haiti did not renege on its debts to North American financial institutions.

Haitians were, and are, almost entirely of African descent, and the bigotry of the marines soon made itself felt. Their harsh regime brought resistance, and Butler's men, he said, hunted dissenters "like pigs."[6] Criticism of his operation was muted in the U.S. press, but with the coming of the New Deal, President Roosevelt began to feel pressure from the National Association for the Advancement of Colored People to end the occupation of the only black republic in the hemisphere. To negotiate removal of the marines and an agreement about debt payments, Roosevelt sent as minister to Haiti Nelson Armour, who shortly wrote to a friend suggesting that he "chuck a couple of burnt corks into your kit bag and come down to Haiti and go native with the rest of us."[7]

At last, in 1934, the occupation forces departed, but they left behind the dictator Stenio Vincent to continue the worst of the marines' abuses and to add a few of his own. He suppressed the press and jailed editors and writers, including — as all the Latin American participants in the League's Fourth Congress knew — the Haitian poet Jacques Romain.

By now Roosevelt's Good Neighbor policy had been well publicized, and it had wide general support at home. For one thing, it promised benefits to the U.S. taxpayer because military occupation in Latin America had been expensive. Benefits for North American enterprises would supposedly continue, thanks to trade agreements with various dictatorial governments; and although actual financial burdens had by no means been lifted from countries to the south, it was assumed that benefits might eventually trickle down.

Doing good for our southern neighbors was supposed to mean the beginning of a new era of democracy. In 1938 the State Department had created a Cultural Relations Division, which was to set up an exchange program involving lectures, research, and fellowships in the United States for Latin American students and professors. Undersecretary of State Sumner Welles explained, "Other Americans must demonstrate a willingness and a desire to understand and appreciate the ideals and life of this country."[8] Accordingly, the Cultural Relations Division initiated a number of programs designed, as Claude Bowers, ambassador to Chile, put it, to "sell the idea that the United States is now the world's most important intellectual center."[9]

Beyond the elitism of Bowers' remark was the State Department's uneasy knowledge that Germany and Italy had been active among our neighbors. By 1940 the Nazis had already established more than 800 German schools throughout Latin America and had set up an anti-U.S.

propaganda program that was handled by German banks and businesses, German cultural centers, and athletic clubs. In some places German-controlled radio stations broadcast programs in Spanish designed to discredit the United States, as did special movies.[10]

Many in the Roosevelt administration were fearful that if Hitler won in Europe, Germany would proceed to take over areas of enterprise that North American business considered its own. In 1939 Roosevelt had promised that the United States would give Latin American countries support and would ensure their economic welfare. The State Department's concept of economic welfare, however, was completely separate from any notion of political freedom. Vicious dictatorships continued to flourish, and for the most part Latin American writers did not find it easy to speak their minds. So it was not surprising that "Yankee imperialism" and the suppression of dissent in their homelands appeared in writers' responses at the League's Fourth Congress.

Among those who spoke at the Latin American session of the congress was Carlos Carrera Benítez, a student at the University of Puerto Rico. Much of his talk was based on the assumption that the audience knew what had been going on ever since the United States took possession of Puerto Rico during the Spanish-American War. All important government executives and officials in the islands were appointed either by the president of the United States or by the governor of Puerto Rico, who was himself a U.S. appointee. In 1930 the governor had been Theodore Roosevelt, son of President Teddy Roosevelt. What this governor found when he took office startled him somewhat. "American corporations," he wrote, "had gathered into their hands the best tracts of land and made handsome earnings thereby. . . . The small farmer had been forced back into the . . . comparatively barren hills. Poverty was widespread and hunger . . . common. . . . Every city or large town had its slum where the squalor and filth were almost unbelievable. . . . The island was disease-ridden."[11]

Governor Theodore Roosevelt set about trying to make some changes — among them an education program, better housing, and health care for children. Ten years later, President Franklin Roosevelt was persuaded that Puerto Ricans, no less unhappy than ever, could be made less hostile to the United States if they were more integrated into mainland culture. He urged the Puerto Rican commissioner of education to have classes conducted in English only. In effect, Spanish-speaking

Puerto Rico was a possession of the United States and was not really to be considered part of Latin America.

This view of cultural relations led to one episode not widely reported in the U.S. press. An Inter-American Writers Conference was convened in San Juan, Puerto Rico, in April 1941, just before the Fourth American Writers Congress in New York. Invitations to the conference went out in the name of two officials of the University of Puerto Rico, but it was no secret that the affair was directed from Washington. Among the carefully chosen Latin American delegates, there was not one Puerto Rican writer. At a special session, however, the floor was open to any member of the Puerto Rican public who wanted to bring a manuscript for discussion.

Puerto Rican university students, already irritated by the makeup of the conference, sent fellow student Carlos Carrera Benítez to the manuscript session. Benítez read an emotional piece protesting the English-in-the-classroom policy and pointing out the failure of the event's planners to invite any local writer to the conference — meetings that were supposed to "stimulate interest in literary production."

Archibald MacLeish, who attended the conference, was no doubt troubled by the uproar the students caused. Several years later, when he was an assistant secretary of state for Public and Cultural Affairs, he admitted that cultural exchanges were devices used for hidden propaganda purposes.[12]

Equally embarrassed by the student's diatribe was the chair of the manuscript session, Cuban writer Jorge Manach, author of a well-known biography of José Martí. The Puerto Rican press did not need to be reminded that Martí, the hero of Cuban independence, would have approved of Benítez's objections to domination by "the Colossus of the North." When interviewers asked Dr. Manach his opinion, he answered that as a guest at the conference he could not interfere in Puerto Rican political affairs.

The controversial Inter-American Writers Conference was still on young Benítez's mind when he spoke a few weeks later at the League's Fourth Congress. In his talk he brought up another cause for skepticism about the administration's Good Neighbor policy. "The so-called bridge to unite the Americas," he said, "has pillars buried in the indescribable misery of a whole people. Such institutions as the Pan-American Union and the [Office for] Coordination of Commercial and Cultural Relations [between the American republics] are but agencies of imperialist greed."[13]

The coordinator of this office, which President Roosevelt had created in 1940, was Nelson Rockefeller. The word sequence in the project's name — commercial before cultural — frankly indicated the focus of its objectives, and the choice of Rockefeller to head the agency seemed ludicrous to those who remembered what the Rockefeller Standard Oil Company meant to Latin Americans. In Venezuela, for example, writers and intellectuals were terrorized during the almost thirty-year dictatorship of Vicente Gómez, nicknamed "The Catfish," a creature of the oil industry. After his death in 1935, Gómez's hundred children began quarreling over his $100 million estate — his payoff for keeping order in his colonial country. A biography of the dictator, *Gómez, Tyrant of the Andes* (William Morrow, 1936), by North American writer Thomas Rourke, had been banned from sale in Venezuela shortly before the Fourth Congress convened.

According to the official history of the coordinator's work, Rockefeller "had his training in the Chase National Bank's foreign department. . . . His interest in the other American republics arose from visits and through the activities of enterprises in which he was concerned . . . [and] problems connected with the affairs of the Standard Oil Company."[14] The name of the agency he headed was later changed to Office of the Coordinator of Inter-American Affairs — CIAA for short. Although "hemisphere defense" was the primary reason for creating it, the CIAA did for a time seem to encourage two-way traffic on what Benítez called "the bridge to unite the Americas." North American young people, however, turned out to be reluctant to go south as exchange students in Latin American universities, and, on the other hand, writers and intellectuals from the south were often not welcomed in the United States.

Early on, the CIAA tossed overboard any notion of reciprocal benefits through a cultural program. Its "cultural" efforts became openly a means of spreading throughout Latin America a rosy picture of life in the United States. One of its efforts was a glossy magazine, *En Guardia*, produced in Spanish and Portuguese, the first issue of which glorified the United States Navy and emphasized this country's military might and its ability to organize for war.

Other early exports of the CIAA were the American Ballet Caravan, which toured some South American countries, the American Lawn Tennis Team, and the Yale Glee Club. Later the agency tried to keep the

Samuel Putnam, biographer, translator, speaker at Fourth American Writers Congress, 1941. From *New Masses*, June 17, 1941.

Hollywood film industry from distributing in Latin America movies that would show anything unfavorable about life north of the border. (Head of the group that was supposed to produce movies for export to Latin America was John Hay Whitney, who had backed the racist film *Gone With the Wind*.)

Knowing at least the thrust of the good neighbor policy, if not all the details, writers from Latin America came to the Fourth Congress with a two-fold message. First, they brought reminders that their North American hosts should be aware of the administration's cultural charade — glorifying democracy to people whose dictators the United States helped to keep in power. Second, but more important, the Latin Americans also brought desperately hopeful pleas for help in resisting oppression in their native countries. The League had sent invitations to a score or more individual writers and writers' organizations. Fourteen responded with great interest. Some of their communications were signed by a dozen or more members of writers' groups. Papers by representatives of four countries were read at a meeting open to the public on June 8, 1941, which was chaired by League member Samuel Putnam, biographer and translator. Two who sent papers were Peruvian novelists Ciro Alegría and César Falcón.

Falcón, unlike many of his fellow writers who were in prison or in exile, had somehow not yet been obliged to flee Peru. His contribution to the congress, entitled "We Do Not Want to Fight Except for Ourselves," read in part:

> Many North-American intellectuals, traveling through the countries of South America, come to me in Lima, and some of them ask me, as no doubt they ask other representative men of this Republic:
> "Who do you want to see win the war, Hitler or President Roosevelt?"
> "They are all the same," I have replied.
> "What!" exclaimed Mr. Callendar of the *New York Times* in amazement. (He was the most explicit or the most impatient of those who have questions.)

"Do you suppose that a political conversation of this sort could be held in Berlin?"

"Certainly not. The Gestapo would interrupt it."

"Well, then? In the United States anyone who wants to can stand up on the steps of the Capitol and say whatever he pleases against President Roosevelt."

"Perhaps. But I have no intention of saying anything against President Roosevelt on the steps of the Capitol. What you offer me, Mr. Callendar, is this, in short: that I should work twelve hours a day for starvation wages, mortgage the economy of my country, hamper its economic development, enslave my people, and surrender, if necessary, the soil and the blood of my kind, so that you may be able to say what you please about President Roosevelt. I don't care to."

John Gunther, journalist, FBI target. *Saturday Review of Literature* photo, August 28, 1937. Reproduced with the permission of the Western Historical Collections, University Archives, University of Colorado at Boulder Libraries.

"What I propose to you is that you should support the cause of humanity in defense of freedom," he replied with some irritation.

"Prove to me first that, if President Roosevelt wins, we shall be able to speak freely on any street against the presidents of our countries."

He could not prove it. Before talking to me, Mr. Callendar had spoken to certain South American politicians who were enthusiastic supporters of the cause of British imperialism and of the policies of President Roosevelt.

"Do you not think," I now asked him, "that all those gentlemen are Fascists at bottom and that, whoever wins, Hitler or President Roosevelt, if they have the power they will use it against those who mean to speak ill of them?"

Mr. Callendar agreed. How could he deny it, when he knows as well as I that, for the North American imperialists and their customers, the struggle against Fascism consists in making democracy fascist?

Mr. John Gunther spoke to me with more imagination.

"We must recognize the experience of Norway, Belgium, and France. If he [Hitler] succeeds in conquering England and destroying the British fleet, he will immediately undertake the invasion of the American continent."

I have lived through the Spanish war, I have seen eight months of war in France, and the little that I learned from those two experiences prevented me from being impressed by Mr. Gunther's eloquence.

"What would you do if German troops were to land in Iquitos?" Mr. Gunther asked me at last, lending an alarming conclusion to our conversation.

"Nothing," I replied calmly.

"Who would defend your country then?"

"The mosquitoes."

I saw in Mr. Gunther's eyes that he understood humor better than our geographical realities. Nevertheless, it is easy to imagine the fate of a Panzer Division in the Amazon jungle. . . .

No, this is not the greatest danger. The close, the immediate danger is much nearer, very much nearer. We hate Fascism in all its forms; we are not fighting merely against Hitler and Mussolini, like Mr. Churchill, but also against the savage regime they represent. Can we free ourselves from that regime merely by fighting against a hypothetical invasion of America by Hitler? . . .

I am writing from a country where perhaps over 50 percent of the population, poor Indians consumed by the most abject ignorance, do not know who Hitler is, or Churchill, or Mr. Roosevelt, or what each of them wants. What we want — our yearning, we men who know — is to work and fight for this people, for all our own people; to serve them, defend them, help them to form and embody themselves, to obtain for them a sure bit of bread, clean work, a decent house, a school, and a free life. How can we do this if we enlist as companions-in-arms with either of the warring imperialisms? No. We can do this only by the labor of peaceful creation. . . .

For this we need the fraternal aid of the other peoples of America, and in the first place that of the North Americans. . . .

You, the free writers of the great North American people . . . must be the voice of the continental call for union of all our intellectual and popular forces.[15]

More an activist than Falcón, his compatriot Ciro Alegría had recently come to the United States from exile in Chile to receive first prize in Farrar and Rinehart's contest for the year's best Latin American novel. Alegría's *Broad and Alien Is the World,* based on his knowledge of Peru's Indian people, was a rambling, compassionate story of life in a village high in the Andes. Its mixture of folk characters, fanciful episodes, and very real problems made it what Carleton Beals, an authority on Latin America, called the best and most poignant picture of life in Peru.[16]

In his paper for the congress, Alegría gave background for his novel — and for his own activities that had resulted in his exile:

Many American writers join us today in the defense of culture, and I believe that it is necessary, first, to consider what culture we defend. . . . Of course, some . . . countries [south of the Rio Grande] are making a praiseworthy effort . . . but they are so few that the fingers of one hand are more than enough to count them. In the others — and they come to twenty-odd — the people are abandoned to an ignorance that is synonymous with chaos. With the Indian tradition dead or half-strangled, and lacking the opportunity to assimilate modern knowledge, people grow up without any definite spiritual character.... Culture is like a lofty and distant tower enclosed in a triple wall of force, economic special interests, and social prejudice.

It begins with denying the people schooling, and consequently they are denied books. And it is thus tragically ironic to refer to the high schools, the universities, and the centers . . . of thought and of art. The man who tills the fields . . . traverses the rivers in his canoe, . . . herds the flocks . . . digs in the earth for ore . . . works at the machine, this man, who constitutes the majority . . . has no culture, and it is no exaggeration to say that he scarcely knows the meaning of the word. . . .

Enrique Gil Gilbert, Ecuadorean novelist, contributor to Fourth American Writers Congress. From *New Masses*, June 17, 1941.

In my own country, in Peru, there are more than seven million inhabitants, of whom six million are illiterate. The colonialists destroyed the Inca culture by plundering the land, by an inquisitional Catholicism, and with a language that still has not been assimilated. It was to be expected that the Republic would take cognizance of the situation and consider what the fate of the people was to be. . . . The Republic was simply the continuation of the Colony through a government of the same class. Not one of the republican regimes that Peru has had . . . has ever made a consistent and effective effort in behalf of the people. Ignorance is essential to exploitation. Thus it is that the number of schools is infamously small, and that for seven million inhabitants there are only four public libraries of any importance, two of which are in Lima. How, then, can one speak of culture? . . . The Peruvian people travail in surroundings in which the roads of culture are obstinately barred to them. . . . Despite everything, if you take the pulse of their spirit, you feel that it is deep and powerful and that there throbs in it the restive yearning for knowledge and for abundance. I have cast my nets in the deepest reaches of my people and I have brought up books which, in the midst of their pain, are a hopeful affirmation.[17]

Much the same message came from Enrique Gil Gilbert, one of a group of Ecuadorean writers who called themselves "Guayaquil Proletarians." Their stories, often in blunt prose, gave realistic, vigorous pictures of ordinary people troubled by poverty and injustice. In his speech Gilbert called on writers to "love peace . . . work for justice . . . and not separate these . . . from . . . liberty. . . . So long as there is a man economically enslaved . . . culture is not possible." He went on to take gently to task fellow writers who, he said, "employed alien thought and language . . . because the land and the wealth were also alienated."[18]

Another book that had been submitted to the judges in the Latin American novel contest was *Mamita Yunai* by Carlos Luis Fallas.[19] Like the Ecuadorean "Proletarians," Fallas wrote in the language of the people who worked on the banana plantations of the United Fruit Company in Costa Rica. (*Yunai* approximates their short-cut pronunciation of the company's name, and *Mamita* — "little mother" — is their bitter word for its harsh rule.) Fallas himself did not participate in the Fourth Congress, but a colleague, Carmen Lyra, sent a letter comparing his novel to *The Grapes of Wrath* and protesting the "Yankee imperialism [that] devotes itself to the conquest of Latin America on the pretext of liberating [us] from Nazism."[20]

A brief, more hopeful message came from Cecilio Carneiro, a Brazilian who had won third prize in a recent *Red Book Magazine*'s short story contest. A writer, he said, should educate people not for war but for resistance to war. "Such a [writer] will not listen to the beguiling voice of false leaders . . . and will fulfill a political mission of tremendous importance, without having been a politician."

That was no easy task in his country, where the dictator Gertulio Vargas suppressed newspapers, jailed editors, sent birthday greetings to Hitler and Mussolini, and claimed he had created a "super democracy." "By abolishing all parties," Vargas said, "I have made it possible for all citizens to come to me."[21] One of his victims was Monteiro Lobato, who spent time in jail for his muckraking book, *The Petroleum Scandal.*

Speaking from the floor, at the meeting where Carneiro's piece was read, North American journalist and League member Isobel Walker Soule gave a colorful but chilling account of her recent visit to Brazil. Not only was the local press censored, she said, but also the press reports of foreign correspondents. The first thing fellow journalists told her was "never to sit near a wall covered with drapery or to eat twice in the same restaurant." In an interview with a Brazilian woman, Soule asked about the fate of 700 people, including a priest, who had recently been arrested. "All my friends are in jail," was the answer. In one of the few bookstores still open in Rio de Janeiro, Soule was astonished to find just two titles by North American writers — *Diamond Lil* by Mae West and *Jews Without Money* by Mike Gold. When asked how many copies of Gold's novel he had sold, the bookstore owner answered that this was the only one he had ever had. A North American woman had brought it in and exchanged it for a mystery story.

Like their Brazilian colleague, two Cuban writers sent messages to the Fourth Congress. For several years before the Fourth Congress, strong men in Cuba had taxed the patience of the Roosevelt administration. After a period of reform, in which peasants revolted and occupied some of the big estates, a dictatorial government was set up, with the approval of Washington. Four men in Franklin Roosevelt's cabinet either had big sugar plantations in Cuba or were connected with companies that did. So it was understandable that two of Cuba's rebellious intellectuals, the poet Nicolas Guillén and literary critic Juan Marinello, could not get U.S. visas when they wanted to attend the congress.

Marinello had been sentenced to ten years in prison for his opposition to the Machado dictatorship in the early 1930s, but there was such a strong public outcry that he was freed after six months and spent some time in exile in Mexico. Back in Cuba in 1941, he was tolerated by the regime, though not welcomed to the United States by the New Deal.

Guillén, like his friend Langston Hughes, was a black poet immensely popular in Latin America. An outspoken critic of racism and of U.S. domination of his country, he was jailed in the early thirties. Hughes had translated a good deal of Guillén's poetry, some of which was read at another session of the Fourth Congress.

The great Chilean poet, Pablo Neruda, also sent greetings to the congress, because he could not afford to attend. Not long after this, the U.S. coordinator of Inter-American Affairs, which had been providing travel grants for chosen Latin American intellectuals, refused to give one to Neruda. Later, even after he received the Nobel Prize for literature, Neruda was denied a visa for travel to the United States.

Many other messages of support for the aims of the Fourth Congress came from individual writers and groups of writers in Venezuela, Mexico, Argentina, Chile, Bolivia, Uruguay, Haiti, and Panama. All of them expressed in one way or another the thoughts of two writers in Mexico — Margarita Nelkin and Jaime Torres Bodet. Nelkin, a former member of the Spanish parliament, now an exile, said:

On behalf of the women who saw thousands of Spanish children blown to bits by Italo-German planes, I ask you not to forget that if Hitler and Mussolini were able to have their lackey Franco triumph, it was only because of the non-intervention policy [of England, France, and the United States]. . . . You have the imperative of conscience to impede . . . [those who promote war under] the pretext of fighting against German imperialism while helping sustain an imperialism that maintains in slavery millions of people in Africa, Asia, and Latin America.

Pablo Neruda, Nobel Prize, 1971, Chilean poet, diplomat, senator, denied U.S. visa. Library of Congress photo.

Mexican poet Bodet, who would later become minister of education for Mexico and director general of UNESCO, wrote in his letter of support: "Not often has the collaboration of intellectuals in defense of liberty been more necessary than it is now."

When the talking was all over, the Fourth Congress resolved to support and take part in a future congress of writers in Latin America — a congress that would not be held because of the tremendous events occurring in far-off Europe.

Notes

1. William Jennings Bryan, *Bryan on Imperialism* (Arno Press and *The New York Times*, 1970), pp. 8, 65, 89.

2. Howard Zinn, *A People's History of the United States* (Harper and Row, 1980), p. 399.

3. Quoted in Page Smith, *Redeeming the Time* (McGraw-Hill, 1987), p. 169.

4. FDR Address at Chautauqua, New York, August 14, 1936, quoted in *The Annals of America* (*Encyclopaedia Britannica*, 1929–1939), vol. 15, p. 352.

5. Irwin F. Gellman, *Good Neighbor Diplomacy: United States Policies in Latin America, 1933–1945* (The Johns Hopkins University Press, 1979), p. 39.

6. Frances MacLean, "They Didn't Speak Our Language; We Didn't Speak Theirs," *Smithsonian* (January 1993): 49.

7. Gellman, p. 71.

8. Gellman, p. 145.

9. Gellman, p. 145.

10. U.S. Government Printing Office, *History of the Office of the Coordinator of Inter-American Affairs*, 1947.

11. Theodore Roosevelt, *Colonial Policies of the United States*, (Arno Press and *The New York Times*, 1970), p. 108.

12. Frank A. Ninkovich, *The Diplomacy of Ideas: U.S. Foreign Policy, 1938–1950* (Cambridge University Press, 1981), p. 84.

13. Carlos Carrera Benítez, *Words to the Fourth Congress*. The original copies of this and other contributions to the Fourth Writers Congress, Latin American panel, are in LAW Papers, Bancroft Library, University of California, Berkeley. Translations from the Spanish by Larry Lomax are in my possession.

14. *History of the Office of the CIAA*, p. 5.

15. César Falcón, *We Do Not Want to Fight Except for Ourselves*. (See note 13.) Falcón went on to write a novel, *El Buen Vecino* [*The Good Neighbor*] that was highly critical of the dictator Manuel Prado.

16. Alegría had been involved in the radical Aprista revolt in 1932, and was arrested and sentenced to ten years in prison. After being freed in a general amnesty a year later, then detained for a while again, he went into hiding and began to work for the underground newspaper published by opponents of the Peruvian dictator. Finally, with the help of American journalist Carleton Beals, he escaped to Chile. There, in spite of tuberculosis and malnournishment, he published four novels in the next eight years, one of which was the prize-winning *Broad and Alien Is the World*, published by Farrar and Rinehart in English in 1941. He spent the following eight years in the United States, where he taught Latin American literature at Columbia University, then at the University of Puerto Rico. After a few years in Cuba, he returned to Peru in 1957; he died there in 1967, having lost in exile the connection with his people that had made his novels so remarkable.

17. Ciro Alegría, *Culture and the People in Latin America*. (See note 13.)

18. Enrique Gil Gilbert, *The Position of the Latin American Writer at the Present Time*. (See note 13.) In the years following the 1941 congress, Gilbert wrote less and less and turned more and more to political activism.

19. Carlos Luis Fallas became a worker for United Fruit at the age of sixteen and was imprisoned for participation in strikes. In 1934 he was freed after he took part in a hunger strike in jail. *Mamita Yunai*, based on his experiences, was published in thirteen languages. In 1944 he was elected deputy to the Costa Rican national congress.

20. Carmen Lyra, author of popular stories based mainly on folklore, was forced to leave her native Costa Rica for exile in Mexico, after a military uprising in 1948.

21. Carleton Beals, *Latin America: World in Revolution* (Abelard-Schuman, 1963), p. 96.

19

The Yanks Are Coming

If we see that Germany is winning, we ought to help Russia. And if Russia is winning, we ought to help Germany, and in that way, let them kill as many as possible.

— Senator Harry S. Truman, quoted in the *New York Times*, June 24, 1941

On June 22, 1941, my phone rang shortly after the radio had carried the bitter news that a German army of three million men had launched an attack on the Soviet Union.

"What do we do now?" asked the voice at the other end of the line.

It was Richard Wright calling. Few people were thrown more off balance than he by the abrupt and violent change on the world scene. Only sixteen days before, interpreting the mood of black Americans, he had passionately opposed the war for which the U.S. government was preparing.

I don't recall how I responded to Dick's disturbed inquiry. I was taken as much by surprise as he was. All the activity of the League for the preceding year — and during the Fourth Congress — had been directed toward trying to keep the United States out of a war that seemed to us a struggle between rival empires, at the expense of the people on both sides. Now the country that we believed had most consistently sought peace had been forced into the martial equation. Willy-nilly, the British Empire found itself allied with the socialist country that it had earlier refused to join in collective security arrangements. Britain could no longer say in effect to Germany, referring to the USSR, "Let's you and him fight." They were fighting, and we could no longer regard the war as a tawdry and terrible contest for power between two sets of pirates. The war was even more terrible than it had been, and the pirates were still in it, but on one side they no longer were in sole charge. The addition in the war of the massive anti-Fascist Soviet population made a tremendous difference.[1] It resulted in the rebirth of attitudes of the Popular Front period. Once again, there was a clear common goal, in pursuit of which most men and women — across class lines — were willing to join in common action.

After a brief period of feeling stunned by the new alignment, the council began to figure out ways in which the League could be of service. The League again had a cause as vital as the defense of Spain, and our experience equipped us to move effectively — or did it?

We were overlooking the power of the anti-League — the anti-Communist — forces in the government, the press, and the literary world. These had gained momentum as the country prepared for war, using anti-Fascist rhetoric, often to hide special agendas that were well this side of nobility.

Not all the League's officers were on hand to help develop plans in the new situation. Vice president Erskine Caldwell, for one, was far away. At the time of the Fourth Congress, he was in China, en route to the Soviet Union to see what was going on there. He reached Moscow just before the Nazi attack, and we were soon hearing his radio reports about events on the eastern front. As we gathered information from Caldwell and many other sources, the League began to press for action on the very quiet western front. On September 15, we released the names of 500 writers who were "enthusiastically behind President Roosevelt for the immediate opening of a second front."

I felt useful as I oversaw the busy work of the League. In October I wrote to my parents saying, "None of your children could be more pleased with life than I am, in spite of the terrible times we face and are entering."

Six weeks later, the terrible times came closer to home with the Japanese attack on Pearl Harbor. Very soon thereafter, a variety of government offices, some newly created, began to ask all writers' organizations, including the League, for help.

Appeals came from the Treasury Department, the new Office of War Information, and at first from the Writers War Board, which had been established with Rex Stout at its head. (Stout had been a League member but was now very hostile to us.) Detailed information about these requests for help — from the government and from others — went out to the League members, along with a questionnaire to find out exactly what kind of writing each member would volunteer to do.

Dashiell Hammett, detective story writer, screenwriter, president of the League, 1941, blacklisted, imprisoned. From *Shadow Man: The Life of Dashiell Hammett*, by Richard Layman (Harcourt Brace Jovanovich).

In a few months, we developed an idea for putting the League's capacity for work into full action. We had seen the value of our stimulating congresses — to Spain, to the People's Popular Front, to the Writers Projects, and to many civil liberties' causes. We decided that a Writers Win-the-War Congress, to be held on the first anniversary of Pearl Harbor, could make a significant contribution to the Allied cause. The congress, we thought, should be broader than the League. With this in mind, some of us and a number of non-League members drew up a call to the congress.[2] To help finance the project, I asked Dashiell Hammett for a contribution. He had enlisted in the army, although he was forty-eight years old, and the night before his induction he invited me to a bar in Greenwich Village to discuss my request. "How in the world did you pass the physical exam?" I asked him. I knew he had earlier suffered from tuberculosis.

"I have had so many X-rays of my chest that I know how to stand in front of the camera so that the scars in my lungs are hidden," Dash said. I wondered. As he handed me a check for $1,000 to help get the congress started, I halfway suspected that some more of his money may have helped an X-ray technician avoid seeing his TB lesions. Be that as it may, Dash was eager to be in the armed forces, and he told Lillian Hellman that the day he was inducted was the happiest day in his life.

To develop plans for the congress, the initiating group gathered in the new and larger League headquarters at 13 Astor Place. Only writers committed to the congress were invited, but one who had not expressed approval of the idea appeared and was admitted. Apparently, he gave his friend Rex Stout a report about the proceedings and the people involved. The next day I got a very imperious call from Stout, demanding that the proposed congress be called off. Stout didn't bother with reasons; he relied on bluster and on the fact that he was now a government official. Soon after he hung up, telegrams withdrawing support for the congress began to flood the League office. Letters followed. One

telegram was from Howard Fast, a militant League member. If Fast could be persuaded to oppose the congress he had just
supported, other League members would
certainly follow his lead. It was clear that
detective-story writer Rex Stout, who held
a high government post, could prevent the
congress that was being helped by detective-story writer Dashiell Hammett, a
lowly private in the United States Army.[3]

Rex Stout, detective story writer;
FBI target. *Saturday Review of Literature* photo, September 18, 1937.
Reproduced with the permission
of the Western Historical Collections, University Archives, University of Colorado at Boulder
Libraries.

We abandoned the congress, at a loss
to the League of Hammett's money and
another $2,500 already invested. Now the
League was financially crippled. The Writers War Board was organizing with ample
funds and all the help it wanted. A few
League members were able to find work
with the board, the Voice of America, or other government agencies, but
there was no place in the government's program for many others no less
competent, and apparently no place for the League.

Donald Ogden Stewart, former president of the League, who had
privately moved toward a pro-Roosevelt position at the time of the
German-Soviet pact, was asked by the Office of War Information (OWI)
to write a morale-building radio script. In his autobiography, *By a Stroke
of Luck*, Stewart tells what happened:

> I chose as my subject an actual happening in a small Ohio town where, in a
> truly joint effort, each person contributed labor according to his or her
> ability: For the first few weeks, the war effort became democratic in the
> sense in which I hoped all of America might some day become, that is, of
> people working together in equality and for each other instead of competing
> in a rat race for financial security and status. I wanted to call my script "This
> is the Real America." When I had finished it was apparently accepted with
> enthusiasm by the Office of War Information which was at that time headed
> by Archibald MacLeish. I remember thinking proudly to myself, while
> flying over the farmhouses and towns of Kansas, "You down there are going
> to be listening to this program in a couple of weeks." I eagerly awaited the
> day of the broadcast. A Program from Washington was announced in the
> papers -- but it was not my sketch. I called Earl Robinson there from
> Hollywood, he seemed a bit embarrassed, but assured me that it had
> probably been postponed. I waited three more weeks, then flew to New

Orson Welles, actor, director, producer, speaker at Exiled Writers Committee Dinner in Hollywood, 1941. National Archives photo.

York at my own expense to see what I could find out. I could find out nothing, except that my contribution would definitely not be broadcast. My last desperate call was to old friend Archie MacLeish in Washington. His irritated response to my appeal for information was "Don, there's a war on," and he hung up.[4]

Malcolm Cowley, who had left the League in protest at its policy following the pact, did get to Washington, summoned by MacLeish. Cowley had been very public in his opposition to the League's stand on the pact, but this did not give him immunity. The Dies committee, among the congressional forces that had been gearing up for war, would not tolerate a former radical on the government payroll. Cowley had to return to private life. Benjamin Appel, one of the most active League members, first went to work not as a writer but in a factory that manufactured airplanes. Only later did Appel find government work in his profession. He became speechwriter for Paul McNutt, governor of the Philippines, after the U.S. Army drove out the Japanese.

The League's role in the war to defeat fascism was clearly not going to be very large. We continued efforts to be useful, but without much success. We held some meetings, and the Writers Schools in New York and Hollywood continued. Many of the younger men in the League were in the armed services, where a few of them functioned as writers, but the League as an organization did not find any activity that was welcomed by those running the war.

I wrote to Dashiell Hammett, who was stationed on the bleak Aleutian Islands, far from where he could render any significant military service — and far from any large body of soldiers he might infect with his ideas. I told Dash I felt useless. I thought I should resign and go to some work that would make a greater contribution to the war effort.

In December 1942, I did resign. Edwin Berry Burgum, literary critic and professor at New York University, became executive secretary, serving just long enough to close up the affairs of the national office in January 1943.[5]

The Hollywood chapter, not seeming to be such a threat to Rex Stout's control over the affairs of writers, continued to run its school. It held forums and conferences, and its members merged into the Hollywood Writers Mobilization. In 1943 League members were prominent at a congress held on the campus of the University of California in Los Angeles. In the end, Hollywood writers, like all others, had to support the war through the Writers War Board and other government agencies. And as the League left the scene, the People's Educational Center in Hollywood carried on classes of the kind the League had been running.

Arch Oboler, radio scriptwriter, speaker at the Third American Writers Congress, 1939. From *Direction* magazine, January 1941.

After my resignation, I went to work for the National Council of American Soviet Friendship, which was headed by Corliss Lamont. The Friendship Council, I felt, was doing a great deal to improve understanding between the United States and the USSR. For a year there, I did many of the things I had learned to do at the League. For example, I helped to organize public meetings, one of which was a protest against the British and U.S. policy of delaying forcing the Nazis to fight on two fronts. In late 1943, artists from various crafts, including writing, joined in the Artists Front to Win the War and held in Carnegie Hall a rally to demand that Britain and the United States open a second

Ruth McKenney, novelist, humorist, member of the National Council, 1941. From *New Masses*.

front in western Europe. A key speaker at this gathering was Charlie Chaplin, who pressed the two governments for action. As he spoke, Chaplin, who had spent a lifetime before audiences, was nervous. I, with other organizers of the meeting, was seated behind him on the stage, and I could see his hands, held behind his back. The fingers nervously clasped each other and twined and intertwined as he spoke. It was not easy for him to tell the governments of two great powers that they should get off their duffs and fight, but he did tell them just that — and he paid for such independence. He had to spend most of his post-war years in exile. He never recanted.

As the time approached when I would be drafted, I considered what had happened to others who had been active in organizations that the attorney general and the Dies committee had labeled subversive. With rare exceptions these men — all devoted anti-Fascists — were not allowed to have any real function in the war effort or to go overseas where the war was being fought. Richard Wright, for example, had tried and failed to get commissioned as an officer.

I decided not to volunteer to serve in the army because I thought my work at the National Council of American Soviet Friendship was more important than anything I would be allowed to do in the military. And now I felt sure that if I were drafted, I would be limited to some meaningless desk job in the States. I could, however, be useful if I could get into the Mountain Troops. I had been a mountaineer in Colorado and could ski; in addition, I had friends who knew I had these skills and would recommend me. They arranged that when my draft number came up, I would be referred to the troops being trained to fight in mountainous terrain and in winter. But before that happened, I tore a ligament in one of my legs. I could not possibly pass the rigorous physical exam that would be required for that special branch of the service.

I had heard, however, that if you could crawl into the examination room of the National Maritime Service, you could get into the Merchant Marine. I hobbled in, concealing my injury as best I could, passed the physical, and was in a service that would allow me to go overseas. Before long, I was on a ship dodging Nazi submarines and helping to deliver munitions through Iran to the Soviet army. I felt useful and I enjoyed the work.

In New York, at a meeting I believe was held in February that I could not attend, the League council had voted the League out of existence. Only Struthers Burt and Benjamin Appel opposed the dissolution. They thought the League could still be useful, and, from a distance of fifty years, I think they were right. The country then — and ever since — I believe, would have had a stronger literature and more democratic practices if citizen-writers had had something like the League through which to work.

Notes

1. Soon after the Nazi attack on the USSR, American writers, responding to the appeal of Alexander Fadayev, president of the Union of Soviet Writers, sent to Moscow statements supporting the struggle of the Soviet Union against the invaders. For a list of signers, see Appendix F.

2. The text of the call and its signers appear in Appendix J.

3. *People's Daily World*, August 24, 1989, published the following letter of mine about Rex Stout:

> In *World Magazine* (June 15) Kate Abel includes some misinformation about Rex Stout in "Mysteries with a Political Punch."
>
> Well before World War II Stout resigned from the anti-fascist League of American Writers. When the United States joined the Soviet Union in the war against fascism, Rex Stout took the lead in stopping the organization of a Win-the-War Congress that members of the League of American Writers and other authors tried to launch. Soon after that Stout became head of the government's Writers' War Board, which persistently discriminated against writers it regarded as Communists. This Board must be what Abel confuses with the Anti-Fascist Writers' League.
>
> In 1964, before going on a research trip to the Soviet Union, I consulted Rex Stout, who was then president of the Author's League of America. I arranged with him to negotiate on behalf of the League with the Union of Soviet Writers on the subject of royalties, which at that time Soviet publishers did not feel obligated to pay to American authors. In the Soviet Union I obtained a letter from the secretary of the Union of Soviet Writers which spoke favorably of a proposal I made that would have solved the royalties problem to the satisfaction of both the Soviet Union and American writers. When I returned with this letter, Stout refused to let me present it at [an Author's] League membership meeting which he chaired. He also told me that the State Department did not favor the proposal. In other words, Stout, in 1964, carried out State Department policy among writers. In this instance the policy was to block steps that would have been beneficial to American writers and to American-Soviet relations. The State Department — and Stout — preferred to maintain a situation which made many U.S. writers understandably irritated with the Soviet Union. No thanks to Stout or to the State Department, the Soviet Union joined the International Copyright Convention in 1973, thus putting the royalties question to rest. Rex Stout was a strong anti-Communist in his most influential years. However, I am glad to learn from Abel that, late in life, Stout wrote a book attacking J. Edgar Hoover and the FBI and that he wrote another book that was favorable to the civil rights movement.

4. Donald Ogden Stewart, *By a Stroke of Luck* (Paddington Press, Ltd., 1975), pp. 260–261.

5. Berry Burgum kept the League papers until I returned from my war service, then turned them over to me. I kept them until 1966, when I sold them to the Bancroft Library. I used the proceeds to support work I was doing for the Council on Interracial Books for Children, of which I was a founder and the first chairperson.

Guy Endore, novelist, teacher in Hollywood Writers School. Photo by Don Ornitz. Courtesy of Marcia Goodman.

Moss Hart, playwright, FBI target. *Saturday Review of Literature* photo, May 8, 1937. Reproduced with the permission of the Western Historical Collections, University Archives, University of Colorado at Boulder Libraries.

Dudley Nichols, screenwriter, Hollywood chapter, 1942. Courtesy of Sheila Schwartz.

George S. Kaufman, playwright. *Saturday Review of Literature* photo, May 8, 1937. Reproduced with the permission of the Western Historical Collections, University Archives, University of Colorado at Boulder Libraries.

FEDERAL BUREAU OF INVESTIGATION

Form No. 1
THIS CASE ORIGINATED AT NEW YORK   FILE NO. 100-5377

REPORT MADE AT	DATE WHEN MADE	PERIOD FOR WHICH MADE	REPORT MADE BY
LOS ANGELES	9/9/43	8/14-17/43	███████

TITLE	CHARACTER OF CASE
LEAGUE OF AMERICAN WRITERS	INTERNAL SECURITY - C

SYNOPSIS OF FACTS: The League of American Writers was originated at Kharkov, Russia, in 1930, and in the United States in 1935.

███████████████████████████████████

It claims association and connection with the Office of War Information and other government organizations.

Attention is called to growing influence of the League of American Writers and propaganda films.

- P -

REFERENCE: Report of Special Agent ██████ Los Angeles, 7/17/42.

COPIES OF THIS REPORT
6 - Bureau
3 - New York
1 - DIO, San Diego
1 - G-2, Los Angeles
1 - San Francisco (Inf.)
3 - Los Angeles

30 NOV 18 1943

596

20

The League and American Literature

In literature the distinguishing mark of the age was its pervasive interest in social ideals.

— Malcolm Cowley, . . . *And I Worked at the Writers Trade*

The accent of politics in literature and criticism has been increasingly more pronounced in these last ten years.

— James T. Farrell, "The End of a Literary Decade," *American Mercury*, December 1939

Hurl your song like a bomb!

— Vladimir Mayakovsky

What steps did the League as an organization take on behalf of the professional work of writers? A glance at Millen Brand's unpublished journal reminds me of one kind of effort the League made:[1]

April 7, 1939

Last night I went to a League of American Writers lecture: Auden, MacNiece, and Isherwood. . . .

Genevieve Taggard was chairman, with Joy Davidman of the large eyes very much in evidence. There was much speaking from behind the curtain. Miss Taggard introduced MacNiece, MacNiece and Auden looked at each other blankly and made signs to Miss Taggard whereupon Miss Taggard said, "I will now introduce Mr. Auden." Auden wanted to speak first.

The first part of the lecture turned into a curious alternation of Auden and MacNiece talking on poets. Auden started with Rimbaud, MacNiece followed with somebody else, and constantly getting up and down, they talked on Kipling, Rilke, Belloc, Yeats, Wilfred Owen, Lawrence, and finally themselves, including Spender. Then Isherwood read something from a new book on China he and Auden had done. Auden had a fallen comb of pale yellow hair and a neat belly; he seemed most obviously the poet and most obviously in command. MacNiece was dark and read his poetry with a nice fall. He seemed more real and Isherwood seemed most real, with a hard, bitter, and humorous face slit by his mouth which widened and opened at the edges. All of them spoke with very much the English accent.

Christopher Isherwood, British poet, lectured for the League. Library of Congress photo.

Sam Sillen was irritable about the whole thing afterward. A symposium previously of 12 American poets hadn't drawn nearly the crowd of the three Englishmen. He said, "We don't know how to promote each other the way they do." Kenneth Fearing said he was going to form a mutual promotion society with Alfred Hayes.

There was a swell party afterwards with free beer and pretzels.

A year later (March 2, 1940), Millen made this entry in his journal:

Second fiction craft session last night given by the League of American Writers at the Newspaper Guild offices — a reproduction of the session at the Congress [in 1939] but open to the public. I gave the first talk, then Dorothy Brewster talked, then Ruth

W. H. Auden, British poet, teacher in the Writers School, FBI target.

McKenney, Ben Appel, Bill Rollins, Jr., Dorothy Thomas [not a League member], Isidor Schneider and Franz Weiskopf. The place was packed. . . . I forgot my rubbers.

Of one of the League lectures, Rolfe Humphries wrote this to Theodore Roethke:

> Granville Hicks spoke last night at the lecture series the League is running
> and maybe we made some money on him. He certainly draws even if he
> looks like a caricature of the younger Theodore Roosevelt. Lewis Gannett
> was chairman and before the evening was over got awfully Rotarian folksy
> and pranksy.[2]

Such sessions or forums or lectures were a regular feature of League life, designed, as Benjamin Appel said, "to draw the general reading public into discussions of current literature." There was one session on Hemingway's latest book, another on "The Frustrated Renaissance of Poetry," and another on "Pulp Markets and the Living Scene." "Readings from Works in Progress" were a continuing feature. At one session Lillian Barnard Gilkes read from a novel dealing with Arkansas sharecroppers, and Ralph Ellison and Lee Hayes commented. At another session Ben Field read a short story of farm life, and Ella Reeve ("Mother") Bloor opened the discussion. On still another occasion Myra Page read from a novel she was writing about the struggles of Tennessee coal miners. At this session William Blake read from a book dealing with the Bryan-Altgeld-Debs era, and Millen Brand read a passage about life in Harlem. One of the commentators was Ralph Ellison. Richard Wright also read from his work about black domestic workers. At another session Philip Van Doren Stern read from a book he was writing about the abolitionist movement. Genevieve Taggard chaired the meeting and commentators were Herbert Aptheker, Henrietta Buckmaster, and Lawrence Reddick, librarian of the Harlem branch of the New York Public Library.

In addition to these recurring lectures, forums, and readings, the League had numerous craft sessions at its biennial congresses. A few of these included demonstrations of new techniques such as poetic dramas for radio. In a craft panel at the Third Congress, Dashiell Hammett read a paper on "Tempo in Fiction," which created considerable interest but which Diane Johnson, when she was at work on a biography of Hammett, had never seen. I was able to lead her to it in the Bancroft Library in Berkeley, where the League papers are deposited.

The League also helped publicize work by League members that seemed to deserve particular attention. It held receptions for authors, voted at congresses on books the members deemed outstanding, and held dinner discussions with influential opinion makers. At one such dinner, held for Henry Seidel Canby, editor of the *Saturday Review of Literature*, discussion focused on *Marching, Marching*, a novel about West Coast lumber workers by Clara Weatherwax.

In other ways the League tried to increase the circulation of books. Led by Benjamin Appel, we campaigned among publishers for paperback editions, which at the time were popular in Europe but not yet accepted by most publishers in the United States. Modern Age Books did, in the late 1930s, bring out low-priced paperback books. Our Book Distribution Committee, headed by Ruth Lechlitner, poet and book reviewer for the New York *Herald Tribune*, also attempted to supply publishers with ideas for expanding writers' markets.

Clara Weatherwax, novelist, Hollywood Chapter, 1940. *Saturday Review of Literature* photo, July 31, 1937. Reproduced with the permission of the Western Historical Collections, University Archives, University of Colorado at Boulder Libraries.

The League itself acted as both publisher and creator of books for trade publishers. Books about the first three of the League's congresses were brought out by three different publishers.[3] *... and Spain Sings* (The Vanguard Press, 1937) was a League-inspired anthology of Spanish poems. *War Poems of the United Nations* (Dial Press, 1943), an anthology of anti-Fascist poems of World War II, had its origin in the League and was edited by Joy Davidman. The League's own publications were substantial pamphlets: *Writers Take Sides, We Hold These Truths, Harry Bridges, Washington's Cliveden Set, Writers Teach Writing, The Citizen Writer*.

Recurring discussions about starting a League magazine resulted, in Hollywood, in *Black and White*, which became *The Clipper*. In the East, *Direction* was close to the League but was not an official League project. Here I will confess that from the day I entered the League, I questioned the idea of an official magazine. I thought it would be as likely to destabilize the organization as to unify it. Members whose works were not accepted for publication would be annoyed with the League, or so I feared, and arguments over aesthetic theories might have a disruptive effect. The editors might be tempted to promote a common theory and drive away members who disagreed with them, even though they supported basic League aims. Whether I was right was never to be known, because plans for an official publication were dropped in 1941. I had to admit that the status of *The Clipper* as the Hollywood chapter's publication did not seem to weaken the League there.

The League did encourage publications that seemed to expand outlets for writers. Support for the WPA Federal Writers Project engaged the League from the beginning to the end of that very fruitful enterprise, with one exception. On April 11, 1938, the head of the Federal

Wellington Roe, novelist, director of New Hampshire Writers School. From *Direction* magazine, May–June 1939.

Writers Project, Henry Alsberg, came to the League office and asked for our support of a Writers Project magazine he wanted to start. I turned him down because he insisted on having a Trotskyist editor. Such an editor, it seemed to me, would surely be hostile to League members and what they stood for. This was not the only incident in which partisan politics affected the work of the Writers Project. Turmoil was frequent in many parts of the country, but the achievements of the project as a whole were notable, and the League's support of the project nationally was firm. A letter dated June 27, 1937, from Rolfe Humphries to Morton Zabel, an editor of *Poetry: A Magazine of Verse*, suggests one of many ways in which the League acted in support of the project:

> Dear Mr. Zabel:
> The executive committee of the League of American Writers has asked me to write you asking that you join us in protest, and/or act independently in the name of *Poetry*, against the federal policy of retrenchment in the WPA [Works Projects Administration] arts projects.
> In particular, we are concerned with the dismissal of [poet and critic] Alfred Kreymborg, a League member and director of the radio project. As you probably know, Mr. Kreymborg had arranged for many poets of recognized standing either to appear personally before large radio audiences on coast-to-coast hookups, or to permit the reading or dramatization

of their poems before such audiences. The opportunities for poets to communicate with America by air are terribly limited, as you know. . . .

If you can write, or better, wire, Secretary [Harry] Hopkins [WPA administrator] in Washington, as well as Director Alsberg, or if you have, through Chicago liberals, any more immediate access to Secretary [of the Interior Harold] Ickes, something might still be done to save the situation. We do not wish to involve the editors of *Poetry* in unseemly political activities, but this seems to us a matter of urgent mutual concern.[4]

Paul Corey, novelist. From *Direction* magazine, December 1939.

Very truly yours,
Rolfe Humphries

The League also campaigned, in collaboration with the Poetry Society of America and the Writers Local of the Workers Alliance, for the establishment of a Federal Bureau of Fine Arts. One result of this collaboration was a conference in May 1938, designed to increase the momentum of the campaign for federal support of the arts. In this and other ways, the League worked with many organizations to expand the areas in which writers could practice their art. Not least in these efforts was our continuous campaign to get our members to join and support the Authors League of America and its constituent guilds. At the Third Congress a whole session was turned over to the Authors League, so that this economic organization could solicit members from among our much more political body.

The League worked with writers' organizations in other countries, first of all through the International Association of Writers for the Defense of Culture, and our congresses attracted delegates from many countries. The Philippine Writers League had a delegation at the Third Congress, where they heard stirring, anti-imperialist words. I don't know what these writers were doing on the day when the Japanese struck at Pearl Harbor, but not long after that some of them sided with the Japanese. My guess is that they welcomed any ally against the domination of their homeland by the imperialist United States. The Fourth Congress brought writers from Latin America. Josephine Herbst represented the League at the launching of a new literary magazine in Canada, and on many occasions our members represented the League in France, Spain, and Mexico.

What was the effect on American literature of the organized efforts of the League? It is not the function of this book to deal with so complex a question, but a few times over the years I have set down my own prejudices on the subject. I include some of them here in the hope that they will provoke others to do a deeper investigation of the subject.

While the League was bristling with political and social activities of many kinds, writers and artists were engaged in an extraordinary renaissance that had come into being, in part, as a result of the federal arts projects. Theatrical shows appeared all over the country where plays had never been seen before. Twelve million people attended WPA performances every year. Some of these were classics. Others were written by new dramatists for the new audience, and all were enthusiastically defended by the League when they came under attack by right-wingers in Congress, which was the source of funds for the arts projects.

In the summer of 1938, I complained, I now think wrongly, in a report I wrote in the League *Bulletin*. I said that League members had acted as pickets and as politicians, but many of them had not been active literary interpreters of the social values dear to anti-Fascists. That is to say, many members supported the League's aims as citizens but had not done so in their role as writers. I was expecting too neat — and too quick — a match between political experience and literary creation. I was also overlooking what was going on around me. For example, already in 1938, there had been these Broadway productions by League members: Steinbeck's *Of Mice and Men,* Odets's *Golden Boy,* and Blitzstein's *The Cradle Will Rock.* Albert Maltz was at work on his novel *Underground Stream.* Hellman would soon complete her anti-Nazi *Watch on the Rhine.* Steinbeck was at work on *The Grapes of Wrath*.

I don't believe I meant — or the League ever said — that good citizenship is a prerequisite to good writing. Good books have come from bad citizens. I do think it is fair to say that the League tried to bring about a fruitful union of good citizenship and literary excellence. Will those who like to point out that the League did not wholly succeed, please list the high-minded social endeavors that have achieved perfection?

The desire for fundamental social change is an aquifer from which writers have received life-giving sustenance. It matters very little whether slow-moving underground water surfaces in a nearby spring or is tapped from a distant source across some political frontier. It is water in either case, and it sustains.

Or put it another way: For a few years a few hundred writers moved toward a magnetic field, call it morality or humanity, or call it the province of those who do the work of the world. Whatever its name, the magnetism was attended by motion among the makers of novels and poems, films and plays, and essays. These men and women in their new alignment also discovered what many had not realized before — that they were citizens and that citizens have duties and also opportunities. One of the duties is to take part in political life. One opportunity is to share the expansion of the general enjoyment of rights that all citizens should have.

As writers had these new experiences, they grew. It would be unrealistic to expect that they would all keep on growing when the popular upsurge exerted less and less of a push, which happened, beginning in the early 1940s. But for most of a decade before that, the League was a not-inconsiderable part of a generous-spirited movement; to ignore this is to accept a limiting vision of the dynamics that operate in our culture. It is to avoid the truth. It is to back away from understanding why an outburst of public art concerned with great issues subsided into an art we still have with us — a private, inward art that is in no way a threat to those who shape our lives by virtue of the control they exercise through ownership and violence and mythmaking.

Critics have dwelt heavily on the assertion that some — or much — of the anti-Fascist propaganda writing done by League members was of poor literary quality. There was indeed some bad anti-Fascist literature. For example, Upton Sinclair's *No Pasaran,* a novel designed to rouse support for the republican government of Spain, is not a great American novel. Nevertheless, it did not give aid and comfort to the social forces that would destroy all literature. Far from it. Perhaps we would be wise to view journalistic efforts like Sinclair's with some generosity of spirit. Would it have been better for Sinclair to remain silent than to do what he could, using words that might help the Spanish people? Literature has survived, although his book has not, and neither the League nor the Communist Party dictated to this very non-Communist socialist that he write second-rate material.

In recent decades many literary critics have happily belabored the role of Communists among writers. Marxist literary theory has been the object of many assaults, and a common theme has been this: The Communist Party served literature poorly by demanding that writers produce works of immediate utility in the struggle against the ruling class. There is no question that some Communist emphasis pointed in the direction of writing that had short-term goals — "agit-prop" (short for agitation and propaganda) writing, it was sometimes called. But there was no unanimity among Marxist theoreticians on this point, as James E. Murphy points out in his study, *The Proletarian Moment*.[5] A whole tradition of Marxist criticism was devoted to the great contributions made by non-Marxist writers of the past and to the belief that it was the function of writers to illuminate society as a whole, not just its working class component.

Within Marxist circles there was a struggle between those who gave precedence to tactics and those who believed long-term strategy was more important. The latter did not require of creative artists any orthodoxy — any hewing to a Party line. They knew that Balzac, a royalist, could write great novels. Marx knew that Aeschylus, living in a slave society, could write great drama. (Marx reread the plays of Aeschylus once every year in the original Greek; he also loved Shakespeare, who was no proletarian writer.)

I do not hear the anti-Marxist critics belaboring artists of the Italian Renaissance because of their ties to the church. And where are the critics who belittle Homer because the *Odyssey* grew out of pre-industrial myths? An anthropologist doesn't turn away from Mayan art — or Nigerian art — because the images and conventions they employ are not those common in the traditions of western Europe. I say this because it seems to me counter-productive to try to show that one trend within the debate over proletarian literature in the 1920s and 1930s was right and everything else was wrong.

Those who saw the new importance of the working class in many parts of the world were entering unfamiliar territory and had few maps to guide them. Moreover, such maps as they did have were often made before exploration had taken place — like the imaginative fifteenth- and sixteenth-century maps of the New World. It seems rather priggish to demand perfection of those who were among the first to delineate areas that were only in the process of becoming known to those who came from other lands. And just as priggish is the assumption that maps drawn from afar will fit territories that were only now being seen for the first time by outsiders. Better, it would seem to me, to acknowledge the searching impulse of the explorers, while guarding against their tendency to be over-enthusiastic and less than careful about recording their discoveries. The critics, full of self-assurance about their knowledge of well-explored territory, might do well to be less scornful of those who were trying to expand, no matter how clumsily, the areas of the world's culture hitherto unknown in their limited circles.

Trying to understand the writers of a dramatic decade is much the same as trying to understand the entirety of the decade. It is an impossible task. Still, I have attempted to do that somewhat in this book. Many others have made this same attempt. Most of them, I believe, have failed, and not only because the task was too great. They failed, I believe, because they tailored their findings to fit the fashion of a bad historic moment. And moments change. The buyers of up-to-the-minute styles have fickle tastes, but they also have in common the ability to buy.

I am fortunate. I am not a connoisseur of styles. My criterion for garments is simple: Can I get another year's wear out of a jacket that keeps me warm and dry and doesn't require onlookers to stare at the singularity of my covering?

In anthropology there has been much debate about whether new fashions or ideas that have appeared in one culture have come from an alien culture or were invented without stimulus from abroad. The fact seems to be that the introduction of ideas from other cultures often has an important effect. At the same time, indigenous invention also takes place. Difficulties arise when zealots claim exclusive credit for one process or the other. Both are important. Cross-fertilization plays an important role in many inventions; on the other hand, direct creativity also exists and can grow out of a local past.

With this in mind, we should not be surprised that influences came to American writers from events and thoughts and organized proselytizing from another culture, let us say from the Russian or Soviet culture. Enrichment of this kind has always gone on. At the same time, American writers of the 1930s responded to the distinct realities in the United States, and they built on a native tradition of protest and solidarity with neighbors and co-workers. They did not need Stalin to tell them that in this country workers were unemployed or that workers were an important resource for those creating literary art. They did not need Trotsky to open their eyes to the existence of exploitation. Mark Twain had seen that, so had William Dean Howells, Upton Sinclair, Jack London, and many others — long before the Russian Revolution.

Just as surely, however, the response of writers to unemployment and to fascism had a heightened intensity because the Russian Revolution had taken place and had stimulated the growth of radical parties in many countries. Stalin and Trotsky did not invent the realities on the American scene. They did, however, influence the quality of response to these events by many people, including writers. It would be folly to deny diffusion of ideas from Moscow. It would be equally wrong to see all literary radicalism in terms of a conspiracy directed from abroad. The upsurge in political activity among writers was the result of both native and foreign influences and is quite worth examining. So, too, is the question of the rejection of myths from abroad and from sources close to home that were in contradiction to reality.

The Depression decade was not the first in which politics and literature in our language have been deeply intertwined. Milton was a revolutionary in his day. Wordsworth wrote his best poems under the stimulus of the French Revolution. Shelley made it very clear that he regarded himself as a voice for revolution. So did the younger Blake. The Scottish poets Burns and Byron were both political revolutionaries. And the United States does not lack for writers who defied authority and spoke out on behalf of the real interests of common people: Thoreau, Whitman, Mark Twain, W.E.B. Du Bois, Harriet Beecher Stowe.

Although I do not recall finding the phrase used by writers in the League, it seems to me that much of what they did and wrote was an effort *to support life*. How to do this was a matter for discussion, often for disagreement, but the goal was there for them, both as creators and as citizens. As international political rivalries increased, writers felt these tensions and were influenced. The result often developed into hostility between groups of writers who saw their responsibilities in different ways. But underlying the differences, with varying degrees of clarity, was a common search by many, in treacherous terrain, for political and artistic ways to support life — even beyond that, to expand life.

After the war good literature appeared in the Fearful Fifties, coming from the same typewriters that produced good books in the Turbulent Thirties. Some authors of the 1950s who had been League members resisted all efforts at thought control. Philip Stevenson, a gentle man who served a term as secretary of the League and quietly carried out the task he took on, also stubbornly carried into the future the spirit of the League. In the years of repression following the League's demise, he was among the blacklisted Hollywood writers. He took on a new name, Lars

Lawrence, and wrote an important but overlooked four-volume novel set in New Mexico.[6] In this work he gives the reader credible radical characters, Unemployed Council actions, Chicanos, native fascist developments. He paints an uncompromising and deeply humane picture of the culturally complex southwestern society — and he remains unknown in a period when great value is placed on trivia. Philip Stevenson did not fail as an artist. The literary marketplace failed him. So, too, it failed another radical writer, John Sanford, who was much less active in the League. He never capitulated artistically or politically, and he never stopped writing and publishing for a limited audience.

Other good books came from authors who had published little or nothing during the League years and hence were not League members. Yuri Suhl was one of these. His *Cowboy on a Wooden Horse* (The Macmillan Company, 1953) is a proletarian novel written with great skill, vitality, and charm at a time when critics were saying that this literary form was long dead. The poet and novelist Kenneth Fearing never ceased his defiance.

No simple generalization can cover what happened to American writers after the demise of the League. It is tempting, however, to emphasize that many of the League's opponents and defectors moved either to the Right or into political silence. League loyalists on the other hand did not move so conspicuously, but they did often become silent politically, having been forced to do so. At the same time, literature became more private and hence less troublesome to upholders of the status quo. Public writing dealing with great themes became something of an oddity in the literary marketplace. Such writing would have to wait for another era, one equipped with readers whose experience had made them more hungry than are many of them today. Writers would have to find channels that do not now exist, through which words can flow freely between their producers and their consumers.

Notes

1. The Millen Brand Journal is with his papers in the Rare Books and Manuscripts section of Butler Library, Columbia University, New York City.

2. Quoted in Richard Gilman and Michael Paul Novak, *Poets, Poetics and Politics* (University Press of Kansas, 1992), p. 129.

3. Henry Hart, ed., *American Writers' Congress* (International Publishers, 1935); Henry Hart, ed., *The Writer in a Changing World* (Equinox Cooperative Press, 1937); Donald Ogden Stewart, ed., *Fighting Words* (Harcourt, Brace and Company, 1940).

4. Gilman and Novak, pp.137–138.

5. James E. Murphy, *The Proletarian Moment* (University of Illinois Press, 1990).

6. Lars Lawrence [Philip Stevenson], *The Seed,* a quartet: *Morning, Noon and Night* (G. P. Putnam's Sons, 1954), *Out of the Dust* (G. P. Putnam's Sons, 1956), *Old Father Antic,* (International Publishers, 1961), and *The Hoax* (International Publishers, 1961).

Myra Page, early writer on proletarian themes who remained
steadily active in the League.
Courtesy of May Kanfer.

Nunnally Johnson, screenwriter,
teacher in Hollywood Writers
School. Courtesy of Sheila
Schwartz.

Oskar Maria Graf, exiled German novelist, president of German-American Writers Association. From *Direction* magazine, January 1941.

Manfred Georg, exiled German writer, general secretary of the German-American Writers Association. From *Direction* magazine, December 1939.

Ramon J. Sender, exiled Spanish novelist. *Saturday Review of Literature* photo, November 13, 1937. Reproduced with the permission of the Western Historical Collections, University Archives, University of Colorado at Boulder Libraries.

21
Aftermath

Who, after 1933, could afford not to read an American book?

— Alfred Kazin, *On Native Grounds*

To omit joy, youth — and love — to concentrate on what was wrong with the 1930's is to *expunge* the heart. Okay, head-minus-heart can look backwards and chalk up the self-seeking, the treachery, the stupidity, the folly. . . . [But] I remember a time when men dared to hope.

— Benjamin Appel, "Miss America and the Look-Back Boys,"
The Literary Review, Fall 1973

At the time the League disappeared, other writers' organizations survived: the Authors League of America, with its constituent guilds of authors, dramatists, radio writers, and screenwriters, and PEN (Poets, Essayists, and Novelists). They — and some local and single-issue writers' groups — had not been active against such powerful forces as the League had chosen to confront. Although these organizations may have been regarded as nuisances, they were only a limited threat to those who wielded power, and they did not have many-faceted programs that gave critics a wide selection of targets at which to take aim. Nor did they have alliances with labor and the Left.

After peaking in the mid-1930s, the influence of labor in the United States had receded. The nourishment it could give to writers also declined and never rose very high in the next fifty years. This does not mean that its influence will not rise again. When stirrings and rumblings again move the producing section of the population, writers, too, will stir; and when they do, they might do well to acquaint themselves not only with the accomplishments of the League but also with the reasons for its disappearance. These include both a lack of skill with which to maneuver when the Establishment stepped up its contradictory effort to be both anti-Nazi and anti-Communist at the same time, and the disillusionment of many writers because of the crimes of Stalin.

The lesson to be learned? Any future activist organization of citizen-writers should avoid accepting illusions as facts, particularly illusions circulated by governments. It should be skeptical. Skepticism, however, can be a powerful inhibitor. Those who stubbornly seek answers to questions are not typically those who plunge into action on the assumption that answers are already in hand. Truth seekers can — and often do — trip up good doers.

It is tempting to wonder how much better off the world, and the world of letters, might be if the League had found a stable balance between skepticism and activism. I wonder if the League's policies would have been very different if it had accepted the dreadful truths about one side of Soviet life, to which the Trotskyists pointed. There were also important positive aspects of Soviet life, and these the anti-Stalinists tended to ignore. No doubt the League could have accomplished more if it had had a complete grasp of reality, but why not just say the League did the best it could?

My belief then — and now — that the Soviet Union was justified, for example, in signing a non-aggression pact with Germany may well cause some eyebrows to be raised. Those who want evidence that I may not be an unbiased reporter can point to these facts: I worked for the National Council of American Soviet Friendship for a year after I left the League. Following the war I worked for two years as a staff writer for TASS, the Soviet news agency. Later I wrote a children's book, *The Soviet Union, A View From Within* (Thomas Nelson, Inc., 1965) and an adult book *Some Basic Rights of Soviet Citizens* (Progress Publishers, Moscow, 1983); two of my books for children have been translated and published in the Soviet Union — *The Language Book* (Grosset and Dunlap, 1963) and *The Story of Archeology in the Americas* (Harvey House, Inc., 1966). I have made five trips to the USSR, two as a guest of Soviet institutions, one as a tourist, and two in connection with preparing for and taking part in a peace walk from Leningrad to Moscow. I very definitely had great hope, and belief, that the type of society that was struggling to mature and survive as a successor to the Russian Empire had much good to offer the suffering billions of people on this planet — jobs for everyone, universal free education and medical care. I admit I was slow to realize that much had gone wrong with the Soviet effort to get rid of exploitation and that

Harold Boner, poet, geographer. From *Coloradoan*, 1927.

Nan Golden, secretary of the Writers School, executive secretary of the New York chapter of the League. Courtesy of Dr. Michael Rohman.

those who managed the Soviet political system engaged in practices that could only lead to a setback, at least temporary, for socialism. These practices included allowing the Soviet state to be enticed into an arms race, which the United States shrewdly expected would bankrupt the Soviet economy and divert it from becoming a success.

I was committed to socialism and so were many League members, but socialism, or communism into which it was supposed to develop, was not the business of the League members generally, either in their work as citizens or in their writing.

One of the things I have discovered as I review my years with the League is how little I knew at the time about the writings of our members and others who created the predominantly social literature of the Depression years. Nor did I know much about the network of personal relationships among the writers it was my duty to organize. I was far too busy to familiarize myself with all the considerable creations and complex lives of many hundreds of women and men who were themselves busy at typewriters when they weren't in committee meetings or on picket lines. I missed, and hence could not fully value, a good number of good things to read. And I had only a sketchy idea of a whole, interactive community life of writers that was in direct contradiction to the prevailing image of them as isolated individuals.

Clearly, I have not played by the rules in preparing this memoir, which bills itself as dealing with the years 1937–1942. I have reached back before 1937 to find a base from which to start. I have reached forward after 1942 to follow some connections that did not end when the League came to formal conclusion. In this spilling over I include now some notes about continuing relationships.

Jane Sherman, who worked with the Exiled Writers Committee and Spanish Intellectual Aid, has been kind enough to look at the manuscript of this book, and she has saved me from several errors. Ellen Conried, another busy volunteer in the League office, still had warm feelings for the organization in 1992, when she taxied me around Los Angeles where I was doing research for this memoir.

Over the years Mary and I have kept in touch with Nan Golden, the very efficient secretary of the New York chapter of the League and of its Writers School. After the League ceased to function, she worked, as I did, for the National Council of American Soviet Friendship. During the League and Council days, Mary and I became good friends with Nan's son, Michael Rohman, who grew up to be a distinguished surgeon. In 1992 he gave me very welcome advice and support when I developed serious cardiac problems.

One friendship of League days — that with Richard Wright — did not survive into the troubled years that followed. I came to know Dick well when we worked together, and Mary and I saw him socially as well. In addition, Mary advised him on his contract for *Black Boy* and introduced him to Paul Reynolds, her boss, who became Dick's literary agent. On one occasion, we lent Dick and his wife a little country place we rented; they needed just such a spot for a rest. My warm relationship with him ended, however, when he left the Party and publicly attacked it, urged on, according to his biographer, Margaret Walker, by Reynolds.

I was in the Merchant Marine when Dick published his attack on the CP, and when I returned to civilian life following an injury at sea, I was in no mood to seek him out. I had time to spare as I hobbled about on crutches while my broken leg healed. Some of this time I used to organize a rent strike at the house on Charles Street where Mary and I shared the top-floor apartment with Beatrice Blum, who managed the CP's Jefferson Bookshop.

The occasion for the strike was the arrival from the Richelieu Estate Company of a notice evicting from the first-floor apartment two impecunious elderly women who had lived there for years. Although the apartment was rent-controlled, an owner could legally put a tenant out if he needed the place for his own use. The Richelieu company did not reveal the name of the owner, but it seemed to us that whoever he was it was unjust to make the two women leave their longtime home simply

Benjamin Appel, novelist, member of Executive Committee, 1937; National Council, 1940, 1941. From *Direction* magazine, May–June, 1939.

to suit his convenience. So we and others refused to pay rent until the eviction notice was withdrawn.

We soon learned, however, that we were not really fighting an estate company. We were fighting Richard Wright. He had used the company to evade the unwritten law that said African-Americans could not own homes in Greenwich Village. The news that Dick was the real buyer came as a complete surprise, and it was confirmed when I ran into him in the building, conferring with an architect about remodeling. We did not speak, but he described in his journal, which I have seen at Yale University, his astonishment at discovering that his adversaries were persons who had befriended and helped him when he first came to New York.[1]

I dropped my rent strike activities when I found I was trying to keep an African-American from integrating an all-white neighborhood, but my withdrawal did not stop stories that the CP was trying to keep blacks from owning property in Greenwich Village. This story has been taken up by at least one of Wright's biographers, who never bothered to check with me or Mary to get our side of the affair.

People even began to say that Folsom and the CP were responsible for Wright's decision to leave the United States and to take up residence in Paris. The fact was that, at precisely this moment, Wright noted in his diary that he had received an invitation from the French government to visit that country. He accepted the invitation, he and his wife liked Paris, and there they remained.[2]

So ended, in the shadow of a sectarian quarrel, one association that had begun in the League. Others had happier outcomes. One friend was Benjamin Appel, who worked hard in the League all the time I was involved and who voted at its last meeting against terminating the organization. Throughout the League years, he was always independent, creative, and humorous, and he remained so in the years that followed. After the League was no more, Ben and his wife Sophie shared a house with us one summer in the country. In time, they moved to

Roosevelt, New Jersey, and when a house in that village fell vacant, we moved in and lived as their neighbors for twenty years.

Friendship with Ralph Roeder began when he became interested in the work of the Exiled Writers Committee. Although Ralph seemed new to organizational work, he labored efficiently on the committee and in the League's National Council and never missed a meeting. His knowledge of Italian helped the committee to correspond with Italian writers who needed aid because they had resisted first Mussolini, then Hitler. Ralph helped us to phrase brochures, letters to important Americans, and appeals for funds. His style said, if nothing else did, that the League was indeed a writers' organization. From diffidence — or a kind of innocence — Ralph had no grievance against

Ralph Roeder, biographer, historian, member of the National Council 1938, 1939. *Saturday Review of Literature* photo, January 9, 1937. Reproduced with the permission of the Western Historical Collections, University Archives, University of Colorado at Boulder Libraries.

this or that faction on the Left. He just wanted to help anyone who suffered because he or she had pushed against the enemies of all writers.

After meeting Ralph as a committee member, Mary and I met Fania, his wife, and we dined many times in their 57th Street apartment, to which Fania clung with ferocity against a rent-hungry landlord. Fania had long-standing credentials as a combatant. She had worked closely with Margaret Sanger in that pioneer's campaign for birth control. Never silent about anything, Fania certainly was not silent about her brother Jacob "Pop" Mindel. Pop was a Communist and a teacher of Marxism in the Workers School. I do not know when he had time to make his living as a dentist, but he did make his way, with dogmatic assurance, among the complexities of political economy.

Theory was not Fania's interest. She wanted justice and her place in the world, but even more she wanted Ralph to be known and recognized as the great writer she believed him to be. Curiously, although he had great presence — he had been a Shakespearean actor — Ralph could not bear to put himself forward. For this, Fania compensated. Acting as his agent, she sold his books to Viking Press, and one at least, *Men of the Renaissance*, became a Book-of-the-Month Club choice.

Rudolf Feistmann, exiled German writer. From *Exil in Lateinamerika*, by Wolfgang Kiessling.

The Roeder apartment seemed to owe very little to Fania. I can't recall any artifacts from her Russian-Jewish background. I do remember knickknacks and family portraits that spoke of Ralph's aristocratic origins in the Old South. The desk on which he wrote, I recall particularly. When he left New York forever and moved to Mexico, he gave me the desk, and I worked at it for twenty-five years before I moved west and passed it along to my son Mike.

Ralph's reasons for mingling with radicals existed before he met Fania — a fact I learned only after I had known him a long time. He had been caught up, as John Reed had been, in the Mexican Revolution. When Woodrow Wilson was sending troops to put a stop to insurgency south of the border, Ralph sided with Pancho Villa. He, a volunteer, was captured at one point by Mexican counter-revolutionaries and was stood against a wall to be shot. By some accident the order to fire was not given, and he survived.

So, too, did his interest in Mexico. When no publisher in New York wanted more of his elegant biographies of Italian Renaissance figures, Ralph turned to writing a biography of Benito Juárez, the Indian who had led a revolution in Mexico and became its president at the time of Abraham Lincoln. Never mind that Ralph was not as fluent in Spanish as in Italian. He would master Spanish soon after Mary and I saw him off on a ship bound for Vera Cruz. When we met him next, in Mexico City, he was completely at home in the language, and Mexicans told me he had a perfect accent.

In Mexico Ralph continued work he had begun for the Exiled Writers Committee in New York. With Fania he visited Anna Seghers during a long stay in the hospital, after she had been struck by a car in traffic. As Seghers recovered, echoing the League days the Roeders gave her support that was needed.

Seghers for her part continued the tradition of writers helping writers. She was very active in organizing relief for fellow refugees in Mexico, and she did much to see that their books got published. In East Germany, where she chose to live after the war, although her pre-war

home had been in West Germany, she became head of the powerful writers' union.
While in that position, she privately organized a rescue effort on behalf of Georg
Lukacs, minister of culture in Hungary,
whose efforts at reform had put him at
odds with the Stalinists. Ute Brandes, professor of German at Amherst College, reports that "Younger colleagues . . . could
always count on her quiet interventions,
personal support, or indirect promotions
of those literary texts Seghers deemed important, despite disfavor by the [Commu-
nist] Party."[3]

Ute Brandes also says:

Alexander Abusch, exiled German writer. From *Exil in Lateinamerika,* by Wolfgang Kiessling.

[Segher's] short story *Der gerechte Richter* first published in 1990, was
apparently written . . . under the influence of the revelations about Stalinist
crimes at the Twentieth Party Congress.

It presents Seghers' reflections on opportunism and communist solidarity, filtered through a fictional form. A court case in an unidentified East-
bloc country . . . is here bitterly condemned as a systemic charade which
attempts to suppress the self-evident truth: an innocent, judicious individual is confronted by a corrupt legal system whose self-serving policies are
enforced by secretive, authoritarian measures. Seghers describes the work-
ings of corruption, opportunism, and lies — a thorough inventory of
Stalinist methods which seek to crush those who refuse to comply.

Yet the novella does not condemn a centrally directed, communist
system. It breaks off, and only a last segment, which takes place some years
later, firmly establishes the principles of justice, humanity, and solidarity.

Seghers publicly supported the Communist Party of East Germany,
hoping always to effect reforms from within. In this she was not successful, but Brandes says:

In view of her continuously passionate advocacy of a utopian socialism
despite her disappointments, and in view of her private actions coupled
with public acquiescence, Anna Seghers today emerges as a representative
figure for the first generation of German communists. Their very idealism,
despite all hardships and disappointments, remains a strong cultural legacy

Anna Seghers, exiled German novelist. From *Exil in Lateinamerika*, by Wolfgang Kiessling.

for the tradition of progressive thought and commitment in twentieth-century Germany.

All of this was far from what either Seghers or Ralph Roeder could have foreseen when they were aiding refugees in Mexico. Ralph helped them with practical plans for fund-raising that he had seen in operation when he was in New York working with the Exiled Writers Committee.

In another way, long after the League had fallen silent, Ralph gave it voice. At the request of Pablo Neruda, speaking for other North American writers, he contributed to a Latin American writers' congress that protested the jailing of the Hollywood Ten and the leaders of the Joint Anti-Fascist Refugee Committee who refused to be made informers.

Ralph's biography of Juárez appeared in the United States and won great praise in Mexico. Indeed, Fania saw to it that Ralph got Mexico's highest award — the Order of the Mexican Eagle, I believe it was. The revolution that Juárez led had so moved Ralph that he went on and wrote a history of its continuation. The last time I saw him and Fania, in Mexico in the late 1960s, he showed me part of the manuscript. What I read seemed to be full of action and detailed insights into Mexican political life.

But who would publish the book? Viking in New York had lost interest in what Ralph was doing; the editors complained that he was writing too much from the Mexican point of view. Why shouldn't a book about the Mexican Revolution be from the point of view of Mexican revolutionists? Still, Ralph had written it in English and wanted a publisher in the States. One day at lunch, he asked me a little shyly if I would hand deliver the manuscript to a New York publisher. He did not trust the Mexican mails, and he knew that I was driving home. He didn't know that I had already undertaken to fill the trunk of my car with Albert Maltz's papers and to take them from Mexico City, where Maltz had been in exile, to Los Angeles. Ralph also didn't know that I would be driving for weeks, doing research in many places on the way from Los Angeles to New York. I was afraid that when I crossed the border and later lived in camp-grounds, possibly followed by the FBI, his manuscript might disappear.

Ralph was visibly hurt when I explained why I was not a secure courier, and clearly my decision was wrong. Fania died shortly after this. On October 22, 1969, when Ralph had completed translating the whole book into Spanish, he put the unpublished manuscript in the center of his desk and shot himself.

Bodo Uhse, exiled German writer. From *Exil in Lateinamerika*, by Wolfgang Kiessling.

The manuscript had not been published years later, when I tried to trace it through Ralph's Mexico City attorney, Leo Benito Noyola. Indeed, it seems to have disappeared quite as completely as the Mexican revolution it celebrated.

My failure to help Ralph Roeder find a publisher for his manuscript is high on the list of regrets I have accumulated over the years. Ralph would probably have ended his life anyway, once his beloved Fania was gone, but I can't help feeling responsible for the death of his beloved book.

So much for personal friendships. I have also looked back on the League in a more general way. There I saw many writers sharing in a fellowship that grew out of a common effort to be useful in a time of great peril and great hope. I saw a number of writers, who had been exceedingly successful, find something they thought more important than success. I saw Don Stewart move out of the playboy world he had conquered in Hollywood and become a caring, daring human being, deeply committed against the corruption in the part of society that had rewarded him so well. I saw Dash Hammett, who knew corruption at firsthand as a detective, aid his fellow writers — and fellow citizens — resist that corruption, which he had escaped. I saw Theodore Dreiser, an angry volcano in disorderly eruption, who had long been drawn by sympathy for suffering and hatred of sham, move from great success to great conviction about how society should evolve. A greatness — beyond their achievements as writers — touched these creators and the

Alfons Goldschmidt, exiled German writer. From *Exil in Lateinamerika*, by Wolfgang Kiessling.

lives of other men and women only a little less well known in the literary world.

The League to which they belonged was for much of the time a happy creation — as harmonious in its parts and in its purpose as a coming-together of highly individual human beings is ever likely to be in our divided society. I like to think that when the history of American culture is written, in some future and more honest time, the steady, persistent effort of our League to be of service will be noted.

I would like to think that the verdict will be that the League was a collective effort, in a time of great disorder on the world scene, to create among writers and their readers a countervailing area of orderly motion, and of hope. Quite possibly, people will find that the League grew out of the spirit that stirred Kenneth Fearing to write:

> Tomorrow, yes, tomorrow, surely we begin at last to live,
> With lots and lots of laughter,
> Solid silver laughter,
> Laughter, with a few simple instructions, and a bona-fide guarantee.[4]

By the time the League left the scene, and coinciding curiously with the government's increasing involvement in World War II, a conservative literary mood began to dominate American writers. But the momentum of the 1930s, which shoved us along in companionship with many, carried over in many families — including mine — in the 1960s. Our son Michael made available to his generation an anthology of the writings of the communist writer Mike Gold. Our daughter Rachel took part in integrating the schools in Chester, Pennsylvania, and went to jail for her trouble.

One day much later, thinking of Rachel, I wrote these lines:

> My grandfather shaped a stone
>   with a sharp point and cutting edge
>   that saved much labor.

My father turned over to machines
   the work that muscles had done.

I have computers to do the work of my brain.

So what remains for my son?

Perhaps tomorrow is for my daughter
   or hers.
   They have been left out of
   this pedigree of power.

With this nod to feminism, I turn back to the League, which was not much ahead of its time in its concern for women's rights and was not at all ahead of its time in its lack of concern for gay and lesbian rights.

So far as I know, very few writers who were continuously active throughout the League's history shifted to the Right — toward the Republicans or beyond. But the same cannot be said of those who departed from the League early and then attacked it from the Left. A number of them moved to positions far to the Right.

As one who was a Stalinist in the 1930s — and was therefore by definition mistrustful of all Trotskyists — I find hope for the world in the fact that today a learned and generous literary investigator of that period, Alan Wald, began his life as a Trotskyist. Originally, he mistrusted Stalinists, but he has come to see beyond the parochial boundaries of the two contending communist camps. Without accepting the rigidities of Stalinism, he has found deep humane inclinations among his erstwhile enemies. And with detailed scholarship he has mapped the intellectual world of the Trotskyists and found much of it rather arid.

Part of the hope I feel for the future has roots in the growth of Wald's spirit. Perhaps there is also a source for hope in the balancing fact that I can find words of praise for a man I once would have thought it my duty to be wary of — indeed to oppose. If Alan Wald and I can learn, so can others; we all need to. In addition, we might pause over, as we note that the League went out not with a bang but a whimper, the following passage, written by League member Mike Quin shortly before dying from the cancer he knew was facing him:

I have often said that were I condemned to execution, no one would be able to get a picture of me walking in proud and courageous dignity to the gallows, electric chair, gas chamber or firing squad that was assigned to dispatch me. I would fight every inch of the way, and a number of strong

THE WHITE HOUSE
WASHINGTON

April 23, 1938

My dear Mr. Brooks:

Please accept my thanks for your letter
of April fifteenth advising me that the League of
American Writers has by unanimous vote conferred
Honorary Membership on me. May I ask you to assure the members of my hearty appreciation of this
action.

Very sincerely yours,

[signature: Franklin D. Roosevelt]

Mr. Van Wyck Brooks,
Vice President,
League of American Writers,
381 Fourth Avenue,
New York, N. Y.

After President Roosevelt accepted honorary membership in the League, this fact was not
announced, partly because the National Council feared its freedom to criticize the president's policies would be compromised and partly to avoid serving the interests of
Roosevelt's right-wing enemies. The original letter is in the LAW Papers, Bancroft Library,
University of California, Berkeley.

Appendix A
Members of the League of American Writers

The official membership and dues records of the League were stolen when the League office was broken into, shortly before the National Council voted to disband the organization in January 1943. The list of members offered here is reconstructed from League *Bulletins*, minutes of League meetings, and other League documents. Partial membership lists from the FBI and HUAC files have also been used, together with a list compiled by Tom Wolfe, whose Ph.D. dissertation relied heavily on FBI and HUAC sources. Following each entry, in this order, are: birth and death dates (the absence of a death date does not necessarily mean the person is still living); pseudonyms, birth names, or full names (e.g., of married women), when known; profession and a sampling of professional achievements, when known; the date of entry into the League, when known; activities in the League (such as attending a congress, a special conference as distinct from a congress, attendance at a council meeting by someone not a council member, or holding the position of teacher, lecturer, etc.); date of exit from the League, when known; membership in an organization hostile to the League; status as a target of FBI investigation, when known; blacklisting, when known; occupation following blacklisting, when known; status as informer, when known; imprisonment.

The list of resignations from the League is not complete. Some members left the organization without formally resigning or making public statements. The names of some non-members who cooperated with the League on at least one project are indicated with asterisks. Non-members who contributed to book and manuscript sales are not listed.

To be eligible for membership, a person must have published enough so that the National Council thought he or she deserved the title of writer. Many who applied for membership were not admitted because their publishing record was deemed too slim. When only scanty information about a member is presented here, it may be 1) that the writer wrote under a name or names that have not been traceable; 2) that the writer died young; or 3) that the writer had work published in little magazines or produced in off-Broadway theaters, which are poorly indexed in reference works.

Information in FBI files on many League members was not available at the time this book went to press. The absence of the notation "FBI target" does not mean that the member was not an FBI target. No attempt has been made to determine whether members were subject to surveillance by other governmental investigative agencies.

After the League ceased to function, many League members became active in the Hollywood Writers Mobilization and took part in a congress held at the University of California, Los Angeles in 1943. Although this congress and the book that came out of it were not LAW activities, I have indicated when LAW members contributed to both. They did not withdraw from the social scene with the demise of the League.

Abels, Cyrilly (?–1975)
> Literary agent; agent of Katherine Anne Porter, Bernard D. N. Grebanier; editor, *40 Best Stories From Mademoiselle, 1935–1960;* LAW National Council, October 20, 1937; executive secretary, Middle Atlantic chapter, 1937; Speaker's Bureau, 1937; resigned as NY secretary, November 1939

Acier, Marcel
> Compiler, *From Spanish Trenches;* LAW 1937

Adamic, Louis (1899–1951)
> Journalist; *House in Antigua; My America;* LAW 1935; 2nd Congress 1937; Committee for Cultural Freedom, May 1939; Advisory Council, Writers War Board, 1942

Adams, Frederic L.
> LAW 1937

Adams, Leonie (1899–1988)
> Poet; *Those Not Elect; Collected Works of Leonie Adams;* LAW 1935; Library of Congress Consultant in Poetry, 1948; FBI target 1921–

**Adler, Irving (1913–) Pseud. Robert Irving
> Children's book writer; *The Secret of Light; Fire in Your Life; How Life Began;* blacklisted as a teacher, then became a writer

Agee, James (1909–1955)
> Poet; *Let Us Now Praise Famous Men; Permit Me Voyage;* LAW 1936; FBI target 1937–

Aiken, Conrad (1889–1973)
> Poet, critic, novelist; *Charnel Rose; Blue Voyage;* Library of Congress Consultant in Poetry, 1950–1952; LAW 1935; FBI target 1945–

Albee, George (1905–1964)
> Free-lance writer; LAW Organization Committee, 1937; chair, Ways and Means Committee, 1937; teacher, New York Writers School, 1939, 1940; 2nd Congress, 1937; chair, Keep America Out of War Committee, 1940

Alberts, Sidney S.
> Second Congress, 1937

Aldrich, Rhoda Truax
> Novelist; *Accident Ward Mystery;* LAW 1938

Alexander, Sidney (1912–)
> Playwright, journalist, poet; *The Third Great Fool; The Celluloid Asylum; Tightrope in the Dark;* 2nd Congress, 1937

Algase, Benjamin
> LAW accountant, briefly

Algren, Nelson (1909–1981) Born Nelson Abraham
> Novelist, poet; *Somebody in Boots; Never Come Morning;* National Book Award for *The Man With the Golden Arm; A Walk on the Wild Side;* signer, Congress Call, 1935, 1941; National Council, 1935–1936; Midwest Writers Congress, 1936; Chicago correspondent, November 3, 1937; executive secretary, Chicago chapter, 1938; FBI target 1935–

Allan, Lewis (1903–1986) Born Abel Meeropol
   Songwriter; "The House I Live In"; "Strange Fruit"; adopted Michael and Robert, the
   sons of the executed Rosenbergs; blacklisted

**Alland, William
   Lecturer, Hollywood Writers School

Allen, James S. (1906–1991) Born Sol Auerbach
   Editor; *Thomas Payne: Selections From His Writings; Reconstruction; Negro Liberation;*
   LAW representative to National Negro Congress, 1937

Allen, Jay (1900–1972)
   Translator, journalist; *New World Theme; Death in the Making*

Allen, Sally Elliot
   LAW 1937

Allen, Sarah Van Alstyne
   Children's poet

Alsberg, Henry (1921–)
   Director, Federal Writers Project; *America Fights the Depression*

Ames, George (1910–)

Amster, Lou (1910–1993)
   Fiction writer, stand-in for the actor Lionel Stander in Hollywood; *The Killer Instinct*

Anderson, A. E. (1905–)
   LAW 1935

Anderson, Maxwell (1888–1959)
   Playwright; *Gods of the Lightning,* with Harold Hickerson; *Winterset; Elizabeth the
   Queen; What Price Glory?;* FBI target 1938–

Anderson, Sherwood (1876–1941)
   Novelist; *Winesburg, Ohio; Beyond Desire;* contributor, *Masses;* member, John Reed
   Club; LAW 1938; Committee for Cultural Freedom, May 1939; FBI target 1932–

Angel, Ruth Olive

Angoff, Charles (1902–1979)
   Editor; *H. L. Mencken: A Portrait From Memory;* LAW 1936

Anshen, Ruth N.
   Journalist; *Beyond Victory; Freedom; Decay of Old Ideas;* LAW 1939

Anthony, Katharine (1877–1965)
   Biographer; 2nd Congress, 1937; signer, Congress Call, 1941

Appel, Benjamin (1908–1977)
   Novelist; *Brain Guy; The Power House; The Dark Stain; Fortress in the Rice;* LAW Writers
   Congress, 1935; Conference December, 1936; Executive Committee, 1937; Organiza-
   tion Committee, 1937; signer, Congress Call, 1939, 1941; chair, Literary Forum, 1937;
   National Council, 1940; Philadelphia civil liberties protest, September 1940; chair,
   Civil Liberties Committee, 1940; lecturer, New York Writers School, 1940; National
   Council, 1940, 1941; teacher, Writers Conference, Highlander Folk School; White
   Mountain Writers Conference, 1941

Appleton, Helen
   2nd Congress Finance Committee, 1937

Aptheker, Herbert (1915–)
   Historian, editor; *A Documentary History of the Negro People in the United States;
   American Negro Slave Revolts;* speaker, Critics Panel, 4th Congress, 1941; teacher, New
   York Writers School, 1942

Aragon, Louis (1897–1982)
   French poet, novelist, journalist; *Residential Quarter; The Bells of Basel; Red Front;* leader,
   International Association of Writers for the Defense of Culture; speaker, 3rd Con-
   gress, 1939

Arent, Arthur (1904–1972)
Novelist, playwright; *Gold Digger's Funeral; One Third of a Nation;* "1935," a Living Newspaper play; "Power," a Living Newspaper play; Federal Theater Project; 2nd Congress, 1937; instructor, New York Writers School, 1939; Organizing Committee, Dramatists Panel, 4th Congress, 1941

Armfield, Eugene
Fiction writer; *Where the Weak Grow Strong;* 2nd Congress, 1937

Armstrong, Arnold B.
Novelist; *Parched Earth;* signer, Congress Call, 1935, 1941

Armstrong, Louise V. (1889–)
Playwright, journalist; *We Too Are the People; The Gold Altar;* LAW 1938

Arnold, Thurman (1891–1969)
Essayist; *The Folklore of Capitalism;* LAW 1938; National Council considered public expulsion, April 17, 1940

Arvin, Newton (1900–1963)
Professor of English, critic, novelist; ed. *The Heart of Hawthorne's Journals; Hawthorne; Whitman; Herman Melville;* signer, Congress Call, 1935, 1937, 1939; 2nd Congress, 1937; resigned 1939

Asch, Nathan (1902–1964)
Novelist, screenwriter; *The Office; Pay Day; Love in Chartres; The Valley; The Road: In Search of America;* signer, Congress Call, 1935; Executive Committee, 1936; Conference, December 1936; investigated by HUAC

Asch, Sholem (1880–1957)
Novelist; *The Mother; Three Novels; Song of the Valley;* LAW 1937

Ashbrook, Harriet (1898–1946)
Fiction writer; *Most Immoral Murder;* LAW 1938; signer, Congress Call, 1941

Asness, George
Free-lance writer; LAW 1938; teacher, New York Writers School, 1938, 1939, 1940; Keep America Out of War Committee, 1940

Atlas, Leopold (1907–1954)
Playwright; *But For the Grace of God;* LAW 1937; signer, Congress Call, 1941

Auden, W. H. (1907–1973)
Poet; *Spain; The Age of Anxiety;* LAW 1939; poetry instructor, New York Writers School, 1939; FBI target 1945–

Ausubel, Nathan (1899–)
Folklorist; *Treasury of Jewish Folklore; Treasury of Jewish Humor; Book of Jewish Knowledge; Treasury of Jewish Poetry*

Babb, Sanora (1907–) Pseud. Sylvester Davis
Fiction writer, poet; *The Lost Traveler;* memoir, *An Owl on Every Post;* LAW 1936; Executive Committee, 1937; executive secretary, Southern California chapter, 1938; secretary-treasurer, Hollywood chapter, 1939, 1940, 1941, 1942

Backus, Georgia
National Council 1941; faculty, Hollywood Writers School, 1941

Baich, Joe
LAW 1935

Balch, J. S. (1909–)
Novelist, poet; *Lamps at High Noon; Castle of Words;* member, John Reed Club

Baker, Robert Lee (1901–)
Fiction writer; *Oil, Blood and Sand;* LAW 1938

**Baldwin, James (1924–1987)
Attended the New York Writers School

Balint, Emery (1892–)
Novelist, science fiction writer, illustrator; *Don't Inhale It; Alpha;* LAW 1936

Ballou, Jenny
Fiction writer; *Spanish Prelude;* LAW 1937

Banning, Margaret Culkin (1891–1982)
Novelist; *The Iron Will; Too Young to Marry; You Haven't Changed;* LAW 1936; member, Advisory Committee, Writers War Board, 1942

Barker, Wayne
LAW 1938

Barlow, Samuel (1892–1982)
Composer, songwriter; "Mon Ami Pierrot"; speaker, Exiled Writers Committee dinner, October 9, 1941

Barnet, Will (1911–)

Barry, John D. (1866–1942)
Free-lance writer; *A Tribute to Albert Bender;* LAW Midwest Writers Conference, 1936

Baruch, Dorothy
Hollywood chapter, 1942

Basshe, Emjo (1900–1939)
Playwright; *Doomsday Circus; Earth;* member, John Reed Club

Basso, Hamilton (1904–1969)
Novelist; *Sun in Capricorn;* LAW 1935; LAW southern representative, 1936

Bates, Ralph (1899–)
British novelist; *Sierra; Lean Men; The Olive Field; Sirocco and Other Stories; Fields of Paradise;* officer, International Brigades; resigned 1939

Baumer, Marie (1905–)
Playwright; *It's an Ill Wind; Creeping Fire*

Beach, Joseph Warren (1880–1957)
Critic; *The Concept of Nature in Nineteenth Century English Poetry; American Fiction: 1920–1940;* LAW 1938

Beals, Carleton (1893–1979)
Journalist; *Rome or Death: The Story of Fascism; Latin America: World in Revolution;* LAW 1935; 2nd Congress, 1937

Becker, Beril (1901–)
2nd Congress, 1937

Becker, Florence (1895–1984) Full name Florence Becker Lennon
Poet, novelist, biographer; *Farewell to Walden; The Life of Lewis Carroll; The Heart in Twain; Forty Years in the Wilderness; Good Green Footstool;* LAW 1938; expelled 1939

Bedford-Jones, Nancy
LAW 1937; 2nd Congress, 1937

Bein, Albert (1902–)
Playwright, screenwriter; *Little Ol' Boy; Let Freedom Ring,* Federal Theater play; *The Heavenly Express;* signer, Congress Call, 1939; Organizing Committee, Dramatists Panel, 4th Congress, 1941; Peace Committee, Hollywood, 1941

Bela, Nicholas
Hollywood chapter, 1942

Belfrage, Cedric (1904–1990)
Journalist; British subject; ed. *The National Guardian; Away From It All; Promised Land; South of God; The Frightened Giant;* LAW January 1938; Hollywood chapter, 1940; faculty, Hollywood Writers School, 1941; after deportation hearings, went to Mexico to avoid imprisonment

Belitt, Ben (1911–)
   Poet, editor; *The Enemy of Joy; The Five-Fold Mesh; Four Poems by Rimbaud; School of the Soldier;* ed. *Selected Poems of Pablo Neruda;* LAW 1938

Beliveau, Emile
   LAW 1939

Bell, Thomas (1903–1961)
   Novelist; *All Brides Are Beautiful; Out of This Furnace;* Conference, December, 1936

Benchley, Robert C. (1889–1945)
   Humorist; *After 1903–What?; My Ten Years in a Quandary and How They Grew;* LAW, 1938

Bendiner, M. R.
   2nd Congress, 1937

Benedict, Agnes E. (1889–1950)
   Anthropologist; LAW, 1936; Arrangements Committee, 2nd Congress, 1937

Benes̆, Eduard (1884–1948)
   Honorary member; Ex-president of Czechoslovakia; speaker, 3rd Congress, 1939

Benet, William Rose (1886–1950)
   Poet, editor; *Oxford Anthology of American Literature;* Pulitzer Prize for *The Dust Which Is God;* LAW, 1938; 3rd Congress, 1939

Bengal, Ben
   Playwright; *Plant in the Sun;* Keep America Out of War Committee, 1940; Organizing Committee, Dramatists Panel, 4th Congress, 1941

Benjamin, Nora (1899–1988) Pseud. of Eleanor Gottheil Kubie
   Fiction and non-fiction for children; *Roving All Day; Fathom Five;* Issac Seigel Award for *King Solomon's Navy;* Executive Committee, 1936; Arrangements Committee, 2nd Congress, 1937; signer, Congress Call, 1939; National Council, 1939; Committee to Organize New York City membership meeting, 1940; resigned March 1940; withdrew resignation, April; resigned July 1940; member, Advisory Committee, Writers War Board, 1942–1943; chair of its Juvenile Book Committee

Bennett, Milly (1909–1989)
   Critic, editor; *The World of Willa Cather;* LAW, 1935

Benson, Rita Romilly

Bentley, Theodore (1916–)
   LAW 1938

Bercovici, Rion Leonardo (1903–1976)
   Journalist; 2nd Congress, 1937; blacklisted, 1951

Bergamin, José (1894–)

Berger, Josef (1903–1971) Pseud. Jeremiah Digges
   Novelist, folklorist; *Copy Boy; Bow Leg Bill;* 2nd Congress, 1937

Bergovoy, Helen
   Radio writer; instructor, New York Writers School, 1939; LAW 1940; signer, Congress Call, 1941

Berkeley, Martin
   Screenwriter; Hollywood chapter, 1942; informer [see Navasky, p. 85; Schwartz, p. 90]

Berman, Harold (1918–)
   Professor, lecturer; *Justice in Russia; The Russians in Focus;* LAW 1937

Berman, Lionel (1906–1968)
   Founder of Frontier Films; editor of *The Good Neighbor,* newspaper of Congressman Vito Marcantonio; LAW 1937

Bernard, Lawrence (1905–1968)
   LAW 1938

Bernstein, Aline (1881–1955)
Novelist, stage designer; *Journey Down; Three Blue Suits;* treasurer, 2nd Congress, 1937; signer, Congress Call, 1939; National Council, 1939

**Bernstein, Joseph (1908–1975)
Editor, translator; teacher, New York Writers School, 1942

Bernstein, Samuel (1905–1977)
Signer, Congress Call, 1941

Bessie, Alvah (1904–1985)
Novelist, screenwriter; *Men in Battle; Bread and a Stone;* ed. *Our Flight: Writings by Veterans of the Abraham Lincoln Brigade, Spain; The un-Americans;* drama critic, *New Masses;* LAW 1937; Abraham Lincoln Battalion; Philadelphia civil liberties protest, September 1940; National Council, 1941; signer, Congress Call, 1941; one of the Hollywood Ten, imprisoned for contempt of Congress; blacklisted in 1954; became stage manager in a nightclub

Bessie, Simon (1916–)
LAW 1941

Bezzerides, A. I.
Novelist, screenwriter; *The Long Haul, Thieves' Market;* Hollywood chapter, 1942

Biberman, Herbert (1900–1971)
Film director; *Meet Nero Wolfe; The Master Race; Salt of the Earth;* Hollywood chapter, 1942; one of the Hollywood Ten; blacklisted after, 1947; imprisoned for contempt of Congress, 1947

Billinger, Karl
Exiled German writer; *Fatherland*

Bimba, Anthony
Labor historian

Birk, Louis P.
Publisher

Birkeland, Joran

Bishop, John Peale (1892–1944)
Poet, novelist, critic; *Green Fruit; Act of Darkness;* LAW 1936

Bisno, Beatrice
Tomorrow's Bread; LAW 1938; resigned

Bjorkman, Edwin (1866–1951)

Black, Algernon D. (1900–)
Professor of Ethics; *The First Book of Ethics; The Young Citizens*

Black, Jean Fergusson (1900–)
Children's poet; *Pennywise;* LAW 1939

Black, Ivan (1904–1979)
Publicity agent, poet; National Council, 1939; signer, Congress Call, 1941

Blake, Clarice (1894–)

** Blake, Eleanor (1899–)
Wherever I Choose

Blake, Ellen
LAW executive secretary, 1937

** Blake, William J. (1894–1968) Born William Blech
Novelist; *The Copperheads;* instructor, New York Writers School, 1941; signer, Congress Call, 1941

Blankfort, Henry, Jr.
Screenwriter, novelist, children's book writer; *Henry, the Smiling Dog;* National Council, 1940; blacklisted

Blankfort, Louise

Blankfort, Michael (1907–1982)
>Novelist, dramatist, screenwriter; *The New Gulliver* (USSR animated feature with English lyrics); *Blind Alley; Adam Had Four Sons; Texas; Flight Lieutenant; Battle Hymn,* a Federal Theater play, with Michael Gold; *A Time to Live;* LAW 1935; National Council, 1935; 3rd Congress, 1939; Executive Committee, Hollywood chapter, 1939, 1940, 1941, 1942; chair, School Council, and lecturer, Hollywood Writers School, 1940; Hollywood School Committee, 1941; blacklisted, then a friendly witness before HUAC [see Maltz, UCLA interview; Navasky, p. 101]

Blitzstein, Marc (1905–1964)
>Composer, lyricist, playwright; *Mack the Knife; The Cradle Will Rock;* Federal Theater Project; LAW 1937; signer, Congress Call, 1941; instructor, White Mountain Conference, 1941; FBI target 1940–

Bliven, Bruce (1889–1977)
>Editor; *New Republic;* LAW 1936; resigned 1939

Bloch, Ernst (1885–1977)
>Free-lance writer, philosopher; *The Principle of Hope*

Block, Anita (1882–1967)
>Journalist, historian; *The Changing World in Plays and Theater;* LAW 1939; investigated censorship in drama for LAW Civil Liberties Committee

Bloom, Pauline
>Mystery writer, creative writing instructor; *Mystery Writers Handbook; Handbook of Short Story Writing; Toby, Law Stenographer;* LAW 1939; signer, Congress Call, 1941

Blossom, Frederick A. (1878–1974)
>Editor; *Memoirs of Casanova;* LAW 1939

Blumberg, Albert E.
>LAW 1937

Bodenheim, Maxwell (1893–1954) Born Maxwell Bodenheimer
>Poet, novelist; *Slow Vision; Run, Sheep, Run;* member, John Reed Club; signer, Congress Call, 1935, 1941; National Council, 1935; 2nd Congress, 1937; FBI target 1936–

Boner, Harold A. (1904–1971)
>Poet; *The Intention of Health;* LAW 1937

Bonsal, Stephen
>LAW 1938

Boothe, Robert O.
>LAW 1937

** Boretz, Allen (1900–1986)
>Playwright, screenwriter; *Room Service; Copacabana;* blacklisted after 1951

Borgese, G. A.
>Novelist; *Goliath;* LAW 1938; president, Chicago chapter, 1938; resigned January 1940

Botkin, B. A. (1901–1975)
>Folklorist; *A Treasury of American Folklore: Stories, Ballads and Traditions of the People;* LAW 1937; 3rd Congress, 1939

Boudin, Louis Boudinoff (1874–1952)
>Lawyer; *The Theoretical System of Karl Marx in the Light of Recent Criticism; Socialism and War;* 2nd Congress, 1937

Bowers, Florence W.
>Second Congress, 1937

Boxer, Herman
>Hollywood chapter, 1942

Boyd, Ruth Fitch
>LAW 1936; Conference December, 1936

Boyd, Thomas (1898–1935)
> Poet, novelist; *In Time of Peace;* signer, Congress Call, 1935, 1941

Boyden, Polly
> LAW 1936

Boyer, Richard Owen (1903–1973)
> Journalist, historian, novelist; *Labor's Untold Story; The Dark Ship; New Yorker* articles; LAW 1938; FBI target 1935–

Boylan, John
> Faculty, Hollywood Writers School, 1942

Brace, Ernest
> LAW 1937

Brady, Robert A.
> LAW 1937

Brand, Millen (1906–1980)
> Novelist, poet, screenwriter; *The Heroes; The Outward Room;* LAW 1936; signer, Congress Call, 1939; National Council, 1940, 1941; delegate, Emergency Peace Mobilization, 1940; Philadelphia civil liberties protest, September 1940; teacher, White Mountain Writers Conference, 1941; teacher, Writers Conference, Highlander Folk School

Braus, Mort
> Hollywood chapter, 1942

**Brecht, Bertolt (1898–1956)
> German playwright, poet, director; founder, The Berlin Ensemble; *The Threepenny Opera; Mother Courage and Her Children; The Caucasian Chalk Circle; Galileo;* unfriendly witness before HUAC

Bresler, Harvey

Breuer, Bessie (1893–1975)
> Fiction writer, editor, playwright; *The Daughter;* signer, Congress Call, 1939

Brewster, Dorothy (1883–1979)
> Critic; Conference December 1936; Executive Committee, 1938; signer, Congress Call, 1939, 1941; National Council, 1938, 1939, 1940, 1941; chair, Young Writers Committee, 1939; Philadelphia civil liberties protest, September 1940; speaker, Critics Panel, 4th Congress, 1941; Committee to Aid *The Clipper,* 1941

Briffault, Robert Stephen (1876–1948)
> Novelist, historian; *Breakdown: The Collapse of Traditional Civilization; Europa; Europa in Limbo; The Decline and Fall of the British Empire;* LAW 1938

Bright, John (1908–)
> Screenwriter; *The Public Enemy; Blonde Crazy; We Accuse,* documentary; National Council, 1941; refugee to Mexico to avoid a HUAC subpoena; blacklisted after 1951

Brinser, Ayers
> Signer, Congress Call, 1941

Brody, Alter
> Member, John Reed Club; LAW 1936; Keep America Out of War Committee, 1940

Bromberger, Anne
> LAW 1937

Bromfield, Louis (1896–1956)
> Novelist; *England; A Dying Oligarchy; The Rains Came;* LAW 1938; 3rd Congress, 1939; signer, Congress Call, 1939; vice president, 1939; speaker, Exiled Writers Committee dinner, Hollywood, 1941; Advisory Council, Writers War Board, 1942

Bronowski, J. (1908–1974)
> Poet, physicist; *The Ascent of Man; Biography of an Atom; Science and Human Values;* contributed poems to *The Clipper,* published by the Hollywood chapter

Brooks, Ernest
 LAW 1937; Chicago chapter, 1938

Brooks, Jerome E. (1895–1983)
 Historian; *The Mighty Leaf;* LAW 1938; treasurer, 1939; chair, Manuscript Sale Committee, 1939; chair, Finance Committee, 1939

Brooks, Marie Short
 LAW 1937

Brooks, Philip (1899–1975)
 Bookseller, columnist, *New York Times Book Review;* LAW 1938

Brooks, Van Wyck (1886–1963)
 Literary critic, historian; *The Confident Years; The Ordeal of Mark Twain; The Life of Emerson;* Pulitzer Prize for *The Flowering of New England,* 1936; LAW 1935; National Council, 1935; Executive Committee, 1935; signer, Congress Call, 1937, 1939; vice president, 1937, 1938, 1939; chair, Connecticut Writers Conference, 1938; resigned 1939; Advisory Council, Writers War Board, 1942; FBI target 1935–

Broun, Heywood (1888–1939)
 Journalist, critic; *Pieces of Hate; Gandle Follows His Nose;* LAW 1935; National Council, 1935; speaker, 3rd Congress, 1939; resigned 1939; FBI target 1935–

Brousseau, Julie

**Browder, Earl (1891–1973)
 General secretary of the Communist Party; *Communism and Culture;* signer, Congress Call, 1935, 1941; speaker, 2nd Congress, 1937

Brown, Bob (1907–)
 Free-lance writer; *Country Cook Book; 10,000 Snacks; Most for Your Money Cook Book;* signer, Congress Call, 1935, 1941; 2nd and 3rd Congresses, 1937, 1939

Brown, Dee (1908–)
 Librarian, writer of westerns, historian, novelist, children's book writer; *Bury My Heart at Wounded Knee; They Went Thataway;* LAW 1936

Brown, John Mason (1900–1969)
 Critic; ed. *Theatre Arts Monthly; The Modern Theatre in Revolt; Letters From Greenwood Ghosts; The Art of Playgoing*

Brown, Sterling A. (1901–1989)
 Poet; *Outline for the Study of Poetry of American Negroes; Southern Road; Collected Poems;* National Council, 1935, 1936, 1939, 1940

Brown, Violet
 LAW 1941

Browne, Waldo R.
 LAW 1938

Bruncken, Herbert
 Novelist; *Last Parade;* LAW 1937, 1938

Buchman, Harold
 Screenwriter; Peace Committee, Hollywood, 1941; blacklisted after 1951

Buchman, Sidney (1902–1975)
 Screenwriter; *Mr. Smith Goes to Washington; The Jolson Story;* signer, Congress Call, 1939; faculty, Hollywood Writers School, 1940, 1941; Exiled Writers Committee, Hollywood, 1941; Hollywood chapter, 1942; found guilty of contempt of Congress, became permanent expatriate; blacklisted after 1952

Buchwald, Nathaniel
 Drama critic, *The Daily Worker;* LAW 1935

Buck, Pearl S. (1892–1973)
 Novelist; *The Good Earth;* Nobel Prize for Literature, 1938; Writers War Board, 1942; FBI target 1937–

Buckmaster, Henrietta (1909–1983) Pseud. of Henrietta Hinkle Stevens
Novelist; editorial staff, *Harper's Bazaar, Reader's Digest; Deep River, Fire in the Heart; Let My People Go, Freedom Bound;* signer, Congress Call, 1941; faculty, New York Writers School, 1942

Bunn, Harriet F.
LAW 1938

Burgum, Edwin Berry (1894–1979)
Critic, professor; *The Novel and the World's Dilemma;* LAW 1935; LAW *Bulletin* editorial board, 1936; Keep America Out of War Committee, 1940; Philadelphia civil liberties protest, September 1940; National Council, 1940, 1941; speaker, Critics Panel, 4th Congress, 1941

Burke, Fielding (1869–1968) Pseud. of Olive Tilford Dargan
Novelist; *Call Home the Heart; Genius and Character; A Stone Came Rolling;* signer, Congress Call, 1935, 1941; National Council 1935

Burke, Kenneth (1897–)
Music critic, essayist; reviewer for *The Dial, The Nation; The White Oxen and Other Stories; Counter Statement; Attitudes Toward History;* lecturer, Writers School; John Reed Club; signer, Congress Call, 1935, 1939, 1941; Executive Committee, 1935; 1st Writers Congress, 1935; LAW *Bulletin* editorial board, 1936; Conference December 1936; Program Committee, 1937

Burnett, Whitney Ewing (Whit) (1899–1973)
Anthologist, fiction writer, editor; LAW 1937

Burns, Paul
Leader, John Reed Club; LAW 1938

Burnshaw, Stanley (1906–)
Drama critic, novelist, playwright, poet; editor, *New Masses; The Iron Land; The Sunless Sea; The Bridge;* LAW 1936

Burnside, Norman
Hollywood chapter, 1942

Burr, Jane

**Burt, Struthers
Present at the last council meeting and voted to continue the League

Burton-Mercur, Paul
LAW 1937; signer, Congress Call, 1941

** Buttitta, Anthony (1907–)
Free-lance newspaper correspondent; founder, editor, *Contempo Magazine; There Were No Elephants,* memoir of the Federal Theater Project; teacher, New York Writers School, 1942

Bynner, Harold Witter (1881–1968)
Poet; *Greenstone Poems; Against the Cold;* LAW 1935; Committee for Cultural Freedom, May 1939; FBI target 1937–

Cahn, Harriet
Second Congress, 1937

Caldwell, Erskine (1903–1987)
Novelist, short story writer; *Journeyman; Southways; North of the Danube; God's Little Acre; Tobacco Road; You Have Seen Their Faces,* with Margaret Bourke-White; signer, Congress Call, 1935, 1937, 1939, 1941; vice president 1937, 1939, 1941; FBI target 1932–

Calmer, Alan. Born Abe Stein
Political activist, editor; *Labor Agitator: The Story of Albert Parsons;* ed. *Salud!; Get Organized;* national officer, John Reed Club; signer, Congress Call, 1935, 1941; National Council, 1935; Committee to Solicit Manuscripts for Labor Periodicals, 1936

Campbell, Victor (1905–)
 Third Congress, 1939
Campbell, Wallace (1910–)
 LAW 1937
Campion, Martha
Cantwell, Robert (1908–1978)
 Novelist; *Laugh and Lie Down; The Land of Plenty;* signer, Congress Call, 1935, 1941;
 National Council, 1935, 1936
Carlisle, Harry (1910–1966?)
 Novelist, journalist, filmwriter; British subject; co-editor, *The Western Worker,* 1935–
 1936; *Darkness at Noon;* LAW 1935; National Council, 1935; 2nd Congress, 1937;
 Executive Committee, 1937; temporary national organizer, 1937; National Council
 correspondent with West Coast chapters, 1938; Legislative Committee, 1939; chair,
 Civil Liberties Committee, 1939; National Council, 1939, 1940; blacklisted; fought
 deportation until departure for London, 1962
Carlisle, Helen Grace
 Novelist; *The Merry, Merry Maidens;* LAW 1936
Carmon, Walter
 Journalist; member, John Reed Club; LAW 1936
Carnicio, Cecilio J.
Carpenter, Marjorie Barth (1896–)
 Educator; *Two Ends of the Log;* LAW 1938
Carse, Robert (1902–1971)
 Fiction writer, journalist; *Siren Song; Horizon; Heart's Desire; The Unconquered; Ama-*
 teurs at War; Exiled Writers Committee; teacher, New York Writers School, 1940, 1941;
 signer, Congress Call, 1941
Carson, Saul (1895–)
 LAW 1938
Caspary, Vera (1904–1987)
 Novelist, playwright, screenwriter; *Laura; Bedelia; Stranger Than Truth; The Weeping*
 and the Laughter; A Chosen Sparrow; Secrets of Grownups; London musical, *Wedding in*
 Paris; LAW 1936; Conference, December 1936; Arrangements Committee, 2nd Con-
 gress, 1937; teacher, New York Writers School, 1938; council member, Hollywood
 chapter, 1940, 1942; faculty, Hollywood Writers School, 1940, 1941; signer, Congress
 Call, 1941; Hollywood Exiled Writers Committee, 1941
Castle, Molly (1908–)
 Screenwriter; *Pigtails;* LAW 1938; signer, Congress Call, 1941; Hollywood School
 Committee, 1941
Chamberlain, John (1904–1959)
 Critic, reporter; *Farewell to Reform: Being a History of the Rise, Life and Decay of the*
 Progressive Mind in America; John Dos Passos: A Biographical and Critical Essay; LAW
 1935; 1st Congress, 1935; resigned 1937; Committee for Cultural Freedom, May 1939
Chapin, Alene Dalton. (1915–1986)
 Educator, television personality; *The Story Princess Book;* 2nd Congress, 1937
Chapin, Katherine Garrison (1891–1978)
 Poet; *Lament for the Stolen; Plain-Chant for America;* signer, Congress Call, 1937, 1939
Cheever, John (1912–1982)
 Novelist, short story writer; *The Wapshot Chronicle; Falconer; Bullet Park;* 2nd Congress,
 1937; FBI target 1965–
Cheney, Ralph
 Member, John Reed Club; signer, Congress Call, 1941; faculty, Hollywood Writers
 School, 1940, 1941

Chevalier, Haakon (1901–1985)
 Translator; tr. *Residential Quarter* by Louis Aragon; LAW 1935; West Coast representative, 1936; Executive Council, 1936; National Council, 1941

Chi, Chao-Ting

** Childs, Marquis W. (1903–1990)
 Journalist; *I Write From Washington;* 2nd Congress, 1937

Childs, Richard S.
 Publisher

Chodorov, Edward (1904–1988)
 Playwright, screenwriter, producer; *Wonder Boy; Kind Lady; Yellow Jack* (adapted from play by Sidney Howard and Paul de Kruif); *Woman Against Woman* (adapted from play by Margaret Culkin Banning); faculty, Hollywood Writers School, 1940, 1941; Organizing Committee, Dramatists Panel, 4th Congress, 1941; signer, Congress Call, 1941; Hollywood chapter, 1942; blacklisted after 1951

Chodorov, Jerome (1911–)
 Playwright, screenwriter, journalist; *Schoolhouse on the Lot* and *Wonderful Town* with Joseph Fields; *3 Bags Full; A Talent for Murder;* Executive and Peace Committees, Hollywood, 1940; Pamphlet and Forum Committee, Hollywood, 1940; Organizing Committee, Dramatists Panel, 4th Congress, 1941; signer, Congress Call, 1941; faculty, Hollywood Writers School, 1942

Christians, Mady

Christman, Henry E. (1906–1980)
 Journalist; editor, *The American Indian,* a journal; *Tin Horns and Calico;* LAW 1937

Christowe, Stoyan (1898–)
 Novelist; *This Is My Country;* LAW Conference, 1936

Clark, Eleanor (1913–)
 Novelist; *Dark Wedding; The Bitter Box; Baldur's Gate;* LAW 1936; 2nd Congress, 1937

Clark, Maurice (1921–)
 Organizing Committee, Dramatists Panel, 4th Congress, 1941

Clarke, Faith
 LAW 1941

Clay, Eugene. Born Eugene Holmes

Clements, Albert Edward
 Poet; *Documents and Dainties I; Documents and Dainties II;* LAW 1936

Clurman, Harold (1901–1980)
 Theater critic, *New Republic;* director of *Orpheus Descending, Golden Boy, Desire Under the Elms, The Iceman Cometh; The Fervent Years: The Story of the Group Theatre and the Thirties; Lies Like Truth; All People Are Famous;* Executive Committee, 1935

Coates, Robert M. (1897–1973)
 Novelist; signer, Congress Call, 1935, 1941; LAW *Bulletin* editorial board, 1936

Cobb, Humphrey (1899–)
 Novelist; *Paths of Glory;* LAW 1937; signer, Congress Call, 1939

Cobb, Lee Jacob (1911–1976)
 Actor, film and TV; *Death of a Salesman; On the Waterfront;* informer [see Navasky, p. 269]

Coblentz, Stanton A. (1896–)
 Poet, free-lance writer, feature writer, book reviewer; founder and editor, *Wings,* 1933–1960; *The Decline of Man; The Literary Revolution; The Answer of the Ages;* 2nd Congress, 1937; Hollywood chapter, 1942

Cohen, Lester (1901–1963)
 Novelist; *Sweepings; Coming Home;* signer, Congress Call, 1935, 1939, 1941; Conference, 1936; National Council, 1939, 1940; instructor, New York Writers School, 1939

Colahan, Charles E. Born Edward Elliot
    Cartoonist; *Blondie;* LAW 1936; Hollywood chapter, 1942

Colby, Merle (1902–1969)
    Novelist; *The Big Secret;* leader, John Reed Club; National Council, 1935; National Council, 1938

Cole, Lester (1904–1985) Pseud. Gerald L.C. Copley
    Novelist; screenwriter; *Sweepings; Coming Home; Charlie Chan's Greatest Case; House of Seven Gables; The Invisible Man Returns; Objective Burma;* signer, Congress Call, 1941; officer, Hollywood chapter, 1941, 1942; National Council, 1941; one of Hollywood Ten; imprisoned for contempt of Congress; blacklisted 1948, subsequently office clerk and cook, then wrote scripts using pseudonyms; *Born Free* as Gerald L.C. Copley

Colehan, Eugene
    LAW 1935

Collins, Lloyd
    LAW 1935

Collins, Richard (Dick) (1914–)
    Screenwriter; *Riot in Cell Block II;* Pamphlet and Forum Committee, Hollywood, 1941; Exiled Writers Committee, Hollywood, 1941; teacher, Hollywood Writers School; Hollywood chapter, 1942; blacklisted 1947; informer before HUAC, 1951, worked steadily thereafter [see Maltz UCLA Interview; Schwartz, p. 282; Navasky, pp. 137, 138, 225]

Colman, Louis (1902–1969)
    Economist; LAW 1936

Commons, David
    Hollywood chapter, 1942

Conklin, Groff (1904–1968)
    Free-lance writer; *All About Subways;* LAW 1937

Connelly, Marc (1890–1980)
    Playwright; Executive Committee, 1935; signer, Congress Call, 1937; 2nd Congress, 1937; Advisory Council, Writers War Board, 1942; Hollywood Writers Congress, 1943; contributor, Hollywood Writers Congress book, 1944

Conover, Harry
    Editorial board; *Science and Society,* 1936; Executive Committee, 1935

Conried, Ellen
    Poet, photographer; Exiled Writers Committee

Conroy, Jack (1899–1990) Pseud. John Wesley
    Novelist, journalist; *The Disinherited; A World to Win;* national officer, John Reed Club; signer, Congress Call, 1935, 1941; National Council, 1935; 1st Congress, 1935; Executive Council, Midwest, 1936; executive secretary, Chicago chapter, 1938

** Copland, Aaron (1900–1990)
    Composer; Third Congress, 1939; lectured for League on American music, December 9, 1935; Hollywood Writers Congress, 1943

** Copstein, Seymour A.
    New York Writers School, 1941

Cordell, Kathryn Coe
    LAW 1937; acting executive secretary, Washington, D.C., chapter, 1938

** Corey, Lewis
    Lectured for League, "Crisis of the Middle Class," January 1936

Corey, Paul (1903–1993)
    Novelist; *Three Miles Square; County Seat; Acres of Antaeus;* LAW 1936

Corwin, Norman (1910–)
    Director, poet, scriptwriter, producer; radio script, *They Fly Through the Air With the Greatest of Ease;* film; *Lust for Life;* books, *Trivializing America, Thirteen by Corwin;* LAW

1938; speaker, 3rd Congress, 1939; National Council, 1939, 1940; lecturer, New York Writers School, 1938, 1940; lecturer, Hollywood Writers School; Advisory Council, Writers War Board, 1942; contributor, Writers Congress book, 1944

Counts, George S. (1889–1974)
Educator; LAW 1935; Committee for Cultural Freedom, May 1939

Cowley, Malcolm (1898– 1989)
Critic, poet; editorial staff, *New Republic; Exile's Return; The Blue Juniata; After the Genteel Tradition,* member, John Reed Club; signer, Congress Call, 1935, 1939; Executive Committee, 1935–1940; 1st Congress, 1935; Lecture Committee, 1935; Conference December, 1936; 2nd Congress, 1937; member, 2nd Congress Program Committee, 1937; vice president, 1937, 1939; LAW representative to International Congress of Writers for Defense of Culture, 1937; National Council, 1938; resigned May 23, 1940; FBI target 1936–

Cox, Marian (1898–1983) Pseud. Marian Monroe
Psychologist, educator; *Dick and Jane* textbooks; *Foundations for Reading;* 2nd Congress, 1937

Cox, Sidney
LAW 1935

Coy, Harold (1902–)
Historian, reporter; executive editor, Federal Writers Project; *The Americans; The Real Book About George Washington Carver;* LAW 1936; instructor in labor journalism, New York Writers School, 1937, 1938

Crampton, C. Ward
Signer, Congress Call, 1941

Crawford, Bruce
LAW 1935

Crawford, Ruth Elizabeth
LAW 1938

Crichton, Kyle (1896–1960) Pseud. Robert Forsythe
Humorist, journalist, critic; editorial staff, *Scribner's, Collier's; Total Recoil; Reading From Left to Right;* LAW 1935; Conference December 1936; Arrangements Committee, 1937; lecturer, "How to Write Articles and Special Features," New York Writers School, 1941; resigned 1939

Crosby, Alexander L. (1906–1980)
Labor journalist; supervisor, Federal Writers Project; *The Rio Grande; Steamboat Up the Colorado;* teacher, New York Writers School, 1941, 1942; signer, Congress Call, 1941; chair, Labor Journalism Panel, 4th Congress, 1941; National Council, 1941

Crosby, Mary Jacob Caresse (1892–1970)
Editor, publisher

Crossen, Ken (1910–) Pseuds. Bennett Barley, M. E. Chaber, Richard Foster, Christopher Monig, Clay Richards
Director, producer; over 400 radio and television dramas; lecturer in adventure and detective fiction, New York Writers School, 1941

Cullen, Countee (1903–1946)
Poet; *The Medea and Some Poems;* Executive Committee, 1935; Committee for Cultural Freedom, May 1939

Cunningham, William
Novelist; *Pretty Boy; The Green Corn Rebellion;* LAW 1935

Curran, Dale (1898–)
Novelist; *A House on a Street;* LAW 1936

Cuthbert, Clifton (1907–)
Novelist; *Another Such Victory*

Dodd, Jr., William E. (1900–)
> Signer, Congress Call, 1941; U.S. Congress stopped his pay, November 1943

Dombrowski, James (1897–1983)
> Civil rights activist; founder, Highlander Folk School, to train labor organizers and civil rights activists; *The Early Days of Christian Socialism in America*; LAW 1938

Donini, Ambrogio (1903–)
> Italian refugee, editor; Exiled Writers Committee

Donahoe, Edward
> LAW 1938

Dos Passos, John (1896–1970)
> Novelist, historian; *The Big Money*; *U.S.A.*; *Airways, Inc*; *The Garbage Man*; member, John Reed Club; signer, Congress Call, 1935; FBI target 1923–; became hostile to League, 1937

Dowdey, Clifford (1904–)
> Novelist; *Gamble's Hundred*

Downes, Olin Edwin (1886–1955)
> Music critic; reviewer for *Boston Post, New York Times*; *The Lure of Music*

Draper, Muriel (1886–1952) Full name Muriel Gurden Sanders Draper
> Feminist, humanitarian; *Music at Midnight*; LAW 1936; 2nd Congress, 1937; Finance Committee, 1937; signer, Congress Call, 1939, 1941; delegate, Emergency Peace Mobilization, 1940; National Council, 1941

Draper, Theodore (1912–)
> Historian, social critic; *The Roots of American Communism*; LAW 1937; liaison in France between the League and the International Association for Defense of Culture, 1939

Dreher, Carl (1896–1976)
> Journalist; *Automation: What It Is, How It Works, Who Can Use It*

Dreiser, Theodore (1871–1945)
> Novelist; *An American Tragedy*; *Tragic America*; *Sister Carrie*; *Jennie Gerhardt*; signer, Congress Call, 1935, 1941; League representative at Paris Writers Conference, 1938; LAW honorary president, 1941; Hollywood chapter, 1942; FBI target 1927–

Drury, John (1898–1972)
> Film critic, poet, historical archivist; *Arclight Dusks*; *Chicago in Seven Days*; *Midwest Heritage*; LAW 1938; Chicago chapter, 1938

Dugan, James (1912–1967)
> Fiction writer; lecturer, "Writing for Picture Magazines," New York Writers School, 1940, 1941; signer, Congress Call, 1941; teacher, Writers Conference, Highlander Folk School

** Dunn, John
> Member, John Reed Club; teacher, New York Writers School, 1942

Dunn, Robert (1877–1955)
> Economist; executive secretary, Labor Research Association; National Council, 1938

Dunne, Philip (1908–1992)
> Screenwriter, union organizer, director; speechwriter for Adlai Stevenson, John F. Kennedy; scripts, *How Green Was My Valley*; *Stanley and Livingston*; co-script, *The Rains Came*; autobiography; *Take Two: A Life in Movies and Politics*; nominated for two Academy Awards; LAW 1938; signer, Congress Call, 1939; resigned; after World War II, co-founded with directors John Huston and William Wyler the Committee for the First Amendment, to protest witch-hunts and vindicate those in danger of imprisonment in the Red Scare

Dupee, F. W. (1904–1979)
> Critic; 2nd Congress, 1937; left LAW in 1937 and became an editor of *Partisan Review*; FBI target 1939–

Duranty, Walter (1884–1957)
Journalist; Moscow correspondent, *New York Times;* Pulitzer Prize for dispatches on the Soviet Union's Five-Year Plan; *Red Economics; The Curious Lottery and Other Tales of Russian Justice;* LAW 1937; 2nd Congress, 1937; resigned 1939; speaker, Exiled Writers Committee, Hollywood, 1941

d'Usseau, Arnaud (1916–1990)
Screenwriter, playwright; *Tomorrow the World; Deep Are the Roots,* with James Gow; signer, Congress Call, 1941; Hollywood chapter, 1942; blacklisted 1950s

du Von, Jay
LAW 1936

Eaton, Horace Ainsworth (1871–)
LAW 1936

Eberhart, Richard (1904–)
Poet, professor of English; *A Bravery of Earth; Reading the Spirit; Dream Journey of the Head and Heart; To Eberhart From Ginsberg*

Edman, Irwin (1896–1954)
Essayist; Committee for Cultural Freedom, May 1939

Efron, David

** Egri, Lajos (1888–1967)
Critic; *How to Write a Play; Art of Dramatic Writing;* teacher, New York Writers School, 1942

Ehrlich, Leonard (1905–)
Novelist; *God's Angry Man;* National Council, 1935; LAW *Bulletin* editorial board, 1936

Ehricos, Emilio

** Einstein, Albert (1879–1955)
Honorary member; message to 2nd Congress, 1937; sponsor of Ludwig Renn tour

Eisenberg, Emanuel
LAW 1935

Eisner, Alfred

**Elby, Harold
Western Writers Congress, 1936

Eliscu, Edward (1902–)
Screenwriter; Executive Committee, Hollywood chapter, 1939, 1940; faculty, Hollywood Writers School, 1940, 1941; signer, Congress Call, 1941; Pamphlet and Forum Committee, Hollywood, 1941; Hollywood chapter, 1942; blacklisted 1951

Eliscu, Stella
LAW 1940; Hollywood chapter, 1942

Ellis, Peter
Second Congress, 1937

Ellison, Ralph (1914–)
Novelist; *Invisible Man; Shadow and Act; Going to the Territory;* National Council, 1941; signer, Congress Call, 1941; committee to plan LAW magazine, 1941; committee to aid *The Clipper,* November 1941

Elting, Mary (1906–) Pseuds. Davis Cole, Campbell Tatham
Children's book writer; editorial staff, *Forum Magazine, Golden Book Magazine; We Are the Government; Ships at Work; Q is for Duck; Mysterious Seas; Snakes and Other Reptiles; The Big Golden Book of Dinosaurs;* LAW 1938; teacher, New York Writers School, 1938–1942

**Endfield, Cyril (1914–)
Blacklisted after 1951

Endore, Guy (1901–1971) Born Samuel Goldstein; pseud. Harry Relis
    Novelist; *Babouk; The Werewolf of Paris; The Sword of God; The Life of Joan of Arc; King of Paris;* signer, Congress Call, 1935, 1939, 1941; Western Writers Congress, 1936; Los Angeles representative, 1936; faculty, Hollywood Writers School, 1942
Engle, Fannie
    Cuisine writer; LAW 1938; Keep America Out of War Committee, 1940; signer, Congress Call, 1941
Engle, Paul (1908–1991)
    Poet, fiction writer, critic; ed. *Ozark Anthology; Corn; Worn Earth;* LAW 1936
Englebrecht, H. C.
    Second Congress, 1937
Engstrand, Stuart (1904–1955)
    Novelist; LAW, 1938
Enters, Angna (1907–1989)
    Performer, sculptor, painter; *Love Possessed Juana; The Unknown Lover; Among the Daughters;* autobiographies, *First Person Plural, Silly Girl, Artist's Life;* LAW 1938
Epstein, Julius
    Hollywood chapter, 1942
Epstein, Philip
    Hollywood chapter, 1942
Essell, Nathan
    Second Congress, 1937
Eulenburg-Weiner, Renie
Eudy, Mary Cummings (1871–1952)
Everts, William (1902–1988)
Ewen, Frederic (1899–1988)
    Bertolt Brecht: His Life, His Art and His Times

Faber, Beatrice
Fadiman, Clifton (1904–)
    Critic; *Any Number Can Play; Party of One; I Believe; Empty Pages,* with James Howard; LAW 1935; 2nd Congress, 1937; Writers War Board, 1942
Fairchild, Henry Pratt (1880–1956)
    Professor of Sociology; *Immigration; Outline of Sociology; Elements of Social Science; The Melting Pot Mistake;* LAW 1938; signer, Congress Call, 1939
Falkowski, Edward
    LAW 1937
Fante, John (1911–1983)
    Novelist, screenwriter; Academy Award nomination for *Full of Life; Wait Until Spring; Bandini; Ask the Dust; Jeanne Eagles; My Six Loves; Walk on the Wild Side*
Faragoh, Francis Edwards
    LAW 1937; signer, Congress Call, 1939; Exiled Writers Committee, Hollywood, 1941; Hollywood chapter, 1942
Farr, Finis (1904–1982) Born Finis King
    Free-lance writer; *A Social History for the 1930's; Black Champion: The Life and Times of Jack Johnson; The Elephant Valley; Frank Lloyd Wright: A Biography*
Farrell, James T. (1904–1979) Pseud. Jonathan Titulescu Fogarty
    Novelist, critic; *Studs Lonigan (trilogy); Bernard Clare; Danny O'Neill (trilogy); My Days of Anger; A World I Never Made; Gas House McGinty; Father and Son;* signer, Congress Call, 1935; National Council, 1935; resigned 1936, and became opponent; FBI target 1934–

Fast, Howard (1914–) Pseud. E. V. Cunningham
Fiction and non-fiction writer; *Freedom Road; Spartacus; The Unvanquished; Citizen Tom Paine; The Last Frontier; The Naked God;* imprisoned for refusing to reveal names to HUAC, 1950; blacklisted; FBI target 1932–

Fauset, Arthur Huff (1899–)
Historian of African-American experience; *For Freedom: A Biographical Story of the American Negro; Folklore From Nova Scotia; Black Gods of the Metropolis; Sojourner Truth; God's Faithful Pilgrim; America: Red, White, Black and Yellow*

Fauset, Jessie Redmon (1884–1961)
Novelist, critic, poet; *There Is Confusion; Comedy, American Style; The Chinaberry Tree; Plum Bun;* first black female to graduate from Cornell University; as literary editor of *The Crisis* magazine, under W.E.B. Du Bois, she published many Harlem Renaissance writers, including Countee Cullen, Langston Hughes, Jean Toomer; LAW 1936

Fearing, Franklin (1892–1962)
Professor of Psychology; *Reflex Action; Influence of Movies on Attitudes and Behaviors;* faculty, Hollywood Writers School, 1942; Hollywood Writers Congress, 1943; contributor, Hollywood Writers Congress book, 1944

Fearing, Kenneth (1902–1961)
Novelist, poet; *Clark Gifford's Body; Dead Reckoning; The Big Clock; Poems; Angel Arms;* national officer, John Reed Club; signer, Congress Call, 1935, 1939; National Council, 1935; faculty, New York Writers School, 1939

Feinberg, Leon (1914–)
Second Congress, 1937

Feinstein, Isidor [see: I. F. Stone]

Fenwick, David
LAW 1940; faculty, Hollywood Writers School, 1940, 1941

Fenwick, Edward
Hollywood chapter, 1942

Ferguson, Otis
LAW 1936

Fergusson, Harvey (1890–1971)
Novelist; *The Life of Riley; The Santa Fe Omnibus: A Trilogy of the Santa Fe Trail; Hot Saturday;* LAW 1938; Hollywood chapter, 1942

Ferrari, Robert
Second Congress, 1937

Ferro, Mathild
LAW 1938

Ferro, Theodore E.
LAW 1938

Feuchtwanger, Lion (1884–1958)
Novelist, playwright, poet; German refugee; *Success; Ugly Duckling; Power; The Pretender;* speaker, Exiled Writers Committee dinner; Hollywood Writers Congress, 1943

Ficke, Arthur Davison (1883–1945)
Poet; translator; tr. *Stormbird;* signer, Congress Call, 1939

Field, Ben (1901–) Born Moe Bragin
Fiction writer; *Cow; The Cock's Funeral; The Last Freshet; The Outside Leaf; Piper Tompkins;* signer, Congress Call, 1935, 1941; Conference December 1936

Field, Frederick Vanderbilt (1905–)
Political scientist; executive secretary, American Peace Mobilization; *Socialist Planning and a Socialist Consortium; Empire in the East; From Right to Left: An Autobiography;* signer, Congress Call, 1941; imprisoned for contempt of Congress

Field, Kathleen
LAW 1938

Field, Sarah Bard (1883–1974)
   Poet; member, John Reed Club; LAW 1935

Fields, Allen A.

Fields, Joseph A. (1895–1966)
   Playwright; *My Sister Eileen;* Organizing Committee, Dramatists Panel, 4th Congress, 1941; Pamphlet and Forum Committee, Hollywood, 1941; Hollywood chapter, 1942

Fineman, Irving (1893–)
   Novelist; *Doctor Addams;* LAW 1936

Finsterwald, Maxine
   Journalist; LAW 1936

Fischer, Bruno (1908–) Pseud. Russell Gray
   Mystery novelist, reporter; editor, *Labor Voice;* editor, *Socialist Call; So Much Blood; The Hornet's Nest;* 3rd Congress, 1937

Fischer, Louis (1896–1970)
   Journalist; *Dawn of Victory; Russia, America, and the World; Gandhi and Stalin; Life of Mahatma Gandhi;* LAW 1937; 2nd Congress, 1937; resigned 1939

Fischer, Marjorie (1903–1961)
   Children's book writer; *Street Fair; Palaces on Monday; Pause to Wonder; Red Feather;* LAW 1936; Executive Committee, 1937; Writers/Artists Ambulance Corps Committee, 1937; chair, Membership Committee, 1937; Film Survey Committee; Conference December 1936; instructor, juvenile story writing, New York Writers School, 1937; National Council, 1938, 1939; signer, Congress Call, 1939; chair, Exiled Writers Committee, 1939; Philadelphia civil liberties protest, September 1940; resigned July 1940

Fisher, Dorothy Canfield (1879–1958)
   Novelist; editor, Book-of-the-Month Club; *The Deepening Stream; An Election on Academy Hill; Seasoned Timber;* LAW 1936; vice president, 1939; Advisory Council, Writers War Board, 1942

Fischer, Vardis (1895–1968)
   Novelist, poet, essayist; *Forgive Us Our Virtues; Odyssey of a Hero; April; Toilers of the Hills; Dark Bridwell; In Tragic Life;* LAW 1937; resigned, date uncertain

Fitts, Dudley (1903–1968)
   Poet, critic, translator; *One Hundred Poems From the Palatine; Antigone;* LAW 1936

Fitzgerald, Robert (1910–1985)
   Second Congress, 1937

Flandrau, Grace Hodgson (?–1971)
   Novelist; *Cousin Julia; Being Respectable; Under the Sun;* Midwest Writers Congress, 1936

Flanell, Rose E.
   Second Congress, 1937

Flanner, Hildegarde (1899–1987) Full name June Hildegarde Flanner Monhoff
   Poet, playwright, essayist; *A Vanishing Land, Young Girl and Other Poems; White Bridge;* Hollywood chapter, 1942

Flato, Charles (1908–1984)
   Journalist, scriptwriter; investigator and report writer for Civil Liberties Subcommittee of Senate Labor Committee from 1937 to 1941; LAW 1936

Fleming, Ethel
   Second Congress, 1937

Fletcher, John Gould (1886–1950)
   Poet; 2nd Congress, 1937

Flexner, Eleanor (1908–)
   Historian, drama critic; *The American Playwrights, 1918–1934; Century of Struggle: The Woman's Rights Movement in the United States;* Keep America Out of War Committee,

1940; secretary, Organizing Committee, Dramatists Panel, 4th Congress, 1941; National Council, 1941

Flores, Angel (1900–)
Critic; ed. *The Philosophy of Art of Karl Marx*; ed. *Literature and Marxism*; National Council, 1935

Floyd, William (1871–)
Political writer; *War Resistance*

Foley, Martha (1897–1977)
Editor; 2nd Congress, 1937

Folsom, Franklin (1907–) Pseuds. Benjamin Brewster, Michael Gorham, Lyman Hopkins, Troy Nesbit, Chase Elwell, Horatio (H. D.) Jones, Philip Stander
Children's book writer, historian, poet; Harriet Monroe Memorial Award, 1937; *Red Power on the Rio Grande; Black Cowboy: The Life and Legend of George McJunkin; Sand Dune Pony; Impatient Armies of the Poor; America's Ancient Treasures*; national executive secretary, September 1937–December 1942; FBI target

Foote, Betsy
LAW 1937; League correspondent, Minnesota chapter, 1938

Forbes-Robertson, Diana
Journalist, novelist; *War Letters From Britain; The Battle of Waterloo Road; A Cat and a King; My Aunt Maxine: Maxine Elliot*; speaker, Exiled Writers Committee dinner, October 9, 1941

Ford, Charles Henri (1913–)
Artist, poet, filmmaker; *The Garden of Disorder & Other Poems*; 2nd Congress, 1937

Foss, Fanya
Faculty, Hollywood Writers School, 1940, 1941; Hollywood chapter, 1942

Foster, Orline Dorman
Economist; *Profits From the Stock Market*; 2nd Congress, 1937

Foster, William Z.
National leader, Communist Party; *Pages From a Worker's Life*; LAW 1938; 3rd Congress, 1939

Fraenkel, Michael (1896–1957)
Novelist; *Anonymous; Death in a Room; Bastard Death; Death Is Not Enough*; LAW 1937

Frank, Bernhard
LAW 1935

Frank, Waldo David (1889–1967)
Novelist, playwright, critic; editor, *Masses*; editor, *New Republic*; *The Bridegroom Cometh; The Re-Discovery of America; The Death and Birth of David Markand: An American Story*; member, John Reed Club; signer, Congress Call, 1935, 1941; Executive Committee, 1935; LAW president, 1935, 1936; American delegate to International Writers Congress, Paris, 1936; resigned as president in 1936; signer, Congress Call, 1937; membership ambiguous but attended later meetings and congresses; FBI target 1932–

Franzen, Erich

Freeman, Frank S.

Freeman, Ira Henry (1906–)
Instructor in labor journalism, New York Writers School, 1939, 1940

Freeman, Joseph (1897–1965)
Novelist, poet, critic; founder, *Partisan Review*; editor, *New Masses*; *Preface to Proletarian Literature in the United States; An American Testament; Never Call Retreat*; national officer, John Reed Club; signer, Congress Call, 1935, 1939, 1941; Executive Committee, 1935; Conference December 1936; 2nd Congress Program Committee, 1937; Executive Committee, 1937; member, National Council, 1938

Freidkin, Emily

Frost, Robert (1874–1963)
    Poet; *A Further Range; A Boy's Will; A Witness Tree;* Library of Congress Consultant in Poetry, 1958; Congressional Gold Medal, 1962; LAW 1935; FBI target 1942–

Fuchs, Daniel (1909–1993)
    Scriptwriter; Academy Award for *Love Me or Leave Me; Interlude; Jeanne Eagels; The Williamsburg Trilogy: Summer in Williamsburg; Homage to Blenholt; Lost Company;* LAW 1936; signer, Congress Call, 1939

Funaroff, Sol (1911–1942) Pseud. Charles Henry Newman
    Poet; *The Spider and the Clock; Exile From a Future Time;* LAW 1937

Funt, Julian (1907–)
    Scriptwriter; dramatic serials, *The Voice of Experience, Search for Tomorrow;* Broadway plays; *The Dancer, The Magic and the Loss*

Gaer, Joseph (1897–1969) Born Joseph Fishman
    Journalist; *The Unconquered: Adapted Folklore Legends;* ed. *Our Federal Government and How It Functions; The Legend Called Meryom; What Uncle Sam Owes You; The First Round;* chief field supervisor and editor-in-chief of Federal Writers Project, 1935–1939; LAW 1935

Gag, Wanda (1893–1946)
    Children's book writer, illustrator; tr. and illus. *Snow White and the Seven Dwarfs; Millions of Cats;* LAW 1936; Conference December 1936

Galantiere, Lewis
    Translator; tr. *Wind, Sand and Stars* by Antoine de Saint Exupery; LAW 1939

Gannett, Lewis (1891–1966)
    Journalist, critic; book reviewer for *New York Herald Tribune; Young China; Sweet Land;* LAW 1938; resigned 1939; Advisory Council, Writers War Board, 1942

Garlin, Sender (1902–)
    Journalist; *The Real Huey P. Long; Is Dewey The Man?; Three American Radicals;* editor, *Partisan Review;* member, John Reed Club

Garrison, Troy

Gaspar, Samuel
    Member, John Reed Club

Gassner, John W. (1903–1967)
    Critic; lecturer, "The Playwright and the Theatre," New York Writers School, 1941

Gates, Michael
    Second Congress, 1937

Gawthorpe, Mary

Geddes, Virgil (1897–)
    Critic, poet; financial editor, *The Paris Tribune; The American Theater: What Can Be Done?; The Melodramadness of Eugene O'Neill; Forty Poems; Poems 4l to 70;* founder, Brookfield Players, 1932; managing producer, Unit A, NYC chapter of the Federal Theater, 1935–1937

Gellert, Lawrence
    Second Congress, 1937

Gellhorn, Martha (1908–)
    Journalist, novelist; *The Heart of Another; What Mad Pursuit;* speaker, 2nd Congress, 1937

Georg, Manfred
    Refugee writer; general secretary, German-American Writers Association

Gerson, Thomas
    LAW 1938

Gessner, Robert (1907–1968)
Poet, novelist; *Upsurge; Broken Arrow; Treason; Some of My Best Friends Are Jews;* LAW 1936; 2nd Congress Program Committee, 1937; Executive Committee, 1937; National Council, 1938; 3rd Congress, 1939

Gibney, Sheridan (1904–1988)
Producer, playwright, screenwriter, critic; shared two Academy Awards in 1936 with Pierre Collings for *The Story of Louis Pasteur; I Am a Fugitive From a Chain Gang; Anthony Adverse; Green Pastures; The Man From U.N.C.L.E.; The Six Million Dollar Man; Police Woman;* president, Hollywood chapter, 1939; faculty, Hollywood Writers School, 1940, 1941; resigned

Gidlow, Elsa (1898–1986)
Poet, journalist; *On a Grey Thread; From Alba Hill; California Valley With Girls*

Gilberta, Helen Earle
Novelist; *Mrs. Wallaby's Birthday;* 2nd Congress, 1937

Gilbert, Leland
LAW 1937

Gilbert, Mercedes
Fiction writer; *Aunt Sara's Wooden God;* LAW 1939

Gilfillan, Lauren (1909–) Pseud. of Harriet Woodbridge Gilfillan
Fiction writer; autobiography, *I Went to Pitt College;* LAW 1936

Gilkes, Lillian Barnard
LAW 1937; chair, Educational Committee, 1937; teacher, "History of Short Story," New York Writers School, 1938; National Council, 1938, 1941; LAW delegate, Emergency Peace Mobilization, 1940; teacher, Writers Conference, Highlander Folk School

Gilliland, Strickland
LAW 1942

Gilman, Mildred
Free-lance writer; *Divide by Two;* LAW 1938

Gingrich, Arnold (1903–1976)
Novelist; *Cast Down Laurel;* LAW 1937

Ginsberg, Louis
Second Congress, 1937

Glaser, Dorothy
LAW 1937; executive secretary, Cambridge, Mass., chapter, 1938

Glassman, Baruch
Second Congress, 1937

Glenn, Charles
Hollywood chapter, 1942

Glenn, Lillian G.
Second Congress, 1937

Glintenkamp, H. H.
Artist; member, John Reed Club; 4th Congress, 1941

Godin, Alexander
Second Congress, 1937

Gold, Michael (1894–1967) Born Irving Granich
Journalist, novelist, playwright, poet; *The Hollow Men; Jews Without Money; Battle Hymn;* member, John Reed Club; signer, Congress Call, 1935, 1941; Executive Committee, 1935; 1st Congress, 1935; Southwest representative, 1936; speaker, Critics Panel, 4th Congress, 1941

Goldberg, David A.
Novelist; *Perish the Jew!;* LAW 1939

Gunther, John (1901–1970)
> Journalist; reporter, *Chicago Daily News; The Red Pavillion; The Bright Nemesis; The High Cost of Hitler; Inside Europe; Inside Asia; Inside Latin America;* 2nd Congress, 1937; Advisory Council, Writers War Board, 1942; FBI target 1936–

Guthrie, Ramon (1896–1973)
> Novelist, poet; *A World Too Old; Parachute; Graffiti;* LAW 1935

Guterman, Norbert (1900–1984)
> Translator; tr. Henri Lefebre's *Sociology of Marx;* with Leo Lowenthal, *Prophets of Deceit: A Study of the Technique of American Agitation;* LAW 1935; Conference, December 1936

Hacker, Louis (1899–1987)
> Historian, professor, editor; *The Farmer Is Doomed; American Problems of Today; The Triumph of American Capitalism;* LAW 1935

Hackett, Albert (1900–)
> Screenwriter; six Academy Award nominations; scripts; *The Thin Man; It's A Wonderful Life; Father of the Bride;* winner of Tony Award, Pulitzer Prize, and New York Drama Critics Award for *The Diary of Anne Frank;* Writers War Board

Haessler, Carl
> Critic, labor journalist; member, John Reed Club; Chicago chapter, 1938

Haldane, John Burdon Sanderson (1892–1964)
> Essayist, professor of Genetics and Biometry; chair of editorial board, *London Daily Worker; The Inequality of Man and Other Essays; The Marxist Philosphy and the Sciences; Why Professional Workers Should Be Communists*

Haldeman-Julius, E. (1889–1951)
> Journalist, publisher; member, John Reed Club; *The First Hundred Million*

Halden, Stuart
> Second Congress, 1937

Hale, Hope
> Free-lance writer; 2nd and 3rd Congresses, 1937, 1939

Hallgren, Mauritz
> LAW 1937; signer, Congress Call, 1939

Halper, Albert (1904–1984)
> Novelist; *The Chute; The Foundry; Union Square;* LAW 1936; resigned 1939

Halperin, Maurice (1906–)
> Professor, journalist; contributor, *New Republic, New York Times Magazine, Foreign Affairs; The Rise and Decline of Fidel Castro;* LAW 1935

Hamilton, Florence

Hammett, Dashiell (1894–1961)
> Novelist; the Nick and Nora Charles series, *The Thin Man;* in his will left funds to aid persecuted writers; LAW 1936; 2nd and 3rd Congresses, 1937, 1939; Philadelphia civil liberties protest, 1940; Keep America Out of War Committee, 1940, 1941; LAW president, 1941; speaker, 4th Congress public meeting, 1941; FBI target 1934–; imprisoned 1951, for refusing to inform on contributors to the Civil Rights Congress; blacklisted thereafter

Hand, Frederic

Handcos, John

Hansen, Harry (1884–1977)
> Journalist, translator; tr. Jacob Wasserman's *Faber* and F. Freksa's *A Peace Congress of Intrigue; Carl Sandburg: The Man and His Poetry;* 2nd Congress, 1937

Hansen, Merlin
> LAW 1939

Harap, Louis (1904–)
    Critic; *Social Roots of the Arts; The Image of the Jew in American Literature*

Harburg, E. Y. (1896–1981)
    Lyricist, playwright, poet; "Brother, Can You Spare a Dime?"; "God's Country";
    Academy Award for "Over the Rainbow" from *The Wizard of Oz;* Henderson Award
    for Best Musical Comedy, *Finian's Rainbow; Rhymes for the Irreverent;* blacklisted

Harlen, Rachel
    Second Congress, 1937

Harris, Jessie Fauset [see Jessie Fauset]

Harris, M. Tjader
    Editor, *Directions;* LAW 1938

Harris, Reed
    Expelled Columbia University student; LAW 1938

Harrison, Alan
    LAW 1938

Harrison, W. F.
    LAW 1936

Harron, Robert
    Second Congress, 1937

Hart, Henry (1903–)
    Novelist; *The Great One, A Novel of American Life;* ed. *The American Writers Congress;*
    ed. *The Writer in a Changing World; Dr. Barnes of Merion;* signer, Congress Call, 1935,
    1939, 1941; 1st Congress, 1935; Executive Committee, 1935, 1937; *Bulletin* editorial
    board, 1936; Program Committee, 1936, 1937; Conference December 1936; chair, 2nd
    Congress Program Committee, 1937; lecturer, New York Writers School, 1940; Keep
    America Out of War Committee, 1940; National Council, 1939, 1940, 1941; resigned
    after June 1941

Hart, Marian (1892–1940)
    LAW Arrangements chair, 1937; 2nd Congress, 1937

Hart, Moss (1904–1961)
    Playwright; *You Can't Take It With You; The Man Who Came to Dinner; Act One; Light
    Up the Sky;* FBI target 1938–

Hart, Walter (1906–1973)
    Stage and television producer

Haste, Gwendolen

Hathaway, Clarence
    Journalist; editor, *The Daily Worker;* signer, Congress Call, 1935, 1941; 1st Congress,
    1935

Havighurst, Walter (1901–)
    Novelist, professor; *Pier 17; The Quiet Shore; Approach to America;* Friends of American
    Writers Award for *Land of Promise*

Hawes, Elizabeth
    Novelist; *Men Can Take It;* LAW 1939

Hawkins, Willard
    LAW 1936

Hawthorne, Edith Garrigues
    Ed. *The Memoirs of Julian Hawthorne;* LAW 1938

Hayes, Alfred (1911–1985)
    Poet, playwright, screenwriter; poetry: *The Big Time;* novel: *Shadow of Heaven;* screen-
    plays: *Paisan; Clash by Night; Human Desire; Joy in the Morning;* LAW 1937

Hays, Howard
    Second Congress, 1937

Hays, Hoffman Reynolds (1904–1980)
> Poet; *12 Spanish American Poets* (an anthology); *From Ape to Angel;* tr. *Bertolt Brecht: Selected Poems; Inside My Own Skin; Crisis;* LAW 1935

Hedley, David

Head, Ethel McCall
> Hollywood chapter, 1942

Helgren, Nora
> Hollywood chapter, 1942

Hellman, George S.
> Second Congress, 1937

Hellman, Lillian (1905–1984)
> Playwright; *The Little Foxes; The Children's Hour; Watch on the Rhine;* LAW 1935; signer, Congress Call, 1939; 3rd Congress, 1939; National Council, 1939, 1940; Keep America Out of War Committee, 1940; co-chair, Exiled Writers Committee dinner, October 9, 1940; Exiled Writers Committee, 1940; called by HUAC, 1942; FBI target 1933–; blacklisted after 1952

Hemingway, Ernest (1898–1961)
> Novelist; *To Have and Have Not; The Spanish Earth; The Green Hills of Africa; The Sun Also Rises; A Farewell to Arms; For Whom The Bell Tolls;* 2nd Congress, 1937; co-chair, Exiled Writers Committee dinner, October 9, 1940; vice president, 1939, 1940; FBI target 1935–

Herald, Leon Srabian
> Poet; LAW 1936; 2nd Congress, 1937

Herbst, Josephine (1897–1969)
> Novelist, critic; *Rope of Gold; Nothing Is Sacred; The Executioner Waits; Satan's Sergeants; Pity Is Not Enough; Somewhere the Tempest Fell;* member, John Reed Club; signer, Congress Call, 1935, 1941; Executive Committee, 1935, 1936; FBI target 1924–

Herndon, Angelo (1913–)
> Journalist; *Let Me Live*

Herrick, Robert (1868–1938)
> Novelist, government secretary, Virgin Islands; *The Common Lot; Together; The End of Desire; The Real World; The Web of Life;* signer, Congress Call, 1935; National Council, 1935; FBI target 1935–

Herrmann, John (1900–1959)
> Novelist; *The Salesman; What Happens; The Big Short Trip;* member, John Reed Club; 2nd Congress, 1937

Herskovits, Melville J. (1895–)
> Anthropologist; 3rd Congress, 1939

Hertz, David
> Novelist; *Valdemar;* LAW 1938; Executive Council, Hollywood chapter, 1941, 1942; Hollywood School Committee, 1941; faculty, Hollywood Writers School, 1941

Hewitt, Allan

Heyward, DuBose (1885–1940)
> Playwright, children's book writer; *Lost Morning; Porgy; Country Bunny and the Little Gold Shoes;* co-author *Mamba's Daughters;* signer, Congress Call, 1939

Hicks, Granville (1901–1982)
> Critic; editorial board, *Science and Society; I Like America;* co-editor, *Letters of Lincoln Steffens; John Reed: The Making of a Revolutionary; The Great Tradition;* ed. *Proletarian Literature in the U.S.;* fired from Rensselaer Polytechnic Institute, 1935; signer, Congress Call, 1935; Executive Committee, 1935; Conference December 1936; resigned December 1939; FBI target 1926–; informer, friendly witness before HUAC, 1953

Hill, James
> Hollywood chapter, 1942

Himes, Norman E.
    Physician; *Practical Birth-Control Methods;* LAW 1939
Hirsch, Alfred
    LAW 1936
Hirschbein, Peretz
    LAW 1936
Hobson, Wilder
    Second Congress, 1937
Hodes, Edward
Hollister, Carroll
Holmes, Eugene C. Pseud. Eugene Clay
    Philosophy professor Howard University; John Reed Club; editorial board, *Science and Society;* Executive Committee, 1936; signer, Congress Call, 1939; National Council, 1940
Holway, Hope
Howard, Milton
    LAW Conference December 1936; 2nd Congress, 1937
Howard, Sidney (1891–1939)
    Playwright; *The Ghost of Yankee Doodle; They Knew What They Wanted; End of Summer; Paths of Glory;* LAW 1935; National Council, 1935
Howe, Quincy (1900–1977)
    Journalist; *England Expects Every American to Do His Duty; World Diary: 1929–1934;* LAW 1936; Finance Committee, 1937
Huberman, Leo (1903–1968)
    Journalist; *Labor Spy Racket; America, Incorporated;* LAW 1936; Finance Committee, 1937
Huddlestone, Warren C.
    Member, John Reed Club; LAW 1936
**Huebsch, B. W.
    Publisher; 3rd Congress, 1939; Committee for Cultural Freedom, May 1939; Exiled Writers Committee, 1940
**Huebsch, Edward
    Screenwriter; novelist; *The Last Summer of Mata Hari;* blacklisted after 1951, subsequently TV repairman
Hughes, Harriet
    3rd Congress, 1939
Hughes, Langston (1902–1967)
    Poet, playwright, novelist; *The Dream Keeper and Other Poems; A New Song; Scottsboro Limited; Shakespeare in Harlem; Not Without Laughter; The Ways of White Folk;* signer, Congress Call, 1935, 1937, 1941; 1st Congress, 1935; vice president, 1937, 1939; 3rd Congress, 1939; FBI target 1925–
Humphries, Rolfe (1894–1969)
    Poet, critic, classics scholar; *Collected Poems of Rolfe Humphries; Out of the Jewel;* tr. Federico Garcia Lorca, Ovid, Virgil; LAW 1935; LAW *Bulletin* editorial board, 1936; Committee for Solicitation of Manuscripts for Labor Periodicals, 1936; Conference December 1936; 2nd Congress, 1937; with Genevieve Taggard organized poetry class for young writers, 1937; editor-in-charge, Spanish Balladry Project, 1937; Ways and Means Committee, 1937; Executive Committee, 1937; National Council, 1938, 1940; teacher, New York Writers School, 1938; chair, Liaison Committee, 1939; secretary, 1939–1940; Exiled Writers Committee; resigned as secretary and council member, September 1940
Hunt, Alice Riggs
    Second Congress, 1937

Hunter, Ian
      Screenwriter; LAW 1940; blacklisted after 1953
Hurlbut, Herman
      LAW 1937
**Hurst, Fannie (1889–1968)
      Novelist, short story writer; *Appassionata; Five and Ten; Humoresque; White Christmas;*
      autobiography, *Anatomy of Me; Back Street; Imitation of Life;* assisted Exiled Writers
      Committee, 1940; Advisory Council, Writers War Board, 1942; FBI target 1930–
Hurwitz, Leo T.
      Documentary filmmaker; *Native Land;* 2nd and 3rd Congresses, 1937, 1939; teacher,
      New York Writers School, 1942
Huston, John Marcellus (1906–1987)
      Director, writer, producer, actor; Academy Awards for *Treasure of the Sierra Madre;*
      The African Queen; The Asphalt Jungle; The Bible; Moby Dick; Prizzi's Honor; The Dead;
      LAW 1937; Hollywood chapter, 1942
Hutchins, Grace (1885–1969)
      Economist; writer on women and race; member, John Reed Club; LAW 1938

Illes, Agatha
      LAW 1938
Ingster, Boris
      Faculty, Hollywood Writers School, 1940, 1941; Hollywood chapter, 1942
Irwin, Theodore (1907–)
      Novelist, magazine writer; *Collusion; Strange Passage;* LAW 1938
Ish-Kishor, Sulamith (1896–1977)
      Novelist; Schwartz Juvenile Award, National Jewish Welfare Book Council, *A Boy of*
      Old Prague; Magnificent Hadrian (intro. by Theodore Dreiser); *Jews to Remember;* LAW
      1935
Ishigaki, Eitaro
      Member, John Reed Club
Ivens, Joris (1898–1989) Born Georg Henri Anton Ivens
      Dutch filmmaker, producer; *Action Stations; Spanish Earth; Power and the Land;* LAW
      1937; 2nd Congress, 1937; Hollywood Writers Congress, 1943

**Jackson, Aunt Molly
      Folksinger; 3rd Congress, 1939
Jackson, Gardner
      Second Congress, 1937
**Jacobs, Lewis
      Lecturer, Hollywood Writers School
Jaffe, Eli
      LAW 1941; signer, Congress Call, 1941
Jaffe, Eugene
      LAW 1936
Jaffe, Henry
Jaffee, Bernard
Jarrico, Paul (1915–)
      Screenwriter; *No Time to Marry; Man of the Timberland;* Executive Council, Hollywood
      chapter, 1941, 1942; Hollywood Exiled Writers Committee, 1941; chair, Hollywood
      Peace Committee, 1941; teacher, Hollywood Writers School; blacklisted; became exile
      in France

Jasper, Phil
    Second Congress, 1937

Jastrow, Joseph

Jay, Verne
    LAW 1938

Jerome, V. J. (1896–1965) Born Jerome Isaac Romaine
    Novelist, poet, cultural director of Communist Party; editor, *The Communist, New Masses,* and *Mainstream; Intellectuals and the War;* novels, *A Lantern for Jeremy; The Paper Bridge;* FBI target; imprisoned under the Smith Act

Joffe, Eugene
    LAW 1935, 1937

Johns, Orrick (1887–1946)
    Poet; New York director, WPA Writers Project; member, John Reed Club; *Time of Our Lives;* signer, Congress Call, 1935, 1941; National Council, 1935; 1st Congress, 1935

Johnson, Edgar (1901–)
    Biographer; LAW 1935

Johnson, Gail
    Second Congress, 1937

Johnson, James Weldon (1871–1938)
    Novelist, poet, historian, critic; *Autobiography of an Ex-Colored Man;* executive secretary, NAACP, 1920–1930; signer, Congress Call, 1937

Johnson, Josephine Winslow (1910–1990)
    Poet, novelist; *Year's End; Now in November; Poems; Jordanstown;* LAW 1936; Executive Committee, 1935

Johnson, Nunnally (1897–1977)
    Screenwriter, director, producer; Academy Award nominations for *The Grapes of Wrath* and *Holy Matrimony;* faculty, Hollywood Writers School, 1940, 1941

Johnson, Oakley
    LAW 1936

Johnston, Winifred

Jones, George Vedder
    Second Congress, 1937

**Jones, Hays
    Labor journalist; 1st Congress, 1935

Jones, Nancy Bedford
    LAW 1937

Jones, Nard (1904–1972) Born Maynard Benedict Jones
    Journalist, editor, novelist; *Oregon Detour; Swift Flows the River;* LAW 1935

Jordan, Henry
    Second Congress, 1937

Jordan-Smith, Paul (1885–1971)
    Journalist, editor; *Anatomy of Melancholy;* columnist, *Los Angeles Times*

Josephson, Matthew (1899–1978)
    Biographer, critic; *The Politicos; The Robber Barons;* 1st Congress, 1935; Executive Committee, 1935; 2nd Congress, 1937; resigned 1940

Kahn, Gordon (1902–1962)
    Screenwriter; *I Stand Accused; Hollywood on Trial;* LAW 1941; faculty, Hollywood Writers School, 1942; blacklisted after 1949

Kallet, Arthur (1902–1972)
    Consumer advocate; signer, Congress Call, 1935, 1941

Kaltenborn, H. V. (1878–1965)
Radio's first news analyst; autobiography, *Fifty Fabulous Years*; *Kaltenborn Edits the News*; *I Broadcast the Crisis*; LAW 1938, speaker, 3rd Congress, 1939

Kamman, Morris
LAW 1938

Kandel, Aben
Hollywood chapter, 1942

Kanin, Michael
Hollywood chapter, 1942

Kang, Younghill (1903–1972)
Novelist; *East Goes West*; LAW 1938

Karsavina, Jean (1908–1992)
Novelist, journalist; *White Eagle, Dark Skies*; LAW 1938; short story instructor, New York Writers School, 1939, 1940, 1941; National Council, 1941

Kats, David
Second Congress, 1937

Kaufman, Charles
Hollywood chapter, 1942

Kaufman, George S. (1889–1961)
Dramatist; co-author *Stage Door*; *The American Way*; *The Fabulous Invalid*; *Of Thee I Sing*; LAW 1938

Kaufman, S. J.

Kaufman, Wolfe (1905–1970)
Critic, press agent, screenwriter; LAW 1940; Executive Committee, Hollywood chapter, 1940; Pamphlet and Forum Committee, Hollywood, 1941; faculty, Hollywood Writers School, 1940, 1941

Kaufmann, Helen Loeb (1887–)
Free-lance writer; co-author *Minute Sketches of Great Composers*; *Artists in Music of Today*; *The Story of Beethoven*; *The Story of Mozart*; LAW 1938

Kaufmann, Jean
LAW 1938

Kay, Helen (1912–) Pseud. of Helen Colodny Goldfrank
Children's book writer; ed. *The Young Pioneer*; *The Secrets of the Dolphin*; *Picasso's World of Children*; *One Mitten for Lewis*; pleaded the Fifth Amendment before McCarthy Committee, "and every other amendment of our lovely constitution"

Kazakevich, Vladimir
Economist

Kazin, Alfred (1915–)
Literary critic, novelist, editor; *On Native Grounds*; editor, *The New Republic*, 1942, 1943; *A Walker in the City*; ed. *The Portable William Blake*; ed. *F. Scott Fitzgerald*; ed. with Charles Shapiro, *The Stature of Theodore Dreiser*; 2nd Congress, 1937; FBI target

Kellogg, Grace

Kelly, Fred C.

Kennedy, Edward
LAW 1936; Conference December 1936

Kennedy, John E.
LAW 1938

Kennell, Ruth Epperson (1893–1977)
Librarian, children's book writer; *Comrade One Crutch*; *That Boy Nikolta and Other Tales of Soviet Children*; *The Secret Farmyard*; 2nd Congress, 1937; delegate, Emergency Peace Mobilization, Chicago, 1940; teacher, New York Writers School, 1942

Kent, Rockwell (1882–1971)
Artist, memoirist; *Rockwellkentiana;* LAW 1938; speaker, 4th Congress public meeting, 1941; White Mountain Writers Conference, 1941

Kibbee, Roland
Hollywood chapter, 1942

Kimbrough, Jess
LAW 1938; signer, Congress Call, 1939; Executive Committee, Hollywood chapter, 1941, 1942; Pamphlet and Forum Committee, Hollywood, 1941

Kingsbury, John A. (1876–1956)
Non-fiction writer; *Red Medicine: Socialized Health in Soviet Russia*

Kinkead, Beatrice
Translator; tr. *Deep Sea Divers* by K. Volotovskii; LAW 1938

Kirstein, Lincoln Edward (1907–)
Poet, dance critic; co-founder, New York City Ballet Company; *Rhymes of a Pfc.; Blast at Ballet;* signer, Congress Call, 1935; member, 2nd Congress Finance Committee, 1937

Klein, Herbert
Hollywood chapter, 1942

Klemmer, Harvey
Fiction writer; *Harbour Nights;* LAW 1938

Klempner, John (1898–1972)
Novelist, screenwriter; *Once Around the Block;* LAW 1939

Kline, Herbert
Leader, John Reed Club; signer, Congress Call, 1935, 1941

Knapp, Elizabeth

**Knight, Eric Mowbray (1897–1943) Pseud. Richard Hallas
Journalist, novelist, illustrator, screenwriter; *You Play Black and the Red Comes Up;* Young Reader's Choice Award in Juvenile Fiction for *Lassie Come Home;* speaker, Exiled Writers Committee dinner, October 9, 1941

Kober, Arthur (1900–)
Fiction writer; *Having a Wonderful Time;* LAW 1938; signer, Congress Call, 1939; Keep America Out of War Committee, 1940; Committee to Organize NYC membership meeting, 1940

Koenig, Lester
Hollywood chapter, 1940; signer, Congress Call, 1941; Executive Committee, Hollywood chapter, 1941, 1942

Konecky, Paul H.
Second Congress, 1937

Kopf, Gladys
LAW 1939; director, Lecture Bureau, 1939

**Kornikov, Captain
Speaker, Exiled Writers Committee dinner, October 9, 1941

Kozlenko, William (1917–)
Editor; founder and editor, *One-Act Play Magazine;* ed. *Contemporary One- Act Plays;* ed. *Best Short Plays of the Social Theatre;* 2nd Congress, 1937

Kraft, H. S. (1899–1975)
Journalist, screenwriter; Organizing Committee, Dramatists Panel, 4th Congress, 1941; Exiled Writers Committee, Hollywood, 1941; Hollywood chapter, 1942

Kramer, Dale

Kresensky, Raymond

Kreymborg, Alfred (1883–1966)
Poet, playwright; member, John Reed Club; *The Planets;* lyrics, *Two New Yorkers,* with Stanley Burnshaw; *Our Singing Strength: An Outline of American Poetry;* LAW 1935;

Executive Committee, 1935, 1936; signer, Congress Call, 1939; instructor, White Mountain Writers Conference, 1941; National Council, 1941

Kronenberger, Louis (1904–1980)
Critic, editor, poet; LAW 1935; Conference December 1936; Executive Committee, 1935

Kruger, Fania
Novelist; *Kosok Laughter*; LAW 1936

Krupp, Nahami

Kunitz, Joshua (1896–1980)
Historian; editor, *New Masses*; *Russian Literature and the Jew*; *Russian Literature Since the Revolution*; lecturer, John Reed Club Writers School; signer, Congress Call, 1935, 1939, 1941; National Council, 1935; teacher, New York Writers School, 1942

Kunitz, Stanley Jasspon (1905–)
Poet; co-editor, *American Authors, 1600–1900*; ed. *Twentieth Century Authors*; member, John Reed Club; Executive Committee, 1935; signer, Congress Call, 1939

Kurnitz, Harry
Hollywood chapter, 1942

La Farge, Oliver (1901–1963)
Novelist; *The Enemy Gods; Laughing Boy; As Long As the Grass Shall Grow*; LAW 1938; National Council, 1939; Philadelphia civil liberties protest, September 1940; resigned July 1940

Laing, Frederick

Lamont, Corliss (1902–1979)
Essayist, philosopher; *The Illusion of Immortality; Remembering John Masefield*; LAW 1936; National Council, 1941; subpoenaed by McCarthy, 1953; American Civil Liberties Union board member, but resigned because they delayed defending him; formed Emergency Civil Liberties Committee

**Lampell, Millard (1919–)
TV, radio, filmwriter; *The Hero; Long Way Home; The Lonesome Train*; Emmy Award for *Eagle in a Cage*; blacklisted for ten years

Lamson, David
Signer, Congress Call, 1939, 1941

Lanham, Edwin (1904–1979)
Journalist, novelist; *Another Ophelia; The Stricklands; Thunder in the Earth*; LAW 1937; National Council, 1939; chair, Publicity Committee, 1939, 1940

Lansang, José A.
Second Congress, 1937

Lapsley, Mary
LAW 1936

Lardner, Ring, Jr., (1915–)
Novelist, screenwriter; Academy Awards for *Woman of the Year*, 1942; *M*A*S*H**, 1970; *The Round-Up; Forever Amber; The Cincinnati Kid*; Exiled Writers Committee, Hollywood, 1941; Hollywood chapter, 1942; one of the Hollywood Ten; imprisoned, 1947, served one year for contempt of Congress; blacklisted

Larkin, Margaret (1899–1967)
Poet, non-fiction writer, folksinger; executive secretary, Theater Union; *Seven Shares in a Gold Mine*; Publicity Committee, 1937

Lasky, Jr., Jesse L. (1910–)
Screenwriter, novelist, poet; *No Angels in Heaven; Singing in Thunder; Curtain of Life*; autobiography, *Whatever Happened to Hollywood?*; LAW 1938; signer, Congress Call, 1939; Hollywood chapter, 1942

Lauren, S. K.
    Hollywood chapter; resigned
Lawson, Elizabeth
    Journalist; LAW 1937
Lawson, John Howard (1895–1977) Born Jacob Levy; Pseuds. Vic Miller,
    Howard Jennings
        Playwright, screenwriter, critic; *Action in the North Atlantic; Theory and Techniques of
        Playwriting and Screenwriting; Processional; Marching Song; Counterattack; Smashup;*
        member, John Reed Club; first president of Screen Writers Guild; signer, Congress
        Call, 1935, 1937, 1939, 1941; Executive Committee, 1935, 1936, 1937; Conference
        December 1936; Program Committee, 1937; National Council, 1938; faculty, Holly-
        wood Writers School, 1939, 1940, 1941; Executive Committee, Hollywood chapter,
        1939, 1940, 1942; National Council, 1940; Philadelphia civil liberties protest, Septem-
        ber 1940; vice president, 1941; chair, Organizing Committee and speaker, Dramatists
        Panel, 4th Congress, 1941; Hollywood Writers Congress, 1943; Hollywood Writers
        Congress book, 1944; FBI target; one of the Hollywood Ten; imprisoned for contempt
        of Congress; blacklisted after 1947
Leaf, Earl H.
    LAW 1938
Lechlitner, Ruth N. (1901–)
    Poet, book reviewer, *New York Herald Tribune; Tomorrow's Phoenix; Only the Years; A
    Changing Season;* LAW 1936; chair, Book Distribution Committee, 1937; Organization
    Committee, 1937; teacher, New York Writers School, 1939; teacher, Writers Confer-
    ence, Highlander Folk School
Leeb, Lee
    Peace Committee, Hollywood, 1941
Leekley, Richard N. (1912–1976)
    Journalist, poet
Lees, Hannah (1904–1973) Pseud. of Elizabeth Head Fetter
    Mystery writer, lecturer; *Women Will Be Doctors; Death in the Doll's House, RX:
    Prescription for Murder;* LAW 1938
Lees, Robert
    LAW 1940; Peace Committee, Hollywood, 1940; faculty, Hollywood Writers School,
    1942; blacklisted 1952, subsequently maitre d' in a hotel
Lengyel, Cornel (1915–)
    Poet, historian, translator, playwright; Federal Writers Project editor; poetry, *Thirty
    Pieces;* history, *The American Self,* with Noah Ben-Tovim; *Four Days in July* (translated
    into thirty languages); LAW 1938; speaker, Exiled Writers Committee dinner, October
    9, 1941
Lengyel, Emil (1895–1985)
    Journalist, professor; *Cattle Car Express: A Prisoner of War in Siberia; Hitler; The Cauldron
    Boils;* LAW 1938
Leo, Ralph C.
    Second Congress, 1937
Leokum, Arkady (1916–)
    Playwright; *Please Send Me, Absolutely Free; Friends and Enemies; Neighbors;* LAW 1936
Lerman, Louis (1906–1988)
    LAW 1936
Lerner, Maxwell Alan (1902–)
    Journalist, essayist; *It Is Later Than You Think;* LAW 1936; Executive Committee, 1936;
    resigned 1939

Lerner, Tillie (1913–) Full name Tillie Lerner Olsen
  Fiction writer; *Tell Me a Riddle; Silences;* member, John Reed Club; signer, Congress
  Call, 1935; National Council, 1935
Leslie, Kenneth (1892–1974)
  Poet; *Windward Rock; Such a Din; By Stubborn Stars*
Leslie, Robert
  Signer, Congress Call, 1941; lecturer, "Analysis of Advertising Copy and Promotion,"
  New York Writers School, 1941
LeSueur, Meridel (1900–)
  Novelist, short story writer, poet; *North Star Country; Salute to Spring;* signer, Congress
  Call, 1935, 1941; National Council, 1935; 1st Congress, 1935; vice president, 1937, 1940,
  1941; Executive Council, Midwest representative, 1936; FBI target; blacklisted
Levin, Meyer (1905–)
  Novelist; *Yehuda; Golden Mountain; New Bridge; The Old Bunch; Citizen;* LAW 1936;
  Chicago chapter, 1938; National Council, 1938, 1940; signer, Congress Call, 1939;
  Chapter representative, Chicago, 1939; council member, Hollywood chapter, 1940;
  Executive Committee, Hollywood, 1941; faculty, Hollywood Writers School, 1941,
  1942
Levinson, Lou
  Pulp writer; instructor, New York Writers School, 1941
**Levitt, Alfred Lewis
  Blacklisted after 1953
Levitt, Saul (1911–1917)
  Playwright; *The Sun Is Silent, The Andersonville Trials;* LAW 1936
Levy, Jack
  Novelist; *Broken Heart;* LAW 1938
Levy, Melvin
  Fiction writer; *The Last Pioneers;* member, John Reed Club; signer, Congress Call, 1935;
  Hollywood chapter, 1942; Hollywood Writers Congress, 1943
Lewis, H. H. (1901–1985)
  Poet; *Poems; Thinking of Russia*
Lewis, Hobard
  LAW 1937
Lewisohn, Ludwig (1883–1955)
  Novelist, editor, critic, translator; *The Broken Snare; This People; Expression in America*
Leyda, Jay (1910–1988)
  Critic, filmmaker; studied at State Film Institute, Moscow, with Sergei Eisenstein,
  1933; *The Melville Log; The Portable Melville; Voices of Film Experience; Sergei Rachman-
  inoff; Kino: A History of the Russian and Soviet Film;* Hollywood Writers Congress, 1943
Lindeman, Eduard C.
  Educator; co-editor, *Problems for Parent Educators;* LAW 1938
Lips, Julius E.
  LAW 1938
**Lipton, Lawrence (1898–1975)
  Poet, novelist, critic; *Brother; The Laugh Is Bitter; The Holy Barbarians;* Midwest Writers
  Congress, 1936
Lloyd, Jessie
  LAW 1935
Locke, Alain Le Roy (1886–1954)
  Professor; Rhodes Scholar, 1907–1910; named to Honor Roll of Race Relations, 1942;
  leader in the Harlem Renaissance; *The New Negro; The Negro in America; Negro Art; The
  Negro and His Music;* LAW 1938; speaker, 3rd Congress, 1939; delegate to fourth

annual conference of the American Committee for the Protection of the Foreign Born, 1940

Loeb, Lee
Hollywood chapter, 1942

Lomax, Alan (1915–)
Folklorist; *American Ballads and Folksongs; Negro Folksongs As Sung By Leadbelly; Our Singing Country; Dear Mr. Lincoln,* CBS documentary; LAW 1939

Long, Haniel Clark (1888–1956)
Poet, essayist; *Pittsburgh Memoranda; Atlantides; Walt Whitman and the Springs of Courage;* LAW 1935

Lorentz, Pare (1905–1992)
Novelist; *The River;* LAW 1938; 3rd Congress, 1939

Lorenzini, Maria
LAW 1937

Lovett, Robert Morss (1870–1956)
Professor of English; editor, *Science and Society; A History of English Literature; American Poetry and Prose;* signer, Congress Call, 1935, 1937, 1941; National Council, 1935; Executive Committee, Chicago chapter, 1936; government secretary, Virgin Islands; Congress stopped his pay November 15, 1943

Lowe-Porter, Helen T.
Translator; tr. *Joseph in Egypt,* by Thomas Mann; tr. *The Day of the King,* by Frank Bruno; tr. *A Man Called Cervantes,* by Frank Bruno; LAW 1938; attended council meeting February 21, 1940, to discuss her differences with League policy

Lowenfels, Walter (1897–1976)
Poet, journalist; *Steel; The Portable Walter: From the Prose and Poetry of Walter Lowenfels;* LAW 1935; Executive Committee, 1936; LAW *Bulletin* editorial board, 1936; Organization Committee, 1937; convicted under the Smith Act; conviction overturned by higher court

Lowenthal, Marvin
Novelist; *The World Passed By;* LAW 1936; 2nd Congress, 1937; resigned October 1939

Lozowick, Louis (1892–1973)
Artist, educator; member, John Reed Club; signer, Congress Call, 1935

Lucas, Eric
Fiction writer; *Corky;* LAW 1938

Luccock, Halford

Lumpkin, Grace
Novelist; *Sign for Cain; The Wedding; To Make My Bread* (adapted for the stage by Albert Bein as *Let Freedom Ring*); *Full Circle;* signer, Congress Call, 1935, 1941; National Council, 1935; Executive Committee, 1936; Conference December 1936; resigned 1941; friendly witness before McCarthy Committee, 1953

Lynd, Helen Merrell (1896–1982)
Sociologist; *Middletown; Middletown in Transition;* LAW 1938; signer, Congress Call, 1939, 1941

Lynd, Robert S. (1892–1970)
Sociologist; *Middletown; Middletown in Transition;* 2nd Congress, 1937

Lyons, J. J.
LAW 1937

Lyon, Peter (1915–)
Radio and television script writer, screenwriter; *Success Story; The U.N. in Action; Alcoholism;* LAW 1938

Maas, Willard (1911–1971)
Poet, filmmaker; *Concerning the Young;* LAW 1937

MacAlbert, Cora

Macdonald, Dwight (1906–1982)
Free-lance writer; editor, *The Partisan Review*; staff writer, *The New Yorker*; *Memoirs of a Revolutionist*; *Against the American Grain*; 2nd Congress, 1937; resigned 1937; leader, League for Cultural Freedom and Socialism; FBI target 1936–

MacGregor, Robert Mercer (1911–1974)
Journalist, publisher; vice president, editor, New Directions Publishing; signer, Congress Call, 1941

MacLeish, Archibald (1892–1982)
Poet, playwright, public official; three Pulitzer Prizes; *Collected Poems*; *Fall of the City*; *Panic*; *Land of the Free*; *Air Raid*; Librarian of Congress, 1939–1944; director, United States Office of Facts and Figures, 1941–1943; assistant director, Office of War Information; assistant secretary of state, 1944–1945; LAW 1935; Executive Committee, 1935; signer, Congress Call, 1937; chair, 2nd Congress public meeting, 1937; resigned 1939; FBI target 1927–

MacLeod, Norman Wicklund (1906–1985)
Poet, novelist; leader, John Reed Club; *You Got What You Asked For*; *Horizon of Death*; *The Bitter Roots*; LAW 1935; 2nd Congress, 1937

MacLeod, William Christie
Second Congress, 1937

MacNichol, Kenneth
Short story instructor, New York Writers School, 1939

Maddow, Ben (1910–) Pseud. David Wolff
Screenwriter, director, novelist, poet; *The Asphalt Jungle*; *The Secret of Santa Vittoria*; *Intruder in the Dust*; 2nd Congress, 1937; teacher, New York Writers School, 1942; contributor, Hollywood Writers Congress book, 1944; blacklisted; informer before HUAC [see Navasky, p. 75]

Magil, A. B.
Journalist; co-author, *The Peril of Fascism: The Crisis of American Democracy*; *Fascism—Made in the USA*, with H. Stevens; member, John Reed Club; LAW 1935; 2nd Congress, 1937; signer, Congress Call, 1941

Maibaum, Richard (1909–1991)
Screenwriter, producer, playwright; *Birthright*; *See My Lawyer*; screenplays, *The Great Gatsby*, James Bond films; Hollywood School Committee, 1941; Hollywood chapter, 1942

Mally, Emma Louise (1908–)
Poet; *The Mockingbird is Singing*; *The Tides of Dawn*; *The Penguin Book of Socialist Verse*; Exiled Writers Committee; financial secretary 1939–1941

Malmberg, Carl (1904–) Pseud. Timothy Trent
Novelist; *Night Boat*; *All Dames Are Dynamite*; *Fall Guy*; *Diet and Die*; LAW 1937

Maltz, Albert (1908–1985)
Novelist, playwright, screenwriter; *The Way Things Are, and Other Stories*; *The Black Pit*; *The Citizen Writer*; *The Happiest Man on Earth*; *Destination Tokyo*; *The Cross and the Arrow*; *The Underground Stream*; O'Henry Award for short stories; 1st Congress, 1935; Executive Committee, 1935; Conference December 1936; National Council, 1939, 1940; signer, Congress Call, 1939, 1941; writer, numerous League documents; lecturer, New York Writers School, 1940; pre-congress press conference, 1941; vice president, 1941; faculty, White Mountain Conference, 1941; Exiled Writers Committee, Hollywood, 1941; Hollywood chapter, 1942; FBI target; blacklisted after 1948; one of the Hollywood Ten; imprisoned 1950–1951 for contempt of Congress; blacklisted in Soviet Union after 1972

Maltzer, Robert
Pamphlet and Forum Committee, Hollywood, 1941

Mamet, Lewis

Mangione, Jerre (1909–) Pseuds. Mario Michele, Jay Gerlando
Journalist, memoirist; Federal Writers Project, 1935–1943; *Night Search; The Dream and the Deal; Mount Allegro; An Ethnic at Large: A Memoir of the Thirties and Forties;* Executive Committee, 1936; Committee to Solicit Manuscripts for Labor Periodicals, 1936; Conference December 1936; chair, Washington, D.C. chapter

Mangold, William P.
LAW 1935

** Mann, Heinrich Luiz (1871–1950)
Exiled German novelist, playwright, satirist; speaker, Exiled Writers Committee dinner, Hollywood, 1941

Mann, Klaus (1906–1949)
Exiled German novelist, essayist, biographer; *Mephisto; Escape to Life;* 3rd Congress, 1939

Mann, Thomas (1875–1955)
Exiled German novelist; *Buddenbrooks; Death in Venice; Living Thoughts of Schopenhauer; The Magic Mountain;* Nobel Prize 1929; speaker, 3rd Congress, 1939; honorary president, 1939; resigned December 6, 1939; contributor, Hollywood Writers Congress book, 1944

*Marcantonio, Vito
Congressman from Harlem; speaker, 4th Congress public meeting, 1941

Margulis, Max
Second Congress, 1937

Markow, Jack

Marrow, Ruth
Fiction writer; lecturer, "Writing for the Confession Market," New York Writers School, 1941, 1942

Marshall, George
LAW 1939

Marshall, Margaret (1901–1974)
Literary editor, *The Nation;* LAW 1937; 2nd Congress, 1937

Marshall, Robert
LAW 1938

Marshall, Rosamond

Martin, Peter
Organizing Committee, Dramatists Panel, 4th Congress, 1941

Martini, Mike

Marvin, Mark
Leader, John Reed Club; LAW 1936

Masters, Dexter Wright (1908–1989)
Journalist; editor, *Consumer's Union; One World or None;* 1947 Peabody Award for *The Accident;* National Council, 1938; signer, Congress Call, 1941

Mateos, Francisco

Matsui, Haru
Second Congress, 1937

Matthews, Herbert Lionel (1900–1977)
Journalist; *The Fruits of Fascism; Two Wars and More to Come;* LAW 1938

Matthiessen, F. O. (1902–1950)
Critic, professor of English; *American Renaissance; From the Heart of Europe;* LAW 1936; FBI target 1935–

Maxwell, Jr., William Keepers (1908–)
　　Novelist, short story writer; editorial staff, *The New Yorker; They Came Like Swallows; The Folded Leaf; Bright Center of Heaven*

McCarthy, Mary Therese (1912–1989)
　　Novelist, short story writer, critic, essayist; *The Oasis; The Group; The Company She Keeps; Cannibals and Missionaries; Memories of a Catholic Girlhood; Venice Observed; Vietnam;* LAW 1937; 2nd Congress, 1937; resigned 1939; FBI target 1939–

McCausland, Elizabeth
　　Signer, Congress Call, 1941

McCleigh, Elwood
　　Second Congress, 1937

McCormick, Myron

McCoy, Horace Stanley (1877–1955)
　　Novelist, short story writer, screenwriter; *They Shoot Horses Don't They?;* faculty, Hollywood Writers School, 1941

McDonald, Angus Henry (1904–1990)
　　Researcher, lobbyist, writer for the National Farmers Union; columnist, *New Republic;* LAW 1938

McFee, William (1881–1966)
　　Marine engineer; *Ocean Tramp;* autobiography, *In the First Watch;* LAW 1935

McGill, V. J.
　　LAW 1937

McHenry, Beth
　　Journalist; *Home Is the Sailor*

McHugh, Vincent (1904–1983)
　　Novelist, editor, poet; editor-in-chief of Federal Writer's Project, New York; staff writer, *The New Yorker; Caleb Catlum's America;* 2nd Congress, 1937

McIntyre, John
　　Novelist; *Drums in the Dawn; Signing Off; Steps Going Down,* LAW 1938

McKay, Claude (1891–1948)
　　Poet, novelist; contributor, *New Masses; Harlem Shadows; Home to Harlem;* signer, Congress Call, 1937; resigned 1937; attacked League June 10, 1939

McKenney, Ruth (1911–1972)
　　Novelist, humorist; *My Sister Eileen; Industrial Valley; Jake Home;* LAW 1938; signer, Congress Call, 1939; lecturer, "The Humorous Essay," New York Writers School, 1940, 1941; National Council, 1941

McNeer, May
　　Children's book writer; *Waif Maid; John Wesley; Martin Luther;* LAW 1937; signer, Congress Call, 1941; instructor, New York Writers School, 1941

McNichol, Kenneth
　　Faculty, New York Writers School, 1939

McWilliams, Carey (1905–1980)
　　Non-fiction writer; editorial staff, *The Nation; Factories in the Field: The Story of Migratory Farm Labor in California;* signer, Congress Call, 1939, 1941; Pamphlet and Forum Committee, Hollywood, 1941; Hollywood Writers Congress, 1943; teacher, Hollywood Writers School

McSorley, Edward (1906–1966)
　　Second Congress, 1937

Meltzer, Lewis
　　Hollywood chapter, 1942

**Meltzer, Milton (1915–)
　　Children's book writer

Meltzer, Robert
Signer, Congress Call, 1941; Hollywood chapter, 1942

Menaker, F. E.
Journalist; LAW 1938; operated Exiled Writers Home in France

Mendes, Alfred H.
LAW 1936

Mendez, Leopold

Menninger, Karl Augustus (1893–1990)
Psychiatrist; co-founder, The Menninger Foundation; *The Human Mind; Man Against Himself; America Now;* LAW 1938

Mercur, Paul Berton
LAW 1941

Merriam, Eve (1916–1992) Pseud. of Eva Moskovitz
Poet, novelist, feminist playwright, children's book writer; *Family Circle; Montgomery, Alabama, Money, Mississippi and Other Places;* winner of Yale Younger Poet's Prize, 1946; *The Inner City Mother Goose,* adapted into Tony Award play; student, New York Writers School

Messick, Ben

Migueis, José Rodriguez (1901–)
Portuguese fiction writer; autobiography, *Milagre;* 2nd Congress, 1937

Milestone, Lewis (1895–1980)
Director, screenwriter; *All Quiet on the Western Front; The Red Pony; Mutiny on the Bounty; Rain;* LAW 1937

Millay, Edna St. Vincent (1892–1950)
Poet, playwright; Pulitzer Prize for *The Harp-Weaver; Aria DaCapo; A Few Figs From Thistles; There Are No Islands Any More;* Advisory Council, Writers War Board, 1942; FBI target 1923–

Miller, Clyde R.

Miller, Fred R.
Second Congress, 1937

Miller, Loren
Alternate member, Hollywood Executive Committee, 1941; Hollywood chapter, 1942

Miller, Louis
Second Congress, 1937

Miller, Sidney
Resigned from LAW, 1941

Millet, Martha
Poet; *Dangerous Jack: A Fantasy in Verse;* LAW 1938

Millspaugh, C. A.
Men Are Not Stars; LAW 1938

**Minor, Robert (1884–1952)
Cartoonist; member, John Reed Club; Midwest Writers Congress, 1936

Mins, Leonard E.
Translator, playwright; *Engels on Capital; The Founding of the First International;* LAW 1938; Exiled Writers Committee; signer, Congress Call, 1941

Minton, Bruce. Pseud. of Richard Bransten
Journalist; *Men Who Lead Labor;* editor, LAW *Bulletin,* with Dorothy Brewster, 1936; Executive Committee, 1937; National Council, 1938; signer, Congress Call, 1939, 1941; teacher, New York Writers School, 1941; National Council, 1941.

Minus, Marian
Fiction writer; 2nd Congress, 1937

Miskell, Alice J.
> LAW correspondent, Midwest Regional group, 1937

Mitchell, John
> Second Congress, 1937

Morais, Herbert Montford (1905–1970)
> Novelist, historian; *Gene Debs, the Story of a Fighting American; Labor's Untold Story,* with Richard Owen Boyer; *History of the Negro in Medicine*

Moran, Dixie

Morang, Alfred
> New England Executive Committee representative, 1936

Morell, Peter

Mori, Toshio (1910–)
> Novelist; *Woman From Hiroshima; The Chauvinist*

Moritz, Henry K.
> Hollywood chapter, 1942

Morley, Christopher Darlington (1890–1957)
> Poet, playwright, essayist, novelist; *Parnassus on Wheels; Human Being; Kitty Foyle;* autobiography, *John Mistletoe*

Muir, Jean (1906–1973)
> Mystery writer, journalist, actress; blacklisted

Mumford, Lewis (1895–1990)
> Social critic, philosopher, historian; *The Culture of Cities; The City in History; Faith For Living; The Myth of the Machine; Men Must Act;* signer, Congress Call, 1935, 1937; National Council, 1935; speaker, League dinner for Spain, March 1939; resigned 1939; FBI target 1923–

Murray, Jack

Murphy, Maurice
> LAW 1941

Muse, Clarence
> Hollywood chapter, 1942

**Myers, Fred
> Labor journalist; teacher, New York Writers School, 1941

Myers, Henry
> Novelist; *Our Lives Have Just Begun;* LAW 1939; Executive Committee, Hollywood chapter, 1939; vice president, Hollywood chapter, 1940, 1942; faculty, Hollywood Writers School, 1940, 1941

Nadir, Moishe (1885–1943)
> First Congress, 1935; National Council, 1935

** Nathan, Robert (1894–1985)
> Novelist; *One More Spring*

Neagoe, Peter (1881–1960)
> Artist, novelist; owner, *New Review,* Paris literary journal; *Easter Sun; There Is My Heart;* ed. *Americans Abroad;* LAW 1935

Nearing, Scott (1883–1983)
> Professor of Social Sciences and Economics; leader, John Reed Club; *Freeborn: An Unpublishable Novel; Fascism; Must We Starve?;* 3rd and 4th Congresses, 1939, 1941

Neruda, Pablo (1904–1973)
> Chilean diplomat, poet, novelist; *Twenty Love Poems and a Song of Despair; Canto General;* Nobel Prize 1971; signer, Congress Call, 1941

Neuberger, Richard (1912–1960)
> Senator, journalist; *Our Promised Land;* LAW 1938; resigned December 1939

Neugass, James (1905–1949)
Novelist; *Give Us This Day; Rain of Ashes;* LAW 1936; Keep America Out of War Committee, 1940

Neville, Helen
Fourth Congress, 1941

Newhouse, Edward (1911–)
Novelist, short story writer; member, John Reed Club; *This Is Your Day; You Can't Sleep Here;* signer, Congress Call, 1935, 1941; Conference December 1936; Publicity Committee, 1937

Newman, Robert (1909–1988)
Radio writer, novelist; *The Japanese: People of the Three Treasures; The Boy Who Could Fly;* LAW 1938

Nichols, Dudley (1895–1960)
Screenwriter; *This Land Is Mine; The Long Voyage Home; The Informer;* LAW 1938; signer, Congress Call, 1941; Hollywood chapter, 1942; contributor, Hollywood Writers Congress book, 1944

Nichols, Gladys

Niebuhr, Reinhold (1892–1971)
Theologian, socialist writer; *Leaves from the Notebook of a Tamed Cynic; The Contribution of Religion to Social Work;* National Council, 1935

Niles, Blair
LAW 1935

Norman, Charles (1904–)
Fiction writer, poet, biographer; *The Savage Century; The Bright World and Other Poems; The Well of the Past;* LAW 1935

Norman, James
Hollywood chapter, 1942

North, Joseph (1904–1976)
Journalist, editor; *No Men Are Strangers; Anthology of Proletarian Literature; New Masses: An Anthology of the Rebel Thirties;* member, John Reed Club; signer, Congress Call, 1935, 1941; National Council, 1939, 1940

Nurnberg, Maxwell (1897–1984)
Professor of English, scriptwriter; *Chalk Dust,* produced by Federal Theater, 1937

Nyland, Naino
LAW 1935

Oaks, Gladys

Oboler, Arch (1907–)
Dramatist, radio writer, producer; *This Freedom; Fourteen Plays by Arch Oboler;* LAW 1939; Hollywood Writers Congress, 1943; contributor, Hollywood Writers Congress book, 1944

O'Connor, Harvey (1897–1987)
Labor journalist; member, John Reed Club; *Mellon's Millions; The Empire of Oil;* won a legal battle against citation for contempt of Congress; LAW 1936; Chicago chapter, 1938; signer, Congress Call, 1939, 1941; National Council, 1941

Odets, Clifford (1906–1963)
Dramatist; *Golden Boy; Rocket to the Moon; Till the Day I Die; Waiting for Lefty; Awake and Sing!;* National Council, 1935, 1941; signer, Congress Call, 1937, 1941; FBI target 1935–; informer before HUAC 1952 [see Navasky, p. 75]

O'Donnell, Peador (1893–1986)
Irish political writer, activist; autobiography, *Salud! An Irishman in Spain; Wrack; On the Edge of the Stream*

Offner, Mortimer
Faculty, Hollywood Writers School, 1940, 1941; Hollywood chapter, 1942

O'Hara, John (1905–1970)
Novelist, screenwriter; Butterfield 8; *From The Terrace; Appointment in Samarra;* Executive Committee, Hollywood, 1939; resigned 1939; FBI target 1939–

Olgin, Moissaye J. (1878–1939)
Editor; member, John Reed Club; signer, Congress Call, 1935; National Council, 1935

Olsen, Tillie [see Tillie Lerner]

O'Neill, Charles
Second Congress, 1937

Opatashu, Joseph
Novelist; *In Polish Woods;* National Council, 1935

Ornitz, Samuel (1891–1957)
Novelist, screenwriter; *Bride of the Sabbath; Haunch, Paunch and Jowl;* signer, Congress Call, 1935, 1941; Hollywood chapter, 1942; one of the Hollywood Ten; imprisoned for contempt of Congress; blacklisted after 1945

O'Rourke, Marian
LAW 1935; Conference December 1936; Executive Committee, 1936

Oser, Martha M.

O'Sheel, Shaemas
LAW delegate, Emergency Peace Mobilization, 1940; Keep America Out of War Committee, 1940

Ossa, Ben
Second Congress, 1937

Otis, Raymond
Novelist, historian; *Fire in the Night; Indian Art of the Southwest; Little Valley;* LAW 1936

Owen, Blaine
Journalist; LAW 1936

Packer, Peter J.
Hollywood chapter

Page, Charles (1909–1992)
Assistant to California lieutenant governor, Ellis E. Patterson; temporary chairman, Exiled Writers Committee, Hollywood, 1940; executive secretary, Hollywood chapter, 1940; U.S. Foreign Service, stationed in Montevideo, Uruguay, 1942

Page, Elizabeth
Hollywood chapter, resigned

Page, Dorothy Myra (1897–1993)
Journalist; *Gathering Storm: A Story of the Black Belt; Soviet Mainstreet; Moscow Yankee; A Daughter of the Hills; A Woman's Part in the Coal Miners' Strike;* ed. *Sunday Worker* 1936; signer, Congress Call, 1935, 1941; Organization Committee, Dramatists Panel, 2nd Congress, 1937; chair, Speakers Bureau, 1937; Council, 1938; chapter representative, New York, 1939; instructor, New York Writers School, 1939–1942; National Council, 1940, 1941; Philadelphia civil liberties protest, 1940; Committee to Aid *The Clipper,* 1941; FBI target

Pampel, George
LAW 1937; correspondent for Seattle, 1938

Paramore, Jr., E. E.

Park, Francis
LAW 1936; Arrangements Committee, 2nd Congress, 1937

Parker, Dorothy (1893–1967)
Poet, screenwriter, critic; *Here Lies; Not So Deep As a Well; Death and Taxes;* left the bulk of her estate to Martin Luther King, Jr; co-founder, Hollywood Anti-Nazi League; LAW 1939; signer, Congress Call, 1939; vice president, 1940; Executive Committee, Hollywood chapter, 1940; Hollywood chapter, 1942; FBI target 1927–; blacklisted after 1951

Parker, Edward L.
Instructor, New York Writers School, 1941

Parry, Tom Jones
LAW 1937

Partnow, Hyde
Folklorist; LAW 1939; faculty, New York Writers School, 1941, 1942

Pascal, Ernest
Faculty, Hollywood Writers School, 1940, 1941

Patchen, Kenneth (1911–1972)
Poet; *Joe Hill Listens to the Praying; First Will and Testament; Before the Brave; Memoirs of a Shy Pornographer*

Paul, Elliot Harold (1891–1958)
Journalist, novelist; *Life and Death of a Spanish Town; Concert Pitch; The Stars and Stripes Forever; All the Brave; The Mysterious Mickey Finn; The Last Time I Saw Paris;* LAW 1938

Paul, Louis (1901–1970) Pseud. of Leroi Placet
Novelist, short story writer, playwright; 2nd Congress, 1937

Pearce, T. M. (1902–)
Professor of English, folklorist; *America in the Southwest, An Anthology*

Peck, James
LAW 1941

Pell, Mike
Novelist; *S.S. Utah;* LAW 1936

Pense, Arthur
LAW 1936; Conference December 1936

Perelman, S. J. (1904–1979)
Humorist; signer, Congress Call, 1939

Perlman, Vee Terry
LAW 1938

** Perry, John (1914–)
Faculty, New York Writers School, 1938

Perry, Tom Jones

Peters, Paul Pseud. Harbor Allen
Playwright; *Stevedore,* with George Sklar; member, John Reed Club; signer, Congress Call, 1935, 1941; National Council, 1935

Peterson, Leroy

Pettis, Ashley
LAW 1937

Phelps, Grace

Phelps, Wallace (1907–) Born William Phillips
National officer, John Reed Club

Phillips, William
Editor; co-editor, *Partisan Review;* member, John Reed Club; LAW 1936; Conference, December 1936; 2nd Congress, 1937; resigned 1937; became opponent of LAW

Pichel, Irving (1891–1954)
Actor, director; *Jezebel; Topper Takes A Trip;* blacklisted after 1951

Pilley, Angela aka Angela Tuckett
  British labor historian; LAW 1938; volunteer worker in League office
Pillin, William (1910–1985)
  Poet; *Dance Without Shoes; Everything Falling;* leader, John Reed Club
Pillionnel, Jacques Henri
**Pitkin, Rex
  Present at Executive Committee, 1937
Pitts, Rebecca
  National Council, 1935; correspondent for Indianapolis, Midwest, 1937
Pizer, L. V.
Plenn, Abel
  Second Congress, 1937
Polakov, Walter N.
  LAW 1938
Pollack, Emanuel
**Polonsky, Abraham Lincoln (1910–)
  Director, screenwriter; Academy Award for *Body and Soul,* Best Picture, 1947; *Season of Fear*
Porter, Alan (1920–)
  Professor of English, poet; *The Signature of Pain and Other Poems;* signer, Congress Call, 1935, 1941
Porter, Katherine Anne (1890–1980)
  Novelist, short story writer; "Pale Horse, Pale Rider"; "Flowering Judas"; *Ship of Fools;* LAW 1937; FBI target 1927–; informed on Josephine Herbst [see Robins, p. 228]
Potter, Edwin, S.
  2nd Congress, 1937
Powell, Dawn (1897–1965)
  Novelist; *The Happy Island; The Wicked Pavillion;* Executive Committee, 1936, 1937; Committee to Solicit Manuscripts for Labor Periodicals, 1936; Finance Committee, 1937; National Council, 1939, 1940; resigned March 1941
Powers, Alfred
  Philosopher; LAW 1937
Prall, D. W.
  LAW 1936
Preece, Harold (1906–)
  Folklorist; *Lighting Up Liberia;* Folklore editor of Texas Writers Project, 1936–1937; signer, Congress Call, 1935, 1941; Chicago chapter, 1938
Preston, John Hyde (1906–1980)
  Novelist, historian; *The Liberals; Revolution, 1776;* 2nd Congress, 1937; Connecticut chapter representative, 1939; National Council, 1940
Prokosch, Frederic (1908–1989)
  Poet, novelist; *The Asiatics; The Seven Who Fled; Night of the Poor;* LAW 1938; signer, Congress Call, 1939; Office of War Information, 1942–1945
Pruette, Lorine
  Second Congress, 1937; signer, Congress Call, 1939
Purcell, Gertrude
  Hollywood chapter, 1942
Putnam, Phelps (1894–1948)
  Poet; signer, Congress Call, 1941
Putnam, Samuel (1892–1950)
  Biographer, translator; *Marguerite of Navarre;* "Brazilian Literature" in the *Third Handbook of Latin American Studies; Bitter Victory; Francois Rabelais;* Executive Commit-

tee, 1935; Conference December 1936; signer, Congress Call, 1939, 1941; speaker, 4th Congress public meeting, 1941; National Council, 1941

Quin, Mike (1906–1947) Born Paul William Ryan; pseuds. Mike Quin, Robert Finnegan
Poet, columnist; "The Sacred They," *Scribner's*, reprinted in O'Brien *Best Short Stories of 1934; Dangerous Thoughts; More Dangerous Thoughts; The Yanks Are Not Coming; The C. S. Case Against Labor; The Big Strike;* member, John Reed Club; signer, Congress Call, 1941

Quince, Peter

Quinn, Kerker

Radin, Paul (1883–1959)
Anthropologist, educator; *Crashing Thunder; Primitive Man As Philosopher;* Executive Committee, 1935

**Radouski, Theodore A.
LAW 1939

Raiziss, Sonia
Signer, Congress Call, 1941; Keep America Out of War Committee, 1940

Rahv, Philip (1908–1973) Born Ilya/Ivan Greenberg
Literary critic, professor of English; member, John Reed Club; co-editor, *Partisan Review;* Executive Committee, 1936; Conference Committee, December 1936; 2nd Congress, 1937; resigned 1937; became opponent of LAW

Rakosi, Carl (see Rawley, Callman)

Ramsey, John Fraser (1907–)
LAW 1938

Rapf, Maurice (1914–)
Film director, screenwriter; *Song of the South; So Dear to My Heart;* signer, Congress Call, 1941; Exiled Writers Committee, Hollywood, 1941; Hollywood chapter, 1942; blacklisted 1951

Raphaelson, Samuel (1896–)
Playwright

Rascoe, Burton (1892–)
Journalist, critic; member, John Reed Club

Rautenstrauch, Walter
Signer, Congress Call, 1941

Ravitch, Michael L.
Journalist; *Romance of Russian Medicine;* LAW 1938

Rawley, Callman (1903–) Born Carl Rakosi
Poet; *Two Poems; Selected Poems;* 2nd Congress, 1937

Ray, Rom

**Raymond, Margaret Elmendorf (1912–)
Psychiatric social worker; *The Healing Alliance*

Reade, Leslie
LAW 1936

Recht, Charles
Journalist; *Right of Asylum; Manhattan Made;* LAW 1939

Reed, Else
LAW 1938

Reeves, George B.
Second Congress, 1937

Regler, Gustav (1898–1963)
    German refugee novelist, historian; *The Great Crusade;* autobiography, *The Owl of Minerva;* veteran, International Brigade; changed political allegiance

Rein, David
    Biographer; *Vardis Fisher: Challenge to Evasion;* Milwaukee correspondent 1937, 1938

Reis, Bernard J.
    Second Congress, 1937; treasurer, resigned 1937

Reis, Irving
    Hollywood chapter, 1942

Reitman, Ben L.
    Biographer, physician, hobo; *Boxcar Bertha;* LAW 1938

Rella, Ettore (1907–1988)
    Educator, playwright, poet; *Here and Now; Communication Please;* LAW 1937

Rendueles, Roberto
    LAW 1938

Renn, Ludwig (1889–1979) Pseud. of Arnold Friedrich Vieth von Golssenau
    Exiled German anthropologist, novelist, political scientist; *War; After War; Warfare: The Relation of War to Society;* chief of staff, International Brigade; LAW lecture tour, 1937

**Rexroth, Kenneth (1905–1982)
    Poet, painter, translator, playwright; *In What Hour; In Defense of the Earth;* member, John Reed Club

Rice, Elmer Leopold (1892–1967) Born Elmer Leopold Reizenstein
    Playwright; *On Trial; The Adding Machine;* Pulitzer Prize for *Street Scene; Judgment Day; Imperial City; Black Sheep; American Landscape; We, the People;* regional director, Federal Theater Project, New York, 1936; president, Dramatists Guild, 1941; LAW 1938; resigned December 1939; FBI target 1925–

Rice, Philip Blair
    LAW 1936

**Richards, Robert L.
    Blacklisted 1951

Ridge, Lola (1871–1941)
    Poet; *Dance of Fire;* Executive Committee, 1935

Riggs, Lynn (1899–)
    Playwright; *Green Grow the Lilacs; Cherokee Night;* LAW 1936

Rinaldo, Fred
    Writer for Abbott and Costello; Executive Committee, Hollywood chapter, 1939, 1940, 1941; vice president, Hollywood chapter, 1941; Peace Committee, Hollywood, 1941; faculty, Hollywood Writers School, 1942; blacklisted 1952, subsequently salesman for a wholesale paper house

River, Walter Leslie (1902–)
    Novelist, screenwriter; *Coffin, Howard Macy, RAF; Transit USA;* LAW 1936; Conference December 1936; chair, Finance Committee, 1937; Executive Committee, 1937; organized discussion group for novel writing, 1937; signer, Congress Call, 1939, 1941; National Council, 1938–1941; chair, Pamphlet and Forum Committee, Hollywood, 1940; faculty, Hollywood Writers School, 1940–1942; Executive Committee, Hollywood, 1940; vice president, Hollywood, 1941; Hollywood School Committee, 1941

Rivington, Ann Pseud. of Alma Weed
    Journalist; *No Gold Stars for Us; Women–Vote For Life;* LAW 1936

Robbin, Edward
    Hollywood chapter, 1942

Roberts, Evan
    LAW 1939

Roberts, Holland D.
Executive Council meeting, 1938; lecturer, White Mountain Writers Conference, 1941

**Roberts, Marguerite (1905–1989)
Screenwriter, playwright; *Red Sky at Morning; Five Card Stud; True Grit;* blacklisted 1951

Roberts, Stanley
Hollywood chapter, 1942

**Robeson, Paul (1898–1976)
Actor, singer, lawyer; *Here I Stand;* speaker, Exiled Writers Committee dinner, October 9, 1941

Robin, Ed
LAW 1941

Robinson, Earl (1910–1991)
Balladeer, singer, composer; "Joe Hill"; "Hurry Sundown"; "The House I Live In"; LAW 1939; signer, Congress Call, 1941; Hollywood Writers Congress, 1943; contributor, Hollywood Writers Congress book, 1944

Robinson, Jack
Hollywood chapter, 1942

Rochester, Anna
Economist; member, John Reed Club; LAW 1936; signer, Congress Call, 1941

Rockwell, Ethel
Second Congress, 1937

Roditi, Edouard Herbert (1910–)
Interpreter at Nuremberg war crimes trial; *Prison Within Prison: Three Elegies on Hebrew Themes;* resigned 1941

Rodman, Selden (1909–)
Poet; co-founder, co-editor, *Harkness Hoot* and *Common Sense,* monthly political magazine, 1930–1943; *Lawrence, the Last Crusade; New Anthology of Modern Poems; 100 American Poems;* 2nd Congress, 1937

Roe, Wellington (1898–1950)
Novelist; *Begin No Day; Juggernaut; The Tree Falls South;* LAW 1938; 2nd Congress, 1937; signer, Congress Call, 1941; instructor, New York Writers School, 1941, 1942; director, White Mountain Writers Conference, 1941

Roeder, Ralph (1890–1969)
Biographer, historian; *The Men of the Renaissance; Juárez;* 2nd Congress, 1937; signer, Congress Call, 1939; Exiled Writers Committee; National Council, 1938, 1939; chair, LAW *Bulletin* editorial board, 1939–1940; chair, Election Committee, 1940; moved to Mexico

Roethke, Theodore Huebner (1908–1963)
Professor of English, poet; *The Lost Son and Other Poems; Words for the Wind; The Far Field; I Am Says the Lamb; Collected Poems; Dirty Dinky and Other Children's Poems;* LAW 1936; FBI target 1941–

Rogers, John C. (1906–)
Artist; *Watercolor Simplified;* member, John Reed Club; LAW 1936

Rolfe, Edwin (1909–1954) Born Solomon Fishman
Poet; veteran, Abraham Lincoln Battalion; *The Lincoln Battalion;* national officer, John Reed Club, 1936; Publicity Committee, 1937

Rollins, William, Jr. (1897–1950)
Novelist; *The Shadow Before; The Wall of Men;* signer, Congress Call, 1935, 1941; National Council, 1935; teacher, New York Writers School, 1940

Romaine, Paul (1906–1986) Pseud. Burton Bleamer
Journalist, bookseller, actor; signer, Congress Call, 1935, 1941; 2nd Congress, 1937; Milwaukee Writers Union; Chicago chapter, 1938

Rome, Harold J.
  Poet; "The Yanks Aren't Coming"; *Pins and Needles;* signer, Congress Call, 1939, 1941; National Council, 1940; faculty, New York Writers School, 1941

Rood, John Hiram (1902–1974)
  Artist, writer; autobiography, *So Brief a Summer;* LAW 1936

**Roosevelt, Franklin Delano (1882–1945)
  Honorary member; resigned March 19, 1940, after LAW protested raids on Abraham Lincoln Battalion recruiters in Detroit

Root, Edward Merrill (1895–1973)
  Novelist; *Dawn Is Forever;* LAW 1938

Root, Wells
  Hollywood chapter, 1942

Rorty, James (1891–1973)
  Journalist; *Where Life Is Better; McCarthy and the Communists,* with Moshe Decter; LAW 1937; 2nd Congress, 1937; Committee for Cultural Freedom, May 1939

Rosen, Aaron T.
  LAW 1938

Rosen, Edward (1906–1985)
  Professor, history of science; 2nd Congress, 1937

Rosenberg, Harold (1906–1978)
  Lecturer, poet; *Trance Above the Streets; The Tradition of the New;* LAW 1935; Lecture Committee, 1935; Executive Committee, 1936

Rosenburg, David
  Second Congress, 1937

Rosenhouse, Betty

Roskolenko, Harry (1907–1980)
  Poet, novelist; *Black Is a Man; Sequence on Violence;* WPA Writers Project; 2nd Congress, 1937; became opponent of LAW

Ross, Jerome D.

Ross, Lillian (1917–)
  Journalist; *Maine Lingo,* with John Gould; LAW 1935

Ross, Sam (1912–) Born Sam Rosen
  Novelist; *Sidewalks Are Free;* LAW 1938; Chicago chapter, 1938

Rossen, Robert (1908–1966)
  Director, producer, screenwriter; *The Hustler;* Academy Award for, *All the Kings Men,* Best Picture, 1947; Hollywood Executive Committee, 1939, 1940; signer, Congress Call, 1941; Exiled Writers Committee, 1941; Organizing Committee, Dramatists Panel, 4th Congress, 1941; Hollywood chapter, 1942; Hollywood Writers Congress, 1943; contributor, Hollywood Writers Congress book, 1944; blacklisted until he became an informer [see Navasky, p. xvii]

Rosten, Norman (1914–)
  Poet, playwright, novelist; *Return Again, Traveler; The Fourth Decade; The Big Road; Love in All Its Disguises;* New York Federal Theater, 1939–1940; signer, Congress Call, 1941

Roth, Claire
  Second Congress, 1937

Roth, Henry (1906–)
  Novelist; *Call It Sleep; Shifting Landscape;* LAW 1935; signer, Congress Call, 1941

Rourke, Constance Mayfield (1885–1941)
  Biographer; *Charles Sheeler, Artist in the American Tradition;* LAW 1938

**Rousseau, Louise
  Blacklisted 1951, subsequently became operator of a printing shop

Rudlin, W. A.

Rudwin, Maximillian
Les Ecrivains Diaboliques de France; LAW 1936

Rukeyser, Muriel (1913–1980)
Poet; *Theory of Flight; U.S.1;* member, John Reed Club; LAW 1937; signer, Congress Call, 1939; FBI target 1932–; questioned by FBI on LAW, February 1943; J. Edgar Hoover ordered additional investigation, May 8, 1943; resigned from Office of War Information, May 17, 1943

Rushmore, Howard (1937–)
Journalist; radio program with Harvey Matusow, *Out of the Red;* informer [see Navasky, p. 40]

Russak, Martin
Member, John Reed Club; LAW 1935

Russell, Charles Edward (1860–1940)
Editor, publisher; *Bolshevism and the United States; The Story of the Non-Partisan League;* LAW 1938

Russell, Alfred

Russell, Philips
LAW 1935

Ruthven, Madeleine
Hollywood chapter, 1940, 1942

Sackheim, Jerry
Hollywood chapter, 1940, 1942; faculty, Hollywood Writers School, 1940-1941; signer, Congress Call, 1941; Hollywood School Committee, 1941

Salemson, Harold J. (1910–1988)
Film critic, translator; 2nd Congress Committee, 1937; Hollywood chapter, 1940; Hollywood School Committee, 1941; signer, Congress Call, 1941

Salt, Sydney
Poet; *Christopher Columbus and Other Poems*

Salt, Waldo (1914–1987)
Screenwriter; *The Shopworn Angel; The Flame and the Arrow;* Academy Award for *Midnight Cowboy;* signer, Congress Call, 1941; faculty, Hollywood Writers School, 1942; blacklisted 1951

Salter, Katherine S.H.
LAW 1938

Sandoz, Mari Suzette (1896–1966) Pseud. of Marie Macumber
Novelist, biographer, editor; *These Were the Sioux; Old Jules; Slogum House; Capital City;* LAW 1938

Sandseff, Ivan
Second Congress, 1937

Sanford, John (1904–) Pseud. of Julian Shapiro
Novelist; *The People From Heaven; Seventy Times Seven; The Old Man's Place; A Man Without Shoes; The Land That Touches Mine;* Executive Council, Hollywood, 1940; signer, Congress Call, 1941; Hollywood chapter, 1942; unfriendly witness before HUAC

**Saroyan, William (1908–1981)
Novelist; *The Daring Young Man on the Flying Trapeze; The Time of Your Life; My Name Is Aram;* LAW manuscript sales; Western Writers Congress, 1936; FBI target 1940–

Saunders, Sallie
Second Congress, 1937

**Sawyer, Thomas Conrad
Lecturer, Hollywood Writers School

Schappes, Morris U. (1907–)
> Instructor in English; *Letters From the Tombs* (intro. by Richard Wright); *The Jews in the United States*; LAW 1936; fired from CCNY for refusing to name names before the Rapp-Coudert Committee

Schary, Dore (1905–1980)
> Playwright, director, producer; *Boys Town; Lassie Come Home; The Spiral Staircase; Father of the Bride*; faculty, Hollywood Writers School, 1940–1941

Scherer, James A.B.
> Journalist; *Japan Defies the World*; LAW 1938

**Schiff, Jack
> Teacher, New York Writers School, 1942

Schindler, Pauline
> Hollywood chapter, 1942

Schlauch, Margaret (1898–1986)
> Professor of English Philology; writer on Chaucer; signer, Congress Call, 1941; went as an exile to Poland

Schneider, Isidor (1896–1977)
> Poet, critic, fiction writer; *Comrade Mister; From the Kingdom of Necessity; The Judas Time*; member, John Reed Club; signer, Congress Call, 1935, 1941; Executive Committee, 1935; Lecture Committee, 1935; Midwest Writers Congress, 1936; Conference December 1936; National Council, 1939–1940; faculty, New York Writers School, 1941; National Council, 1941

Schoenfeld, Bernard
> Screenwriter; LAW 1938; resigned 1939; informer before HUAC

Schor, Sol
> Hollywood chapter, 1940

Schorer, Max

Schreiber, Florence
> LAW 1941

Schubert, David
> Second Congress, 1937

Schulberg, Budd Wilson (1914–)
> Screenwriter, novelist; *What Makes Sammy Run; The Disenchanted; Waterfront*; film, *On the Waterfront*; Western Writers Congress, 1936; LAW 1938; signer, Congress Call, 1939; Hollywood chapter, 1940; Exiled Writers Committee, Hollywood, 1941; Hollywood chapter, 1942; informed before HUAC [see Maltz, UCLA interview, p. 836; Schwartz, p. 171]

Schulberg, Sonya
> Novelist; *They Cried a Little*; LAW 1938; Hollywood chapter, 1942

Scott, Adrian (1912–1973)
> Producer, screenwriter; *Crossfire; Mr. Lucky*; Pamphlet and Forum Committee, Hollywood, 1941; one of the Hollywood Ten; imprisoned; blacklisted 1947

Scott, Allan (1906–)
> Playwright, screenwriter; Academy Award for *So Proudly We Hail*; Hollywood Executive Council, 1939; faculty, Hollywood Writers School, 1940–1941; Exiled Writers Committee, Hollywood, 1941; Hollywood chapter, 1942

Scott, Evelyn (1893–1963)
> Novelist; *A Calendar of Sin; The Narrow House; Breathe Upon These Slain*; member, John Reed Club; 2nd Congress, 1937

Scott, Virginia
> LAW 1938

Scudder, Vida Dutton (1861–1954)
    Literary critic; *Socialism and Character; Privilege of Age;* LAW 1937; signer, Congress Call, 1939, 1941

Scully, Frank (1892–1964)
    Columnist; "Scully's Scrapbook," *Variety,* 1944–1964; signer, Congress Call, 1941

Seaver, Edwin (1906–)
    Novelist; *Between the Hammer and the Anvil; The Company;* member, John Reed Club; signer, Congress Call, 1935, 1939, 1941; Executive Committee, 1935; LAW *Bulletin* editorial board, 1936; Conference December 1936; Ways and Means Committee, 1937; Executive Committee, 1937; National Council, 1940; Philadelphia civil liberties protest, 1940; faculty, New York Writers School, 1941; testified against LAW and his own books as friendly witness before the McCarthy Committee, March 1953

**Seeger, Pete
    Folksinger; 2nd Congress, 1939

Seldes, George (1890–)
    Journalist; *You Can't Do That; Your Money or Your Life; Witness to a Century: Encounters With the Noted, the Notorious, and Three SOBs; Facts and Fascism;* LAW 1935; vice president, 1939, 1940, 1941; chair, New York chapter, 1940; signer, Congress Call, 1941

Seligmann, Herbert J. (1891–1984)
    Journalist; *The Negro Faces America; Race Against Man;* LAW 1938

Sellers, Charles Coleman (1903–1980)
    Researcher, librarian; *Artist of the Revolution;* LAW 1937

Sender, Ramon (1902–1982)
    Spanish exiled novelist, professor of Spanish; refugee in U.S., 1942; *Seven Red Sundays*

Settel, Arthur

Shaftel, George
    Hollywood chapter, 1942

Shapin, Irwin
    Second Congress, 1937

Shapiro, Meyer
    Member, John Reed Club; Executive Committee, 1935

Shapiro, Victor
    Hollywood chapter, 1942

Shapley, Harlow (1885–1972)
    Astronomer, educator; author of books on science

Shaw, Irwin (1913–1984)
    Playwright, screenwriter, novelist; *The Gentle People; Bury the Dead; The Young Lions* (book and film); *Rich Man, Poor Man* (book and film); LAW 1937; signer, Congress Call, 1939; faculty, Hollywood Writers School, 1941; FBI target 1935–

Shay, Edith
    Second Congress, 1937

Shay, Frank
    Second Congress, 1937

Sheean, Vincent (1899–1975)
    Journalist, historian; *The Thunder and the Sun; Personal History; Pieces of a Fan; San Felice; A Day of Battle;* signer, Congress Call, 1937, 1939; speaker, 3rd Congress, 1939; vice president, 1939–1940; resigned March 1941; FBI target 1927–

Sheckman, Arthur

Sheffington, Hanna S.

Sheldon, Sidney

Shepard, Odell (1884–1967)
    Professor of English; Connecticut lieutenant governor, 1940–1943

Sher, Sol
    Peace Committee, Hollywood, 1941
Sherman, Hiram
Sherman, Jane (1908–)
    Dancer, writer on dance, children's book writer; *Soaring: The Diary of a Denishawn
    Dancer in the Far East; The Drama of Denishawn Dance;* Exiled Writers Committee
Sherman, Nathaniel
Shiffrin, A. B.
Shipman, Evan
    Poet; LAW 1935
Shirer, William L. (1904–)
    Journalist, historian; columnist: *New York Herald Tribune; Rise and Fall of the Third Reich;
    Berlin Diary;* assisted Exiled Writers Committee
Shires, Henry (1913–1980)
Shore
    Viola Brothers Screen writer; Western Writers Congress, 1936; signer, Congress Call,
    1939, 1941; faculty, Hollywood Writers School, 1939; Executive Committee, Holly-
    wood chapter, 1940, 1942; faculty, Hollywood Writers School, 1940–1941; National
    Council, 1941; Hollywood School Committee, 1941
Shore, Wilma
    Hollywood chapter, 1942
Shreiber, David
    Second Congress, 1937
Shulimson, M.
    Member, John Reed Club; LAW 1936
Siegel, Eli (1902–1978)
     Poet, columnist; 2nd Congress, 1937
Sifton, Claire (1897–1980)
    Journalist; first female to teach journalism at a university; signer, Congress Call, 1935
Sifton, Paul (1893–1972)
    Journalist, labor lobbyist; signer, Congress Call, 1935
Sigerist, Henry E. (1891–1957)
    Medical writer; *The Great Doctors; On the History of Medicine; Civilization and Disease;
    Socialized Medicine and the Soviet Union;* LAW 1938
Sigrist, Joe
    LAW 1938
Sillen, Samuel (1911–1973)
    University instructor, Marxist literary critic; 2nd Congress, 1937; faculty, New York
    Writers School, 1938; signer, Congress Call, 1941; speaker, Critics Panel, 4th Congress,
    1941; National Council, 1941
Simmons, Ernest Joseph (1903–1972)
    Translator from the Russian, professor; *English Literature and Culture in Russia; Russian
    Fiction and Soviet Ideology;* LAW 1938
Simonson, Lee (1888–1967)
    Artist, theater designer; founder and director of Theater Guild, Garrick Theater, and
    Guild Theater of New York, 1919–1940; Executive Committee, 1935
Sims, Blackburn
Simpson, Clinton
    LAW 1936; Conference December 1936; Membership Committee, 1937
Sinclair, Upton (1878–1968)
    Novelist, journalist; *Flivver King; Little Steel; Our Lady; The Brass Check; The Goose Step;
    The Jungle;* member, John Reed Club; Western Writers Congress, 1936; signer, Con-

gress Call, 1937, 1939; vice president, 1937, 1939; resigned September 1940; FBI target 1923–

Sinks, Alfred
LAW 1938

Skidelsky, Bernice C.
Signer, Congress Call, 1941

Sklar, George (1908–1988)
Playwright, screenwriter; *Peace on Earth,* with Albert Maltz; *The Life and Death of an American; Stevedore,* with Paul Peters; *The Identity of Dr. Frazier; The Triumph of Willie Pond;* signer, Congress Call, 1935, 1941; National Council, 1935; Conference December 1936; Keep America Out of War Committee, 1940; faculty, Hollywood Writers School, 1940–1941; Organizing Committee, Dramatists Panel, 4th Congress, 1941; Hollywood chapter, 1942; blacklisted, became novelist

Slade, Caroline Beach (1886–1975)
Social worker, welfare executive, novelist; LAW 1936

Sleslinger, Frank Davis
Hollywood chapter, 1942

Slesinger, Tess (1905–1945)
Screenwriter, novelist; *The Unpossessed;* signer, Congress Call, 1939; Hollywood chapter, 1940; faculty, Hollywood Writers School, 1940–1941; National Council, 1941; Hollywood chapter, 1942

Slochower, Harry (1900–1991)
Psychologist, professor of German, comparative literature; German refugee; *Thomas Mann's Joseph Story; Three Ways of Modern Man;* LAW 1937

Slocum, Rosalie
Novelist; co-author, *Key to New York,* with Ann Todd

Small, Sasha
Journalist; LAW 1938

Smart, Charles Allen (1904–1967)
Novelist; *The Brass Cannon; RFD,* essays; LAW 1938

Smedley, Agnes (1894–1950)
Journalist; *Daughter of Earth; China's Red Army Marches;* National Council, 1935; FBI target

Smith, Bernard
Critic; *Forces in American Criticism;* LAW 1936; Conference December 1936; Publicity Committee, 1937

Smith, Charles Edward
LAW 1938

Smith, Frank

Smith, Henry

Smith, Jessica (1895–)
Journalist; *Women in Soviet Russia;* tr. *Over the North Pole;* 2nd Congress, 1937

Smith, Mathieu
Second Congress, 1937

Smith, Paul Jordan
Hollywood chapter, 1942

Smitter, Wessel
Executive Committee, Hollywood, 1940, 1941; Hollywood School Committee, 1941; Hollywood chapter, 1942

Smyth, Joseph Hilton
Third Congress, 1939; Committee for Cultural Freedom, May 1939

Snow, Edgar (1905–1972)
Journalist; *Red Star Over China;* speaker, Exiled Writers Committee dinner, October 9, 1941; speech rejected, 4th Congress, 1941; FBI target 1931–

Snow, Walter
Member, John Reed Club; LAW 1936

Solow, Herbert (1903–1964)
Journalist; editorial board of *Fortune;* LAW 1937

Soule, George
LAW 1936

Soule, Isobel Walker (1898–1972)
Journalist; LAW 1936; National Council, 1938; New York Writers School, 1938; Exiled Writers Committee, 1941

Spector, Herman (1895–1959)
Poet, editor; *We Gather Strength; Bastard in the Ragged Suit;* member, John Reed Club

Speer, Robert K.
Fourth Congress, 1941

Spencer, Ray
Hollywood chapter, 1942

Spender, Stephen (1909–)
British poet; *The Destructive Element; European Witness; Collected Poems;* LAW 1935

Spengler, Joseph J.

Sperling, Milton
Hollywood chapter, 1942

Spewack, Bella (1899–1990)
Publicist, journalist, playwright, screenwriter; co-scriptwriter, *Kiss Me Kate,* with Samuel Spewack; Tony Award for *Kiss Me Kate;* as a free-lance publicist, she suggested that the Girl Scouts sell cookies

Spewack, Samuel (1899–1971)
Novelist, screenwriter, playwright; co-scriptwriter, *Kiss Me Kate,* with Bella Spewack; Tony Award for *Kiss Me Kate*

Spitzer, Antoinette

Spitzer, Esther
Teacher, New York Writers School, 1942

Spitzer, Marian
Exiled Writers Committee, Hollywood, 1941; Hollywood chapter, 1942

Spivak, John L. (1891–1981)
Journalist, novelist; *On the Chain Gang; Europe Under the Terror; Georgia Nigger; Plotting America's Pogroms;* signer, Congress Call, 1935, 1941

Stalmaster, Irvin
Hollywood chapter, 1942

Stander, Lionel
Actor

Stavis, Barrie (1906–)
Playwright; *Refugee; The Man Who Never Died: A Play About Joe Hill;* faculty, New York Writers School, 1939, 1940; Organizing Committee, Dramatists Panel, 4th Congress, 1941

Stead, Christina (1902–1983)
Australian novelist, short story writer, translator; LAW 1939; National Council, 1941

Stebbins, Robert (1915–)
Second Congress, 1937

Steegmuller, Francis Pseuds. David Keith, Bryan Steel
Novelist, critic; *American Relief; Flaubert and Madame Bovary*

Steele, James (1910–) Pseud. Robert Cruden
Novelist; *Conveyor;* LAW 1936

**Steele, Johannes
Speaker, Exiled Writers Committee dinner, October 9, 1941

Steffens, Lincoln (1866–1936)
Journalist; contributor to *Masses; The Autobiography of Lincoln Steffens; The Shame of Cities;* signer, Congress Call, 1935; National Council, 1935; FBI target 1917–

Steig, Arthur Ebel
Second Congress, 1937

Steig, Henry
LAW 1941

Steiger, Andrew J. (1900–)
Journalist; *Soviet Asia; American Engineers in the Soviet Union;* signer, Congress Call, 1941

Steinbeck, John (1902–1968)
Novelist; *In Dubious Battle; Of Mice and Men; Red Pony; The Grapes of Wrath;* Western Writers Congress, 1936; LAW 1937; National Executive Council, 1937; vice president, 1939–1940; FBI target 1936–

Stern, Bernhard J. (1894–1956)
Sociologist; *The Family, Past and Present;* signer, Congress Call, 1935, 1941; Executive Committee, 1936; Conference December 1936; National Council, 1941

Stern, Edith M. (1901–1975)
Editor, lecturer; 2nd Congress, 1937

Stern, Philip Van Doren (1900–1984)
Free-lance writer, critic; ed. *Selected Writings of Thomas De Quincy; The Man Who Killed Lincoln;* LAW 1936; faculty, New York Writers School, 1941

Stevenson, Philip (1896–1965) Pseud. Lars Lawrence
Novelist, playwright; *God's in His Heaven; You Can't Change Human Nature; Morning, Noon, and Night; Transit; The Seed;* national officer, John Reed Club; signer, Congress Call, 1935, 1939; secretary, 1937; National Council, 1939–1940; Ways and Means Committee, 1937; Executive Committee, 1937; Writers-Artists Ambulance Corps Committee, 1937; faculty, New York Writers School, 1938; blacklisted, thereafter wrote as Lars Lawrence

Stewart, Donald Ogden (1894–1980)
Humorist, screenwriter, playwright; *Parody Outline of History; Philadelphia Story;* Western Writers Congress, 1936; signer, Congress Call, 1937, 1939; Executive Committee, Hollywood, 1939; 3rd Congress, 1939; LAW president, 1937–1940; vice president, 1941; president, Hollywood chapter, 1940, 1941; faculty, Hollywood Writers School, 1940–1941; Exiled Writers Committee, Hollywood, 1941; Pamphlet and Forum Committee, Hollywood, 1941; Hollywood chapter, 1942; FBI target 1936–; blacklisted after 1949

Stewart, Kenneth
Teacher, New York Writers School, 1941

Stoddard, John M.
LAW 1938

Stone, I. F. (1907–1989) Born Isidor Feinstein
Journalist, editor; editor, *I. F. Stone's Weekly; In A Time of Torment;* LAW 1936

Stone, Irving (1903–1989)
Professor of economics, creative writing; biographer, novelist; *Lust for Life; False Witness; The Agony and the Ecstasy;* LAW 1937; signer, Congress Call, 1939; vice president, Hollywood chapter, 1939; chair, School Council, Hollywood Writers School, 1939; resigned December 1940

Storm, Hans Otto (1895–)
> Exiled German novelist; *Pity the Tyrant*; Executive Committee, 1935

Stout, Rex (1886–1975)
> Detective story writer; Nero Wolf detective novels; *The Doorbell Rang; The Hand in the Glove; Some Buried Caesar*; president, Authors Guild and Authors League; chair, Writers War Board; LAW 1938; resigned, date uncertain; became opponent of League; FBI target 1920–

Stowe, Leland (1899–)
> Journalist; Pulitzer Prize for foreign correspondent, 1930; *Nazi Means War; No Other Road to Freedom; While Time Remains; Conquest by Terror*; LAW 1938; signer, Congress Call, 1939; 3rd Congress, 1939; possible informer about LAW [see Robins, p. 443]

Strand, Paul (1890–1976)
> Photographer, cinematographer; *Portfolio of Mexican Photographs*; 3rd Congress, 1939

Strauss, Theodore
> LAW 1938

Strawn, Arthur
> Hollywood chapter; blacklisted 1953

Strong, Anna Louise (1885–1970)
> Journalist; *I Change Worlds; Wild River; Dictatorship and Democracy in the Soviet Union*; LAW representative, International Congress of Writers for Defense of Culture, 1937

Stroud, Sally
> Second Congress, 1937

Stuart, John
> Political writer; *Men Who Lead Labor*, with Bruce Minton; LAW 1937

Suckow, Ruth (1892–1960)
> Novelist; *The Odyssey of a Nice Girl; The Folks; New Hope*; LAW 1937

Suhl, M. A.
> Second Congress, 1937

Swerling, Jo
> Hollywood chapter, 1942

Swing, Raymond Gram (1887–1968)
> Broadcaster, journalist; *How War Came; In the Name of Sanity; Good Evening*

Swinson, Henry
> Second Congress, 1937

Sydnor, Earl Lawson
> LAW 1936

Taggard, Ernestine

Taggard, Genevieve (1894–1948)
> Poet, professor; *Words for the Chisel; Not Mine to Finish; Calling Western Union*; member, John Reed Club; signer, Congress Call, 1935, 1937, 1939, 1941; Executive Committee, 1935, 1937; Ways and Means Committee, 1937; treasurer 1937; Publicity Committee, 1937; New York Writers School, 1938; chair, Radio Committee, 1939; National Council, 1939, 1940, 1941

Talmadge, I.D.W.
> LAW 1938

Tao, H. C.
> Second Congress, 1937

Tarnoff, Harry

Tasker, Robert
> Hollywood chapter, 1942

Thompson, Jim (1906–1976)
Pulp writer; *Now and On Earth*

Thompson, Ralph (1904–1979)
Book club executive, reviewer; editor, *Book-of-the-Month Club* 1951–1979; LAW 1938; resigned, date uncertain

Thompson, Randall (1899–1984)
Composer, conductor, educator

Thornbury, Ethel M.

Thurber, James Grover (1894–1961)
Humorist, cartoonist, playwright, short story writer; *Let Your Mind Alone; The Male Animal; The 13 Clocks;* "The Secret Life of Walter Mitty"; LAW 1938; signer, Congress Call, 1939; 3rd Congress, 1939; FBI target 1938–

Titterton, Lewis
Third Congress, 1939

Todd, Ann (1909–)
Actress, producer; film, *Danny Boy;* autobiography, *The Eighth Veil;* co-author, *Key to New York,* with Rosalie Slocum

Toller, Ernst (1893–1939)
Exiled German poet, playwright; *Man and the Masses;* autobiography, *I Was a German; Pastor Hall;* LAW 1939

Tompkins, Warwick M.
Signer, Congress Call, 1941

Totheroh, Dan
LAW 1938

Trachtenberg, Alexander (1884–1966)
Publisher; *Looking Forward;* a founder and leader, American Communist Party, 1921–; signer, Congress Call, 1935, 1941; Conference December 1936; Executive Committee, 1935–1937; imprisoned under the Smith Act

Traube, Mildred
School council, Hollywood chapter, 1940

Traube, Shepard
Hollywood chapter, 1942

Treat, Lawrence (1903–) Born Lawrence Arthur Goldstone
Mystery writer; *Run Far, Run Fast; Mystery Writer's Handbook;* signer, Congress Call, 1941

Trent, Lucia (1897–)
Faculty, Hollywood Writers School, 1940–1941

Trivers, Paul
Peace Committee, Hollywood, 1941

Trosper, Guy

Troy, William (1903–1961)
Educator, critic; Executive Committee, 1935

Trowbridge, W. D.
LAW 1936; Chicago chapter, 1938

Trumbo, Dalton (1905–1976) Pseud. Robert Rich
Screenwriter, playwright, novelist; *Johnny Got His Gun; A Man to Remember; Kitty Foyle; The Flying Irishmen;* Academy Award for *The Brave One,* 1966; *Exodus; Spartacus;* faculty, Hollywood Writers School, 1940–1941; Hollywood Writers Congress, 1943; contributor, Hollywood Writers Congress book, 1944; one of the Hollywood Ten; blacklisted after 1945; imprisoned for contempt of Congress, 1950; in 1993 the fountain in a free speech area on the campus of the University of Colorado at Boulder was named in his honor

Tsiang, H. T.
  Novelist; *The Hanging on Union Square* (privately printed)
Turner, Ethel Sybill (1872–1958)
  Australian editor; Western Writers Congress, 1936; LAW correspondent for Northern
  California, 1939
Tuttle, Jr., Frank Day (1902–)
  Actor, director, producer; signer, Congress Call, 1939; Pamphlet and Forum Commit-
  tee, Hollywood, 1941; Hollywood chapter, 1942; informer before HUAC [see Maltz,
  UCLA interview, p. 836]
Tyler, Parker (1907–1974)
  Film critic, poet, novelist; *The Young and Evil; Three Examples of Love Poetry; The
  Hollywood Hallucination;* 2nd Congress, 1937
Tyson, Robert

Uhse, Bodo
  Exiled German writer
Untermeyer, Jean Starr (1886–1970)
  Poet; *Private Collection;* LAW 1936; signer, Congress Call, 1937, 1939; Membership
  Committee, 1937; Executive Committee, 1937; National Council, 1938, 1939; faculty,
  New York Writers School, 1938, 1939; resigned July 1940
Untermeyer, Louis (1885–1977)
  Poet, anthologist; *The Book of Living Verse; New Modern American and British Poetry;*
  member, John Reed Club; signer, Congress Call, 1939; FBI target 1921–
Uris, Michael
  Pamphlet and Forum Committee, Hollywood, 1941; Hollywood chapter, 1942

Van Auw, Ivan
  Second Congress, 1937
Van Doren, Carl (1885–1950)
  Critic, biographer; Pulitzer Prize for *Benjamin Franklin,* 1938; literary editor, *The
  Nation,* 1912–1922; *American and British Literature Since 1890;* signer, Congress Call,
  1937, 1939; Congress, 1937, 1939; FBI target 1927–
Vetch, M.
  LAW 1936
Vilaplana, Antonio R.
Vogel, Joseph (1904–)
  Novelist; *Man's Courage; At Madame Bonnard's;* member, John Reed Club; LAW 1936
Von Ulm, Gerith
  Hollywood chapter, 1942
Von Wiegand, Charmion (1898–1983)
  Journalist, artist, translator; Hearst correspondent, Moscow 1929–1932; art critic, *New
  Masses;* LAW 1937
Vorse, Mary Heaton (1873–1966)
  Labor journalist; *Footnote to Folly; Labor's New Millions; Strike!; The Ninth Man;* mem-
  ber, John Reed Club; 2nd Congress, 1937

Wagner, Bob
  Hollywood chapter, 1942
Wagner, Dorothy
Wagner, Charles Abraham (1901–)
  LAW 1938; Keep America Out of War Committee, 1940
Waldman, Seymour
  LAW 1938

Walker, Margaret (1915–)
> Poet, social worker, reporter, professor of English; director, Institute for the Study of the History, Life, and Culture of Black Peoples; Yale Younger Poets Award, 1942, for *For My People*; LAW 1938; Chicago chapter, 1938

Wallace, Henry Agard (1888–1965)
> United States vice president; editor, *New Republic*, 1946–1948; *America Must Choose; Paths to Plenty*

Walsh, J. Raymond (1901–)
> Labor journalist; *C.I.O.: Industrialized Unionism in Action*; LAW 1938

Walton, Eda Lou (1898–)
> Professor of English, poet, critic; *Dawn Boy; City Day*; LAW 1935; faculty, New York Writers School, 1940; White Mountain Writers Conference, 1941

Ward, Harold
> LAW 1938

Ward, Harry Frederick (1873–1966)
> Theologian; *Labor Movement; New Social Order; In Place of Profit; Democracy and Social Change*

Ward, Lem (1907–1942)
> Director; *The Eve of St. Mark; Uncle Harry; Processional; One Third of a Nation*; Organizing Committee, Dramatists Panel, 4th Congress, 1941

Ward, Lynd (1905–1985)
> Illustrator, graphic artist; director of Federal Art Project, New York, 1937–1939

Ward, Theodore James (1902–1983)
> Playwright; *Big White Fog: A Negro Tragedy; Our Lan'*; LAW 1938

Ware, Alice Holdship
> LAW 1938; Organizing Committee, Dramatists Panel, 4th Congress, 1941

Warner, Sylvia Townsend (1893–1978)
> British novelist; *Summer Will Show; The True Heart*; poems, *Whether a Dove or a Seagull*; Loyalist Red Cross in Spanish Civil War; speaker, 3rd Congress, 1939

Warren, Brett
> Playwright; faculty, White Mountain Writers Conference, 1941; faculty, New York Writers School, 1941

Watson, George Lardon
> LAW 1939

**Watson, Maurice
> Teacher, New York Writers School, 1942

Weatherwax, Clara (1905–1958)
> Novelist; *Marching, Marching*; LAW 1936; Hollywood chapter, 1940, 1942; signer, Congress Call, 1941

Weatherwax, Jack
> Pamphlet and Forum Committee, Hollywood, January 1941

Wechsler, James Arthur (1915–1983)
> Journalist, editor; *Revolt on the Campus*; editor, *New York Post; War, Our Heritage; The Age of Suspicion*; 2nd Congress, 1937; FBI target 1937–; informer before McCarthy Committee [see Navasky, p. 5]

Weidman, Jerome (1913–)
> Novelist, playwright, short story writer, essayist; *I Can Get It for You Wholesale; Letter of Credit*

**Weil, Richard
> Hollywood Writers Congress, 1943; blacklisted 1952

Weinstock, Helen
> LAW 1939

Weiskopf, F. C. (1900–1955)
    Exiled Czechoslovak novelist; *Dawn Breaks; The Firing Squad; Hundred Towers;* 1949
    Czech ambassador to Sweden; Czech minister plenipotentiary to Washington; Czech
    ambassador to China; Exiled Writers Committee

Weiss, Paul (1901–)
    Professor of philosophy; *Reality;* LAW 1938

Welch, Marie de L.
    LAW 1937; National Executive Committee, 1937

Welles, Orson (1915–1985)
    Actor, director, producer; Academy Award for *Citizen Kane,* 1941; *The Shadow; Jane
    Eyre;* speaker, Exiled Writers Committee dinner, Hollywood 1941

Wellington, Amy
    Second Congress, 1937

Wells, Hulett M.
    Second Congress, 1937

Wells, Lee E.
    LAW 1938

Wentworth, Franklin H.

West, Dorothy (1907–)
    Novelist, short story writer; *The Living Is Easy;* 2nd Congress, 1937

West, Nathanael (1902–1940) Born Nathaniel Wallenstein Weinstein
    Novelist; *The Day of the Locust; Miss Lonelyhearts; The Dream of Balso Snell;* signer,
    Congress Call, 1935, 1941; Western Writers Congress, 1936

Wexley, John (1907–1985)
    Screenwriter, playwright, historian; *They Shall Not Die; The Last Mile; Angels With Dirty
    Faces; The Judgment of Julius and Ethel Rosenberg;* national officer, John Reed Club, 1935;
    signer, Congress Call, 1939; Executive Committee, Hollywood chapter, 1939, 1940,
    1942; Organizing Committee, Dramatists Panel, 4th Congress, 1941; Hollywood
    Writers Congress, 1943

Wharton, Elizabeth H.

Wheelright, John B. (1897–1940)
    Poet; *Rock and Shell; Mirror of Venus; Political Self-Portrait*

**Whipple, Chandler Henry (1905–)
    Editor, *Argosy* magazine, 1937–1939; teacher, New York Writers School, 1942

White, Kenneth
    LAW 1937; resigned from LAW *Bulletin* committee, October 20, 1937

White, Leigh
    LAW 1936

White, Max
    Second Congress, 1937

White, W. L. (1900–1973)
    LAW 1938

Whitehand, Robert
    Second Congress, 1937

Whitsett, George
    LAW 1937; Publicity Committee, 1937; Executive Committee, 1937

Wickes, Frances

Widen, Ruth
    Exiled Writers Committee, 1940

Wilder, Isobel
    Resigned 1941

Wilder, Lucy

Wilder, Thornton (1897–1975)
Novelist, playwright; Pulitzer Prizes for *Our Town* and *The Bridge of San Luis Rey; The Merchant of Yonkers;* LAW 1937; 2nd Congress, 1937; FBI target 1933–

Williams, Albert Rhys (1883–1962)
Historian; *Through the Russian Revolution; Russian Land; Soviets;* 2nd Congress, 1937

Williams, Alexander
Second Congress, 1937

Williams, Wesley
Second Congress, 1937

Williams, William Carlos (1883–1963)
Poet, physician; *The Poems of William Carlos Williams; Selected Essays; The William Carlos Williams Reader; Paterson;* LAW 1936; signer, Congress Call, 1939; Committee for Cultural Freedom, May 1939; FBI target 1930–

Willison, George Findlay (1896–1972)
Educator, historian; member, John Reed Club; LAW 1938; 2nd Congress, 1937

Wilson, Michael (1914–1978)
Screenwriter; Academy Award for *A Place in the Sun; It's a Wonderful Life; Five Fingers; Lawrence of Arabia; Salt of the Earth;* Hollywood chapter, 1942; blacklisted 1952, and denied Oscar for screenplay of *Bridge on the River Kwai*

Wilson, Walter
LAW 1938

Winkler, Jean
LAW 1935

Winspear, Alban Dewes (1899–)
Professor of classics; *Who Was Socrates?;* LAW 1937

Winter, Ella (1898–1980)
Journalist, memoirist, fiction writer; *Red Virtue; I Saw the Russian People;* ed. *Lincoln Steffens Speaking;* ed. *Letters of Lincoln Steffens;* signer, Congress Call, 1935, 1937, 1939, 1941; Western Writers Congress, 1936; Executive Committee, 1937; National Council, 1938, 1941; Council contact with West Coast chapters 1938; Executive Council, Hollywood chapter, 1939, 1941, 1942; FBI target 1927–

Winther, Sophus Keith (1893–)
Professor of English; *The Realistic War Novel; Mortgage Your Heart;* LAW 1937

Winwar, Frances (1900–) Born Francesca Vinceguerra
Novelist, biographer; *Poor Splendid Wings; The Romantic Rebels; Farewell the Banner; Life of the Heart: George Sand and Her Time;* LAW 1936; Conference December 1936; Executive Committee, 1936; Arrangements Committee, 1937; National Council, 1938; Regional Executive Committee, 1939; resigned 1939

Wirth, Nicholas
Second Congress, 1937

Wise, James Waterman (1901–1983)
Journalist, art dealer; editor, *Opinion;* correspondent, *New York Post; Swastika! and Nazism: The Assault on Civilization;* National Council, 1935

Wolfe, Philip
LAW 1938

Wolff, David (see Ben Maddow)

Wood, Charles Erskine Scott (1852–1944)
Essayist; *Heavenly Discourses; Earthly Discourses;* contributor to *Masses;* member, John Reed Club; LAW 1936; Western Writers Congress, 1936

Woodburn, John (1914–)

Woodward, Helen (1914–1982)
Journalist, editor; *The Bold Women;* LAW 1936; Committee for Cultural Freedom, May 1939

Wormser, Richard
Novelist; *All's Fair;* LAW 1938

Wright, Ernest
LAW 1936

Wright, Milton

Wright, Richard (1908–1960)
Novelist, poet; *Uncle Tom's Children; Native Son;* autobiography, *Black Boy; Twelve Million Black Voices;* signer, Congress Call, 1935, 1939, 1941; National Council, 1935; Midwest Writers Congress, 1936; Committee for *American Stuff,* 1938; Executive Committee, 1938; National Council, 1939–1941; vice president, 1941; lecturer, New York Writers School, 1940, 1941; Philadelphia civil liberties protest, 1940; speaker, 4th Congress, 1941; FBI target 1935–

Wylie, Max Melville (1904–1975)
Novelist, TV producer, director; *Hindu Heaven; Radio Writing;* 3rd Congress, 1939

Yakhontoff, Victor A. (1881–)
Historian; *Russia and the Soviet Union in the Far East; Chinese Soviets; USSR Foreign Policy;* LAW 1937; signer, Congress Call, 1941

Yellen, Samuel (1906–)
Professor of English, poet, historian; *American Labor Struggles; In the House and Out;* LAW 1937

Yerby, Frank Garvin (1916–1991)
Novelist; *The Foxes of Harrow; The Vixens;* Chicago chapter

Young, Art (1866–1944)
Artist; member, John Reed Club; 4th Congress, 1941; faculty, White Mountain Writers Conference, 1941; speaker, 4th Congress public meeting, 1941

Young, Lenore Kay
Hollywood chapter, 1942

Young, Stanley (1906–1975)
Poet, playwright, literary critic; signer, Congress Call, 1939; Connecticut chapter representative, 1939; National Council, 1940; resigned 1941

Zacharoff, Lucien
Faculty, New York Writers School, 1939, 1940

Zacks, Robert
LAW 1938

Zara, Louis (1910–)
Novelist, editor; *Blessed Is This Man; Give Us This Day; This Land Is Ours;* LAW 1937

Zerwick, Mortimer
Second Congress, 1937

Zinberg, Len (1912–1956) Pseud. Ed Lacy
Novelist; *Walk Hard–Talk Loud; Hold With the Hares;* LAW 1939; Keep America Out of War Committee, 1940

Zugsmith, Leane (1903–1969)
Novelist; *A Time to Remember; The Summer Soldiers;* LAW 1935; Conference December 1936; faculty, New York Writers School, 1938; signer, Congress Call, 1939; representative, WPA Writers Project Sponsoring Committee

Zukofsky, Louis (1904–1978)
    Poet, critic; *All: The Collected Poems; A;* LAW 1935; Executive Committee, 1936; FBI target 1935–

Appendix B
Officers Elected
at the Biennial Congresses
of the League of American Writers

First Americans Writers Congress, April 26–27, 1935

Chair: Waldo Frank
National Council: Nelson Algren, Michael Blankfort, Maxwell Bodenheim, Van Wyck Brooks, Sterling Brown, Fielding Burke, Alan Calmer, Robert Cantwell, Harry Carlisle, Eugene Clay, Merle Colby, Jack Conroy, Edward Dahlberg, Leonard Ehrlich, James T. Farrell, Kenneth Fearing, Angel Flores, Horace Gregory, Robert Herrick, Sidney Howard, Orrick Johns, Joshua Kunitz, Tillie Lerner, Meridel LeSueur, Robert Morss Lovett, Grace Lumpkin, Lewis Mumford, Moishe Nadir, Clifford Odets, M. J. Olgin, Joseph Opatoshu, Paul Peters, Rebecca Pitts, William Rollins, Jr., George Sklar, Agnes Smedley, Lincoln Steffens, James Waterman Wise, Richard Wright
Executive Committee: Kenneth Burke, Harold Clurman, Malcolm Cowley, Joseph Freeman, Michael Gold, Henry Hart, Josephine Herbst, Granville Hicks, Matthew Josephson, Alfred Kreymborg, John Howard Lawson, Albert Maltz, Isidor Schneider, Edwin Seaver, Genevieve Taggard, Alexander Trachtenberg
Executive Secretary: Katherine Buckles (retained after the congress)

Second American Writers Congress, June 4–6, 1937

President: Donald Ogden Stewart
Vice Presidents: Van Wyck Brooks, Erskine Caldwell, Malcolm Cowley, Langston Hughes, Paul de Kruif, Meridel LeSueur, Upton Sinclair
Secretary: Philip Stevenson
Treasurer: Bernard J. Reis (chosen by the Executive Council, succeeded by Aline Bernstein)
Executive Secretary: Ellen Blake
Executive Council: Dorothy Brewster, Kyle Crichton, George Dangerfield, Marjorie Fischer, Joseph Freeman, Robert Gessner, Henry Hart, Rolfe Hum-

Some changes made between Congresses are not indicated.

phries, John Howard Lawson, Dexter Masters, W. L. River, Genevieve Taggard, Jean Starr Untermeyer

Third American Writers Congress, June 2–4, 1939

Honorary President: Thomas Mann
President: Donald Ogden Stewart
Secretary: Rolfe Humphries
Treasurer: Jerome E. Brooks
Executive Secretary: Franklin Folsom
Vice Presidents: Van Wyck Brooks, Louis Bromfield, Malcolm Cowley, Dorothy Canfield Fisher, Ernest Hemingway, Langston Hughes, George Seldes, Vincent Sheean, Upton Sinclair, John Steinbeck
National Board: Nora Benjamin, Aline Bernstein, Ivan Black, Dorothy Brewster, Sterling Brown, Harry Carlisle, Lester Cohen, Norman Corwin, George Dangerfield, Martha Dodd, Marjorie Fischer, Henry Hart, Lillian Hellman, Oliver La Farge, Edwin Lanham, Albert Maltz, Joseph North, Dawn Powell, W. L. River, Ralph Roeder, Philip Stevenson, Isidor Schneider, Genevieve Taggard, Jean Starr Untermeyer, Richard Wright
Chapter Representatives: New York — Benjamin Appel, Myra Page; Connecticut — J. H. Preston, Stanley Young; Chicago — George Dillon, Meyer Levin. Representatives from Hollywood, San Francisco, and Washington, D.C., still to be elected by the chapters.

Fourth American Writers Congress, June 5–8, 1941

Honorary President: Theodore Dreiser
President: Dashiell Hammett
National Executive Secretary: Franklin Folsom
Vice-Presidents: Erskine Caldwell, John Howard Lawson, Meridel LeSueur, Albert Maltz, George Seldes, Donald Ogden Stewart, Richard Wright
National Board: Benjamin Appel, Georgia Backus, Thomas Bell, Alvah Bessie, Marc Blitzstein, Millen Brand, Dorothy Brewster, John Bright, Edwin Berry Burgum, Haakon Chevalier, Lester Cole, Alexander Crosby, Henry Wadsworth Longfellow Dana, Joy Davidman, Martha Dodd, Muriel Draper, Ralph Ellison, Eleanor Flexner, Lillian Barnard Gilkes, Henry Hart, Jean Karsavina, Alfred Kreymborg, Corliss Lamont, Ruth McKenney, Bruce Minton, Harvey O'Connor, Clifford Odets, Myra Page, Samuel Putnam, W. L. River, Isidor Schneider, Viola Brothers Shore, Samuel Sillen, Tess Slesinger, Christina Stead, Bernhard J. Stern, Philip Stevenson, Genevieve Taggard

Appendix C
Members of Some League of American Writers Committees

... and Spain Sings

Those who took part in translating or adapting the ballads in ... *and Spain Sings* were: Rolfe Humphries, John Peale Bishop, Katherine Anne Porter, William Carlos Williams, Stanley Kunitz, George Dillon, Millen Brand, Muriel Rukeyser, Willard Maas, Kenneth Porter,* Ethel Turner, Maxwell Singer,* Shaemas O'Sheel, Allen Dowling,* Genevieve Taggard, Edna St. Vincent Millay, Katherine Garrison Chapin, Eli Siegel, Jean Starr Untermeyer, Bernard Guilbert Guerney, Hugh J. Perry,* Charles Preston,* James Neugass, E. Merrill Root, Myra G. Marini,* Ruth Lechlitner, David Efron.

* An asterisk after a name indicates contributors to the anthology who, with M. J. Benardete, were not League members.

Exiled Writers Committee

These League members all helped at one time or another in the work of the Exiled Writers Committee: Nathan Ausubel, Robert Carse, Martha Dodd, Ambrogio Donini, Marjorie Fischer, Rolfe Humphries, Louise Mally, F. E. Menaker, Leonard Mins, Ralph Roeder, Isidor Schneider, Isobel Walker Soule, Christina Stead, Jean Starr Untermeyer, Ruth Widen, Lucien Zacharoff. To help with fundraising and with getting jobs for refugee writers, an Exiled Writers Committee of the League's Hollywood chapter included Sidney Buchman, Vera Caspary, Lester Cole, Richard Collins, Francis Faragoh, Paul Jarrico, Hy Kraft, Ring Lardner, Jr., Albert Maltz, Maurice Rapf, Robert Rossen, Budd Schulberg, Allan Scott, Marian Spitzer, Donald Ogden Stewart, and Ella Winter (chair). Also active with the committee was Jane Sherman from the League's staff. In Chile Nancy Cunard, not a League member, gave valuable assistance, as did Constancia de la Mora, a Spanish refugee in Mexico.

Keep America Out of War Committee

By January 1940, these League members had been active on the Keep America Out of War Committee: Ben Bengal, Lillian Hellman, Arthur Kober,

Dashiell Hammett, Alter Brody, Lawrence A. Goldstone, Henry Hart, Edwin Berry Burgum, Henry Goodman, George Sklar, Charles A. Wagner, Fannie Engle, George Asness, Eleanor Flexner, Len Zinberg, Shaemas O'Sheel, James Neugass, Sonia Raiziss.

Appendix D
Writers Active in the Sacco-Vanzetti Case

Among the writers taking active part as picketers or protesters in the campaign in the 1920s to save Sacco and Vanzetti were Katherine Anne Porter, Gardner Jackson, John Dos Passos, Heywood Broun, Edna St. Vincent Millay, Louis Mumford, Elinor Wylie, Lola Ridge, and Paxton Hibben. A great outpouring of writings accompanied and followed the Sacco-Vanzetti campaign. Among those who did this writing were E. Merrill Root, Malcolm Cowley, Lucia Trent, Edna St. Vincent Millay, Upton Sinclair, and Maxwell Anderson.

Appendix E
The League of Professional Groups for Foster and Ford

The League of Professional Groups for Foster and Ford, the Communist candidates in the 1932 presidential election, included Leonie Adams, Sherwood Anderson, Newton Arvin, Em Jo Basshe, Maurice Becker, Slater Brown, Fielding Burke, Erskine Caldwell, Robert Cantwell, Lester Cohen, Louis Colman, Lewis Corey, Malcolm Cowley, Kyle Crichton, Countee Cullen, Henry Wadsworth Longfellow Dana, M. A. de Ford, John Dos Passos, Theodore Dreiser, Waldo Frank, Eugene Gordon, Louis Grudin, Horace Gregory, John Herrmann, Granville Hicks, Sidney Hook, Sidney Howard, Langston Hughes, Orrick Johns, Matthew Josephson, Alfred Kreymbourg, Grace Lumpkin, Felix Morrow, Samuel Ornitz, James Rorty, Isidor Schneider, Frederick Schuman, Edwin Seaver, Lincoln Steffens, Charles R. Walker, Robert Whitaker, Edmund Wilson, and Ella Winter.

Appendix F
Signers of Certain League Statements

Statement drafted November 1940, by the National Council, in which anti-Fascism remained the core of the League's work, was submitted to League membership with these signatures:

Benjamin Appel	Oliver La Farge
Nora Benjamin	Edwin Lanham
Dorothy Brewster	John Howard Lawson
Ivan Black	Albert Maltz
Michael Blankfort	Joseph North
Jerome Brooks	Dawn Powell
Sterling Brown	John Hyde Preston
Harry Carlisle	Myra Page
Lester Cohen	W. L. River
Norman Corwin	Ralph Roeder
Malcolm Cowley	George Seldes
George Dillon	Philip Stevenson
Martha Dodd	Isidor Schneider
Marjorie Fischer	Vincent Sheean
Franklin Folsom	Donald Ogden Stewart
Henry Hart	Genevieve Taggard
Lillian Hellman	Jean Starr Untermeyer
Eugene Holmes	Richard Wright
Rolfe Humphries	Stanley Young

Wartime Support of the USSR

Among writers forwarding statements to the Union of Soviet Writers via the League were: Benjamin Appel, Jenny Ballou, Silas Bent, Michael Blankfort, Millen Brand, Struthers Burt, Witter Bynner, H.W.L. Dana, Angna Enters, Howard Fast, Hutchins Hapgood, Robert Hillyer, Alexander Kaun, Ernest Poole, Eric Knight, Frederic Arnold Kummor, John Howard Lawson, William Ellery Leonard, Albert Maltz, F. O. Matthiessen, Harvey O'Connor, Samuel Putnam, Jules Romains, Norman Rosten, Christina Stead, Bernhard J. Stern, Philip Stevenson, Eda Lou Walton, William Carlos Williams.

Appendix G
Contributors to Writers Take Sides

Supporters of the elected government of Spain:

Franklin P. Adams
Herbert Agar
George Albee
Nelson Algren
Sally Elliott Allen
Henry G. Alsberg
A. E. Anderson
Eugene Newton Anderson
J. L. Anderson
Maxwell Anderson
Sherwood Anderson
Benjamin Appel
Newton Arvin
Herbert Asbury
Nathan Asch
H. Ashbrook
Brooks Atkinson
Sanora Babb
George Backer
Leonard Bacon
Emery Balint
Jenny Ballou
Margaret Culkin Banning
John D. Barry
Joseph Warren Beach
Carleton Beals
Carl Becker
May Lamberton Becker
Albert Bein
Cedric Belfrage
E. T. Bell
Henry Bellaman
Agnes E. Benedict
Stephen Vincent Benet
William Rose Benet

Nora Benjamin
Rion Bercovici
Aline Bernstein
Dean Beshlich
Beatrice Bisno
Marc Blitzstein
Bruce Bliven
Ralph Block
R. Blucher
Louise Bogan
G. A. Borgese
Percy H. Boynton
Millen Brand
Dorothy Brewster
Louis Bromfield
Van Wyck Brooks
Alice Brown
Bob Brown
Dee Brown
J. F. Brown
Earl Browder
Herbert Bruncken
Pearl S. Buck
Harriet Foster Bunn
Fielding Burke
Kenneth Burke
Stanley Burnshaw
Witter Bynner
Nev Campbell
Harry Carlisle
Helen Grace Carlisle
Vera Caspary
Katherine Garrison Chapin
Haakon M. Chevalier
Richard S. Childs

Samuel Chotzinoff
Stoyan Christowe
Albert E. Clements
Robert M. Coates
Humphrey Cobb
Lester Cohen
Morris R. Cohen
Lincoln Colcord
Alice Ross Colver
Groff Conklin
Marc Connelly
Jack Conroy
Paul Corey
George S. Counts
Harold Coy
Bruce Crawford
George Creel
Kyle Crichton
Rachel Crothers
Countee Cullen
William Cunningham
Dale Curran
Clifton Cuthbert
H.W.L. Dana
Elmer Davis
Frank Marshall Davis
Jerome Davis
Miriam Allen de Ford
Paul de Kruif
Floyd Dell
Leon Dennen
August Derleth
Alvaro de Silva
Babette Deutsch
George Dillon
Martha Dodd
William E. Dodd, Jr.
Muriel Draper
Theodore Dreiser
R. L. Duffus
Robert W. Dunn
Walter Duranty
Howard Edminster
Leonard Ehrlich
Paul Eldridge
Mary Elting

Guy Endore
H. C. Engelbrecht
Dorothy Erskine
Clifton Fadiman
Henry Pratt Fairchild
Ed Falkowski
William Faulkner
Leon Feinberg
Edna Ferber
Harvey Fergusson
Theodore E. Ferro
Ben Field
Kathleen Field
Sara Bard Field
Irving Fineman
Charles J. Finger
Louis Fischer
Marjorie Fischer
Dorothy Canfield Fisher
Vardis Fisher
Dudley Fitts
Grace Flandrau
Hildegarde Flanner
John Gould Fletcher
William Floyd
Franklin Folsom
Hulbert Footner
Charles Henri Ford
Felix Frankfurter
Joseph Freeman
Beatrice Frohlich
Frances Frost
Daniel Fuchs
John W. Gassner
Elizabeth Young George
Harrison George
Clifford Gessler
Robert Gessner
Elsa Gidlow
Helen Earle Gilbert
Lauren Gilfillan
Lillian Barnard Gilkes
Arnold Gingrich
Louis Ginsberg
Alexander Godin
Morton S. Goldstein

Joseph Gollomb
Henry Goodman
Don Gordon
Emmett Gowen
Edith K. Grafton
Samuel Grafton
Harry Granick
Bernard D.N. Grebanier
David Greenhood
Horace Gregory
John J. Gross
B. H. Haggin
Albert Halper
Maurice Halperin
Dashiell Hammett
Sibyl Croly Hanchett
Harry Hansen
Hutchins Hapgood
Reed Harris
Henry Hart
Willard E. Hawkins
Ernest Hemingway
Leon Srabian Herald
Josephine Herbst
Robert Herrick
John Herrmann
Granville Hicks
Hilaire Hiler
Sydney Hillyard
Peretz Hirshbein
Parks Hitchcock
John Haynes Holmes
Leo Huberman
Langston Hughes
Rolfe Humphries
Alice Riggs Hunt
Fannie Hurst
Inez Haynes Irwin
Theodore Irwin
Will Irwin
V. J. Jerome
Orrick Johns
Alvin Johnson
James Weldon Johnson
Josephine Johnson
Paul Jordan-Smith

Matthew Josephson
Joseph Kalar
H. V. Kaltenborn
MacKinlay Kantor
George A. Kaufman
Alexander Kaun
Alfred Kazin
Grace Kellogg
Ruth Epperson Kennell
Rockwell Kent
Sophie Kerr
Beatrice Kinkead
Manuel Komroff
William Kozlenko
Alfred Kreymborg
Fania Kruger
Stanley J. Kunitz
Oliver La Farge
Corliss Lamont
Edwin Lanham
Mary Lapsley
John Howard Lawson
Ruth Lechlitner
Hannah Lees
William Ellery Leonard
Max Lerner
Meyer Levin
Frank Grant Lewis
Eduard C. Lindeman
Lewis Lindsay
Leo Lipp
Alain Locke
Walter Lowenfels
Marvin Lowenthal
Grace Lumpkin
Ferdinand Lundberg
Norman MacLeod
William Christie MacLeod
A. B. Magil
Albert Maltz
Jerre Mangione
Fred T. Marsh
Marguerite Mooers Marshall
Robert Marshall
Daniel Gregory Mason
Edgar Lee Masters

Henry McCarty
William McFee
V. J. McGill
Vincent McHugh
Carey McWilliams
Peveril Meigs
Alfred H. Mendes
Karl A. Menninger
Martha Millet
Omer Mills
Bruce Minton
Broadus Mitchell
Marianne Moore
Alfred Morang
Oliver A. Morris
Robert A. Muir
Robert Nathan
Peter Neagoe
Scott Nearing
Reinhold Neibuhr
Charles G. Norris
Kathleen Norris
Harvey O'Connor
Clifford Odets
Moissaye J. Olgin
Charles O'Neill
Sam Ornitz
Shaemas O'Sheel
Raymond Otis
Walter Pach
Myra Page
Frances Park
Tom Jones Parry
Donald Culross Peattie
Arthur Pense
Ashley Pettis
William Lyon Phelps
Walter N. Polakov
Alan Porter
Anna Norma Porter
Katherine Anne Porter
John Hyde Preston
Lorine Pruette
Michael Quin
Carl Rakosi
Jackson H. Ralston

Michael I. Ravitch, M.D.
Leslie Reade
George B. Reeves
Cale Young Rice
Philip Blair Rice
Lynn Riggs
W. L. River
Ralph Roeder
Paul Romaine
John Rood
Edward Rosen
David Rosenberg
Paul Rosenfeld
Charles Edward Russell
Nahum Sabsay
Harold J. Salemson
Ivan Sandrof
Morris U. Schappes
Margaret Schlauch
Isidor Schneider
Mark Schorer
David Schubert
Budd Wilson Schulberg
Frederick L. Schuman
Vida D. Scudder
Edwin Seaver
George Seldes
Charles Coleman Sellers
Irwin Shaw
Vincent Sheean
Odell Shepard
Ruth Forbes Sherry
M. Shulimson
Eli Siegel
Joe Sigrist
Lee Simonson
Upton Sinclair
George Sklar
Tess Slesinger
Bernard Smith
Wilbert Snow
William Soskin
George Soule
Isobel Walker Soule
J. E. Spingarn
Robert G. Spivack

Wilbur Daniel Steele
John Steinbeck
Bernhard J. Stern
Philip Van Doren Stern
Philip Stevenson
Maxwell S. Stewart
I. F. Stone
Hanns Otto Storm
John Stuart
Ruth Suckow
Earl Lawson Sydnor
Genevieve Taggard
Norman Thomas
Dorothy Thompson
Gertrude Tonkonogy
Dan Totheroh
Ruth Tucker
Ethel Turner
Frank Tuttle
Jean Starr Untermeyer
Louis Untermeyer
Rena Vale
Carl Van Doren
Dorothy Van Doren
Mark Van Doren
Joseph Vogel
Mary Heaton Vorse
Lillian D. Wald
Webb Waldron
Paula Walling

Eda Lou Walton
Harry F. Ward
C. E. Warne
Richard Watts, Jr.
Clara Weatherwax
James Wechsler
Amy Wellington
M. R. Werner
John Hall Wheelock
Max White
William Allen White
Ruth Widen
Percival Wilde
Thornton Wilder
Carl Wilhelmson
William Carlos Williams
Wythe Williams
Ella Winter
Frances Winwar
Phil Wolfe
Charles Erskine Scott Wood
Richard Wormser
Richard Wright
Victor A. Yakhontoff
Avrahm Yarmolinsky
Samuel Yellen
Marya Zaturenska
Len Zinberg
Leane Zugsmith
Louis Zukofsky

Writers who said they were neutral about the Civil War in Spain:

Eleanor Carroll Chilton
e. e. cummings
Walter D. Edmonds
T. Swann Harding

Robinson Jeffers
Channing Pollock
Stewart Edward White

Writer who supported Franco in the Spanish Civil War:

Gertrude Atherton

Appendix H
The Writers Schools

The teachers in the Writers Schools were:

The Writers School (New York): George Albee, Benjamin Appel, Herbert Aptheker, Arthur Arent, George Asness, W. H. Auden, Helen Bergovoy, Joseph Bernstein, William J. Blake, Henrietta Buckmaster, Anthony Buttitta, Robert Carse, Vera Caspary, Lester Cole, Dorothy Brewster, Norman Corwin, Harold Coy, Alexander L. Crosby, Joy Davidman, James Dugan, John Dunn, Lajos Egri, Mary Elting, Ira Henry Freeman, Lillian Gilkes, Harry Granick, Bernard D.N. Grebanier, William Gresham, Kenneth Fearing, Rolfe Humphries, Leo Hurwitz, Jean Karsavina, Ruth Epperson Kennell, Joshua Kunitz, Ruth Lechlitner, Ruth Marro, May McNeer, Kenneth McNichol, Bruce Minton, Fred Myers, Myra Page, Edward L. Parker, Hyde Partnow, John Perry, Wellington Roe, William Rollins, Jr., Jack Schiff, Isidor Schneider, Edwin Seaver, Samuel Sillen, Isobel Walker Soule, E. E. Spitzer, Barrie Stavis, Philip Van Doren Stern, Philip Stevenson, Genevieve Taggard, Jean Starr Untermeyer, Eda Lou Walton, Lem Ward, Brett Warren, Morris Watson, Chandler Whipple, David Wolfe, Lucien Zacharoff, Leane Zugsmith.

Highlander Folk School (Tennessee): Benjamin Appel, Barrie Stavis, James Dugan, Millen Brand.

White Mountain Conference (New Hampshire): Wellington Roe, director; Genevieve Taggard, Art Young, Millen Brand, Benjamin Appel, Lee Atlas. Visiting lecturers: Rockwell Kent, Albert Maltz, Holland D. Roberts, Richard Wright, Eda Lou Walton, Marc Blitzstein, Vida D. Scudder, Irwin Shaw.

At one time or another, the following taught in the Hollywood Writers School: *Georgia Backus, *Cedric Belfrage, John Boylan, Michael Blankfort, Sidney Buchman, Vera Caspary, *Ralph Chaney, Edward Chodorov, Jerome Chodorov, Lester Cole, Richard Collins, Norman Corwin, *Danny Dare, Frank Davis, Guy Endore, Edward Eliscu, Dr. Franklin Fearing, *David Fenwick, *Fanya Foss, Sheridan Gibney, *Jay Gorney, Don Gordon, Morton Grant, David Hertz, Boris Ingster, Paul Jarrico, *Nunnally Johnson, Gordon Kahn, *Wolf Kaufman, John Howard Lawson, Meyer Levin, Milton Morlin, Carey McWilliams, Henry Myers, Albert Maltz, Dudley Nichols, Arch Oboler, *Mortimer Offner, *Ernest Pascal, Irving Reis, Fred Rinaldo, W. L. River, Robert Rossen, *Jerry Sachheim, Harold J. Salemson, *Dore Schary, Allan Scott, *Viola Brothers Shore, Budd Wilson Schulberg, *George Sklar, Tess Slesinger, Waldo Salt, George Sklar, Donald Ogden Stewart, *Lucien Trent, Dalton Trumbo.

The FBI compiled a list of teachers in the Hollywood Writers School but missed all those whose names are preceded by an asterisk.

Appendix I
Exiled Writers

Exiled Writers Interned in Le Vernet

Some who endured stays in Le Vernet were Rudolf Feistman, Bruno Frei, Rudolf Leonhard, Gustav Regler, Max Schroeder, Friedrich Wolf. The list of internees in this or other camps continues — Herman Budzislawski, Hermann Dunker, Lion Feuchtwanger, Leonhard Frank, Adolf Hofmeister, Alfred Kantorowicz, Peter Kast, Kurt Kersten, Hermann Kesten, Walter Mehring, Balder Olden, Bruno Von Saloman, Franz Werfel, Paul Westheim.

Exiled Writers Arrested in France

In November 1939 the League of American Writers knew of these German and Austrian writers who had been taken into custody in France (some were later released under surveillance): Franz Werfel, Friedrich Wolf, Hermann Dunker (who was very ill), Balder Olden, Gustav Regler, Alfred Kantorowicz, Peter Kast, Paul Westheim, Hermann Kesten, Leonhard Frank, Walter Mehring, H. W. Katz, Erich Keisch, Rudi Feistmann, Karl Obermann, Kurt Stern, Elizabeth Karr, Kurt Kersten, Hans Natonek, Hermann Budzislawski, Alfred Wolfenstein, Rudolf Leonhard, Wolf Frank, Maria Frank, Felix Timpe, Theo Balk, Hasen Clever, Bruno Saloman, Lion Feuchtwanger, Adolf Hofmeister.

Roster of Exiled Writers

The Exiled Writers Committee helped, in one way or another, eighty-four writers and fourteen dependents to escape from Europe. The amount and kind of help given varied from person to person, and the EWC was not alone in helping a number of them. The types of assistance given included money for transportation, visas (exit, entry, and transit), shelter (in the League house in France and in a co-op hotel in Mexico City), food packages, monthly cash payments, grants in support of writing projects, affidavits of support required by the U.S. government, book contracts, screenwriting contracts, and introductions to persons able to give help. Those aided in at least one of these ways were:

Alexander Abusch, wife, and
child
Friedrich Alexan

Julius Bab
Theodore Balk
Max Barth

Johannes Becher
Max Beer
Ernest Bloch
Bertolt Brecht
Willi Bredel
Ferdinand Bruckner
Hermann Budzislawski,
    wife, and child
Pierre de Lanu
Emilio Delgado
Alfred Doeblin
Ambrogio Donini
Hermann Dunker
E. N. Dzelepy
Rudolph Feistmann
Lion Feuchtwanger
Dragotin Fodor
Bruno Frank
Leonhard Frank
Wolf Frank
Bruno Frei (Benedict Freistadt)
    and two children
Claire Goll
Ivan Goll
Oskar Maria Graf
Professor Gumbel
Martin Gumpert
Wieland Herzfelde
Adolf Hoffmeister
Egon Hostovsky
Ruth Jerusalem
Alfred Kantorowicz and wife
Otto Katz (André Simone)
Hermann Kesten
Toni Kesten
Egon Erwin Kisch and wife
Rudolf Leonhard
Heinrich Mann
Klaus Mann
Hans Marchwitza
Jacques Maritain

Karin Michaelis
Walter Mehring
Franz Molnar
Mario Montagnana and wife
André Monze
Alfred Neumann
Rudolf Neumann
Albert Norden and wife
Franz Pfempffert
Alfred Polgar
Vladimir Pozner
Gustav Regler
Helene Reiner
Ludwig Renn
Otto Sattler
Will Schabel
Walther Schleiper
A. Schreiner
Max Schroeder
Leopold Schwarzchild
Anna Seghers, her husband, and
    two children
Ramon Sender
Helene Stoecker
Aladar Tamas
Adrienne Thomas
Julian Tuvim
Bodo Uhse
Sigrid Undset
Fritz von Unruh
Berthold Viertel
Arnold Wadler
Hilde Walter
Alex Wedding
Franz C. Weiskopf and wife
Franz Werfel
Paul Westheim
Joseph Wittlin
Friedrich Wolf
Milly Zirker
Otto Zoff

After they rescued the authors listed above, the Exiled Writers Committee and its members kept in touch with all of them and also with the following writers or publishers, many of whom had reached this hemisphere without being directly assisted by the EWC:

Rafael Alberti
Vicki Baum
José Bergamín
S. Bermann-Fischer
Henri Bernstein
Emile Bure
Constancia de la Mora
Enrique Diez-Canedo
Albert Einstein
Konrad Keiden
Gina Kaus
Leo Lania
Maria Teresa Leon
Prince Hubertus zu Loewenstein
Maurice Maeterlinck
Erika Mann
Thomas Mann

Pertinax
Erich Reiss
Erich Maria Remarque
Alfredo Reyes
Jules Romains
Jacques Roumains
Walter Schoenstedt
Genevieve Tabouis
Navarro Tomas
Tristan Tzara
Amadeo Ugolini
Jiri Voskovec
Ernst Waldinger
Paul Zech
Carl Zuckmayer
Stefan Zweig

Appendix J
Call to the Writers Win-the-War Congress

Signed as of November 3, 1942 — Not Released

In the interest of sharpening our effectiveness as writers against fascism, we are issuing this Call to a Writers Win-the-War Congress to be held in New York on the anniversary of Pearl Harbor (December 4-5-6). At this urgent hour no American, and least of all the writer, can rest until he has explored every possible means of contributing to Victory. Our Congress will provide an opportunity to pool the experiences of writers during the past year, to weigh our contribution and to formulate a program of action in the light of our country's need.

It is our function as writers to articulate the will and desires of the people, to strengthen public morale by clarifying and imaginatively projecting the issues of this war. We shall seek to relate the talent of the writer to the role he must perform on the home front and in the armed forces. Together with writer representatives of our Allies, we shall endeavor to strengthen the fellowship and full cooperation of the United Nations on which our victory depends.

Supporting President Roosevelt and his policy of swift offensive action to insure a quick and complete Axis defeat, we urge the immediate opening of a Second Front in Europe. Our Congress will seek ways and means of crushing our internal enemies who would sow disunity among the American people by spreading apathy, confusion, appeasement and defeatism. We shall demand the democratic integration in this people's war of the total energies of the Negro people, by fighting with them against discrimination in any form whether in civil life or in the armed forces. Our great heritage of democratic culture is violently threatened by Hitlerism; it is a fighting heritage which we plan to bring to the forefront of our deliberations.

Our words are weapons, and we offer our Congress as a weapon, for the defense of our cultural achievement and for Victory. The measure of our success will be the degree to which we can link our writing energies to the universal fight against the fascist enslavers and murderers of mankind. We shall strive not only to remember Pearl Harbor and Lidice and Stalingrad, but to avenge them. For that pressing purpose we issue this Call to American writers.

Nelson Algren	Sholom Asch
Hervey Allen	Harry Bailey
Benjamin Appel	Jenny Ballou

Thomas Bell
Silas Bent
Konrad Bercovici
Josef Berger
Aline Bernstein
Alvah Bessie
Edwin Bjorkman
William Blake
Arna Bontemps
Asa Bordages
Richard O. Boyer
Lowell Brentano
Bessie Breuer
Dorothy Brewster
John Bright
Louis Bromfield
Henrietta Buckmaster
Edwin Berry Burgum
Struthers Burt
Fanny Benable Cannon
Robert Carse
Vera Caspary
Haakon Chevalier
Edward Chodorov
Blake Clark
Lester Cole
Jack Conroy
Paul Corey
Countee Cullen
H.W.L. Dana
Joy Davidman
Frank Marshall Davis
Paul de Kruif
Merrill Denison
August Derleth
Albert Deutsch
Gertrude Diamant
Martha Dodd
Olin Downes
Muriel Draper
Carl Dreher
Robert W. Dunn
Arnaud D'Usseau
Lajos Egri
Edward Eliscu
Ralph Ellison

DeForest Ely
Guy Endore
Henry Pratt Fairchild
Howard Fast
Ben Field
Sara Bard Field
Wanda Gag
Sheriden Gibney
Lillian Barnard Gilkes
Strickland Gilliland
Harry Granick
Morton Grant
E. Haldeman-Julius
Mauritz Hallgren
Florence Hamilton
William Harrison
Langston Hughes
Albert Kahn
Gordon Kahn
Jean Karsavina
Harry Kemp
Rockwell Kent
William Kozlenko
H. S. Kraft
Alfred Kreymborg
Corliss Lamont
Ring Lardner, Jr.
John Howard Lawson
Ruth Lechlitner
Robert Lees
Emil Lengyel
William Ellery Leonard
Meridel LeSueur
Percy MacKaye
Albert Maltz
F. O. Matthiessen
Elizabeth McCausland
Ruth McKenney
May McNeer
Carey McWilliams
Lyon Mearson
Bruce Minton
Henry Myers
Robert Newman
Joseph North
Arch Oboler

Harvey O'Connor
Samuel Ornitz
Myra Page
Ernest Poole
Phelps Putnam
Samuel Putnam
Mike Quinn
Wellington Roe
Harold J. Rome
Robert Rossen
Norman Rosten
Waldo Salt
Michael Sayers
Margaret Schlauch
Isidor Schneider
Edwin Seaver
George Seldes
Elie Siegmeister
Samuel Sillen
George Sklar
Sarah Smith
Wessel Smitter

Christina Stead
Bernhard J. Stern
Philip Stevenson
Donald Ogden Stewart
Anna Louise Strong
Jesse Stuart
Genevieve Taggard
Ida M. Tarbell
Orin Tovrov
Shepard Traube
Lawrence Treat
Ethel Turner
Frank Tuttle
Michael Uris
Harry F. Ward
Lem Ward
John Wexley
Ella Winter
C.E.S. Wood
Victor A. Yakhontoff
Louis Zara
Leane Zugsmith

Appendix K
Permissions for Quotations

For permission to quote I am indebted to:

Millen Brand Papers, Rare Books and Manuscripts Library, Columbia University, for passages from Millen Brand's Journal in Chapter 8, Chapter 15, and Chapter 20;

Peter Stimson Brooks and Pacific Research Institute, for letters from Van Wyck Brooks in Chapters 14 and 15;

Theodore Draper Papers, Special Collections, Robert W. Woodruff Library, Emory University, and to Felix E. Browder for remarks by Earl Browder in Chapter 9;

Special Collections, Newberry Library and the Estate of Malcolm Cowley, for letters by Malcolm Cowley in Chapters 9 and 15;

Indiana University Press, for poems by Kenneth Fearing in Chapters 11 and 21;

Poetry: A Magazine of Verse, for poem by Franklin Folsom in Chapter 1;

Indiana University Press, for poem by Rolfe Humphries in Chapter 15;

Special Collections, Morris Library, Southern Illinois University, for letters of Dalton Trumbo in Chapter 9, Donald Ogden Stewart in Chapter 13, and Martha Dodd in Chapter 13;

Special Collections, University Research Library, University of California, Los Angeles, for quotation from Albert Maltz interview in Chapter 13.

Albert Maltz Papers, Special Collections, Mugar Memorial Library, Boston University, Chapter 13;

Yale Collection of American Literature, Beinecke Rare Book and Manuscript Library, Yale University, and Ellen Wright for the estate of Richard Wright for the lines from "The BI Eye Blues" in Chapter 13.

Acknowledgments

If I had died when statisticians decreed that I should, you would have been spared this book. It follows that one charge cannot be brought against me — that I was too eager to rush into print. There is, however, a disadvantage to waiting half a century before putting pen to paper. Memory fades and time distorts.

To fill in blanks in my recollections and to try to keep me honest, I have had important help.

This book, like the organization about which it is written, is a collaborative effort. In part, it is what a reader has a right to expect of a memoir. It contains recollections and reflections, but others have labored to keep them in harmony with the facts. In this effort my wife, Mary Elting Folsom, has given a great deal of time, using her considerable skills as an editor and offering her own recollections. She, too, was a member of the League of American Writers. Also helpful in jogging my memory have been Betty Bacon, Sender Garlin, Jane Sherman — all survivors from the days of the League. For helpful suggestions, I thank my daughter, Rachel Folsom, and my daughter-in-law, Marcia McClintock Folsom, who were not in the League generation. To all these at the University Press of Colorado I am indebted: to publisher Luther Wilson for decisive encouragement; to Jody Berman, managing editor, for patient editorial assistance; to Laurie Sirotkin, editorial assistant, for her care in solving many problems; to Carol Humphrey for her care with book design; and to Pete Hammond, marketing director, for his plans to find an audience for what I have written.

For translating relevant portions of books in German about exiled writers, I am indebted to Margarete Moller.

For finding many of the illustrations, and for checking much of the information about League members that appears in the membership list, I am indebted to Matthew Beata, Candace Holland, Carrie Jenkins, and John Wheeler. Their help, and my research trips to Los Angeles, Palo Alto, Chicago, Madison, Ann Arbor, Carbondale, Washington, New York, New Haven, and Amherst to look into papers left by League members were made possible by grants from the Margaret S. Mahler Institute of the Gray Panthers, the American Philosophical Society, and the Neodata Endowment for the Arts and Humanities. Professor Alan Wald of the University of Michigan generously gave information and encouragement as I worked, and I have made considerable use of books by Herbert Mitgang, Victor Navasky, and Natalie Robins, all of whom have made important contributions to the record of the repressive steps taken against writers in this century.

A Ph.D. dissertation by Arthur Casciato, "Citizen Writer: A History of the League of American Writers," University of Virginia, 1986, and graduate papers at the University of Colorado by Larry Lomax, on part of the unpublished proceedings of the Fourth American Writers Congress, and by Corinne M. Adler, on Anna Seghers, have been useful. I am grateful also to Ute Brandes, professor of German, Amherst College, for information contained in her then-unpublished article on Anna Seghers. Others who facilitated my research are: Deborah Pelletier, Special Collections and Archives, Amherst College Library; Karen Mix, archivist, Special Collections, Mugar Memorial Library, Boston University; Ronald J. Grele, director, Oral History Research Service, Butler Library, Columbia University; Rare Books and Manuscripts, Butler Library, Columbia University; the Darien Historical Society, the Darien Public Library, the convent of Saint Birgitte, all in Darien, Connecticut; Beverly B. Allen, reference archivist, Robert W. Woodruff Library, Emory University, and Professor Harvey Klehr, Emory University, Atlanta, Georgia; J. Kevin O'Brien, chief, Freedom of Information–Privacy Acts Section, Information Managerial Division, Federal Bureau of Investigation; Mrs. Lee, Carolyn Thompson, Mary Zeger, librarians, FOIPA Reading Room, Federal Bureau of Investigation, Washington, D.C.; Allen Seaburg, curator of manuscripts, and Glen MacAfee, Harvard Divinity School Library, Cambridge; Ghanda DiFiglia, Department of Philosophy, Harvard University; Hoover Institution, Library and Archives, Palo Alto, California; Betty Smith, International Publishers; Jane E. Hodes, director, Marxist Library for Social Research, Berkeley, California; Margaret Kulis, Special Collections, The Newberry Library, Chicago, Illinois; Rare Books and Manuscripts Division, The New York Public Library; Tamiment Library, New York University; Ann Maitlin, librarian, Reference Center for Marxist Studies, New York, New York; Karen D. Drickamer, curator of manuscripts, Morris Library, Special Collections, Southern Illinois University at Carbondale; Bonnie Hardwick, head of Manuscripts Division, The Bancroft Library, University of California, Berkeley, California; John Skarstad, assistant department head/archivist, Department of Special Collections, The University Library, University of California, Davis; Susan Dean, head, and Kris McCusker, library technician, Special Collections, Norlin Library, University of Colorado at Boulder; Professor Manning Marable and Professor John Stevenson, University of Colorado, Boulder; Helen Ballew, ALA Archives graduate assistant, University Library, University of Illinois at Urbana-Champaign; Nancy M. Shawcrosse, Charles Patterson Van Pelt Library; University of Pennsylvania; Patricia Willis, The Beinecke Rare Book and Manuscript Library, Yale University; Arthur M. Zipser.

For typing, re-typing and typing again, I am indebted to Abby Fountain, who saw the manuscript through from beginning to end.

The writers whose words I have borrowed are also collaborators. If these quotations, a few of which are extensive, make the book seem like something other than a personal memoir, so be it. The League itself was not a one-person performance, so a book about it may surely be excused for reflecting this reality.

To all my collaborators go my sincere thanks, but none of them can be held responsible for errors or shortcomings in the pages of this volume. Such lapses are entirely my doing — or undoing.

Bibliography

As I prepared this memoir, I consulted these manuscript collections in addition to my own files:

Millen Brand Papers. Rare Books and Manuscripts Library, Butler Library, Columbia University, New York.

Earl Browder Tapes. Oral History Research Office, Columbia University.

Earl Browder Papers. The Draper Collection, Robert W. Woodruff Library, Emory University, Atlanta.

Malcolm Cowley Papers. Special Collections, The Newberry Library, Chicago.

Theodore Dreiser Papers. Special Collections Department, Van Pelt Library, University of Pennsylvania.

Federal Bureau of Investigation. Freedom of Information Act Reading Room, Washington, D.C., limited files on Cedric Belfrage, Erskine Caldwell, Theodore Dreiser, Langston Hughes, Dwight Macdonald, F. O. Matthiessen, Clifford Odets, Myra Page, Dorothy Parker, Ludwig Renn, Elmer Rice, Muriel Rukeyser, Upton Sinclair, John Steinbeck, Rex Stout.

Franklin Folsom FBI file. Special Collections, Norlin Library, University of Colorado at Boulder.

Joseph Freeman Papers. Hoover Institution of War, Revolution and Peace, Stanford University.

Bernard D.N. Grebanier Papers. Special Collections, Mugar Memorial Library, Boston University.

Rolfe Humphries Papers. Special Collections and Archives, Amherst College Library, Amherst, Massachussetts.

V. J. Jerome Papers. The Beinecke Rare Book and Manuscript Library, Yale University.

Matthew Josephson Papers. The Beinecke Rare Book and Manuscript Library, Yale University.

John Howard Lawson Collection. Special Collections, Morris Library, Southern Illinois University at Carbondale.

League of American Writers FBI file. Special Collections, Norlin Library, University of Colorado at Boulder.

League of American Writers Papers. Manuscripts Division, The Bancroft Library, University of California, Berkeley.

Albert Maltz Papers. Special Collections, Mugar Memorial Library, Boston University.

Mercury Theater/Theater Union Oral History Project. Oral History Research Office, Columbia University.

Isidor Schneider Collection. Rare Book and Manuscript Library, Butler Library, Columbia University.

Ella Winter Collection. Rare Book and Manuscript Library, Butler Library, Columbia University.

Richard Wright Papers. The Beinecke Rare Book and Manuscript Library, Yale University.

I also consulted the following materials:

Aaron, Daniel. "The Thirties — Now and Then." *American Scholar,* Summer 1966.

————. *Writers on the Left: Episodes in American Literary Communism.* Harcourt Brace and World, 1961. Reprint. Columbia University Press, 1992.

Aaron, Daniel, and Robert Bendiner, eds. *The Strenuous Decade: A Social and Intellectual Record of the Nineteen-Thirties.* Anchor Books, 1970.

Adickes, Sandra. "Grace Lumpkin, Myra Page, and Josephine Herbst: Commitment and Its Aftermath." Paper presented at the Conference on the Thirties, Youngstown Ohio State University, 1992.

Adler, Corinne M. "Antifascist German Writers in Exile: Life and Work." Paper submitted in the graduate course in American Literature and Politics, University of Colorado, 1987.

Alegria, Ciro. *Broad and Alien Is the World.* Farrar and Rinehart, Inc., 1941.

Appel, Benjamin. "Miss America and the Look-Back Boys." *The Literary Review,* Fairleigh Dickinson University, Fall 1973.

Bak, Hans. *Malcolm Cowley: The Formative Years.* University of Georgia Press, 1993.

Beals, Carleton. *Latin America: World in Revolution.* Abelard-Schuman, 1963.

Belfrage, Cedric. *American Inquisition: 1945–1960.* Thunder's Mouth Press, 1989.

Bell, Thomas. *In the Midst of Life.* Atheneum, 1961.

Benardete, M. J., and Rolfe Humphries, eds. *. . . and Spain Sings: Fifty Loyalist Ballads Adapted by American Poets.* Vanguard Press, 1937.

Benson, Frederick R. *Writers in Arms: The Impact of the Spanish Civil War.* New York University Press, 1967.

Bentley, Elizabeth. *Out of Bondage.* Devin Adair, 1951.

Bentley, Eric, ed. *Thirty Years of Treason: Excerpts From Hearings Before the House Committee on Un-American Activities, 1938–1960.* The Viking Press, 1971.

Bessie, Alvah. *Men in Battle.* Charles Scribner's Sons, 1939.

Bloom, James D. *Left Letters: The Culture Wars of Mike Gold and Joseph Freeman.* Columbia University Press, 1992.

Bogardus, Ralph F., and Fred Hobson, eds. *Literature at the Barricades: The American Writer in the 1930s.* The University of Alabama Press, 1982.

Bourne, Randolph. "The War and the Intellectuals." In *Untimely Papers.* B. W. Huebsch, 1919. Limited reprint by Robert L. Leslie distributed to all writers at the Fourth American Writers Congress 1941.

Boyers, Robert, ed. *The Legacy of the German Refugee Intellectuals.* Schocken Books, 1972.

Brandes, Ute. "Anna Seghers and the Politics of Affirmation in the GDR." In *Coming to Terms With the Present,* edited by Marilyn Fries and Patricia Anne Simpson. Forthcoming.

Brooks, Howard L. *Prisoners of Hope: Report on a Mission.* L. B. Fischer, 1942.

Bryan, William Jennings. *Bryan on Imperialism.* Arno Press and *The New York Times,* 1970.

Buhle, Mari Jo, and Paul Buhle, eds. *Encyclopedia of the American Left.* Garland Publishers, 1990.

Calverton, V. F. *The Liberation of American Literature.* Charles Scribner's Sons, 1932.

Casciato, Arthur Dominic. "Citizen Writer: A History of the League of American Writers." Ph.D. diss., University of Virginia, 1986.

Caute, David. *The Fellow-Travellers: Intellectual Friends of Communism.* Rev. ed. Yale University Press, 1988.

———. *The Great Fear: The Anti-Communist Purge Under Truman and Eisenhower.* Simon and Schuster, 1978.

Cazden, Robert E. R. *German Exile Literature in America, 1933–1950.* American Library Association, 1970.

Ceplair, Larry, and Steven Englund. *Inquisition in Hollywood: Politics in the Film Community, 1930–1960.* Anchor Press/Doubleday, 1980.

Chafee, Zachariah, Jr. *Free Speech in the United States.* Harvard University Press, 1941. Reprint. Atheneum, 1969.

Churchill, Ward, and Jim Vander Wall. *The Cointelpro Papers: Documents From the FBI's Secret War Against Domestic Dissent.* Boston: South End Press, 1990.

Clurman, Harold. *Fervent Years: The Story of the Group Theatre and the Thirties.* Alfred A. Knopf, 1945. Reprint. Hill and Wang, 1957.

Colodny, Robert G. *Spain: The Glory and the Tragedy.* Humanities Press, 1970.

Conquest, Robert. *The Great Terror: A Reassessment.* Oxford University Press, 1990.

Conroy, Jack, and Curt Johnson, eds. *Writers in Revolt: The Anvil Anthology.* Lawrence Hill and Company, 1973.

Cook, Bruce. *Brecht in Exile.* Holt, Rinehart and Winston, 1982.

Cooper, Wayne F., ed. *The Passion of Claude McKay: Selected Poetry and Prose, 1912–1948.* Schocken Books, 1973.

Cowley, Malcolm. — *And I Worked at the Writer's Trade: Chapters of Literary History, 1918–1978.* The Viking Press, 1963.

———. *The Dream of the Golden Mountain: Remembering the 1930's.* Reprint. Viking Press, 1980.

———. *Exile's Return.* W. W. Norton and Company, 1934. Reprint. The Viking Press, 1956.

———. *Think Back on Us . . . A Contemporary Chronicle of the 1930's.* Southern Illinois University Press, 1967.

Crichton, Kyle. *Total Recoil.* Doubleday and Company, 1960.

Crossman, Richard, ed. *The God That Failed.* Bantam, 1965.

Dahlberg, Edward. *The Confessions of Edward Dahlberg.* George Braziller, 1971.

Daniels, Roger. *Concentration Camps USA: Japanese Americans and World War II.* Holt, Rinehart and Winston, 1972.

Davis, Frank Marshall. *Livin' the Blues.* University of Wisconsin Press, 1992.

de la Mora, Constancia. *In Place of Splendor: The Autobiography of a Spanish Woman.* Harcourt Brace and Company, 1939.

Diamont, Sigmund. *Compromised Campus: The Collaboration of Universities With the Intelligence Community, 1945–1955.* Oxford University Press, 1992.

Divine, Robert A. *Roosevelt and World War II.* The Johns Hopkins Press, 1969.

Donaldson, Scott. *Archibald MacLeish: An American Life.* Houghton Mifflin Company, 1992.

Donner, Frank. *Protectors of Privilege: Red Squads and Police Repression in Urban America.* University of California Press, 1990.

Dos Passos, John. *The Best Times: An Informal Memoir.* The New American Library, 1966.

Draper, Theodore. *American Communism and Soviet Russia.* The Viking Press, 1960.

———. *The Roots of American Communism.* The Viking Press, 1957.

Dreiser, Theodore. *America Is Worth Saving.* Modern Age Books, 1941.

———. *Tragic America.* Horace Liveright, 1932.

Drew, Bettina. *Nelson Algren: A Life on the Wild Side.* G. P. Putnam's Sons, 1989.

Dunne, Philip. *Take Two (An Autobiography).* McGraw-Hill, in association with San Francisco Book Co., 1980.

Endore, Guy. *Let's Skip the Next War.* Hollywood Peace Forum, 1940.

———. "Life on the Blacklist," *The Nation,* December 20, 1952.

Fabre, Michel. *The Unfinished Quest of Richard Wright.* William Morrow, 1977.

Fallas, Carlos Luis. *Mamita Yunai.* Fondo de Cultura Popular, Mexico, 1957.

Farrell, James T. *The League of Frightened Philistines.* Vanguard Press, 1945.

———. *A Note on Literary Criticism.* Columbia University Press, 1936.

Fast, Howard. *The Naked God.* Frederick A. Praeger, 1957.

Fearing, Kenneth. *Afternoon of a Pawnbroker and Other Poems.* Harcourt, Brace and Company, 1943.

———. *New and Selected Poems.* Indiana University Press, 1966.

Felgar, Robert. *Richard Wright.* Boston: Twayne Publishers, 1980.

Field, Frederick Vanderbilt. *From Right to Left: An Autobiography.* Lawrence Hill and Co., 1983.

Fittko, Lisa. *Escape Through the Pyrenees.* Northwestern University Press, 1991.

Foster, William Z. *History of the Communist Party of the United States.* International Publishers, 1952.

Freeman, Joseph. *An American Testament: A Narrative of Rebels and Romantics.* Farrar and Rinehart, Inc., 1936.

———. *Never Call Retreat.* Farrar and Rinehart, Inc., 1943.

Fried, Emmanuel. *The Un-American: Autobiographical Non-Fiction Novel.* Buffalo, N.Y.: Labor Center Books, 1992.

Fry, Varian. *Surrender on Demand.* Random House, 1945.

Gaer, Joseph, ed. *Our Lives: American Labor Stories.* Boni and Gaer, 1948.

Gellman, Irwin F. *Good Neighbor Diplomacy: United States Policies in Latin America, 1933–1945.* The Johns Hopkins University Press, 1979.

Gilbert, James Burkhart. *Writers and Partisans: A History of Literary Radicalism in America.* John Wiley and Sons, 1968.

Gilman, Richard, and Michael Paul Novak. *Poets, Poetics and Politics: A Selection of Rolfe Humphries' Letters.* University Press of Kansas, 1992.

Gold, Michael. *The Hollow Men.* International Publishers, 1972.

Goldstein, Robert Justin. *Political Repression in Modern America From 1870 to the Present.* Schenkman Publishing Co., Inc., 1978.

Gurko, Leo. *The Angry Decade.* Dodd, Mead, 1947.

Halper, Albert. *Good-Bye, Union Square: A Writer's Memoir of the Thirties.* Quadrangle Books, 1970.

Hamilton, John Maxwell. *Edgar Snow: A Biography.* Indiana University Press, 1988.

Hart, Henry, ed. *American Writers' Congress*. International Publishers, 1935.

————, ed. *The Writer in a Changing World*. New York: Equinox Cooperative Press, 1937.

Hart, John E. *Albert Halper*. Boston: Twayne Publishers, 1980.

Hayden, Sterling. *Wanderer*. Alfred A. Knopf, 1963.

Healey, Dorothy, and Maurice Isserman. *Dorothy Healey Remembers: A Life in the American Communist Party*. Oxford University Press, 1990.

Heilbut, Anthony. *Exiled in Paradise: German Refugee Authors and Intellectuals in America From the 1930's to the Present*. The Viking Press, 1983.

Hicks, Granville. *Part of the Truth*. Harcourt, Brace and World, Inc., 1964.

————. *Where We Came Out*. The Viking Press, 1954. Reprint. Greenwood Press, 1973.

Hicks, Granville, et al., eds. *Proletarian Literature in the United States*. International Publishers, 1935.

Himelstein, Morgan Y. *Drama Was a Weapon: The Left-Wing Theatre in New York 1929–1941*. Rutgers University Press, 1963.

Hitler, Adolf. *My Battle (Mein Kampf)*. Houghton Mifflin Company, 1933.

Hollywood Writers' Mobilization. *Writers' Congress: The Proceedings of the Conference Held in October 1943 Under the Sponsorship of the Hollywood Writers' Mobilization and the University of California*. University of California Press, 1944.

Howe, Irving, and Lewis Coser. *The American Communist Party*. Praeger, 1962.

Humphries, Rolfe. *Collected Poems of Rolfe Humphries*. Indiana University Press, 1965.

Ickes, Harold. *The Secret Diary of Harold L. Ickes*. Vol. 3, *The Lowering Clouds, 1939–1941*. Simon and Schuster, 1954.

Ilma, Viola. *The Political Virgin*. Duell, Sloan and Pearce, 1958.

Jaffe, Philip. *The Rise and Fall of American Communism*. Horizon Press, 1975.

Jarrico, Paul, Sylvia Jarrico, Sonja Dahl Biberman, and Helen Blair, eds. *A Salute to John Howard Lawson*. Privately printed, November 12, 1955.

Jerome, V. J. *Intellectuals and the War*. Workers Library Publishers, 1940.

Josephson, Matthew. *Infidel in the Temple: A Memoir of the Nineteen-Thirties*. Alfred A. Knopf, 1967.

Jungk, Peter Stephan. *Franz Werfel: A Life in Prague, Vienna, and Hollywood*. Translated by Anselm Hollo. New York: Grove Weidenfeld, 1990.

Kahn, Gordon. *Hollywood on Trial*. Arno Press and *The New York Times*, 1972.

Kazin, Alfred. *On Native Ground: An Interpretation of Modern American Prose Literature*. Harcourt, Brace and Company, 1942.

Kempton, Murray. *Part of Our Time: Some Monuments and Ruins of the Thirties*. Simon and Schuster, 1955. Reprint. Delta, 1967.

Kiessling, Wolfgang. *Exil in Lateinamerika*. Leipzig: Verlag Philipp Reclam jun, 1980.

Krispyn, Egbert. *Anti-Nazi Writers in Exile*. University of Georgia Press, 1978.

Kutulas, Judy. "Becoming 'More Liberal': The League of American Writers, the Communist Party, and the Literary People's Front." *Journal of American Culture*. Spring 1990.

LaBahn, Kathleen J. *Anna Seghers' Exile in Literature: The Mexican Years (1941–1947)*. New York: Peter Lacy, 1986.

Langer, Elinor. *Josephine Herbst: The Story She Could Never Tell*. Warner Books, Inc., 1983.

Lardner, Ring, Jr. *The Lardners: My Family Remembered*. Harper and Row, 1976.

———. "My Life on the Blacklist," *The Saturday Evening Post*, October 14, 1961.

Layman, Richard. *Shadow Man: The Life of Dashiell Hammett*. Harcourt Brace Jovanovich, 1981.

Leonhard, Wolfgang. *Betrayal: The Hitler-Stalin Pact of 1939*. St. Martin's Press, 1989.

Linfield, Michael. *Freedom Under Fire: U.S. Civil Liberties in Times of War*. South End Press, 1990.

Lingeman, Robert. *Theodore Dreiser: An American Journey, 1908–1945*. Putnam, 1990.

Lovett, Robert Morss. *All Our Years: The Autobiography of Robert Morss Lovett*. The Viking Press, 1948.

Lyon, James K. *Bertolt Brecht in America*. Princeton University Press, 1980.

MacLean, Frances. "They Didn't Speak Our Language; We Didn't Speak Theirs," *Smithsonian*. January 1993.

Madden, David, ed. *Proletarian Writers of the Thirties*. Southern Illinois University Press, 1968.

Maltz, Albert. *The Citizen Writer*. International Publishers, 1950.

———. "The Citizen Writer in Retrospect." Interview by Joel Gardner. Reports of the University of California, 1983. Typescript in UCLA Library.

Mangione, Jerre. *The Dream and the Deal*. Little, Brown and Company, 1972.

———. *An Ethnic at Large, A Memoir of America in the Thirties and Forties*. University of Pennsylvania Press, 1983.

McCarthy, Mary. *Intellectual Memoirs: New York 1936–1938*. Harcourt Brace Jovanovich, 1992.

McGilligan, Pat. *Backstory: Interviews With Screenwriters of Hollywood's Golden Age*. University of California Press, 1986.

Menaker, Daniel. *The Old Left*. Alfred A. Knopf, 1987.

Mitford, Jessica. *A Fine Old Conflict*. Alfred A. Knopf, 1977.

Mitgang, Herbert. *Dangerous Dossiers: Exposing the Secret War Against America's Greatest Authors*. Donald L. Fine, Inc., 1988.

Morrow, Felix. *Revolution and Counter-Revolution in Spain*. Pioneer Publishers, 1938. Reprint. Pathfinder Press, 1974.

Murphy, James E. *The Proletarian Moment: Leftism and the Debates Over Literature and Politics Before and During the Great Depression*. University of Illinois Press, 1990.

Naison, Mark. *Communists in Harlem During the Depression*. University of Illinois Press, 1983.

Navasky, Victor S. *Naming Names*. Penguin Books, 1981.

Nelson, Cary. *Repression and Recovery: Modern American Poetry and the Politics of Cultural Memory, 1910–1945*. University of Wisconsin Press, 1989.

Nelson, Raymond. *Van Wyck Brooks: A Writer's Life*. E. P. Dutton, 1981.

Ninkovich, Frank A. *The Diplomacy of Ideas: U.S. Foreign Policy, 1938–1950*. Cambridge University Press, 1981.

North, Joseph, ed. *New Masses: An Anthology of the Rebel Thirties*. International Publishers, 1969.

O'Connor, Jessie Lloyd, Harvey O'Connor, and Susan M. Bowler. *Harvey and Jessie: A Couple of Radicals*. Temple University Press, 1988.

Odets, Clifford. *The Time Is Ripe: The 1940 Journal of Clifford Odets*. Grove Press, 1988.

Peck, David R. *American Marxist Literary Criticism: 1926–1941: A Bibliography.* California State University, 1968.

Polonsky, Abraham. "How the Blacklist Worked in Hollywood." *Film Culture* 50-51 (Fall–Winter 1970).

Quigley, Carroll. *Tragedy and Hope: A History of the World in Our Time.* The Macmillan Company, 1966.

Quin, Mike. *On the Drum Head: A Selection From the Writing of Mike Quin.* Edited by Harry Carlisle. San Francisco: Pacific Publishing Foundation, 1948.

Rampersad, Arnold. *The Life of Langston Hughes.* 2 vols. Oxford University Press, 1988.

Ravitz, Abe C. *Leane Zugsmith: Thunder on the Left.* International Publishers, 1992.

Regler, Gustav. *Owl of Minerva.* Farrar, Straus and Cudahy, 1960.

Reich-Ranicki, Marcel. *Thomas Mann and His Family.* Translated by Ralph Manheim. London: Collins, 1989.

Rideout, Walter. *The Radical Novel in the U.S.* Hill and Wang, 1966.

Roberts, Geoffrey. *The Unholy Alliance: Stalin's Pact With Hitler.* Indiana University Press, 1989.

Robins, Natalie. *Alien Ink: The FBI's War on Freedom of Expression.* William Morrow and Company, Inc., 1992.

Roosevelt, Theodore. *Colonial Policies of the United States.* Arno Press and *The New York Times,* 1970.

Roskolenko, Harry. *When I Was Last on Cherry Street.* Stein and Day, 1965.

Salzman, Jack, and Barry Wallenstein, eds. *Years of Protest.* Pegasus, 1967.

Sanford, John. *A Very Good Land to Fall With: Scenes From the Life of an American Jew.* Vol. 3. Santa Rosa, Calif.: Black Sparrow Press, 1967.

Schneider, Isidor. *The Judas Time.* Dial Press, 1946.

Schrecker, Ellen W. *No Ivory Tower: McCarthyism and the Universities.* Oxford University Press, 1986.

Schultz, Bud, and Ruth Schultz. *It Did Happen Here: Recollections of Political Repression in America.* University of California Press, 1989.

Schwartz, Anne Laura. "The League of American Writers: A Study of the Literary Left in the Late Thirties." B.A. thesis, Brown University, June 1983.

Schwartz, Nancy Lynn. *The Hollywood Writers' Wars.* Alfred A. Knopf, 1982.

Seeger, Pete. *The Incompleat Folksinger.* Edited by Jo Metcalf Schwartz. University of Nebraska Press, 1992.

Segal, Errol. "George Sklar: Playwright for a Socially Committed Theatre." Ph.D. diss., University of Michigan, 1986.

Shachtman, Tom. *The Phony War.* Harper and Row, 1982.

Simon, Rita, ed. *As We Saw the Thirties.* University of Illinois Press, 1967.

Smith, Page. *Redeeming the Time.* McGraw-Hill, 1987.

Sontag, Raymond, and James Beddie, eds. *Nazi-Soviet Relations, 1939–1941.* Documents from the Archives of the German Foreign Office, European and British Commonwealth Series No. 6. U.S. Department of State, 1948.

Spender, Stephen. *Journals 1939–1983.* Edited by John Goldsmith. London and Boston: Faber and Faber, 1985.

Sporn, Paul. "The Writer and the Left in the 1930's: The Failure of a Promise." Senior thesis, Wayne State University, Detroit, 1991.

Steinbeck, John. *Working Days: The Journals of "The Grapes of Wrath," 1938–1941.* Edited by Robert DeMott. Penguin, 1989.

Steven, Stewart. *Operation Splinter Factor: The Untold Story of America's Most Secret Cold War Intelligence Operation.* J. B. Lippincott Company, 1974.

Stewart, Donald Ogden. *By a Stroke of Luck: An Autobiography.* Paddington Press, Ltd., 1975.

———, ed. *Fighting Words.* Harcourt Brace and Company, 1940.

Summers, Anthony. *Official and Confidential: The Secret Life of J. Edgar Hoover.* G. P. Putnam's Sons, 1993.

Summers, Robert E., comp. *Wartime Censorship of Press and Radio.* The H. W. Wilson Company, 1942.

Swados, Harvey. *The American Writer and the Great Depression.* Bobbs-Merrill, 1966.

Theoharis, Athan G. *Seeds of Repression: Truman and the Origins of McCarthyism.* Quadrangle Books, 1971.

———. *Spying on Americans: Political Surveillance From Hoover to the Huston Plan.* Temple University Press, 1978.

Theoharis, Athan G., and John Stuart Cox. *The Boss: J. Edgar Hoover and the Great American Inquisition.* Temple University Press, 1988.

Thorp, Willard. "American Writers on the Left." In *Socialism and American Life,* Vol. 1, edited by Donald Drew Egbert and Stow Persons. Princeton University Press, 1952.

Trotsky, Leon. *Literature and Revolution.* International Publishers, 1925. Reprint. University of Michigan Press, 1960.

Trumbo, Dalton. *Harry Bridges: A Discussion of the Latest Effort to Deport Civil Liberties and the Rights of American Labor.* Hollywood: League of American Writers, 1941.

———. *The Time of the Toad: A Study of Inquisition in America and Two Related Pamphlets.* Perennial Library, 1972.

U.S. Congress. House. Special Committee on Un-American Activities. *Investigation of Un-American Propaganda Activities in the U.S.* Vol. 7. March 23, 29–31, April 1, 2, 5–9, 16, 1943. (On the League of American Writers)

———. Senate. Committee of the Judiciary. *Hearing Before the Subcommittee to Investigate the Administration of the Internal Security Act and Other Internal Security Laws.* 84th Cong. 2d. sess. On Scope of Soviet Activity in the United States, April 17, 1956, p. 15, U.S. Government Printing Office, 1956.

Untermeyer, Jean Starr. *Private Collection: A Memoir.* Alfred A. Knopf, 1965.

U.S. Government Printing Office. *History of the Office of the Coordinator of Inter-American Affairs,* 1947.

Wagner, Linda W. *Dos Passos: Artist as American.* University of Texas Press, 1979.

Wald, Alan M. *The New York Intellectuals: The Rise and Decline of the Anti-Stalinist Left From the 1930's to the 1980's.* University of North Carolina Press, 1987.

———. *The Responsibility of Intellectuals: Selected Essays on Marxist Traditions in Cultural Commitment.* Atlantic Heights, N.J.: Humanities Press, 1992.

Walker, Margaret. *Richard Wright Daemonic Genius: A Portrait of the Man, A Critical Look at His Work.* Warner Books, 1988.

Wilkinson, James D. *The Intellectual Resistances in Europe.* Harvard University Press, 1981.

Wilson, Edmund. *The American Earthquake.* Doubleday Anchor Books, 1958.

Winter, Ella. *And Not to Yield: An Autobiography.* Harcourt, Brace and World, 1963.

Wolfe, Thomas Kennerly, Jr. "The League of American Writers: Communist Organizational Activity Among American Writers." Ph.D. diss., Yale University, 1956.

World Committee for the Victims of German Fascism. *The Brown Book of the Hitler Terror and the Burning of the Reichstag.* Alfred A. Knopf, 1933.

Wrenn, John H. *John Dos Passos.* Boston: Twayne Publishers, 1961.

Wright, Richard. *American Hunger.* Harper and Row, 1977.

———. "Backing the Hitler-Stalin Pact." *Daily Worker.* February 11, 1940.

———. *Richard Wright Reader.* Harper and Row, 1978.

Wright, William. *Lillian Hellman: The Image, The Woman.* Simon and Schuster, 1986.

Zinn, Howard. *A People's History of the United States.* Harper and Row, 1980.

Zugsmith, Leane. *The Summer Soldier.* Random House, 1938.

———. *A Time to Remember.* Random House, 1936.

Index